Routledge Revivals

The English-American

The English-American

A New Survey of the West Indies,
1648

Thomas Gage

First published in 1928 by George Routledge & Sons, Ltd.

This edition first published in 2018 by Routledge
2 Park Square, Milton Park, Abingdon, Oxon, OX14 4RN
and by Routledge
711 Third Avenue, New York, NY 10017

Routledge is an imprint of the Taylor & Francis Group, an informa business

© 1928 Taylor & Francis

All rights reserved. No part of this book may be reprinted or reproduced or utilised in any form or by any electronic, mechanical, or other means, now known or hereafter invented, including photocopying and recording, or in any information storage or retrieval system, without permission in writing from the publishers.

Publisher's Note
The publisher has gone to great lengths to ensure the quality of this reprint but points out that some imperfections in the original copies may be apparent.

Disclaimer
The publisher has made every effort to trace copyright holders and welcomes correspondence from those they have been unable to contact.

A Library of Congress record exists under ISBN: 30007119

ISBN 13: 978-1-138-60372-1 (hbk)
ISBN 13: 978-1-138-60375-2 (pbk)
ISBN 13: 978-0-429-46195-8 (ebk)

THOMAS GAGE
THE
ENGLISH-AMERICAN
1648

BROADWAY TRAVELLERS

THE BROADWAY TRAVELLERS

EDITED BY SIR E. DENISON ROSS
AND EILEEN POWER

*TRAVELS AND ADVENTURES
OF PERO TAFUR*, 1435–1439

*AKBAR AND THE JESUITS
BY FATHER P. DU JARRIC*

*DON JUAN OF PERSIA,
A SHI'AH CATHOLIC*, 1560–1604

THE DIARY OF HENRY TEONGE, 1675–1679

*MEMOIRS OF AN XVIII CENTURY
FOOTMAN, BY JOHN MACDONALD*

*NOVA FRANCIA
BY MARC LESCARBOT*, 1606

*TRAVELS IN TARTARY, THIBET AND
CHINA*, 1844–6, *BY M. HUC*

*THE CONQUEST OF MEXICO
BY BERNAL DIAZ DEL CASTILLO*, 1517–21

*TRAVELS IN PERSIA
BY SIR THOMAS HERBERT*, 1627–9

TRUE HISTORY OF HANS STADEN, 1557

*THE ENGLISH AMERICAN
BY THOMAS GAGE*, 1648

*THE EMBASSY OF
CLAVIJO TO TAMERLANE*, 1403–6

*LADY'S TRAVELS INTO SPAIN
BY MADAME D'AULNOY*, 1691

The above volumes are ready or nearing publication.
A complete list will be found at the end of this volume.

Published by
GEORGE ROUTLEDGE & SONS, LTD.

PLATE 1

THOMAS GAGE RECEIVING GIFTS FROM HIS PARISHIONERS
(*Frontispiece of the First German Edition*)

Front.

THE BROADWAY TRAVELLERS
EDITED BY SIR E. DENISON ROSS
AND EILEEN POWER

THOMAS GAGE
THE ENGLISH-AMERICAN
A NEW SURVEY OF THE WEST INDIES, 1648

Edited with an Introduction by
A. P. NEWTON
D.Lit., F.S.A., Rhodes Professor of Imperial History in the University of London

Published by
GEORGE ROUTLEDGE & SONS, LTD.
BROADWAY HOUSE, CARTER LANE, LONDON

First published in the Broadway Travellers, 1928

CONTENTS

	PAGE
INTRODUCTION	ix

CHAPTER ONE
Of the mission sent by the Dominicans to the Philippines in the year 1625 5

CHAPTER TWO
Of the Indian Fleet that departed from Cadiz, Anno Dom. 1625, and of some remarkable passages in that voyage . . 12

CHAPTER THREE
Of our discovery of some islands, and what trouble befell us in one of them 18

CHAPTER FOUR
Of our further sailing to St John de Ulhua, alias Vera Cruz; and our landing there 25

CHAPTER FIVE
Of our landing at Vera Cruz, otherwise St John de Ulhua, and of our entertainment there 31

CHAPTER SIX
Of our journey from St John de Ulhua to Mexico; and of the most remarkable towns and villages in the way . . 37

CHAPTER SEVEN
A description of the town of Tlaxcala . . . 45

CHAPTER EIGHT
Concluding the rest of our journey from Tlaxcala to Mexico, through the City of Angels, and Guacocingo . . 50

CHAPTER NINE
Shewing some particulars of the great and famous City of Mexico in former times, with a true description of it now, and of the state and condition of it the year 1625 . . . 59

v

CONTENTS

CHAPTER TEN
Shewing my journey from Mexico to Chiapa southward, and the most remarkable places in the way . . . 109

CHAPTER ELEVEN
Describing the country of Chiapa, with the chiefest towns and commodities belonging unto it 149

CHAPTER TWELVE
Shewing my journey from the city of Chiapa unto Guatemala, and the chief places in the way 169

CHAPTER THIRTEEN
Describing the dominions, government, riches, and greatness of the city of Guatemala, and country belonging unto it . . 187

CHAPTER FOURTEEN
Shewing the condition, quality, fashion, and behaviour of the Indians of the country of Guatemala since the Conquest, and especially of their feasts and yearly solemnities . . 228

CHAPTER FIFTEEN
Shewing how and why I departed out of Guatemala to learn the Poconchi language, and to live among the Indians, and of some particular passages and accidents whilst I lived there 271

CHAPTER SIXTEEN
Shewing my journey from the town of Petapa into England; and some chief passages in the way 333

CHAPTER SEVENTEEN
Shewing how, and for what causes, after I had arrived in England, I took yet another journey to Rome, and other parts of Italy, and returned again to settle myself in this my country . . 383

INDEX 403

LIST OF ILLUSTRATIONS

	FACING PAGE
1. Thomas Gage receiving Gifts from his Parishioners *Frontispiece* (*Frontispiece of the first German edition.*)	
2. Frontispiece to the First English Edition	viii
3. The Attack of the Savages at Guadaloupe (*From the Dutch edition of* 1700.)	22
4. Riot in Mexico City. (*Ibid.*)	106
5. The Hermitage of the Indians. (*Ibid.*)	176
6. Funeral Procession of the King of Mechaocan. (*Ibid.*)	208
7. The Christmas Festival in the Church of Petapa. (*Ibid.*)	262
8. Thomas Gage in the Dominican Habit (*Frontispiece of the Dutch edition of* 1700.)	272
9. Flying Locusts. (*Ibid.*)	288

MAPS

(*From the Second English Edition*)

1. The Islands of the West Indies (*Drawn by Michael Sparkes from a mixture of Spanish and Dutch material.*)	18
2. New Spain (*Shewing only the region between Mexico City and the Pacific coast.*)	64
3. The Spanish Main, New Granada and Popayan	344

·The *Englifh-American his Travail by Sea and Land*:

OR,

A NEW SVRVEY
OF THE

WEST-INDIA'S,

CONTAINING

A Journall of Three thousand and Three hundred
Miles within the main Land of AMERICA.

Wherin is fet forth his Voyage from *Spain* to *S^t. Iohn de Ulhua*;
and from thence to *Xalappa*, to *Tlaxcalla*, the City of *Angeles*, and
forward to *Mexico*; With the defcription of that great City,
as it was in former times, and alfo at this prefent.

Likewife his Journey from *Mexico* through the Provinces of *Guaxaca*,
Chiapa, *Guatemala*, *Vera Paz*, *Truxillo*, *Comayagua*; with his
abode Twelve years about *Guatemala*, and efpecially in the
Indian-towns of *Mixco*, *Pinola*, *Petapa*, *Amatitlan*.

As alfo his ftrange and wonderfull Converfion, and Calling from thofe
remote Parts to his Native COUNTREY.

With his return through the Province of *Nicaragua*, and *Cofta Rica*,
to *Nicoya*, *Panama*, *Portobelo*, *Cartagena*, and *Havana*, with divers
occurrents and dangers that did befal in the faid Journey.

ALSO,

A New and exact Difcovery of the Spanifh Navigation to
thofe Parts; And of their Dominions, Government, Religion, Forts,
Caftles, Ports, Havens, Commodities, fafhions, behaviour of
Spaniards, Priefts and Friers, Blackmores, Mulatto's, Meftifo's,
Indians; and of their Feafts and Solemnities.

With a Grammar, or fome few Rudiments of the *Indian* Tongue,
called, *Poconchi*, or *Pocoman*.

By the true and painfull endevours of THOMAS GAGE, now *Preacher of
the Word of God at* Acris *in the County of* KENT, Anno Dom. 1648.

London, Printed by *R Cotes*, and are to be fold by *Humphrey Blunden* at the
Caftle in *Cornhill*, and *Thomas Williams* at the Bible in *Little Britain*, 1648.

(*Frontispiece to the First English Edition*)

INTRODUCTION

By PROFESSOR A. P. NEWTON

To Englishmen of the first half of the seventeenth century the term "America" usually signified the regions discovered by the Spaniards whose possession had made the King of Castile the richest monarch in Europe. In the popular imagination America was a land of wonders whence a stream of gold and silver poured into his coffers. The real circumstances in the New World were so little known that fancy could paint its marvels almost as it would. Eden, Hakluyt and Purchas had translated the adventurous stories of the *Conquistadores* and painted in vivid prose the wonders of Mexico and Peru, but no foreign traveller had ever been permitted by the Spaniards to visit and describe the new lands as they really were after their conquest. For half a century the ambition of English sailors was to capture the rich spoils of the annual treasure fleet, and the profits of even smaller prizes made the English public associate the Indies with the idea of inexhaustible riches.

The residence of all foreigners and especially of Englishmen in the Spanish colonies was stringently forbidden, and though in the pages of Hakluyt we occasionally get glimpses of some men of English descent living in New Spain under Philip II, they were humble merchants or traders who had become denationalised and had neither the power nor the opportunity to describe for English readers the real America as it was. The sailors who raided and robbed the cities on the coast could give but fragmentary descriptions of the interior, and the few survivors of Drake's and Hawkins' crews who escaped,

INTRODUCTION

knew more of the prisons of the Inquisition than the glories of the country. When they got back to England, some of them had to draw largely on their imaginations to satisfy their questioners, and so the tale of America's marvels grew. As his boon companion Thomas Chaloner wrote in his advertisement in verse which precedes the first edition of Gage's *English American* :

> "Those who have describ'd these parts before
> Of trades, winds, currents, hurricanes do tell,
> Of headlands, harbours, trendings of the shore,
> Of rocks and isles, wherein they might as well
> Talk of a nut, and only shew the shell;
> The kernel neither tasted, touched nor seen."

That there was a widespread curiosity as to the interior of the New World and its inhabitants is clear from the care with which any fragmentary accounts by Englishmen were collected and printed, but they were always bald and unsatisfying, and their readers turned with relief to translations of Gomara or Oviedo's vivid pages where the tale of the conquest was told. There they could sate themselves with wonders or with adventures such as Raleigh told of his search for the city of *El Dorado*.

The publication in 1648 of the first authentic account of the provinces of New Spain and Central America by a well-known and educated Englishman excited widespread interest, and *The English American* found many readers even though the country was in the midst of revolution. It had an important share in reviving the anti-Spanish policy of Elizabeth, and when Cromwell had restored England once more to power in international affairs, he caused the publication of a second edition of Gage's book (1655) in order to excite public opinion in favour of his "Western Design" against the Indies. Twenty years later, when Colbert was planning the extension of French power overseas at the expense of Spain, he

INTRODUCTION

commanded the publication of a French translation of the book (1677), and during the long struggle between England and France for the trade of the Spanish Indies this was several times reprinted. (Paris editions of 1680, 1691, 1721, 1722.) Dutch and German translations also appeared during the same period, and new English editions in 1677, 1699 and 1711. Gage's work owed its popularity to its monopoly of first-hand information about regions with which national interests were concerned, but after the Peace of Utrecht (1713) the book was less read, and its popularity was eclipsed by stories of the buccaneers in the highly coloured pages of Esquemeling and Dampier. Our author has suffered at the hands of subsequent writers the fate of most of those who have changed their party or their creed. The writers of the Restoration despised him for his polemical passages in favour of the unpopular Puritan cause, while Roman controversialists damned him unfeignedly for his apostacy, and the Jesuits whom he had especially attacked were relentless in pouring scorn upon his memory. Subsequent writers both in English and French have occasionally quoted from the book, but it has never been reprinted in a modern edition. Edward Long referred to it in his *History of Jamaica* (1774), and Robert Southey used its information for his Mexican epic *Madoc* (1805), though he unfairly disparaged its originality. The comparative neglect of a book that on its first appearance caused such a sensation and that undoubtedly exercised an influence on public policy has been undeserved. Though it can hardly be claimed that Gage's account of his adventures can rank in liveliness with the stories of the most celebrated travellers, it is filled with touches of acute observation, and it describes at first hand a stage of American society so little known that it amply deserves the modern dress that is here given to it for the first time.

INTRODUCTION

The main features of Gage's career are outlined in his own pages, but they appear in a light that is strongly coloured by the circumstances of religious and political controversy. To understand many of his allusions it is necessary to place his story against the background of its time, and this can be done best by tracing something of the history of his family, one of the most celebrated among the English recusants. It will recall the incidents of a forgotten persecution and do something to justify Chaloner's claim of reality for the book.

> "... It so befell
> That these relations to us made have been
> Differing as much from what before y'have heard
> As doth a land-map from a seaman's card.
>
> . . . . . .
>
> Sure the prescience of that power Divine
> Which safely to those parts did him convey,
> Did not for naught his constant heart decline
> There twelve whole years so patiently to stay
> That he each thing exactly might survey.
> Then him return'd, nay more did turn to us,
> And to him shew'd of bliss the perfect way,
> Which of the rest seems most miraculous,
> For had the last of these not truly been,
> These fair relations we had never seen."

The course of events which made a quondam priest of the Roman Church describe Spanish America to Puritan England must be explained by attention to his family and associations, and we must try to amplify the somewhat imperfect notices of him in the biographical dictionaries.

The Gage family was sprung from the county of Sussex and rose to wealth and prominence in the service of the House of Tudor. The founder of the family fortunes was Sir John Gage, who succeeded his father in the estate of Firle Place, Sussex, while still a minor. He was trained in the household of the

INTRODUCTION

Duke of Buckingham, and passed thence to the brilliant Court of the young King Henry VIII, with whom he became associated on terms of close personal friendship. For the rest of his life he served the Crown at home and in the field with the ability and loyalty of a well-trained soldier, and his fortunes prospered like those of most of the "new men" of Henry's household. That he did not go further was possibly due to the fact that he was lukewarm in the matter of the Divorce. While accepting without question the royal supremacy in the Church, he strongly adhered to the old doctrines and was opposed to the Protestant party who came into power on the accession of Edward VI. This is of importance in the history of the family, for the Gages thenceforward were strongly identified with the Catholic party and took a prominent place among the recusant gentry and the supporters of Roman missions. Sir John Gage retired into private life until the accession of Mary, but then his religious views assured him of high favour. He held one of the foremost positions at Court until his death in 1556, and warmly supported the Queen's marriage with Philip II. This brought his family into an association with Spain that was maintained for several generations. By his wife Philippa Guldeford Sir John had a family of four sons and four daughters.

The second son, Robert Gage, under his father's will, succeeded to the estate of Haling Park near Croydon in Surrey. There he and his wife, the daughter of a merchant of Liège,[1] with many of the neighbouring gentry, were diligent in the practice of the old faith. They often afforded harbourage to the priests who passed back and forth to the Low Countries, and thus they came under the unfavourable notice of the authorities. Their younger son Robert was implicated in Antony Babington's plot for the assassination of Elizabeth and the release of Mary Queen

[1] St. Pap., Dom., Eliz. cxcv. no. 102.

INTRODUCTION

of Scots, and in September 1586 he was tried for high treason, attainted and hanged.

Robert Gage the elder died in the following year and Haling then passed to his son John,[1] who married Margaret Copley, daughter of Sir Thomas Copley of Gatton, Surrey. The Copleys were notorious recusants and probably the most devoted supporters of the Jesuits in the South of England. In 1590, three years after John Gage had succeeded to his estate, he and his wife were arrested on suspicion of concealing a missionary priest, one Richard Garnet, in their house, and for two years they were closely imprisoned. In 1592 they were tried and convicted under the savage laws against recusants and were sentenced to death. While they were being carried in a cart to the place of execution with their hands ignominiously bound, Margaret received a letter respiting the sentence, and she and her husband were released.[2] This favour had been obtained by the intercession of the Lord Admiral, Charles Howard, Earl of Nottingham, and he obtained his price by the grant of a lease for a period of 21 years of Haling House, which was forfeited on John's attainder, and it never came back to the Gages.[3] Mr. and Mrs. Gage were greatly impoverished by the confiscation of their property, but they were more confirmed than ever in their recusancy and their attachment to the cause of the proscribed Jesuits. They were helped by their relatives, and after a time of banishment in the Spanish Netherlands they returned to live quietly with their friends in London. Their eldest son Henry was born in 1597, and Thomas, the second, probably in 1600. In 1601 Margaret was again in trouble for her religion, being arrested with one Mrs. Line for harbouring a Jesuit priest, Father Page. Mrs. Line

---

[1] *Vict. County Hist. of Surrey*, iv. 222.
[2] *Records of the English Province, S.J.*, i. 425.
[3] *V.C.H., Surrey*, iv. 222.

INTRODUCTION

and the priest were hanged, but Mrs. Gage was set at liberty by the influence of the Howards.[1]

Henry was sent in 1609 when twelve years old to be educated by the English Jesuits at their seminary at St. Omer, and there he remained until 1615 when he proceeded to the English College in Rome.[2] He entered the Spanish service as an officer in the English Legion in the Low Countries and earned a high reputation among the soldiers of his time. He did much to organise and train the Royalist armies in the Civil War, and was killed in action in 1644 when Governor of Oxford.

Thomas was destined by his father and mother for the priesthood from the beginning and followed his brother to St. Omer. He was trained under the severe but effective discipline of the seminary along with Thomas Holland and other English boys who were devoted by their parents for the conversion of England and many of whom were to suffer a martyr's fate. Though he acquired some sound learning, Thomas does not seem to have won any special reward or to have attracted notice as Henry had done. Three other brothers were ordained to the priesthood, William, a Jesuit, George, a secular priest, and Francis, who became one of the most celebrated preachers among the English Roman Catholics after the Restoration. Thomas came back to England to see his family in 1617, and his intention of returning to St. Omer becoming known, he was arrested and brought before the Privy Council. After a few days' detention he was released and went back to his studies.[3]

At that period the pupils of the Jesuits who were destined for the priesthood were passed from St. Omer to complete their preparation in Spain. The English College at Valladolid had been founded by Father Robert Parsons, S.J., in 1589, with the aim of infusing

[1] *Records, S.J.*, i. 425.   [2] *Ibid.*, i. 184.
[3] *Acts of the Privy Council*, 1616-7, pp. 264, 299.

INTRODUCTION

its students with an admiration of Spanish glory and an obedience to Spanish discipline which would make them fitting tools for the projected conquest and conversion of their nation.[1] But Parsons's plans had miscarried, and the College was troubled with dissensions and lack of means from the first. The Spanish Jesuits were determined to keep the education of the students in their own hands, but English Catholics had little liking for young priests who had been " hispaniolated," and they were none too warmly welcomed when they came to take up their work of proselytization. The College was also unpopular with the regular religious Orders, and their lack of sympathy with its political aims led to frequent difficulties and disorders among the students. Before 1620, when Gage arrived at Valladolid, these disorders had become so acute as to result in open scandal. The Benedictines in particular were ready to receive deserters from the Jesuit College into their novitiate, and, to quote the words of their Rector, " the students, seeing they were so run after, began to be somewhat puffed up and to neglect the discipline of the house, or rather to despise it altogether. They began to get lax in their zeal for study and prayer, and to hold meetings among themselves " to concert measures to annoy their superiors.[2] Coming into such an atmosphere, young Gage was confirmed in the dislike of the Jesuit system and its insidious discipline that he had felt at St. Omer. The College was insanitary, and the students suffered badly in recurrent attacks of plague which swept Valladolid, while the endowments were so slender that there was a dearth of food and all conveniences. The English youths were distracted from their theological studies and mixed in political disputes between the Spanish Jesuits and the English Rector. Under such forbidding circumstances it was

[1] Taunton, E. L., *Hist. of Jesuits in England*, p. 136.
[2] Fr. Blackfan, *cit.* Taunton, p. 339.

INTRODUCTION

natural that the prevailing tone was not high, and that the weaker sort came to look to their future career rather as a means of gaining promotion and spiritual influence for political ends than as a vocation. Possibly we may attribute some of the flaws of character that appeared in Gage's later life and his selfish lack of scruple to these defects in his upbringing.

As he himself tells us,[1] " No hatred is comparable to that which is between a Jesuit and a friar, and above all between a Jesuit and a Dominican. . . . For these owe unto them an old grudge for that when Ignatius Loyola lived, he was questioned by the Dominicans and by a Church censure publicly and shamefully whipped about their cloisters for his erroneous principles." All over Spain at this time the Jesuits were stirring up the people against their rivals " in so much that the Dominicans were in the very streets termed heretics, stones cast at them, . . . and they, poor friars, forced to stand upon their guard in their cloisters in many cities to defend themselves from the rude and furious multitude."

The friars were ready to welcome any deserters who came to them from the opposite camp, and even did not disdain to take active steps to encourage them. It appears that Gage was still resident in the Jesuit College at Valladolid when Prince Charles and Buckingham came to Madrid, and Thomas Holland, his old schoolfellow from St. Omer, was chosen to express in a Latin oration the loyalty of the English students and their hopes for more favourable times for their religion.[2] It must have been within the next few months that Gage followed the example of so many of his fellows and left the Jesuit College to pass over to the Dominicans. His secession was a bitter blow to his father, who was passionately devoted to the Jesuit schemes and had hoped that his sons would be the

[1] *English American*, ed. 1648, p. 4.   [2] *Records, S.J.*, i. 551.

INTRODUCTION

foremost of the apostles for the conversion of England. He reproached Thomas in unmeasured terms. "My father's angry and harsh letter," Gage tells us,[1] "signified unto me the displeasure of most of my friends and kindred, and his own grievous indignation against me, for that having spent so much money in training me up to learning, I had not only refused to be of the Jesuits' Order (which was his only hopes), but had proved in my affections a deadly foe and enemy unto them. He said that if I should prove a General of the Order of Dominicans, that I should never think to be welcome to my brothers nor kindred in England nor to him, that I should not expect ever more to hear from him, nor dare to see him if ever I returned to England, but expect that he would set upon me even the Jesuits whom I had deserted and opposed to chase me out of my country, that Haling House, though he had lost it with much more means for his religion during his life, yet with the consent of my eldest brother he would sell it away,[2] that neither from the estate or money made of it I might enjoy a child's part due unto me."

These remonstrances and threats were of no effect, and early in 1625 we find Thomas fully received into the Dominicans and resident in one of their convents at Jeres. Thither there came at the end of May 1625 a commissary of the Pope with licence to recruit priests to serve as missionaries for the conversion of the natives of the Philippine Islands. Among those already recruited was one Antonio Melendez, a near acquaintance of Gage's from Valladolid. Although the passage of Englishmen to the Spanish Indies was strictly forbidden, Gage yielded to his persuasion and resolved to accept service with the mission. He planned to journey through Mexico

---

[1] *English American*, p. 8.
[2] The reversion was sold by John Gage and his son Henry in 1626 to Christopher Gardiner. *V.C.H., Surrey*, iv., 222, note 61.

INTRODUCTION

and across the Pacific to the islands and possibly to get even as far as Japan, of whose wonders and riches he had heard.

As it is at this point that the story of his travels begins, it is unnecessary for us here to trace the succeeding events in detail. Our only knowledge of the next twelve years of his life is derived from his own pages, though possibly a careful search of the unexplored archives in Guatemala and Mexico might yield further evidence. As he relates, he abandoned his intention of proceeding with the Philippine mission when he reached Mexico, and gave his leaders the slip, preferring to avoid the dangers and hardships of the long passage and to remain amidst the rich opportunities of America. We may there leave him and pass on to the time when, twelve years later, having amassed something of a fortune from the credulity of his Indian parishioners, he returned to Europe in 1637. Gage travelled extensively in the New World, and availed himself fully of his opportunities of observing the character and riches of the Spanish dominions, but his first interest seems always to have been in the endless jealousies and disputes of the various religious orders who were at work among the Indians, and his pages abound in unfavourable comments upon the superstition and the general self-indulgence of the ecclesiastics among whom he served. A convert is usually more hostile to the faith that he has left than an impartial observer, and there need be no excuse for our use of the pruning knife to spare the modern reader many of the malicious diatribes, couched in the approved scriptural jargon of his day, which were most relished by his Puritan readers. The reason for their inclusion in the original will appear when we trace the story of our author's later career.

After some twelve years' service as a priest in various charges in and around Guatemala, Gage was weary of the country and anxious to return to Europe. He

INTRODUCTION

implies that he was moved by concern at some points of religion and desired to fly from " that place of daily idolatry " into England and be at rest. " I weighed the affliction and reproach which might ensue to me," he says, " after so much honour, pleasure and wealth which I had enjoyed for about twelve years in that country, but in another balance of better consideration I weighed the trouble of a wounded conscience and the spiritual joy and comfort that I might enjoy at home with the people of God, and so resolutely concluded . . . to choose rather to suffer affliction . . . than to enjoy the pleasures of sin for a season, esteeming the reproach of Christ greater riches than the treasures in Egypt." It is to be feared that these were afterthoughts intended to be palatable to his Puritan readers, and that they were ante-dated to convince his patrons of his sincerity. In 1637 he did not yet contemplate the abandonment of the Catholic faith in which he had been reared, but in all probability he was moved rather by discontent with the hard work and monotony of the missionary life for which he no longer felt a vocation.

After some months of danger and adventure which he describes for us in detail, he arrived at last at San Lucar near Seville on 28 November 1637, and a month later he set foot again on English soil for the first time in twenty years. He could speak but a few words of his native tongue, and he had little left of the money that he had made in America. He therefore addressed himself to his relations, the Gages and the Copleys, to find what portion his father had left him at his death four years before. But he was disappointed, for he learnt that his claims to a share in the inheritance had been wholly ignored and that his father had done as he threatened when he refused to be a Jesuit, and had wholly thrust him from his memory.[1] For a year or more Gage lived with one

[1] *English American*, p. 383.

INTRODUCTION

or another of his relations in Surrey and in London in close contact with many of the English and Irish Dominicans, Benedictines and Jesuits who gathered round the Court of Queen Henrietta Maria. He still exercised his priestly functions and preached and celebrated Mass from time to time. After one of his London sermons the Jesuit Father Thomas Holland, his old schoolfellow, came to congratulate him in a particular manner for his good success and to ask him to say Mass for him at a chapel in Holborn.[1] He was thus still in full communion with his co-religionists.

But he was discontented with his somewhat dependent circumstances and the non-fulfilment of the promises of favour that he received from the Catholic Secretary of State, Sir Francis Windebanke, and other persons of influence. He wrote to the General of the Dominicans for a licence to visit him in Rome, and, provided with money for his journey by his uncle Copley of Gatton, he left England again early in the spring of 1639 and passed over into the Low Countries. His elder brother, Colonel Henry Gage, whom he had not seen since they were boys at St. Omer together, was now in command of the English Legion in the Spanish service and was in camp against the Hollanders near Ghent. There Thomas received a warm welcome and the promise of financial support. Colonel Gage had many friends in high quarters and he presented his brother in the best circles in Brussels and procured for him many introductions to assist him in Rome. Like his father and mother the Colonel was a firm adherent of the Jesuits and had chosen his chaplain, Father Peter Wright, from the Society.[2] Thomas saw much of him during his stay with the army, and also had a wide acquaintance among the missionary priests who passed backward and forward

---
[1] *Records, S.J.*, i. 551.
[2] *Ibid.*, iv. 525.

INTRODUCTION

into England, which was to prove unfortunate for some of them in future years.

Our traveller resumed his journey towards Italy in August 1639, but it is unnecessary to follow his adventures; in February 1640 he was stricken down with ague at Trent and suffered a long illness. He reached Rome in April and was received cordially by many belonging to the inner circles of the Curia. He came into close contact with the English ecclesiastics who were deeply involved in political intrigues for bringing England back to obedience to the Holy See.[1] His younger brother, the Rev. George Gage,[2] was well known in Rome as a plotter, and Thomas was anxious to earn promotion by his service to the cause. In later years he maintained that his time in Germany was spent in a search after truth from Lutherans and other Protestants, but we have only his word for it, and it seems more probable that as late as 1640 he still thought only of opportunities to gratify his ambition within the Catholic Church. There is no doubt that his roving life had weakened, if it had not destroyed, any sincere attachment to religion, and that his main object was his own worldly advantage. This he was ready to pursue with little care for conscience or scruple, and when the Scottish war brought shipwreck to the hopes of Charles I and his Queen and the Catholic plotters alike, Gage saw that the time had come to change his side.

At first he thought of making his home in France for a time, and he procured a licence from the General of the Dominicans and a letter of commendation to a convent of his Order at Orleans. He soon relinquished this plan, however, as the news from England

---

[1] *English American*, p. 393.

[2] The Rev. George Gage, who was Thomas's half-brother, has sometimes been identified with the Rev. George Gage who was one of James I's agents for procuring the Papal dispensation for the Spanish match in 1621-2. A comparison of dates shews that this identification is incorrect.

INTRODUCTION

became more and more adverse to Catholic hopes. As he tells us with a somewhat odious mixture of piety and self-seeking, " Upon this good purpose of mine I presently perceived the God of truth did smile with what I heard He was ordering in England by an army of Scotland raised for reformation and by a new Parliament called to Westminster; at which I saw the Papists and Jesuits there began to tremble and to say it would blast all their designs and all their hopes of settling Popery. . . . With all this good news I was much heartened and encouraged to leave off my journey to France and to return to England where I feared not my brother nor any kindred nor any power of the Papists, but began to trust on the protection of the Parliament which I was informed would reform religion and make such laws as should tend to the undermining of all the Jesuits' plots and to the confusion of the Romish errors and religion."[1]

The time had evidently come for a new attempt to swim to fortune with the stream, and when Gage reached England again on Michaelmas Day 1640, his mind was made up for the plunge. Again we may let him speak for himself. " My brother's spirit I found was not much daunted with the new Parliament, nor some of the proudest Papists', who hoped for a sudden dissolving of it. But when I saw their hopes frustrated by His Majesty's consent to the continuing of it,[2] I thought the acceptable time was come for me, wherein I ought not to dissemble any further with God, the world and my friends, and so resolved to bid adieu to flesh and blood, and to prize Christ above all my kindred, to own and profess him publicly maugre all opposition of Hell and kindred to the contrary." But he had to wait nearly two years before he could convince the Anglican bishops of the sincerity of his conversion, and it was not until

[1] *English American*, p. 397.
[2] November 1640.

INTRODUCTION

28 August 1642 that he was permitted to preach his recantation sermon in St. Paul's.¹

He could find no influential patron among the Parliamentary leaders, and when his sermon was published in October 1642, his only sponsor was an unimportant country member, Sir Samuel Oldfield. " I thought I must yet do more to satisfy the world of my sincerity," he says, " knowing that converts are hardly believed by the common sort of people, unless they see in them such actions which may further disclaim Rome for ever for the future." He tried to win confidence therefore by entering " into the state of marriage which the Church of Rome disavows to all her priests." This helped him to some extent, for soon after he was appointed by Parliament to the substantial living of Acrise in Kent. But he still spent much of his time in London, and from internal evidence we know that it was at this period that he wrote a large part of his book.

The apostacy of one of their family was regarded with horror by the Gages, who were intensely proud of their devotion to the Old Faith for which they had suffered so much. Colonel Gage wrote offering his brother £1,000 ready money if he would come over again to Flanders, but he had gone too far to retrace his steps, and in a further attempt to convince his new friends of his worthiness for promotion Gage now lent himself to an act of treachery that was utterly unforgivable. For some months he had been secretly giving information against his acquaintances in the English mission. In October 1642 Father Thomas Holland, of whom we have already spoken, was arrested and charged under the Penal Laws with the capital crime of being a Romish priest who had celebrated Mass on English soil. The trial came on

---

¹ *The Tyranny of Satan, Discovered by the Tears of a Converted Sinner.* Printed by Thomas Badger for Humphry Mosley . . . in Paul's Churchyard, MDCXLII.

INTRODUCTION

in December, and mainly on Gage's testimony the Jesuit was condemned to death. He was hanged and quartered at Tyburn a few days later praying that his death might bring back " that apostate religious " Thomas Gage to the bosom of Mother Church.

The family was filled with bitter anger that one of them should have sold himself so basely, and since they could not get hold of him by fair means they resolved to make away with him by foul. He was assaulted in Aldersgate Street, and another time he tells us he " was like to be killed in Shoe Lane by a Captain of my brother's regiment who came over from Flanders on purpose to make me away or convey me over . . . from whom God graciously delivered me by the weak means of a woman, my landlady."[1] About this time he became friendly with Thomas Chaloner, the regicide who was prominent among the Parliament men but " who was as far from being a puritan or presbyterian as the east is from the west, for he was a boon companion, . . . was of the natural religion, and loved to enjoy the comfortable importances of this life."[2] Though not yet a Councillor of State it was at his prompting that Gage published the account of his travels, and he wrote the advertisement from which we have already quoted. The book was dedicated to " His Excellency Sir Thomas Fairfax, Knight, Lord Fairfax of Cameron, Captain-General of the Parliament's Army and of all their Forces in England and the Dominion of Wales," and that there was a definite political purpose in its publication is clear from the terms of the Epistle Dedicatory. " I humbly pray . . . that the same God who hath led your Excellency through so many difficulties towards the settlement of the peace of this Kingdom, and reduction of Ireland, will after the perfecting thereof direct your noble thoughts to employ the soldiery of this

---

[1] *English American*, p. 399.
[2] Wood, A., *Athenæ Oxonienses*.

INTRODUCTION

Kingdom upon such just and honourable designs in those parts of America, as their want of action at home may neither be a burden to themselves nor the Kingdom. To your Excellency therefore I offer a New World."

Chaloner attempted to strike both a patriotic and a prophetic note:

> " And though we now lie sunk in civil war,
> Yet you the worthy Patriots of this land,
> Let not your hearts be drownèd in despair,
> And so your future happiness withstand.
>
> . . . . .
>
> Your Drums which us'd to beat their martial dance
> Upon the banks of Garonne, Seine and Soane,
> Whilst you trode measures through the Realm of France,
>
> . . . . .
>
> Now shall the tawny Indians quake for fear
> Their direful march to beat when they do hear;
> Your brave Red-Crosses on both sides display'd
> The noble Badges of your famous Nation,
> Which you yet redder with your bloods have made,
> And dy'd them deep in drops of detestation
> You shall advance with reputation
> And on the bounds of utmost Western shore
> Shall them transplant and firmly fix their station,
> Where English Colours ne'er did fly before.
> Your well-built ships, companions of the Sun,
> As they were chariots to his fiery beams,
> Which oft the Earth's circumference have run,
> And now lie moor'd in Severn, Trent and Thames,
> Shall plough the Ocean with their gilded stems,
> And in their hollow bottoms you convey
> To Lands enrich'd with gold, with pearls and gems,
> But above all where many thousands stay
> Of wronged Indians, whom you shall set free
> From Spanish yoke and Rome's idolatry."

The attack upon the Spanish Indies that *The English American* was designed to promote had, however, to wait until Cromwell had brought Scotland, Ireland and the Colonies into subjection.

Meanwhile our author continued his ministry at Acrise, but he was often in London[1] and more than

---

[1] *Cal. St. Pap., Dom.*, 1649-50, pp. 388, 437, 511.

INTRODUCTION

once was called upon by the authorities for information about the English Catholics. His testimony against Father Holland was neither forgotten nor forgiven by his family, but he eclipsed it in infamy at the trial of his late brother's regimental chaplain, Father Peter Wright. The persecution of the Catholics had been somewhat relaxed during the later years of the Civil War, but it broke out with renewed violence at the end of 1650. Father Wright was arrested and was sent for trial along with Father Dade, the Provincial of the Dominicans in England. The authorities ordered Thomas Gage to come up from Kent and give evidence against them. But his brother George determined to do what he could to prevent this. To quote a Jesuit historian: "He did not shrink, though at considerable personal risk, to go to the haunt of vice where the wretched debauchee was lodging and to warn him of the divine judgments that were hanging over him if he should make himself guilty of innocent blood."[1]

It was upon the destruction of Father Dade that the "apostate" was more set, on account of some ancient grudge, but George's entreaty in his own name and the names of other friends not to commit so enormous a crime as to give evidence against the priests of God in court so far prevailed that Thomas solemnly pledged his word to his brother that he would not injure either of them, and he suggested a means to avoid the force of the evidence forthcoming. He kept his word so far as the Dominican was concerned, and in his evidence at the trial astutely contrived to argue that though certainly a friar, he might not be a priest, quoting to the jury the case of St. Francis of Assisi. Dade was acquitted, but Father Wright was not so fortunate. Probably owing to pressure from Bradshaw, the regicide President of the Council of State, Gage attacked the prisoner with

[1] *Records, S.J.*, iv. 520-1.

INTRODUCTION

virulence and testified fully to his previous acquaintance with him. He did this ostensibly not because of his priesthood but because the state of public affairs required it, and he was compelled by lawful authority to appear. " I would not assert against you," he had told Wright on the day before the trial, " that you had resolved upon my death, but you were my brother's confessor, and it was notified to you that he had on foot certain designs upon my life, and had suborned one Vincent Burton to commit the crime, you ought to have dissuaded them from that wicked intention; therefore I have a right to act as I do."[1]

After he had given his evidence, Gage professed himself so much in fear of assassination that he prayed the court to afford him military protection; but he was so despised and disliked that no notice was taken of his application. Father Wright was found guilty and sentenced to death under the Penal Laws, and his hanging at Tyburn caused an immense sensation not unmingled with pity among all but the most extreme sectaries.

The notoriety of the trial had made Gage more disliked and feared than ever, and he endeavoured to justify himself by the publication of a tract explaining how he had been compelled to give evidence. It bore the cumbrous title: " *A Duel between a Jesuit and a Dominic, begun at Paris, gallantly fought at Madrid, and victoriously ended at London* by Thomas Gage, alias the English American, now Preacher of the Word at Deal in Kent."[2] His arguments with Father Wright were likened to the conflict between the Jesuit Florentia and the Dominican Domingo de Torres before the King of Spain in 1622, and Gage concluded the eight pages of the tract by attributing

---

[1] *Records, S.J.*, iv. 523.
[2] LONDON: *Printed for Tho: Williams dwelling at the Bible in Little Britain*, 1651.

INTRODUCTION

the butchery that he feared to the spite, malice and hatred of his Jesuit enemies.

After the publication of his tract Gage returned to continue his ministry at Deal, and we hear nothing further of him for about three years until Cromwell entered in earnest on his "Western Design" and called upon him for information and advice. The idea of attacking the Indies had often been considered by the Long Parliament, and it was much discussed in 1648 before the Naval revolt rendered it out of the question. It was this circumstance that promoted the publication of the first edition of *The English American* in that year. In December 1654 Cromwell directed Gage to prepare a reasoned report on the proper objects of attack and the best methods to be pursued, and this has been preserved for us among the Thurloe Papers.[1] He must have discussed it with Milton, then Foreign Secretary, and he may have been personally consulted by the Lord Protector, but we have no information as to this. Limitations of space forbid us to devote attention to the further progress of the "Western Design," and we can only note one or two points.[2] The memorandum was to a considerable extent a summary of parts of his book presented in the pious language fashionable at the time. The missionary motive was emphasized to take away the taint of mere gold-seeking. " I pray that these few observations may by your Highness be accepted as from one who for these many years hath observed, yea, admired the activity of your Highness his faith, who waits for the conversion of the poor Indians who long to see the light of the Gospel run yet more and more forwards, till it come to settle in the

[1] *Thurloe State Papers*, ed. Birch, iii. 59. Reprinted in Watts A. P., *Hist. des Colonies Anglaises aux Antilles*, 1649-60, pp. 452-7.

[2] For discussion of Gage's share in the genesis of the Design see Newton, A. P., *The Colonizing Activities of the English Puritans*, especially the final chapter, and Watts, A. P., *op. cit.*, pp. 95-6.

INTRODUCTION

West among those poor, simple and truly purblind Americans."

The writer was appointed to accompany the expedition as chaplain to General Venables, and a frigate was ordered to transport him from Deal to Portsmouth where the expedition was fitting out.[1] After it had sailed, a new edition of his book was published under the direct inspiration of the Government bearing the alteration in title that was to be borne by all subsequent English editions. It was now called *A New Survey of the West India's or the English American*, and was embellished with three maps, which we reproduce. The dedication to Fairfax and Chaloner's verses were retained, and the edition was in fact little more than a corrected reprint[2] of the original.

The expedition, it will be remembered, failed completely in its attempt on Hispaniola, and its only achievement was the occupation of Jamaica. There Gage died early in 1656, as we know from the fact that in July of that year the Council of State arranged to pay the debts owing to him to his widow Mary Gage and she was granted a pension of 6s. 8d. a week.[3] His long-cherished scheme for the founding of an English empire in America had come to nothing, but he had lived to see the Red Crosses floating over the island that was to become the centre of England's naval power in the Caribbean, and we may justly credit him with a share in the founding of the largest of our West Indian colonies. But only his book remained to preserve his memory as the first foreigner to describe the Spanish colonies from within.

We have already mentioned the later English editions, but it is of interest to add a few words concerning the French versions. Girard Garnier was

---

[1] *Cal. St. Pap., Dom.*, 1654, Dec. 20, p. 586.
[2] London: *Printed by E. Cotes and sold by J. Sweeting at the Angel in Pope's Head Alley*, 1655.
[3] *Cal. St. Pap., Dom.*, 1656-7, 1656, July 18.

INTRODUCTION

licensed to print the first of these at Paris in 1663, and this version was collected by Thevenot for his *Relation des divers Voyages curieux* (1672). The title was changed to *Relation de Mexique et de la Nouvelle Espagne par Thomas Gages*. The text was considerably abridged and the declamatory passages suppressed, notably the early chapters and the chapter at the end relating to the author's activities in Europe after his return.[1]

In 1677 a new translation was made for M. le Sieur de Beaulieu, Huës O'Neil, by one M. de Carcavi, and published in two volumes. It was entitled *Nouvelle Relation des Indes Occidentales contenant les Voyages de Thomas Gage dans la Nouvelle Espagne*, and contained practically the whole of the original but the early chapters and the expressions most offensive to Roman Catholics. The dedication to Colbert shews that it was by his command that the publication was undertaken. "Voici ce fameux voyager qui a traversé la mer sous vos heureux auspices et a qui j'ay appris a parler François par votre commandement." So in the Preface: "Notre nation auroit esté privé de la connoissance de tant de choses curieuses qu'il nous apprend sans la soin qu'a pris Monseigneur Colbert parmi tant d'autres . . . d'en faire ordonner la traduction." It was from this French version that the later translations into Dutch and German were made. The chapter divisions of the original were abandoned and the whole redivided into shorter chapters with fresh headings.

The work as here printed for the first time in modern dress has necessarily demanded some abridgment, for none but specialists in the controversies of the seventeenth century would find much of interest in the writer's polemics. We have shewn in the Table of Contents the full chapter headings of the First Edition and have preserved the original numbering. It will

[1] Thevenot, tom. iv.

INTRODUCTION

therefore be possible to see at once where a considerable section has been omitted. Omissions of minor passages have been indicated in the usual way by dots [. . .].

Robert Southey maintained in the notes to his poem *Madoc* that Gage's account of Mexico which he pretends to have collected on the spot is copied verbatim from T. Nicholas's translation of Gomara, published as *The Conquest of the West Indies* in 1576.[1] This, however, is not the case, and Gage's translation was made independently from the Spanish authorities. He certainly used Gomara and Oviedo and may also have known Herrera. Doubtless a careful collation would enable us to identify the source of his information in each case. Many of those well-known stories of Cortez and his *Conquistadores* have here been omitted, and only those are retained that are of direct interest in connection with their context. For further accounts our readers may be appropriately referred to the graphic pages of Prescott.

The sources of our contemporary illustrations are sufficiently indicated in the notes attached to each.

[1] Southey, R., *Madoc* (1st ed. 1805), p. 468.

Thomas Gage
The English-American

To His Excellency

SIR THOMAS FAIRFAX, Knight,

LORD FAIRFAX OF CAMERON

CAPTAIN-GENERAL OF THE PARLIAMENT'S ARMY, AND OF ALL THEIR FORCES IN ENGLAND, AND THE DOMINION OF WALES

May it please your Excellency,
The Divine Providence hath hitherto so ordered my life, that for the greatest part thereof I have lived (as it were) in exile from my native country: which happened partly by reason of my education in the Romish religion, and that in foreign universities; and partly by my entrance into monastical orders. For twelve years' space of which time I was wholly disposed of in that part of America called New Spain, and the parts adjacent. My difficult going thither, being not permitted to any but to those of the Spanish nation; my long stay there; and lastly my returning home, not only to my country, but to the true knowledge and free profession of the Gospel's purity, gave me reason to conceive that these great mercies were not appointed me by the Heavenly Powers to the end I should bury my talent in the earth, or hide my light under a bushel, but that I should impart what I there saw and knew to the use and benefit of my English countrymen. And which the rather I held myself obliged unto, because in a manner nothing hath been written of these parts for these hundred years last past, which is almost ever since the first Conquest thereof by the Spaniards,

EPISTLE DEDICATORY

who are contented to lose the honour of that wealth and felicity they have there since purchased by their great endeavours, so they may enjoy the safety of retaining what they have formerly gotten in peace and security. In doing whereof, I shall offer no collections but such as shall arise from mine own observations, which will as much differ from what formerly hath been hereupon written as the picture of a person grown to man's estate from that which was taken of him when he was but a child; or the last hand of the painter to the first or rough draft of the picture. I am told by others that this may prove a most acceptable work; but I do tell myself that it will prove both lame and imperfect, and therefore had need to shelter myself under the shadow of some high protection, which I humbly pray your Excellency to afford me; nothing doubting, but as God hath lately made your Excellency the happy instrument not only of saving myself, but of many numbers of godly and well-affected people in this county of Kent (where now I reside by the favour of the Parliament) from the imminent ruin and destruction plotted against them by their most implacable enemies, so the same God who hath led your Excellency through so many difficulties towards the settlement of the peace of this kingdom, and reduction of Ireland, will, after the perfecting thereof (which God of his mercy hasten), direct your noble thoughts to employ the soldiery of this kingdom upon such just and honourable designs in those parts of America as their want of action at home may neither be a burden to themselves nor the kingdom. To your Excellency therefore I offer a New World, to be the subject of your future pains, valour, and piety, beseeching your acceptance of this plain but faithful relation of mine, wherein your Excellency, and by you the English nation, shall see what wealth and honour they have lost by one of their narrow-hearted princes, who, living in peace and abounding in riches did notwithstanding reject the offer of being first discoverer of America, and left it unto Ferdinand of Aragon, who at the same time was wholly

EPISTLE DEDICATORY

taken up by the wars in gaining of the city and kingdom of Granada from the Moors; being so impoverished thereby that he was compelled to borrow with some difficulty a few crowns of a very mean man to set forth Columbus upon so glorious an expedition. And yet, if time were closely followed at the heels, we are not so far behind but we might yet take him by the fore-top. To which purpose our plantations of the Barbados, St Christophers, Nevis, and the rest of the Caribbean Islands, have not only advanced our journey the better part of the way, but so inured our people to the clime of the Indies as they are the more enabled thereby to undertake any enterprise upon the firm land with greater facility. Neither is the difficulty of the attempt so great as some may imagine; for I dare be bold to affirm it knowingly that with the same pains and charge which they have been at in planting one of those petty islands they might have conquered so many great cities and large territories on the main continent as might very well merit the title of a kingdom. Our neighbours the Hollanders may be our example in this case; who whilst we have been driving a private trade from port to port, of which we are likely now to be deprived, have conquered so much land in the East and West Indies that it may be said of them, as of the Spaniards, That the sun never sets upon their dominions. *And to meet with that objection by the way,* That the Spaniard being entitled to those countries, it were both unlawful and against all conscience to dispossess him thereof, *I answer that (the Pope's donation excepted) I know no title he hath but force, which by the same title and by a greater force may be repelled. And to bring in the title of first discovery, to me it seems as little reason that the sailing of a Spanish ship upon the coast of India should entitle the King of Spain to that country, as the sailing of an Indian or English ship upon the coast of Spain should entitle either the Indians or English unto the dominion thereof. No question but the just right or title to those countries appertains to the natives themselves, who, if they shall willingly*

EPISTLE DEDICATORY

and freely invite the English to their protection, what title soever they have in them no doubt but they may legally transfer it or communicate it to others. And to say that the inhuman butchery which the Indians did formerly commit in sacrificing of so many reasonable creatures to their wicked idols was a sufficient warrant for the Spaniards to divest them of their country, the same argument may by much better reason be enforced against the Spaniards themselves, who have sacrificed so many millions of Indians to the idol of their barbarous cruelty, that many populous islands and large territories upon the main continent are thereby at this day utterly uninhabited, as Bartholomeo de las Casas, the Spanish Bishop of Guaxaca in New Spain, hath by his writings in print sufficiently testified. But to end all disputes of this nature; since that God hath given the earth to the sons of men to inhabit, and that there are many vast countries in those parts not yet inhabited either by Spaniard or Indian, why should my countrymen the English be debarred from making use of that which God from all beginning no question did ordain for the benefit of mankind?

But I will not molest your Excellency with any further argument hereupon, rather offering myself, and all my weak endeavours (such as they are), to be employed herein for the good of my country. I beseech Almighty God to prosper your Excellency, who am

The most devoted and humblest of
your Excellency's servants,
THO. GAGE.

CHAPTER I

Of the mission sent by the Dominicans to the Philippines in the year 1625

IN the year of our Lord 1625 it was my fortune to reside among the Dominicans in Jerez in Andalusia. The Pope's Commissary for their Mission was Friar Matheo de la Villa, who having a commission for thirty and having gathered some twenty-four of them about Castile and Madrid, sent them by degrees well stored with money to Cadiz, to take up a convenient lodging for himself and the rest of his crew, till the time of the setting forth of the Indian fleet. This Commissary named one Friar Antonio Calvo to be his substitute, and to visit the cloisters of Andalusia lying in his way, namely, Cordova, Seville, St Lucar, and Jerez, to try if out of them he could make up his complete number of thirty, which was after fully completed.

About the end of May came this worthy Calvo to Jerez, and in his company one Antonio Melendez of the College of St Gregory in Valladolid, with whom I had formerly near acquaintance. This Melendez greatly rejoiced when he had found me; and being well stocked with Indian patacones, the first night of his coming invited me to his chamber to a stately supper. The good Jerez sack, which was not spared, set my friend in such a heat of zeal of converting Japanese, that all his talk was of those parts never yet seen, and at least six thousand leagues distant. Bacchus metamorphosed him from a Divine into an orator, and made him a Cicero in parts of rhetorical eloquence. Nothing was omitted that might exhort me to join with him in that function, which he thought was apostolical. *Nemo propheta in patria sua* was a great argument with him; sometimes he propounded martyrdom for the Gospel sake, and the glory after it to have his life and death printed, and of poor Friar Anthony, a clothier's son of Segovia, to be styled St Anthony by the Pope, and made collateral with the Apostles in heaven; thus did Bacchus make him ambitious of honour upon the earth, and preferment in heaven. But when he thought this rhetoric had not prevailed, then would he act a Midas and Crœsus, fancying the Indies paved with tiles of gold and silver, the stones to be pearls, rubies, and diamonds, the trees to be hung with clusters of nutmegs bigger than the clusters of grapes of Canaan, the fields to be planted with sugar-canes, which should so sweeten the chocolate that it should far exceed the milk and honey of the land of promise; the silks of China he conceited so common that the sails of the ships were nothing else; finally he dreamed of Midas' happiness, that whatsoever he touched should be turned to gold. Thus did Jerez nectar make my friend and mortified friar a covetous worldling. And yet from a rich covetous merchant did it shape him to a courtier in pleasures; fancying the Philippines to be the Eden, where was all joy without tears, mirth without sadness, laughing without sorrow, comfort without grief, plenty without want, no not of Eves for Adams, excepted only that in it should be no forbidden fruit, but all lawful for the taste and sweetening of the palate; and as Adam would have been as God, so conceited Melendez himself a God in that Eden; whom travelling, Indian waits and trumpets should accompany, and to whom, entering into any town, nosegays should be presented, flowers and boughs should be strewed in his way, arches should be erected to ride under, bells for joy should be rung, and Indian knees for duty and homage, as to a God, should be bowed to the very ground. From this inducing argument, and representation of a Paradise, he fell into a strong rhetorical point of curiosity, finding out

SURVEY OF WEST INDIES

a tree of knowledge, and a philosophical maxim, *Omnis homo naturaliter scire desiderat*, man naturally inclines to know more and more; which knowledge he fancied could be nowhere more furnished with rare curiosities than in these parts, for there should the gold and silver, which here are fingered, in their growth in the bowels of the earth be known; there should pepper be known in its season; the nutmeg and clove; the cinnamon as a rind or bark on a tree; the fashioning of the sugar from a green growing cane into a loaf; the strange shaping the cochineal from a worm to so rich a scarlet dye; the changing of the *tinta*, which is but grass with stalk and leaves, into an indigo black dye should be taught and learned; and without much labour thus should our ignorance be instructed with various and sundry curiosities of knowledge and understanding. Finally, though Jerez liquor (grapes' bewitching tears) had put this bewitching eloquence into my Anthony's brain, yet he doubted not to prefer before it his wine of the Philippines, growing on tall and high trees of *coco*, wherein he longed to drink a Spanish *brindis* in my company to all his friends remaining behind in Spain. Who would not be moved by these his arguments to follow him, and his Calvo, or bald-pated Superior?

Thus supper being ended, my Melendez desired to know how my heart stood affected to his journey; and breaking out into a *Voto á Dios* with his converting zeal, he swore he should have no quiet night's rest until he were fully satisfied of my resolution to accompany him. And having learned the poet's expression, *Quid non mortalia pectora cogis, Auri sacra fames?* he offered unto me half-a-dozen of Spanish pistoles, assuring me that I should want nothing, and that the next morning Calvo should furnish me with whatsoever moneys I needed for to buy things necessary for the comfort of so long and tedious a journey. To whom I answered: sudden resolutions might bring future grief and sorrow, and that I should that night lie down and take counsel with my pillow, assuring him that for his sake I would do much, and that if I resolved to go, my resolution should draw on another friend of mine, an Irish friar, named Thomas de Leon. Thus took I my leave of my Melendez, and retired myself to my chamber and bed, which that night was no place of repose and rest to me as formerly it had been.

I must needs say Melendez his arguments, though most of them moved me not, yet the opportunity offered me to hide myself from all sight and knowledge of my dearest friends stirred up in me a serious thought of an angry and harsh letter, which not long before I had received out of England from mine own father, signifying unto me the displeasure of most of my friends and kindred, and his own grievous indignation against me, for that having spent so much money in training me up to learning, I had not only utterly refused to be of the Jesuits' Order (which was his only hopes) but had proved in my affections a deadly foe and enemy unto them; and that he would have thought his money better spent if I had been a scullion in a college of Jesuits than if I should prove a General of the Order of Dominicans; that I should never think to be welcome to my brothers nor kindred in England, nor to him; that I should not expect ever more to hear from him, nor dare to see him if ever I returned to England, but expect that he would set upon me even Jesuits, whom I had deserted and opposed, to chase me out of my country; that Haling House, though he had lost it with much more means for his religion during his life, yet with the consent of my eldest brother (now Governor of Oxford, and Mass-founder in that our famous University) he would sell it away that neither from the estate, or money made of it, I might enjoy a child's part due unto me. These reasons stole that night's rest from

SURVEY OF WEST INDIES

my body, and sleep from my eyes, tears keeping them unclosed and open, lest Cynthia's black and mourning mantle should offer to cover, close, and shut them. To this letter's consideration was joined a strong opposition, which serious studies and ripeness of learning, with a careful discussion of some schoolpoints and controversies, had bred in me against some chief of the Popish tenets. Well could I have wished to come to England, there to satisfy and ease my troubled conscience; well considered I that if I stayed in Spain when my studies were completely finished, the Dominicans with a Pope's mandamus would send me home for a missionary to my country. But then well considered I the sight of a wrathful father, the power of a furious brother, a colonel, who (as now landed in England to search me out, and do me mischief) then, when Zephyrus with a pleasant gale seconded his Popish zeal, might violently assault me. Well considered I the increased rout and rabble of both their great friends, the Jesuits, who what with Court friends' power, what with subtle plots and policies, would soon and easily hunt me out of England. Lastly, well considered I my Melendez his last inducing argument of the increase of knowledge natural by the insight of rich America and flourishing Asia, and of knowledge spiritual by a long contemplation of that new-planted Church, and of those Church planters' lives and conversations. Wherefore, after a whole night's strife and inward debate, as the glorious planet began to banish night's dismal horror, rising with a bright and cheerful countenance, rose in my mind a firm and settled resolution to visit America, and there to abide till such time as Death should surprise my angry father, Ignatius Loyola his devoted Maecenas, and till I might there gain out of Potosi or Zacatecas treasure that might counterpoise that child's part which, for detesting the four-cornered cap and black coat of Jesuits, my father had deprived me of.

THE ENGLISH-AMERICAN

So in recompense of the supper which my friend Anthony had bestowed upon me, I gave him a most pleasing breakfast by discovering unto him my purpose and resolution to accompany him in his long and naval journey. And at noon I feasted him with a dinner of one dish more than his breakfast, to wit, the company also of my Irish friend Thomas de Leon. After dinner we both were presented to Calvo, the bald-pate Superior, who immediately embraced us, promised to us many curtesies in the way, read unto us a memorandum of what dainties he had provided for us, what varieties of fish and flesh, how many sheep, how many gammons of bacon, how many fat hens, how many hogs, how many barrels of white biscuit, how many jars of wine of Casalla, what store of rice, figs, olives, capers, raisins, lemons, sweet and sour oranges, pomegranates, comfits, preserves, conserves, and all sorts of Portugal sweetmeats; he flattered us that he would make us Masters of Arts and of Divinity in Manila. Then opened he his purse, and freely gave us to spend that day in Jerez, and to buy what most we had a mind to, and to carry us to Cadiz. Lastly, he opened his hands to bestow upon us the Holy Father's benediction, that no mischief might befall us in our way; I expected some relique or nail of his great toe, or one of his velvet pantofles to kiss, but peradventure with frequent kissing through Italy and all Castile it was even worn threadbare. Much were we frowned at by the Dominicans our chiefest friends of Jerez, but the liberty which with Melendez we enjoyed that day about the city of Jerez took from us all sad thoughts, which so sudden a departure from our friends might have caused in us. And Calvo with cunning policy persuaded us to depart from Jerez the next morning. Which willingly we performed in company of Melendez and another Spanish friar of that city (leaving our chests and books to Calvo to send after us), and

SURVEY OF WEST INDIES

that day we travelled like Spanish Dons upon our little *boricoes*, or asses, towards Puerto de Santa Maria, taking in our way that stately Convent of Carthusians, and the river of Guadalethe, the former poets' river of oblivion, tasting of the fruits of those Elysian fields and gardens and drinking of Guadalethe's crystal streams, that so perpetual oblivion might blind and cover all those abstractive species which the intuitive knowledge of Spain's and Jerez's pleasant objects had deeply stamped in our thoughts and hearts.

At evening we came to that *puerto* so famous for harbouring Spain's chief galleys, and at that time Don Frederique de Toledo, who, hearing of the arrival of four Indian Apostles, would not lose that occasion of some soul-sanctification (which he thought might be his purchase) by entertaining us that night at supper. The town thought their streets blessed with our walking in them, and wished they might enjoy some reliques from us, whom they beheld as appointed to martyrdom for Christ and Anti-Christ's sake together; the galley slaves strived who should sound their waits and trumpets most joyfully. Don Frederique spared no cost in fish and flesh that night, doubting not but that receiving four prophets, he should receive a fourfold reward hereafter. Supper being ended, we were by Don Frederique his gentlemen conveyed to the cloister of the Minims appointed by Don Frederique to lodge us that night, who, to shew their brotherly love, washed our feet, and so recommended us to quiet and peaceable rest. The next morning, after a stately breakfast bestowed upon us by those poor mendicant friars, a boat was prepared for us and Don Frederique his gentlemen to wait on us, and to convey us to Cadiz, where we found out our fellow Apostles, and the Pope's Commissary, Friar Matthew de la Villa, who welcomed us with Rome's indulgences, *a culpa & a pena*, and with a flourishing table stored with fish and flesh for dinner.

There we continued in daily honour and estimation, enjoying the sights most pleasant which Cadiz both by sea and land could afford unto us, until the time of the fleet's departing. Which when it drew near, our Grand Apostle Friar Matthew de la Villa (whom we thought burned with zeal of martyrdom) took his leave of us, shewing us the Pope's commission to nominate in his place whom he list, and naming bald Calvo for Superior, returning himself to Madrid with more desire to enjoy a bishopric in Spain (as we understood) than to sacrifice his life in Japan. His departure caused a mutiny among us, and cooled the spirit of two of our missionaries, who privily fled from us. The rest were pleased with honest Calvo, for that he was a simple and ignorant old man (whom they could more jeer than any way respect), more scullion-like in daily greasing his white habit with handling his fat gammons of bacon than like a Pope's Commissary; for his master's toe the proudest of our missioners then would willingly have kissed, yet Calvo's greasy fists the humblest would loath to have kissed. Thus under a sloven was that Apostolical Mission to be conveyed first to Mexico, three thousand Spanish leagues from Spain, and afterwards three thousand leagues further from thence to Manila, the Metropolitan and Court-City of the Philippine Islands.

CHAPTER II

Of the Indian Fleet that departed from Cadiz, Anno Dom. 1625, and of some remarkable passages in that voyage

UPON the first of July in the afternoon, Don Carlos de Ybarra, Admiral of the Galleons that then lay in the Bay of Cadiz, gave order that a warning piece should be shot off to warn all passengers, soldiers, and mariners to betake themselves the next morning to their ships. O, what was it to see some of our apostolical company who had enjoyed much liberty for a month in Cadiz: now hang down their heads, and act with sad and demure looks, loath to depart, and cry out, *Bonum est nos hic esse*, It is good for us to be here; and amongst them one Friar John de Pacheco made the warning piece to be a warning to him to hide himself (who could no more be found amongst his fellow missioners), thinking it a part of hard cruelty to forsake a young Franciscan nun to whom he had engaged and wholly devoted his heart. The second of July in the morning early, notice was given unto us that one Friar Pablo de Londres, an old crab-faced English friar living in St Lucar, had got the Duke of Medina his letter and sent it to the Governor of Cadiz charging him to search for me and to stay me, signifying the King of Spain's will and pleasure that no English should pass to the Indies, having a country of their own to convert; this did that old friar to stop my passage, having before wrote unto me many letters to the same purpose, and got a letter from that father master that was in England before, with the Count of Gondomar, alias Friar Diego de la Fluente, then Provincial of Castile, and sent it unto me, wherein that Superior offered me many kind offers of preferment if I would desist from my journey, and return to him to Castile; but none of these letters could prevail with me, nor the Governor's searching stop me; for immediately I was conveyed alone to our ship, and there closely hid in a barrel that was emptied of biscuit to that purpose; so that when the Governor came a shipboard to enquire for an Englishman, Friar Calvo, having the father of liars in my stead about him, resolutely denied me, who would not be found, because not sought for in a barrel's belly. Thus found our Apostles sport and talk that first day. Then went out the ships one by one crying *A dios, A dios*, and the town replying

Buen viaje, buen viaje; when all were out and no hopes of enjoying more Cadiz' pleasures and liberty, then began my young friars to wish themselves again aland: some began presently to feed the fishes with their nuns' sweet dainties; others to wonder at the number of stately ships, which with eight galleons that went to convey us beyond the Canary Islands were forty-one in all, some for one port of the Indies, and some for another. To Porto Rico went that year two ships; to Santo Domingo three, to Jamaica two, to Margarita one, to Havana two, to Cartagena three, to Campeche two, to Honduras and Trujillo two, and to St John de Ulhua, or Vera Cruz, sixteen; all laden with wines, figs, raisins, olives, oil, cloth, kerseys [carsies], linen, iron, and quicksilver for the mines, to fetch out the pure silver of Zacatecas from the earthen dross from whence it is digged.

The persons of most note that went that year was first the Marquess de Serralvo with his lady, who went for Viceroy of Mexico instead of the Conde de Gelves then retired to a cloister for fear of the common people, who the year before had mutinied against him. This Marquess went in the ship called 'St Andrew,' and with him in the same ship went Don Martin de Carrillo, a priest and inquisitor of the Inquisition of Valladolid, who was sent for Visitor-General to Mexico to examine the strife between the Conde de Gelves and the Archbishop, and the mutiny that for their sakes had happened, with full commission and authority to imprison, banish, hang, and execute all delinquents. In the ship called 'Santa Gertrudis' went Don John Nino de Toledo, who was sent to be President of Manila in the Philippines, and in the same ship with him went the whole Mission of thirty Jesuits sent to the Philippines, who had already got the favour of the President, and politicly sought to be passengers in the same ship, that so they might the

SURVEY OF WEST INDIES

more ingratiate themselves to him; for this cunning generation studies purposely how to insinuate themselves with kings, princes, great men, rulers, and commanders. In the ship called 'St Anthony' went my Dominican Mission of twenty-seven friars. In the ship called 'Nuestra Señora de Regla' went four and twenty Mercenarian friars bound for Mexico; part of those that afterwards drew their knives to slash and cut the Creoles of their profession.

Thus with the convoy of eight galleons for fear of Turks and Hollanders (whom the Spanish Dons shake and tremble at) set forward our fleet with a pleasant and prosperous gale, with a quiet and milken sea, until we came to the gulf called Golfo de Yeguas, or of Kicking Mares, whose waves and swelling surges did so kick our ships that we thought they would have kicked our St Anthony's gilded image out of our ship, and bereaved my Antonio Melendez of his gilt and painted idol (to whom he daily bowed and prayed against the merciless element), and that all our ship's galleries would have been torn from us with these spurnings and blows of that outrageous gulf. But at last, having overcome the danger of this gulf, the eight galleons took their leave of us, and left our merchant ships now to shift for themselves. The departure of these galleons was most solemnly performed on each side, saluting each other with their ordnance, visiting each other with their cock-boats, the Admiral of the Fleet feasting with a stately dinner in his ship the Admiral of the Galleons; and the like performing most of the other ships to the several colonels and captains and other their allied friends that were of the Royal Fleet. Here it was worth noting to hear the sighs of many of our Indian Apostles, wishing they might return again in any of those galleons to Spain; their zeal was now cold, and some endeavoured many ways for Calvo his licence to return (which could not be granted), others employed themselves most of that day in writing letters to their friends and sisters in Cadiz.

Thus dinner being ended, and the two Admirals solemnly taking their leaves, the warning piece being shot off for the galleons to join together, and turn their course to Spain, we bad mutual adieu, crying one to another *Buen viaje, Buen pasaje.* We kept our course towards America, sailing before the wind constantly till we came to America. A thing worth noting in that voyage from Spain to the Indies: that after the Canary Islands are once left, there is one constant wind continuing to America still the same without any opposition or contrariety of other winds, and this so prosperous and full on the sails, that did it blow constantly and were it not interrupted with many calms, doubtless the voyage might be ended in a month or less. But such were the calms that many times we had that we got not to the sight of any land till the twentieth day of August: so that near six weeks we sailed as on a river of fresh water, much delighting and sporting ourselves in fishing many sorts of fishes, but especially one, which by the Spaniards is called *dorado*, the golden fish, for the skin and scales of it that glitter like gold. Of this sort we found such abundance that no sooner was the hook with any small bait cast into the sea, when presently the *dorado* was caught, so that we took them many times for pleasure and cast them again into the sea, being a fish fitter to be eaten fresh than salted. Many were the feasts and sports used in the ships, till we discovered the first land, or island called Deseada.

The last day of July (being according to the Jesuits' Order, and Rome's appointment, the day of Ignatius their patron and founder of their religion), the gallant ship called 'Sta Gertrudis' (wherein went thirty Jesuits) for their and their saint's sake made to all the rest of the fleet a most gallant shew, she being trimmed round about with white linen, her flags and top-

SURVEY OF WEST INDIES

gallants representing some the Jesuits' arms, others the picture of Ignatius himself, and this from the evening before, shooting off that night at least fifty shot of ordnance, besides four or five hundred squibs (the weather being very calm), and all her masts and tacklings hung with paper lanthorns having burning lights within them; the waits ceased not from sounding, nor the Spaniards from singing all night. The day's solemn sport was likewise great, the Jesuits increasing the Spaniards' joy with an open procession in the ship; singing their superstitious hymns and anthems to their supposed saint, and all this seconded with roaring ordnance, no powder being spared for the completing of that day's joy and triumph. The fourth of August following, being the day which Rome doth dedicate to Dominic, the first founder of the Dominicans or Preachers' Order, the ship wherein I was, named 'St Anthony,' strived to exceed 'Sta Gertrudis' by the assistance of the twenty-seven Dominicans that were in her. All was performed both by night and day as formerly in 'Sta Gertrudis' both with powder, squibs, lights, waits, and music. And further did the Dominicans' joy and triumph exceed the Jesuits', in that they invited all the Jesuits, with Don John Nino de Toledo, the President of Manila, with the Captain of the ship of 'Sta Gertrudis' to a stately dinner both of fish and flesh; which dinner being ended, for the afternoon's sport they had prepared a comedy out of famous Lope de Vega, to be acted by some soldiers, passengers, and some of the younger sort of friars; which I confess was as stately acted and set forth both in shews and good apparel, in that narrow compass of our ship, as might have been upon the best stage in the Court of Madrid. The comedy being ended, and a banquet of sweetmeats prepared for the closing up of that day's mirth, both ours, and 'Sta Gertrudis'' cock-boat carried back our invited friends, bidding each other adieu with our waits and chiefest ordnance.

THE ENGLISH-AMERICAN

Thus went we on our sea voyage without any storm, with pleasant gales, many calms, daily sports and pastimes till we discovered the first land called Deseada upon the twentieth day of August.

CHAPTER III

Of our discovery of some islands, and what trouble befell us in one of them

THE Admiral of our Fleet wondering much at our slow sailing, who from the second of July to the 19 of August had seen nor discovered any land, save only the Canary Islands, the same day in the morning called to council all the pilots of the ships, to know their opinions concerning our present being, and the nearness of land. The ships therefore drew near unto the Admiral one by one, that every pilot might deliver his opinion. Here was cause of laughter enough for the passengers to hear the wise pilots' skill; one saying we were three hundred miles, another two hundred, another one hundred, another fifty, another more, another less, all erring much from the truth (as afterward appeared) save only one old pilot of the smallest vessel of all, who affirmed resolutely that with that small gale wherewith we then sailed we should come to Guadeloupe the next morning. All the rest laughed at him, but he might well have laughed at them, for the next morning by sun-rising we plainly discovered an island called Deseada by the Spaniards, or the Desired Land, for that at the first discovery of the Indies it was the first land the Spaniards found, being then as desirous to find some land after many days' sailing as we were. After this island presently we discovered another called Marie Galante, then another called Dominica, and lastly, another named Guadeloupe, which was that we aimed

THE ISLANDS OF THE WEST INDIES

(Drawn by Michael Sparkes from a mixture of Spanish and Dutch material)

at to refresh ourselves in, to wash our foul clothes, and to take in fresh water, whereof we stood in great need. By two or three of the clock in the afternoon we came to a safe road lying before the island, where we cast our anchors, no ways fearful of the naked barbarians of that and the other islands, who with great joy do yearly expect the Spanish fleet's coming, and by the moons do reckon the months, and thereby make their guess at their coming, and prepare some their sugar-canes, others the plantain, others the tortoise, some one provision, some another to barter with the Spaniards for their small haberdashery, or iron, knives, or such things which may help them in their wars, which commonly they make against some other islands. Before our anchors were cast, out came the Indians to meet us in their canoes, round like troughs, some whereof had been painted by our English, some by the Hollanders, some by the French, as might appear by their several arms, it being a common road and harbour to all nations that sail to America.

Before we resolved to go to shore we tasted of those Indian fruits, the plantain above all pleasing our taste and palate. We could not but much wonder at that sight never yet seen by us of people naked, with their hair hanging down to the middle of their backs, with their faces cut out in several fashions, or flowers, with thin plates hanging at their noses, like hog-rings, and fawning upon us like children, some speaking in their unknown tongue, others using signs for such things as we imagined they desired. Their sign for some of our Spanish wine was easily perceived, and their request most willingly granted to by our men, who with one reasonable cup of Spanish sack presently tumbled up their heels, and left them like swine tumbling on the deck of our ship. After a while that our people had sported with these rude and savage Indians, our two cock-boats were ready to carry to shore such as either had clothes to wash, or a desire to bathe themselves in a river of fresh water which is within the island, or a mind to set their feet again upon unmovable land, after so many days of uncertain footing in a floating and reeling ship. But that day being far spent, our friars resolved to ſtay in the ship, and the next whole day to visit the island; many of the mariners and passengers of all the ships went that evening to shore, some returning at night, and some without fear continuing with the Indians all night on shore. The next morning myself and moſt of our friars went, and having hired some Spaniards to wash our clothes, we wandered sometimes all together sometimes two and two, and sometimes one alone about the island, meeting with many Indians, who did us no hurt, but rather like children fawned upon us, offering us of their fruits, and begging of us whatsoever toys of pins, points, or gloves they espied about us. We ventured to go to some of their houses which ſtood by a pleasant river, and were by them kindly entertained, eating of their fish, and wild deer's flesh.

About noon we chanced to meet with some of the Jesuits of 'Santa Gertrudis' ship in the midſt of the mountain, who were very earneſt in talk with a mulatto, all naked like the reſt of the Indians. This mulatto was a Chriſtian, born in Seville in Spain, and had been slave there formerly to a rich merchant; his name was Lewis; and spoke the Spanish language very perfeƈtly. Some twelve years before he had run away from his maſter by reason of hard and slavish usage, and having got to Cadiz, offering his service to a gentleman then bound for America, the gentleman fearing not that his true maſter should ever have more notice of him from a new world, took him a shipboard with him as his slave. The mulatto remembering the many ſtripes which he had suffered from his firſt cruel maſter, and fearing that from America he might by some intelligence or other be sent back again to Spain, and also jealous of his second master (whose blows he had begun to suffer in the ship) that he would prove as cruel as his first; when the ships arrived at Guadeloupe, resolved rather to die among the Indians (which he knew might be his hardest fortune) than evermore to live in slavery under Spaniards. So casting his life upon good or bad fortune, he hid himself among the trees in the mountain till the ships were departed; who after being found by the Indians, and giving them some toys which he had got by stealth from his master, he was entertained by them, they liking him, and he them. Thus continued this poor Christian slave among those barbarians from year to year; who had care to hide himself at the coming of the Spanish fleet yearly. In twelve years that he had thus continued amongst them he had learned their language, was married to an Indian, by whom he had three children living. The Jesuits by chance having met with him, and perceiving more by the wool upon his head that he was a mulatto than by his black and tawny skin (for those Indians paint themselves all over with a red colour), they presently imagined the truth that he could not come thither but with some Spaniard, so entering into discourse with him, and finding him to speak Spanish, they got the whole truth of him. Then we joining with the Jesuits, began to persuade the poor Christian to forsake that heathenish life, wherein his soul could never be saved, promising him if he would go along with us he should be free from slavery for ever. Poor soul, though he had lived twelve years without hearing a word of the true God, worshipping stocks and stones with the other heathens, yet when he heard again of Christ, of eternal damnation in hell's torments, and of everlasting salvation in Heaven's joys, he began to weep, assuring us that he would go with us, were it not for his wife and children, whom he tenderly loved, and could not forsake them. To this we replied that he might be a means of saving likewise their souls, if he would bring them with him; and further that we would assure him that care should be taken that neither he, his wife, nor children should ever want means competent for the maintenance of their lives. The mulatto hearkened well to all this, though a sudden fear surprised him, because certain Indians passed by, and noted his long conference with us. The poor and timorous mulatto then told us that he was in danger for having been known by us, and that he feared the Indians would kill him, and suspect that we would steal him away; which if they did, and it were noised about the island, we should soon see their love changed into cruel rage and mutiny. We persuaded him not to fear anything they could do to us, who had soldiers, guns, and ordnance to secure ours and his life also, wishing him to resolve to bring his wife and children but to the seaside, where our men were drying their clothes, and would defend him, and a boat should be ready to convey him with his wife and children a shipboard. The mulatto promised to do as we had counselled him, and that he would entice his wife and children to the seaside to barter with us their wares for ours, desiring some of the Jesuits (whom he said he should know by their black coats) to be there ready for him with a cock-boat. Lewis departed; as to us he seemed resolute in what he had agreed our joy likewise was great with the hope of bringing to the light of Christianity five souls out of the darkness of heathenish idolatry.

The Jesuits who had begun with this mulatto were desirous that the happy end and conclusion might be their glory. So taking their leaves of us, they hastened to the sea to inform the Admiral of what they had done, and to provide that the cock-boat of their ship might be in readiness to receive Lewis

PLATE 3

THE ATTACK OF THE SAVAGES AT GUADALOUPE

(From the Dutch Edition of 1700)

[*Face p.* 22]

SURVEY OF WEST INDIES

and his family. We likewise returned to the shore to see if our shirts and clothes were dry. Most of us (among whom myself was one) finding our linen ready and our boat on shore went aboard to our ship, leaving two or three of our company with many of other ships on shore, especially the Jesuits waiting for their prey. When we came to our ship, most of our friars with what love that they had found in the barbarians, were inflamed with a new zeal of staying in that island, and converting those heathens to Christianity, apprehending it an easy business (they being a loving people), and no ways dangerous to us, by reason of the fleet that yearly passeth that way, and might enquire after our usage. But by some it was objected that it was a rash and foolish zeal with great hazard of their lives, and many inconveniences were objected against so blind and simple an attempt. But those that were most zealous slighted all reasons, saying that the worst that could happen to them could be but to be butchered, sacrificed, and eaten up; and that for such a purpose they had come out of Spain to be crowned with the crown of martyrdom for confessing and preaching Jesus Christ. While we were hot in this solemn consultation, behold an uproar on the shore; our people running to and fro to save their lives, leaving their clothes, and hasting to the cock-boats, filling them so fast and so full that some sunk with all the people in them. Above all, most pitiful and lamentable were the cries of some of our women, many casting themselves to the sea, choosing rather to venture to be taken up by some boat, or at worst to be drowned, than to be taken and to be cruelly butchered by the Indians. We wondering at this sudden alteration, not knowing the cause of it, at last perceived the arrows to come out thick from the wood from behind the trees, and thereby guessed at the truth that the barbarians were mutinied. The uproar lasted not half an hour, for presently our Admiral shot off two or three pieces of ordnance and sent a company of soldiers to shore to guard it and our people with their muskets; which was well and suddenly performed, and all the Indians soon dispersed.

Three of our friars who had remained on the land, our cock-boat brought them to us with more of our passengers, among whom one Friar John de la Cueva, was dangerously shot and wounded in one of his shoulders; this friar had been earneſt with me to ſtay on shore with him, which I refused, and so escaped that cruel and fiery onset of the Indians. Besides those that were drowned and taken up at shore (which were fifteen persons) two Jesuits were found dead upon the sand, three more dangerously wounded, three passengers likewise slain, ten wounded, besides three more of the fleet which could never be found alive or dead, and were thought to have been found in the wood by the Indians, and to have been murdered by them. Our mulatto Lewis came not according to his word; but in his ſtead a sudden army of treacherous Indians, which gave us motive enough to think that either Lewis himself had discovered the Jesuits' plot to take him away with his wife and children, or that the Indians suspecting it by his talk with us had made him confess it. And certainly this was the ground of their mutiny; for whereas Lewis before had said that he would know the Jesuits by their black coats, it seems he had well described them above all the reſt unto the Indians, for (as it was after well observed) moſt of their arrows was directed to the black marks, and so five of them in little above a quarter of an hour were slain and wounded. All that night our soldiers guarded the coaſt, often shooting off their muskets to affright the Indians, who appeared no more unto us. All that night we slept little, for we watched our ship, leſt the Indians in their canoes should set upon us and take us asleep. Some lamented the dead and drowned, others pitied our wounded Friar John de la Cueva, who all that night lay in great

SURVEY OF WEST INDIES

torment and misery, others laughed and jeered at those zealous friars who would have stayed in that island to convert the barbarians, saying they had had their full desire of martyrdom, for had they been but that night with the Indians doubtless they had been shred for their suppers. But now we perceived their zeal was cool, and they desired no more to stay with such a barbarous kind of people, but rather wished the Admiral would shoot off the warning piece for us all to take up our anchors, and depart from so dangerous a place. In the morning all the ships made haste to take in such fresh water as was necessary for their voyage yet to America, a strong watch being kept along the coast, and a guard guarding our men to the river; and all the morning while this was doing not one Indian could be found or seen, nor our three men that were missing, appeared. Thus at noon with a pleasant and prosperous gale we hoisted up our sails, leaving the islands and harbour of Guadeloupe.

CHAPTER IV

Of our further sailing to St John de Ulhua, alias Vera Cruz; and of our landing there

UPON the 22 day of August, we sailed so pleasantly that we soon left the sight of the islands. The Indians' uproar had weaved for us a thread of long discourse. It made some hate their calling to teach and convert Indians. But Calvo he encouraged us, telling us many stories of the good and gentle nature of the Indians of the Philippines, to whom we were going, and that most of them were Christians already, who esteemed their priests as gods upon the earth; and that those that were not as yet converted to Christianity were kept in awe by the power of the Spaniards. Our chief care the first two or three days was to look to our plantains which we got from the Indians. This fruit pleased us all exceedingly, judging it to be as good or better than any fruit in Spain. It is not gathered ripe from the tree; but being gathered green, it is hung up some days, and so ripens and grows yellow and mellow, and every bit as sweet as honey. Our sugar-canes were no less pleasing unto us, whilst chewing the pith, we refreshed and sweetened our mouths with the juice. We fed for the first week almost upon nothing but tortoise; which seemed likewise to us, that had never before seen it, one of the sea monsters, the shell being so hard as to bear any cart-wheel, and in some above two yards broad; when first they were opened, we were amazed to see the number of eggs that were in them, a thousand being the least that we judged to be in some of them. Our Spaniards made with them an excellent broth with all sorts of spices. The meat seemed rather flesh than sea fish, which being corned with salt, and hung up two or three days in the air, tasted like veal. Thus our hens, our sheep, our powdered beef, and gammons of bacon, which we brought from Spain, were some days slighted, while with greedy stomachs we fell hard to our sea veal.

After four days' sail, our Friar John de la Cueva, who had been shot by the Indians, died, all his body being swelled, which gave us just occasion to think that the arrow which was shot into his shoulder was poisoned. His burial was as solemnly performed as could be at sea. His grave being the whole ocean, he had weighty stones hung to his feet, two more to his shoulders, and one to his breast; and then the superstitious Romish dirge and requiem being sung for his soul, his corpse being held out to the sea on the ship side with ropes ready to let him fall, all the ship crying out three times, *Buen Viaje* (that is, a good voyage) to his soul chiefly, and also to his corpse ready to travel to the deep to feed the whales: at the first cry all the ordnance were shot off, the ropes on a

SURVEY OF WEST INDIES

sudden loosed, and John de la Cueva with the weight of heavy stones plunged deep into the sea, whom no mortal eyes ever more beheld. The like we saw performed in the ship of 'Santa Gertrudis' to another Jesuit, one of the three who had been dangerously wounded by the Indians of Guadeloupe; who likewise died like our friar, his body being swelled as with poison.

Now our sailing was more comfortable than before; for we passed in the sight of the land of Porto Rico, and then of the great island of Sto Domingo; and here our company began to be lessened, some departing to Porto Rico, and Sto Domingo, others to Cartagena, and Havana, and Honduras, Jamaica, and Yucatan. We remained now alone the fleet for Mexico; and so sailed till we came to what the Spaniards call *La Sonda*, or the Sound of Mexico; for here we often sounded the sea; which was so calm that a whole week we were stayed for want of wind, scarce stirring from the place where first we were caught by the calm. Here likewise we had great sport in fishing, filling again our bellies with *dorados*, and saving that provision which we had brought from Spain. But the heat was so extraordinary that the day was no pleasure unto us; for the repercussion of the sun's heat upon the still water and pitch of our ships kindled a scorching fire, which all the day distempered our bodies with a constant running sweat, forcing us to cast off most of our clothes. The evenings and nights were somewhat more comfortable, yet the heat which the sun had left in the pitched ribs and planks of the ship was such, that under deck and in our cabins we were not able to sleep, but in our shirts were forced to walk, or sit, or lie upon the deck. The mariners fell to washing themselves and to swimming, till the unfortunate death of one in the ship called 'St Francisco' made them suddenly leave off that sport. The nearer we come to the mainland, the sea abounds with a monstrous fish called by the Spaniards *tiburon*. Some mistake this fish for the cayman, or crocodile, holding them both for one and thinking that it is only the cayman or crocodile (by abuse called *tiburon*) which devours man's flesh, a whole joint at a bite in the water. But the mistake is gross, for the cayman is plated all over with shells, whereas the *tiburon* hath no shells, but only like other great sea fishes, hath a thick skin. The cayman though the Indians eat of it, yet the Spaniards hate it, who eat of the *tiburon*; and in our ship catching one with a tridental iron fork, and haling him with a cable rope to the ship side, and then binding him with it (being as much as a dozen or fifteen men could do to hoist him up into the ship), we found him to be a most monstrous creature, twelve ells long at least, which we salted, and found likewise to eat like flesh, as hath been said of the tortoise. This kind is as ravenous after man's flesh as the crocodile, and many of them were to be seen in this Sound of Mexico.

The Spaniards bathing themselves daily by the ship's side (where there is no such danger of the *tiburon*; who useth not to come too near the ships), one mariner of the ship called 'St Francisco' being more venturous than the rest, and offering to swim from his ship to see some friends in another not far off, chanced to be a most unfortunate prey to one of them, who before any boat could be set out to help him, was thrice seen to be pulled under water by the monster, who had devoured a leg, an arm, and part of his shoulder; the rest of the body was after found and taken up, and carried to 'St Francisco' and there buried in the form and manner as hath been said of our Friar John de la Cueva. This mischance sadded all our fleet for three days till it pleased God to refresh our burning heat with a cool and prosperous wind, driving us out of that calm sound, which (if we had continued in it with that excessive heat) might have proved most unsound and unhealthy to our bodies.

SURVEY OF WEST INDIES

Three days after we had sailed, being Monday in the morning about seven of the clock, one of our friars saying Mass, and all the people in the ship kneeling to hear it, and to adore their bread-God, one mariner with a loud and sudden voice crieth out *Tierra, Tierra, Tierra,* 'Land, Land, Land,' which rejoiced the hearts of all that were in the ship, as it seemed, more than their Mass, for leaving that, and their God upon the altar with the priest to eat him alone, they arose from their knees to behold the continent of America. Great was the joy of all the ships that day; and great was the slaughter which our old Calvo made among his fowls (which he had spared formerly), to feast that day his friars. About ten of the clock the whole face of the land was visibly apparent, and we with full sail running to embrace it. But our wise Admiral, knowing the danger of the coast, and especially the dangerous entering into the haven, by reason of the many rocks that lie about it, and are known only by marks and flags set out to give all ships warning of them, perceiving that with the wind wherewith we sailed then we should not come till towards evening to the port; and, lastly, fearing lest some north wind (which is dangerous upon that coast, and ordinary in the month of September) should in the night arise and endanger all our ships upon the rocks, he therefore called to council all the pilots, to know whether it were best to keep on our sailing with full sail that day, with hopes to get that day in good time into the haven, or else with the middle sail only to draw near, that the next morning with more security we might with the help of boats from land be guided in. The result of the council was not to venture that day too near unto the port, for fear of being benighted, but to pull down all but the middle sail. The wind began to calm, and our ships to move slowly towards land, and so we continued till night.

A double watch was kept that night in our ship,

and the pilot was more watchful himself and more careful than at other times. But our friars betook themselves to their rest, which continued not long, for before midnight the wind turned to the north, which caused a sudden and general cry and uproar in ours, and all the other ships. Their fear was more for the appehension of danger by that kind of wind, and of what might happen, than for what as yet the wind threatened, which was not strong nor boisterous; however, hallowed wax candles were lighted by the friars, knees bowed to Mary, litanies and other hymns and prayers sung aloud unto her till towards the dawning of the day, when behold the north wind ceased, our wonted gale began to blow again, it being God's will and pleasure, and no effect of the howling friars' prayers to Mary, who yet superstitiously to deceive the simple people cried out, *Milagro, Milagro, Milagro,* ' A miracle, a miracle, a miracle.' By eight o'clock in the morning we came to the sight of the houses, and made signs for boats to convey us into the haven; which immediately with great joy came out, and guided us one by one between those rocks which make that port as dangerous as any I have discovered in all my travels both upon the North and South Sea. Our waits played most pleasantly, our ordnance saluted both town and fort over against it, our hearts and countenances reciprocally rejoiced; we cast our anchors, which yet were not enough to secure our ships in that most dangerous haven, but further with cable ropes we secured them to iron rings, which for that purpose are fastened into the wall of the fort, for fear of the strong and boisterous northern winds. And thus welcoming one another to a new world, many boats waiting for us, we presently went with joy to set footing in America.

SURVEY OF WEST INDIES

CHAPTER V

Of our landing at Vera Cruz, otherwise St John de Ulhua, and of our entertainment there

UPON the 12 day of September, we happily arrived in America in that famous town called St John de Ulhua, otherwise Vera Cruz; famous for that it was the first beginning of the famous conquest of that valiant and ever renowned conqueror, Hernando Cortez. Here first was that noble and generous resolution, that never heard of policy, to sink the ships which had brought the first Spaniards to that continent, greater than any of the other three parts of the world, to the intent that they might think of nothing but such a conquest as after followed, being destitute of the help of their ships, and without hopes evermore to return to Cuba, Yucatan, or any of those parts from whence they had come. Here it was that the first five hundred Spaniards strengthened themselves against millions of enemies, and against the biggest fourth part of all the world. Here were the first magistrates, judges, aldermen, officers of justice named. The proper name of the town is St John de Ulhua, otherwise called Vera Cruz, from the old harbour and haven of Vera Cruz, six leagues from this, and so called for that upon Good Friday it was first discovered. But the old Vera Cruz proving too dangerous an harbour for ships, by reason of the violence of the northern winds, it was utterly forsaken by the Spaniards, who removed to St John de Ulhua, where their ships found the first safe road by reason of a rock, which is a strong defence against the winds. And because the memory of the work of that Good Friday should never be forgotten, to St John de Ulhua they have added the name also of Vera Cruz, taken from that first haven which was discovered upon Good Friday, anno 1519.

THE ENGLISH-AMERICAN

As soon as we came to shore we found very solemn preparations for entertainment, all the town being resorted to the seaside, all the priests and canons of the cathedral church, all the religious orders of the several convents (which are there Dominicans, Franciscans, Mercenarians, and Jesuits) being in a readiness, with their crosses borne before them, to guide the new Viceroy of Mexico, in procession, to the chief cathedral church. The friars and Jesuits were quicker in going to land than the great Don, the Marquess de Serralvo, and his lady. Some of them kissed the ground as holy in their opinion, for the conversion of those Indians to Christianity, who before had worshipped idols and sacrificed to devils; others kneeled upon their knees making short prayers, some to the Virgin Mary, others to such saints as they best affected; and so betook themselves to the places and stations of those of their profession. In the meantime all the cannon playing both from ships and castle, landed the Viceroy and his lady and all his train, accompanied with Don Martin de Carrillo the Visitor-General for the strife between the Count of Gelves, the last Viceroy, and the Archbishop of Mexico. The great Don and his lady being placed under a canopy of state, began the *Te Deum* to be sung with much variety of musical instruments, all marching in procession to the Cathedral, where with many lights of burning lamps, torches, and wax candles, was to the view of all set upon the high altar their God of bread; to whom all knees were bowed, a prayer of thanksgiving sung, holy water by a priest sprinkled upon all the people, and lastly a Mass with three priests solemnly celebrated. This being ended, the Viceroy was attended on by the Chief High Justice, named *Alcalde Mayor*, by the officers of the town, some judges sent from Mexico to that purpose, and all the soldiers of the ships and town unto his lodging. The friars likewise in procession with their cross before them were conducted to their several cloisters. Friar Calvo presented his Dominicans to the Prior of the cloister of St Dominic, who entertained us very lovingly with some sweetmeats, and everyone with a cup of the Indian drink called chocolate, whereof I shall speak hereafter. This refreshment being ended, we proceeded to a better, which was a most stately dinner both of fish and flesh; no fowls were spared, many capons, turkey cocks, and hens were prodigally lavished, to shew us the abundance and plenty of provision of that country. The Prior of this cloister was no staid, ancient, grey-headed man, such as usually are made Superiors to govern young and wanton friars, but he was a gallant and amorous young spark, who (as we were there informed) had obtained from his Superior, the Provincial, the government of that convent with a bribe of a thousand ducats. After dinner he had some of us to his chamber, where we observed his lightness and little favour of religion or mortification in him. We thought to have found in his chamber some stately library, which might tell us of learning and love of study; but we found not above a dozen old books, standing in a corner covered with dust and cobwebs, as if they were ashamed that the treasure that lay hid in them should be so much forgotten and undervalued, and the *guitarra* (the Spanish lute) preferred and set above them. His chamber was richly dressed and hung with many pictures, and with hangings, some made with cotton-wool, others with various coloured feathers of Michoacan; his tables covered with carpets of silk; his cupboards adorned with several sorts of China cups and dishes, stored within with several dainties of sweetmeats and conserves.

This sight seemed to the zealous friars of our Mission most vain, and unbeseeming a poor and mendicant friar; to the others, whose end in coming from Spain to those parts was liberty, and looseness, and covetousness of riches, this sight was pleasing and gave them great encouragement to enter further into that country, where soon a mendicant Lazarus might become a proud and wealthy Dives. The discourse of the young and light-headed Prior was nothing but vain boasting of himself, of his birth, his parts, his favour with the chief Superior or Provincial, the love which the best ladies, the richest merchants' wives of the town bare unto him, of his clear and excellent voice, and great dexterity in music, whereof he presently gave us a taste, tuning his *guitarra* and singing to us some verses (as he said, of his own composing) to some lovely Amaryllis, adding scandal to scandal, looseness to liberty, which it grieved some of us to see in a Superior who should have taught with words and in his life and conversation examples of repentance and mortification. No sooner were our senses of hearing delighted well with music, our sight with the objects of cotton-wool, silk, and feather-works, but presently our Prior caused to be brought forth of all his store of dainties, such variety as might likewise relish well and delight our sense of tasting. Thus as we were truly transported from Europe to America, so the world seemed truly to be altered, our senses changed from what they were the night and day before when we heard the hideous noise of the mariners hoisting up sails, when we saw the deep and monsters of it, when we tasted the stinking water, when we smelt the tar and pitch; but here we heard a quivering and trembling voice and instrument well tuned, we beheld wealth and riches, we tasted what was sweet, and in the sweetmeats smelt the musk and civet wherewith that epicurean Prior had seasoned his conserves.

Here we broke up our discourse and pastimes, desirous to walk abroad and take a view of the town, having no more time than that and the next day to stay in it. We compassed it round about that afternoon; and found the situation of it to be sandy, except on the south-west side, where it is moorish ground, and full of standing bogs, which, with the great heats that are there, cause it to be a very unhealthy place. The number of inhabitants may be three thousand, and amongst them some very rich merchants, some worth two hundred, some three hundred, and some four hundred thousand ducats. Of the buildings little we observed, for they are all, both houses, churches, and cloisters, built with boards and timber, the walls of the richest man's house being made but of boards, which with the impetuous winds from the North hath been cause that many times the town hath been for the most part of it burnt down to the ground. The great trading from Mexico, and by Mexico from the East Indies, from Spain, from Cuba, Sto Domingo, Yucatan, Portables, and by Portobello from Peru, from Cartagena, and all the islands lying upon the North Sea, and by the River Alvarado going up to Zapotecas, St Ildefonso, and towards Oaxaca, and by the river Grijalva, running up to Tabasco, Los Zoques and Chiapa de Indios, maketh this little town very rich and to abound with all the commodities of the continent land, and of all the East and West Indies' treasures.

The unhealthiness of the place is the reason of the paucity of inhabitants, and the paucity of them, together with the rich trading and commerce, the reasons that the merchants therein are extraordinary rich; who yet might have been far richer had not the town been so often fired, and they in the fire had great losses. All the strength of this town is first the hard and dangerous entrance into the haven; and secondly, a rock which lieth before the town less than a musket-shot off, upon which is built a castle, and in the castle a slight garrison of soldiers. In the town there is neither fort nor castle, nor scarce any people of warlike minds. The rock and castle are as a wall, defence, and enclosure to the haven, which otherwise

THE ENGLISH-AMERICAN

lieth wide open to the ocean, and to the northern winds. No ship dares cast anchor within the haven, but only under the rock and castle, and yet not sure enough so with anchors, except with cables also they be bound and fastened to rings of iron for that purpose to the side of the rock; from whence sometimes it hath happened that ships floating with the stream too much on one side the rock have been driven off and cast upon the other rocks or out to the ocean, the cables of their anchors, and those wherewith they have been fastened to the castle being broken with the force of the winds. This happened to one of our ships the first night after we landed; who were happy that we were not then at sea; for there arose such a storm and tempest from the North, that it quite broke the cables of one ship and drove it out to the main sea, and we thought it would have blown and driven us out of our beds after it, for the slight boarded houses did so totter and shake that we expected every hour when they would fall upon our heads. We had that first night enough of St John de Ulhua, and little rest, though feasted as well at supper as at dinner by our vain, boasting Prior, who before we went to bed had caused all our feet to be washed, that now in easier beds than for above two months together the strait and narrow cabins of the ship had allowed us, our sleep might be more quiet and more nourishing to our bodies; but the whistling winds and tottering chambers, which made our beds uneasy cradles to us, caused us to fly from our rest at midnight, and with our bare (though washed) feet to seek the dirty yard for safer shelter.

In the morning the friars of the cloister, who were acquainted with those winds and storms, laughed at our fearfulness, assuring us that they never slept better than when their beds were rocked with such-like blasts. But that night's affrightment made us weary already of our good and kind entertainment; we desired to remove from the seaside; which our Superior Calvo yielded to, not for our fear sake so much as for his fear, lest with eating too much of the fruits of that country, and drinking after them too greedily of the water (which causeth dangerous fluxes, and hasteneth death to those that newly come from Spain to those parts) we should fall sick, and die there, as hundreds did after our departure for want of temperance in the use of those fruits which before they had never seen or eaten. Thirty mules were ready for us, which had been brought a purpose from Mexico, and had waited for us in St John de Ulhua six days before ever the fleet arrived. Calvo that day busied himself a shipboard in sending to shore our chests, and such provision as had been left of wines, and biscuit, gammons of bacon, and salted beef, whereof there was some store, besides a dozen hens and three sheep, which was much wondered at, that so much should be left after so long a voyage. In the meantime we visited our friends and took our leaves of them in the forenoon; and after dinner seats were prepared for us in the cathedral church to sit and see a comedy acted, which had been on purpose studied and prepared by the town for the entertainment of the new Viceroy of Mexico. Thus two days only we abode in St John de Ulhua, and so departed.

CHAPTER VI

Of our journey from St John de Ulhua to Mexico; and of the most remarkable towns and villages in the way

UPON the 14 day of September we left the town and port of St John de Ulhua, entering into the road to Mexico, which we found the first three or four leagues to be very sandy, as wide and open as is our road from London to St Albans. The first Indians we met with was at the old Vera Cruz, a town seated by the seaside, which the Spaniards that first conquered that country thought to have made their chief harbour; but afterwards by reason of the small shelter they found in it for their ships against the north winds they left it, and removed to St John de Ulhua. Here we began to discover the power of the priests and friars over the poor Indians, and their subjection and obedience unto them. The Prior of St John de Ulhua had writ a letter unto them the day before of our passing that way, charging them to meet us in the way, and to welcome us into those parts; which was by the poor Indians gallantly performed. For two miles before we came to the town there met us on horseback some twenty of the chief of the town, presenting unto every one of us a nosegay of flowers; who rid before us a bow-shot, till we met with more company on foot, to wit, the trumpeters, the waits (who sounded pleasantly all the way before us), the officers of the church, such as here we call church-wardens, though more in number, according to the many sodalities or confraternities of saints whom they serve; these likewise presented to each of us a nosegay; next met us the singing men and boys, all the choristers [quiristers], who softly and leisurely walked before us singing, *Te Deum laudamus*, till we came to the midst of the town, where were two great elm trees, the chief market-place; there was set up one long arbour with green bows, and a table ready furnished with boxes of conserves, and other sweetmeats, and diet-bread to prepare our stomachs for a cup of chocolate, which while it was seasoning with the hot water and sugar, the chief Indians and officers of the town made a speech unto us, having first kneeled down and kissed our hands one by one. They welcomed us into their country, calling us the Apostles of Jesus Christ, thanked us for that we had left our own country, our friends, our fathers and mothers for to save their souls; they told us they honoured us as gods upon earth; and many such compliments they used till our chocolate was brought. We refreshed ourselves for the space of one hour, and gave hearty thanks to the Indians for their kind respects unto us, assuring them that nothing was more dear unto us in this world than their souls, which that we might save we regarded not sea, nor land dangers, nor the unhuman cruelties of barbarous and savage Indians (who as yet had no knowledge of the true God), no nor our own lives.

And thus we took our leaves, giving unto the chief of them some beads, some medals, some crosses of brass, some *Agnus Dei*, some reliques brought from Spain, and to every one of the town an indulgence of forty years (which the Pope had granted unto us, to bestow where and upon whom, and as often as we would), wherewith we began to blind that simple people with ignorant, erroneous, and Popish principles. As we went out of the arbour to take our mules, behold the market-place was full of Indian men and women, who as they saw us ready to depart, kneeled upon the ground as adoring us for a blessing, which as we rid along we bestowed upon them with lifted up hands on high, making over them the sign of the cross. And this submission of the poor Indians unto the priests in those parts, this vainglory in admitting such ceremonious entertainment and public worship from them, did so puff up some of our young friars' hearts that already they thought themselves better than the best bishops in Spain, who though proud enough, yet never travel there with such public acclamations as we did. The waits and trumpets sounded again before us, and the chief of the town conducted us a mile forward, and so took their leaves.

The first two days we lodged but in poor small Indian towns, among whom we still found kind entertainment and good store of provision, especially of hens, capons, turkeys, and several sorts of fruits. The third day at night we came to a great town consisting of near two thousand inhabitants, some Spaniards, some Indians, called Jalapa de la Vera Cruz. This town in the year 1634 was made a new bishop's see (the bishopric of the city called La Puebla de los Angeles being divided into two) and this being not above the third part of it, is thought to be worth ten thousand ducats a year. It stands in a very fertile soil for Indian wheat called maize, and some Spanish wheat. There are many towns about it of Indians; but what makes it rich are the many farms of sugar, and some which they call *estancias*, rich farms for breeding of mules and cattle; and likewise some farms of cochineal. In this town there is but one great church and an inferior chapel, both belonging to a cloister of Franciscan friars, wherein we were lodged that night and the next day, being the Lord's Day. Though the revenues of this cloister be great, yet it maintains not above half a dozen friars, where twenty might be plentifully maintained, that so those few lubbers might be more abundantly, and like epicures, fed and nourished. The Superior or Guardian of this cloister was no less vain than the Prior of St John de Ulhua; and though he were not of our profession, yet he welcomed us with stately entertainment.

Here and wheresoever further we travelled, we still found in the priests and friars looseness of life, and their ways and proceedings contrary to the ways of their profession, sworn to by a solemn vow and covenant. This Order especially of the mendicant Franciscan friars voweth (besides chastity and obedience) poverty more strictly to be observed than any other Order of the Romish Church; for their clothing ought to be coarse sackcloth, their girdles made of hemp should be no finer than strong halters, their shirts should be but woollen, their legs should know no stockings, their feet no shoes but at the most and best either wooden clogs or sandals of hemp, their hands and fingers should not so much as touch any money, nor they have the use or possession or propriety of any, nor their journeys be made easy with the help of horses to carry them, but painfully they ought to travel on foot; and the breach of any of these they acknowledge to be a deadly and mortal sin, with the guilt of a high soul-damning and soul-cursing excommunication. Yet for all these bonds and obligations, those wretched imps live in those parts as though they had never vowed unto the Lord, shewing in their lives that they have vowed what they are not able to perform. It was to us a strange and scandalous sight to see here in Jalapa a friar of the cloister riding in with his lackey boy by his side, upon a goodly gelding (having gone but to the town's end, as we were informed, to hear a dying man's confession), with his long habit tucked up to his girdle, making shew of a fine silk orange-colour stocking upon his legs, and a neat Cordovan shoe upon his foot, with a fine holland pair of drawers, with a lace three inches broad at knee. This sight made us willing to pry further into this and the other friars' carriages, under whose broad sleeves we could perceive their doublets quilted with silk, and at their wrists the laces of their holland shirts. In their talk we could discern no mortification, but mere vanity and worldliness.

After supper some of them began to talk of carding and dicing; they challenged us, that were but new-comers to those parts, to a primera, which though most of ours refused, some for want of money, some for ignorance of that game, yet at last with much ado they got two of our friars to join with two of theirs. So the cards were handsomely shuffled, the vies and revies were doubled, loss made some hot and blind with passion, gain made others eager and covetous; and thus was that religious cloister made all night a gaming house, and sworn religious poverty turned into profane and wordly covetousness. We that beheld some part of the night the game, found enough to observe, for the more the sport increased, scandals to the sport were added, both by drinking, and swearing that common oath *Voto á Cristo, Voto á Dios*, and also by scoffing and jeering at the religious vows of poverty which they had vowed; for one of the Franciscans, though formerly he had touched money, and with his fingers had laid it to the stake on the table, yet sometimes to make the company laugh, if he had chanced to win a double vie (and sometimes the vies and revies went round of twenty patacones) then would he take the end of one sleeve of his habit and open wide the other broad sleeve, and so with his sleeve sweep the money into his other sleeve, saying: ' I have vowed not to touch money, nor to keep any, I meaned then a natural contact of it; but my sleeve may touch it, and my sleeve may keep it ': shewing with scoffs and jests of his lips what religion was in his heart. My ears tingled with hearing such oaths; my tongue would have uttered some words of reproof, but that I considered myself a guest and stranger in a strange house, and that if anything I should say, it would do no good. So silently I departed to my rest, leaving the gamesters, who continued till sun-rising, and in the morning I was informed that the jesting friar, that rather roaring boy than religious Franciscan, fitter for Sardanapalus or Epicurus his school than to live in a cloister, had lost fourscore and odd patacones, his sleeve (it seems) refusing to keep for him what he had vowed never to possess. Here I began to find out by experience of these Franciscans that liberty and looseness of life it was that brought yearly so many friars and Jesuits from Spain to those parts, rather than zeal of preaching the Gospel and converting souls to Christ, which indeed being an act of highest charity, they make a special badge of the truth of their religion. But the looseness of their lives sheweth evidently that the love of money, of vainglory, of power and authority over the poor

SURVEY OF WEST INDIES

Indians, is their end and aim more than any love of God.

From Jalapa we went to a place called by the Spaniards La Rinconada, which is no town nor village, and therefore not worth mentioning in such a road as now I am in; yet, as famous in two things, it muſt not be omitted amongſt greater places. This place ſtands so far from any other town that travellers can scarce make their journeys without either baiting there at noon, or lying there at night, or declining three or four miles out of the road to some Indian town. It is no more than one house, which the Spaniards call *venta*, or as our English inns, seated in the corner of a low valley, which is the hotteſt place from St John de Ulhua to Mexico; about it are the beſt springs and fountains in all the road, and the water though warm with the heat of the sun, yet as sweet as any milk. The inn-keepers, knowing well the Spaniards' heat, that it seeks cool and refreshing drink, have special care so to lay in water in great earthen vessels, which they set upon a moiſt and waterish sand, that it is so cold that it maketh the teeth to chatter. This sweetness and this coolness together of that water in so hot and scorching a country was to us a wonder, who could find no other refreshment from that extraordinary heat. Besides our provision here of beef, mutton, kid, hens, turkeys, rabbits, fowls, and especially quails, was so plentiful and cheap that we were aſtonished at it. The valley and country about it is very rich and fertile, full of Spanish farms of sugar, and cochineal, Spanish and Indian wheat. But what maketh me more especially remember this *venta*, or inn, is, for that though art and experience of man have found a way to provide for travellers in so hot a place cool and refreshing water, and God have given it the sweetness of milk, and to the place such abundance of provision, yet all this in the day only is comfortable and pleasant; but in the night the Spaniards call it

THE ENGLISH-AMERICAN

Cumfites en infierno, that is to say, cumfits in hell, for not only the heat is so extraordinary that it is impossible to be feeding without wiping away the continual sweat of the face, whose drops from the brows are always ready to blind our eyes and to fill with sauce our dishes, but the swarms of gnats are such that waking and sleeping no device of man is able to keep them off. True it is, most of us had our pavilions which we carried with us to hang about and over our beds, but these could not defend us from that piercing and stinging vermin, which like Egypt's plague of frogs would be sure to be in every place, and through our curtains to come upon our very beds. Yet in the day they are not; but just at sun-setting they begin to swarm about, and at sun-rising away they go. After a most tedious and troublesome night, when we found the rising of the sun had dispersed and banished them away, we thought it best for us to flee away from that place with them; and so from thence early we departed to a town as pleasant and fertile and abounding with provision as this Rinconada, and free from such busy guests and individual mates and companions as the night before had intruded themselves upon us.

The next night we got to a town called Segura, inhabited both by Indians and Spaniards, consisting of about a thousand inhabitants; here again without any charges we were stately entertained by Franciscan friars, as light and vainglorious as those of Jalapa. This town had its first beginning and foundation from Hernando Cortez, and is called Segura de la Frontera, being built up by him for a frontier town to secure the Spaniards, that came from St John de Ulhua to Mexico, against the Culiacans and people of Tepeacao, who were allied to the Mexicans, and so much annoyed the Spaniards. This town likewise, as all the rest from St John de Ulhua to Mexico, is very plentiful of provision, and many sorts of fruits, namely plantains, sapotes, and chicosapotes, which have within a great black kernel as big as our horse plums, the fruit itself is as red within as scarlet, as sweet as honey; but the chicosapote is less and some of them red, some brown-coloured, and so juicy that at the eating the juice like drops of honey fall from them, and the smell is like unto a baked pear. Here likewise were presented unto us clusters of grapes as fair as any in Spain, which were welcome unto us, for that we had seen none since we came from Spain, and we saw by them that the country thereabouts would be very fit for vineyards, if the King of Spain would grant the planting of vines in those parts; which often he hath refused to do, lest the vineyards there should hinder the trading and traffic between Spain and those parts, which certainly had they but wine, needed not any commerce with Spain. This town is of a more temperate climate than any other from Vera Cruz to Mexico, and the people who formerly had been eaters of man's flesh, now as civil and politic, as loving and courteous as any in the road. From whence we declined a little out of our way more westward (the road being north-westward) only to see that famous town of Tlaxcala, whose inhabitants joined with Cortez, and we may say were the chief instruments of that great and unparalleled conquest.

CHAPTER VII

A description of the town of Tlaxcala.

TLAXCALA being worth all the rest of the towns and villages between St John de Ulhua and Mexico, I thought it not fit to parallel it with the others in naming it briefly and passing by it as a traveller, but rather I judged it convenient, and beseeming my present history, to record to posterity with one whole chapter the greatness of it, and the valour of its inhabitants, from the conquest of America made by Hernando Cortez.

Tlaxcala was subdued and sworn to the power and command of the Spaniards, being in those times one of the chiefest, though not richest, towns in America; whose inhabitants after clave most faithfully to Cortez, and were chief instruments for the subduing of Mexico, and therefore to this day are freed from tribute by the Kings of Spain, paying not the money which as a tribute tax is laid upon every Indian to be paid yearly, but only in acknowledgment of subjection they pay yearly one corn of maize, which is their Indian wheat.

This great town of Tlaxcala is properly in the Indian tongue as much as to say, as bread well baked, for there is more grain called *centli* gathered than in all the province round about. In times past the town was called Texcallan, that is to say, a valley betwixt two hills. It is planted by a river side, which springeth out of a hill called Atlancapetec, and watereth the most part of the province, and from thence issueth out into the South Sea, by Zacatula. This town hath four goodly streets, which are called Tepeticpac, Ocotelulco, Tizatlan, Quiahuiztlan. The first street standeth on high upon a hill, far from the river which may be about half a league, and because it standeth on a hill it is called Tepeticpac, that is to say, a hill, and was the first population, which was founded there on high because of the wars. Another street is situated on the hill-side towards the river; because at the building thereof there were many pine trees, they named it Ocotelulco, which is to say, a pineapple plot. This street was beautiful, and most inhabited of all the town, and there was the chiefest market-place, where all the buying and selling was used, and that place they called *tianquiztli*; in that street was the dwelling house of Maxixca. Along the river side in the plain standeth another street called Tizatlan, because there is much lime and chalk. In this street dwelled Xicotencatl, Captain-General of the whole commonwealth. There is another street named, by reason of the brackish water, Quiahuiztlan; but since the Spaniards came thither, all those buildings are almost altered after a better fashion, and built with stone. In the plain by the river side standeth the town house, and other offices, as in the city of Venice. This Tlaxcala was governed by noble and rich men; they used not that one alone should rule, but did rather flee from that government as from tyranny, and therefore hated Montezuma as a tyrant. In their wars they had four captains, which governed each one street, of the which four they did elect a Captain-General. Also there were other gentlemen that were under-captains, but a small number. In the wars they used their standard to be carried behind the army, but when the battle was to be fought, they placed the standard where all the host might see it, and he that came not incontinent to his ancient paid a penalty. Their standard had two cross-bow arrows set thereon, which they esteemed as the reliques of their ancestors. This standard two old soldiers and valiant men, being of the chiefest captains, had the charge to carry, in the which an abuse of soothsaying either of loss or victory was noted. In this order they shot one of these arrows against the first enemies that they met, and if with that arrow they did either kill or hurt, it was a token that they should have the victory, and if it neither did kill nor hurt, then they assuredly believed that they should lose the field.

This province or lordship of Tlaxcala had twenty-eight villages and towns, wherein were contained 150,000 householders. They are men well made, and were good warriors, the like were not among the Indians. They are very poor, and have no other riches but only the grain and corn called *centli*, and with the gain and profit thereof they do both clothe

THE ENGLISH-AMERICAN

themselves and provide all other necessaries. They have many market-places, but the greatest and most used daily standeth in the street of Ocotelulco, which formerly was so famous that 20,000 persons came thither in one day to buy and sell, changing one thing for another, for they knew not what money meaned. They have now, and had formerly, all kind of good policy in the town; there are goldsmiths, feather-dressers, barbers, hot houses, and potters, who make as good earthen vessel as is made in Spain. The earth is fat and fruitful for corn, fruit, and pasture, for among the pine trees groweth so much grass that the Spaniards feed their cattle there, which in Spain they cannot do. Within two leagues of the town standeth a round hill of six miles of height, and five and forty miles in compass, and is now called St Bartholomew's Hill, where the snow freezeth. In times past they called that hill Matealcucie, who was their God for water. They had also a God for wine, who was named Ometochtli, for the great drunkenness which they used. Their chiefest God was called Camaxtlo; and by another name Mixcovatl, whose temple stood in the street of Ocotelulco, in the which temple there was sacrificed some years above eight hundred persons.

In the town they speak three languages, that is to say, Nahualh, which is the courtly speech, and chiefest in all the land of Mexico; another is called Otomir, which is most commonly used in the villages; there is one only street that speaketh Pinomer, which is the grossest speech. There was also formerly in the town a common jail, where felons lay in irons, and all things which they held for sin were there corrected. At the time that Cortez was there it happened that a townsman stole from a Spaniard a little gold; whereof Cortez complained to Maxixca, who incontinent made such enquiry that the offender was found in Cholula, which is another great town five leagues from thence; they brought the prisoner with the gold, and delivered him

SURVEY OF WEST INDIES

to Cortez to do with him his pleasure. Cortez would not accept him, but gave him thanks for his diligence; then was he carried with a crier before him, manifesting his offence, and in the market-place upon a scaffold they brake his joints with a cudgel. The Spaniards marvelled to see such strange justice, and began to be more confident that as in this point they had endeavoured to pleasure and right them, so likewise they should afterwards find them very forward to do their wills and pleasures for the better conquering of Mexico and Montezuma.

Ocotelulco and Tizatlan are the two streets which now are most inhabited. In Ocotelulco standeth a cloister of Franciscan friars who are the preachers of that town; they have there joining to their cloister a very fair church, to which belong some fifty Indians, singers, organists, players on musical instruments, trumpeters and waits, who set out the Mass with a very sweet and harmonious music, and delight the fancy and senses, while the spirit is sad and dull as little acquainted with God, who will be worshipped in spirit and in truth. In Tepeticpac and Quiahuiztlan are two chapels only, to which on the Lord's Day, and upon other occasions, the friars of the cloister resort to say Mass. In this cloister we were entertained a day and two nights with great provision of flesh and fish, which is very plentiful by reason of the river. The friars are allowed by the town a dozen Indians who are free from other services only to fish for the friars. They change their turns by weeks, four one week and four another, except they be called upon for some special occasion, and then they leave all other work and attend only with fish upon the friars. The town now is inhabited by Spaniards and Indians together; and is the seat of a chief Officer of Justice sent from Spain every three years, called *Alcalde Mayor*, whose power reacheth to all the towns within twenty leagues about. Besides him the Indians have likewise among themselves *Alcaldes*, *Regidores* and *Alguaziles*, superior and inferior officers of justice appointed yearly by the *Alcalde Mayor*, who keeps them all in awe, and takes from them for his service as many as he pleaseth without paying anything for the service done unto him. The hard usage of this *Alcalde Mayor* and other Spaniards hath much decayed that populous town, which should rather have been cherished than disheartened by the Spaniards, who by means of it gained all the rest of the country.

CHAPTER VIII

Concluding the rest of our journey from Tlaxcala to Mexico, through the City of Angels, and Guacocingo

THE next place most remarkable in the road wherein we travelled was the city called by the Spaniards La Puebla de los Angeles, the City of Angels. To the which we were desirous to go, knowing that in it there was a convent of Dominicans of our profession, not having met with any such since the day we departed from St John de Ulhua. Here we refreshed ourselves at leisure three days, finding ourselves very welcome to our own brethren, who spared nothing that was fit for our entertainment. We visited all the city, and took large notice of it, judging of the wealth and riches of it not only by the great trading in it, but by the many cloisters both of nuns and friars which it maintaineth, such being commonly very burdensome to the places where they live, an idle kind of beggars who make the people believe the maintaining of them is meritorious and saving to their souls, and that their prayers for them is more worth than the means and sustenance which they receive from them. Of these there is in that city a very great cloister of some fifty or threescore Dominicans, another of more Franciscans, another of Augustines, another of Mercenarians, another of Discalced Carmelites, another of Jesuits, besides four of nuns.

This city is seated in a low and pleasant valley, about ten leagues from a very high mountain, which is always covered with snow. It standeth twenty leagues from Mexico. It was first built and inhabited in the year 1530 by the command of Don Antonio de Mendoza, Viceroy of Mexico, together with the consent of Sebastian Ramirez who was a Bishop, and had been President in time past in Sto Domingo, and was that year instead of Nunnio de Guzman (who had behaved himself very evil both with the Indians and Spaniards) sent to be President of the Chancery of Mexico with these other four judges, the Licenciates John de Salmeron, Gasco Quiroga, Francisco Ceynos, and Alonso Maldonado. These judges governed the land far better than Nunnio de Guzman before them had done; and among other remarkable things they did was to cause this city to be inhabited; and set at liberty the Indians who inhabited there before, and were grievously suppressed and enslaved by the Spaniards, and therefore many of them departed from thence who had inhabited there before, and went to seek their living at Xalixco, Honduras, Guatemala and other places where war then was.

This city was formerly called by the Indians Cuetlaxcoapan, that is to say, a snake in water; the reason was because there are two fountains, the one of evil water and the other of good. This city is now a bishop's see, whose yearly revenues since the cutting off from it Jalapa de la Vera Cruz are yet worth above twenty thousand ducats. By reason of the good and wholesome air it daily increaseth with inhabitants, who resort from many other places to live there; but especially the year 1634, when Mexico was like to be drowned with the inundation of the lake, thousands left it, and came with all their goods and families to this City of the Angels, which now is thought to consist of ten thousand inhabitants. That which maketh it most famous is the cloth which is made in it, and is sent far and near, and judged now to be as good as the cloth of Segovia, which is the best that is made in Spain, but now is not so much esteemed of nor sent so much from Spain to America by reason of the abundance of fine cloth which is made in this City of Angels. The felts likewise that are made are the best of all that country; there is likewise a glass house, which is there a rarity, none other being as yet known in those parts. But the mint house that is in it, where is coined half the silver that cometh from Zacatecas, makes it the second to Mexico; and it is thought that in time it will be as great and populous as Mexico. Without it there are many gardens, which store the markets with provision of salads [salets], the soil abounds with wheat, and with sugar farms, among the which not far from this city there is one so great and populous (belonging to the Dominican friars of Mexico) that for the work only belonging unto it, it maintained in my time above two hundred blackamoor slaves, men and women besides their little children.

The chief town between this City of Angels and Mexico is called Guacocingo, consisting of some five hundred Indians and one hundred Spaniards inhabitants. Here is likewise a cloister of Franciscans, who entertained us gallantly, and made shew unto us of the dexterity of their Indians in music. Those fat friars wanted not like the rest all provision necessary for the body. But their greatest glory and boasting to us was the education which they had given to some children of the town, especially such as served them in their cloister, whom they had brought up to dancing after the Spanish fashion at the sound of the *guitarra*. And this a dozen of them (the biggest not being above fourteen years of age) performed excellently for our better entertainment that night; we were there till

SURVEY OF WEST INDIES

midnight, singing both Spanish and Indian tunes, capering and dancing with their castanets, or knockers on their fingers, with such dexterity as not only did delight, but amaze and astonish us. True it is, we thought those Franciscans might have been better employed at that time in their choir [quire] at their midnight devotions according to their profession; but we still found vowed religious duties more and more neglected, and worldliness too too much embraced by such as had renounced and forsaken the world and all its pleasures, sports, and pastimes.

This town of Guacocingo is almost as much as Tlaxcala privileged by the Kings of Spain; for that it joined with Tlaxcala against the Mexicans in defence of Hernando Cortez, and the rest of the Spaniards that first conquered that land. From hence we made our last journey to the city of Mexico, passing over the side of that high hill which we had discovered at the City of Angels, some thirty miles off. There are no alps like unto it for height, cold, and constant snow that lieth upon it. From Spain to that place we had not felt any such extremity of cold, which made the Spaniards that had come out of the hot climate of Spain, and endured excessive heat at sea, wonder and admire. This last journey from Guacocingo to Mexico we reckoned to be thirty English miles, and of the thirty miles we judged at least the fifteen to be up and down the hill; and yet the top of it (whither we ascended not) was far higher. From that highest part of it which we travelled over, we discovered the city of Mexico, and the lake about it, which seemed to us to be near at hand, standing some ten English miles in a plain from the bottom of this mountain. The first town we came to below the hill was Quahutipec, of the jurisdiction of Texcoco; where we also called to mind that this was the place near unto which was pitched the camp of the Indians of Culhua, which was near a hundred thousand men of war, who were sent by the seniors of Mexico and Texcoco to encounter Cortez, but all in vain, for his horsemen broke through them, and his artillery made such havoc among them that they were soon put to flight.

Three leagues from hence on our right hand as we travelled, we discovered Texcoco by the side of the lake and out of the road; yet it ministered unto us matter of a large discourse, taken from the time of Cortez and the first conquerors, who found it a great city, and at that time even as big as Mexico; though in it Cortez met with no resistance, for as he journeyed towards it four principal persons inhabitants of it met with his forces, bearing a rod of gold with a little flag in token of peace, saying that Coacuacoyocin their Lord had sent them to desire him not to make any spoil in his city, and towns about it; and likewise to offer his friendship, praying also that it might please him with his whole army to take his lodging in the town of Texcoco, where he should be well received. Cortez, rejoicing at this message, yet jealous of some treachery, and mistrusting the people of Texcoco (whose forces joined with the Mexicans and Culiacans he had met with a little before) went forward on his way and came to Quahutichan and Huaxuta (which then were suburbs of the great city Texcoco, but now are pretty villages by themselves), where he and all his host were plenteously provided of all things necessary, and threw down the idols. This done he entered into the city, where his lodging was prepared in a great house, sufficient for him and all the Spaniards, with many other his Indian friends. And because that at his first entry he saw neither women nor children, he suspected some treason, and forthwith proclaimed upon pain of death that none of his men should go out. In the evening the Spaniards went up into the *zoties* and galleries to behold the city, and there they saw the great number of citizens that fled from thence with their stuff, some towards the mountains, and others to the water side to take boat, a thing strange to see the great haste and stir to provide for themselves. There were at that time at least twenty thousand little boats (called *canoas*) occupied in carrying household-stuff and passengers; Cortez would fain have remedied it, but the night was so nigh at hand that he could not. He would gladly also have apprehended the Lord, but he was one of the first that fled unto Mexico.

This town of Texcoco to this day is famous among the Spaniards; for that it was one of the first, if not the first (which according to the histories of those parts is very probable), that received a Christian King to rule and govern. For Cortez, hearing that Coacuacoyocin then King of that city and towns adjacent was fled, caused many of the citizens to be called before him, and having in his company a young gentleman of a noble house in that country, who had been lately christened, and had to name Hernando (Cortez being his god-father, who loved him well), said unto the citizens that this new Christian lord Don Hernando was son unto Nezavalpincintli their loving lord, wherefore he required them to make him their King, considering that Coacuacoyocin was fled unto the enemies, laying also before them his wicked fact in killing of Cacuza, his own brother, only to put him from his inheritance and kingdom, through the enticement of Quahutimoccin, a mortal enemy to the Spaniards. In this sort was that new Christian Don Hernando elected King, and the fame thereof being blown abroad, many citizens repaired home again to visit their new prince, so that in short space the city was as well replenished with people as it was before, and being also well used at the Spaniards' hands, they served them diligently in all things that they were commanded. And Don Hernando abode ever after a faithful friend unto the Spaniards in their wars against Mexico, and in short time learned the Spanish tongue.

Now Cortez was strong both with Spaniards and

Indians; and his court at Texcoco was as great or greater than Montezuma's formerly had been at Mexico. And here Cortez made his preparation for the siege of Mexico with all haste, and furnished himself with scaling ladders and other necessaries fit for such a purpose. His brigantines [vergantines] being nailed and thoroughly ended, he made a sluice, or trench, of half a league of length, twelve foot broad and more, and two fathom in depth. This work was fifty days a doing, although there were four hundred thousand men daily working; truly a famous work and worthy of memory, which hath made Texcoco gloriously mentioned, though now almost decayed in the great number of inhabitants. The dock or trench being thus finished, the brigantines were caulked with tow and cotton-wool, and for want of tallow and oil they were (as some authors report) driven to take man's grease, not that Cortez permitted them to slay men for that effect, but of those which were slain in the wars, and of such as sallied daily out of Mexico to hinder this work, and fighting were slain. The Indians, who were cruel and bloody butchers, using sacrifice of man's flesh, would in this sort open the dead body and take out the grease. The brigantines being launched, Cortez mustered his men, and found nine hundred Spaniards, of the which were fourscore and six horsemen, and a hundred and eighteen with cross-bows, and harquebuses [hargabushes]; and all the residue had sundry weapons, as swords, daggers, targets, lances, and halberds. Also they had for armour, corslets, coats of mail, and jacks. They had moreover three great pieces of cast iron, fifteen small pieces of brass, and ten hundred-weight of powder, with store of shot, besides a hundred thousand Indians, men of war. On Whit-Sunday all the Spaniards came into the field, that great plain below the high mountain spoken of before, where Cortez made three chief captains, among whom he divided his whole army. Unto Pedro de Alvarado, the first Captain, he appointed thirty horsemen, and a hundred and seventy footmen of the Spaniards, two pieces of ordnance, and thirty thousand Indians, commanding him to camp in Tlacopan. Unto Christoval de Olid, the second Captain, he gave three and thirty horsemen, and a hundred and eighteen footmen of the Spanish nation, two pieces of ordnance and thirty thousand Indians, and appointed him to pitch his camp in Culiacan. To Gonzalo de Sandoval, who was the third Captain, he gave three and twenty horsemen, and a hundred and threescore footmen, two pieces of ordnance, and forty thousand Indians, with commission to choose a place to pitch his camp. In every brigantine he planted a piece of ordnance, six harquebuses, or cross-bows, and three and twenty Spaniards, men most fit for that purpose. He appointed also captains for each, and himself for General, whereof some of the chiefest of his company began to murmur, that went by land, thinking that they had been in greater danger; wherefore they required him to go with the main battle, and not by water. Cortez little esteemed their words; for although there was more danger in the land than in the water, yet it did more import to have greater care in the wars by water than on the land, because his men had been in the one, and not in the other. Besides, the chiefest hopes that Cortez had to win Mexico were these vessels, for with them he burned a great part of the canoes of Mexico, and the rest he so locked up that they were no help unto the Mexicans, and with twelve only brigantines he did annoy his enemy as much by water as the rest of his army did by land.

All this preparation for the siege of Mexico by land and water, with above a hundred thousand Indians, besides the Spaniards above mentioned, and the twelve brigantines by water, was finished in this city of Texcoco, which is a sufficient argument of the greatness of it at that time, maintaining with provision fit and necessary so many thousands of people, and it yielded matter enough unto us for a large discourse, whilst not far from the sight of it we travelled in the open and direct plain road to Mexico. And as we talked of the greatness of it in former times, so likewise we now wondered to consider it to be but a small government, where doth constantly reside a Spanish Governor sent from Spain, whose power reacheth to those borders of Tlaxcala and Guacocingo, and to most of the petty towns and villages of the plain, which were formerly under the command and power of a King, but now are not able to make up above a thousand ducats a year, which is supposed to be the yearly revenues of the Governor; and Texcoco itself this day judged to consist only of a hundred Spaniards, and three hundred Indian inhabitants, whose chief riches come by gardening, and sending daily in their canoes herbs and salads to Mexico. Some wealth likewise they get by their cedar trees which grow there, and are ready timber for the buildings of Mexico. Yet now also are these cedars much decayed by the Spaniards, who have wasted and spoiled them in their too too sumptuous buildings. Cortez only was accused by Pamfilo de Narvaez for that he had spent seven thousand beams of cedar trees in the work of his own house. Gardens there were in Texcoco formerly, that had a thousand cedar trees for walls and circuit, some of them of a hundred and twenty foot long, and twelve foot in compass from end to end; but now that garden that hath fifty cedar trees about it is much regarded. At the end of this plain we passed through Mexicalcinco, which formerly was a great town, but now not of above an hundred inhabitants, and from thence to Guetlavac, a petty village, yet most pleasant for the shade of many fruit trees, gardens, and stately houses which for their recreation some citizens of Mexico have built there, being at the foot of the causeway [cawsey] which from this town through the lake reacheth about five English miles to Mexico.

And thus upon the third day of October, 1625, we entered into that famous and gallant city, yet not abiding in it, but only passing through it, till we came to a house of recreation, standing among the gardens in the way to Chapultepec, named Saint Jacintho, belonging to the Dominicans of Manila in the East Indies (whither our course was intended), where we were stately entertained, and abode till after Candlemas Day, the time of our second shipping at Acapulco (eighty leagues from Mexico) by the South Sea to Manila, the chief city of the islands named Philippines.

CHAPTER IX

Shewing some particulars of the great and famous City of Mexico in former times, with a true description of it now, and of the state and condition of it the year 1625

IT hath been no small piece of policy in the friars and Jesuits of Manila and the Philippine Islands to purchase near about Mexico some house and garden to carry thither such missionary priests as they yearly bring from Spain for those parts. For were it not that they found some rest and place of recreation, but were presently closed up in the cloisters of Mexico to follow those religious duties (which sore against their wills most of them are forced to), they would soon after a tedious journey from Spain by sea and land relent of their purposes of going forward, and venturing upon a second voyage by the South Sea; and would either resolve upon a return to Spain, or of staying in some part of America; as myself and five more of my company did, though secretly and hiddenly, and sore against the will of Friar Calvo and others, who had the tutoring and conducting of us. Therefore that all such as come from Spain to be shipped again at Acapulco for the Philippines may have all manner of encouragement, rest, and recreations becoming their professions, whilst they do abide in America, and may not be disheartened by those that live about Mexico (who do truly envy all that pass that way to Asia), the friars and Jesuits have purchased for their missions houses of recreation among the gardens, which are exempted from the power and command of the Superiors of Mexico, and are subordinate unto the government of the Provincials of the Philippines, who send from thence their substitute vicars to rule, and to look to the aforementioned houses and gardens. To the Dominicans belonged this house called St Jacintho, whither we were carried, and where we did abide near five months, having all things provided that were fit and necessary for our recreations, and for our better encouragement to a second voyage by sea. The gardens belonging to this house might be of fifteen acres of ground, divided into shady walks under the orange and lemon trees; there we had the pomegranates, figs, and grapes in abundance, with the plantain, sapote, chicosapote, pine-fruit, and all other fruits that were to be found in Mexico. The herbs and salads and great number of Spanish *cardoes* which were sold out, brought in a great rent yearly; for every day there was a cart attended to be filled and sent to the market of Mexico; and this not at seasons of the year, as here in England and other parts of Europe, but at all times and seasons, both winter and summer, there being no difference of heat, cold, frosts, and snow, as with us, but the same temper all the whole year, the winter differing only from the summer by the rain that falls, and not by excessive frosts that nip. This we enjoyed without doors; but within we had all sorts and varieties both of fish and flesh.

What most we wondered at was the abundance of sweetmeats, and especially of conserves, that were provided for us; for to every one of us during the time of our abode there was brought on Monday morning half a dozen boxes of conserve of quinces, and other fruits, besides our biscuits, to stay our stomachs in the mornings and at other times of the day; for in our stomachs we found a great difference between Spain and that country. For in Spain and other parts of Europe a man's stomach will hold out from meal to meal, and one meal here of good cheer will nourish and cherish the stomach four and twenty hours, but in Mexico and other parts of America we found that two or three hours after a good meal of three or four several dishes of mutton, veal or beef, kid, turkeys, or other fowls, our stomachs would be ready to faint, and so we were fain to support them with either a cup of chocolate, or a bit of conserve or biscuit, which for that purpose was allowed us in great abundance. This seemed to me so strange (whereas the meat seemed as fat and hearty, excepting the beef, as ours in Europe), that I for some satisfaction presently had recourse to a doctor of physic, who cleared my doubt with this answer: That though the meat we fed on was as fair to look on as in Spain, yet the substance and nourishment in it came far short of it, by reason of the pasture, which is drier and hath not the change of springs which the pastures of Europe have, but is short and withers soon away. But secondly, he told me that the climate of those parts had this effect, to produce a fair shew but little matter or substance. As in the flesh we fed on, so likewise in all the fruits there, which are most fair and beautiful to behold, most sweet and luscious to taste, but little inward virtue or nourishment at all in them, not half that is in a Spanish *camuesa*, or English Kentish pippin. And as in meat and fruit there is this inward and hidden deceit, so likewise the same is to be found in the people that are born and bred there, who make fair outward shews, but are inwardly false and hollow-hearted.

THE ENGLISH-AMERICAN

Which I have heard reported much among the Spaniards to have been the answer of our Queen Elizabeth of England to some that presented unto her of the fruits of America, that surely where those fruits grew the women were light, and all the people hollow and false-hearted. But further reasons I omit to search into for this; of experience only I write, which taught me that little substance and virtue is in the great abundance and variety of food which there is enjoyed, our stomachs witnessing this truth, which ever and anon were gaping and crying, 'Feed, feed.' Our conserves therefore and dainties were plentifully allowed us and all other encouragements, and no occasion denied us of going to visit Mexico (which was not two full miles from us), all the while we abode there. It was a pleasant walk for us to go out in the morning, and to spend all the day in the city and come home at night; our way lying by arches made of stone, three miles long, to convey the water from Chapultepec unto the city. Take therefore, gentle Reader, from me what for the space of five months I could learn concerning it in former and present times.

The situation of this city is much like that of Venice, but only differs in this, that Venice is built upon the sea-water, and Mexico upon a lake, which seeming one, indeed is two; one part whereof is standing water, the other ebbeth and floweth according to the wind that bloweth. That part which standeth is wholesome, good, and sweet, and yieldeth store of small fish. That part which ebbeth and floweth is of saltish, bitter, and pestiferous water, yielding no kind of fish, small or great. The sweet water standeth higher than the other, and falleth into it, and reverteth not backward, as some conceive it doth. The salt lake containeth fifteen miles in breadth, and fifteen in length, and more than five and forty in circuit; and the lake of sweet water containeth even as much; in such sort that the whole lake containeth much about a hundred miles. The Spaniards are divided in opinions concerning this water and the springs of it; some hold that all this water hath but one spring out of a great and high mountain which ſtandeth south-weſt within sight of Mexico, and that the cause that the one part of the lake is brackish or saltish is that the bottom or ground is all salt. But however this opinion be true or false, certain it is and by experience I can witness that of that part of the salt water great quantity of salt is daily made, and is part of the great trading of that city into other parts of the country, nay it is sent part of it to the Philippine Islands. Others say that this lake hath two springs, and that the fresh water springeth out of that mountain which ſtandeth south-weſt from Mexico, and the salt brackish water springeth out of other high mountains which ſtand more north-weſt. But these give no reason for the saltness of it, without it be the agitation of it in the ebbing and flowing; which not being with tides like the sea, but with the winds only (which indeed make it as ſtormy sometimes as is the sea), why may not the winds produce the same effeƈt in the fresh water lake? I think rather if it spring from a different spring from that from whence springeth the fresh water, the brackishness and saltishness of it may proceed from some brackish and sulphurous minerals through which it passeth in those mountains. For by experience I know the like in the province of Guatemala, where by a town called Amatitan there is a ſtanding lake of water not altogether sweet and fresh, but a little brackish, which certainly hath its spring from a fiery mountain called there a *volcún* (whose burning proceeds from the mines of brimſtone that are within it), from whence spring near the same town likewise two or three springs of exceeding hot water, which are resorted to for wholesome baths, as coming through a sulphurous mine, and yet the ſtanding lake proceeding from the same mountain is of that quality that it maketh the ground about it salt, and especially in the mornings the people go to gather up the salt which lieth upon the ground by the water side like unto a hoary frost. But thirdly, others conceive that that part of the Lake of Mexico which is saltish and brackish comes through the earth from the North Sea; and though springs of water which come from the sea lose their brackishness through the earth, yet this may keep some brackishness by reason of the minerals, which are many in those parts; or by reason of the great, wide, and open concavities of those mountains, which being very hollow within (as we find by experience of the earthquakes which are more frequent there than here by reason of the wind that getteth into those concavities, and so shake the earth to get out) give no way to the water to sweeten through the earth, or to lose all that saltness which it brought with it from the sea. But whatsoever the true reason be, there is not the like lake known of sweet and saltish water, one part breeding fish, the other breeding none at all.

This lake had formerly some fourscore towns, some say more, situated round about it; many of them containing five thousand households, and some ten thousand, yea and Texcoco (as I have said before) was as big as Mexico. But when I was there, there might be thirty towns and villages about it, and scarce any of above five hundred households between Spaniards and Indians; such hath been the hard usage of the Spaniards towards them that they have even almost consumed that poor nation. Nay two years before I came from those parts, which were the years of 1635 and 1636, I was credibly informed that a million of Indians' lives had been lost in an endeavour of the Spaniards to turn the water of the lake another way from the city, which was performed by cutting a way through the mountains, for to avoid the great inundations that Mexico was subject unto, and especially for that the year 1634 the waters grew so high that they

NEW SPAIN

(Shewing only the region between Mexico City and the Pacific Coast)

threatened destruction to all the city, ruinating a great part, and coming into the churches that stood in the highest part of it, in so much that the people used commonly boats and canoes from house to house. And most of the Indians that lived about the lake were employed to strive against this strong element of water, which hath been the undoing of many poor wretches, but especially of these thirty towns and villages that bordered near upon the lake which now by that great work is further from the houses of the city, and hath a passage made another way, though it was thought it would not long continue but would find again its old course towards Mexico.

This city when Cortez first entered into it was (as some say) of sixty, but more probably it is reported to have been of fourscore thousand houses. Montezuma his palace was very great, large, and beautiful, which in the Indian language was named *tepac*; and that had twenty doors or gates, which had their outcoming into the common streets. It had three courts; and in the one stood a fair fountain, many halls, and a hundred chambers of three and twenty, and thirty foot long, an hundred baths, and hot-houses, and all this without nails, yet very good workmanship. The walls were made of mason's work, and wrought of marble, jasper, and other black stone, with veins of red, like unto rubies and other stones, which glistered very fair; the roofs were wrought of timber, and curiously carved, being of cedar, cypress, and pine tree; the chambers were painted and hung with cloth of cotton, and of coneys' hair and feathers. The beds only were unseeming this great state, very poor and of no value, such as to this day the best and richest Indians use; for they wear nothing but mantles laid upon mats, or upon hay, or else mats alone. Within this palace lived a thousand women, nay some affirm three thousand, reckoning gentlewomen, servants, and slaves, all together. But the most were principal

Indians' daughters; of whom Montezuma took for himself those that liked him best, and the others he gave in marriage to gentlemen his servants. It is credibly reported among the Spaniards that he had at one time a hundred and fifty women his wives with child, who commonly took medicines to cast their creatures, because they knew that they should not inherit the State; and these had many old women to guard them, for no man was permitted to look upon them.

Besides this *tepac*, which signifieth palace, Montezuma had yet in Mexico another house with very curious lodgings and fair galleries, built upon pillars of jasper, which looked towards a goodly garden, in the which there were at least a dozen ponds, some of salt water for sea fowls, and others of fresh water for river fowls and lake fowls, which ponds were devised with sluices to empty and to fill at pleasure for the cleanness of the fowls' feathers; and these fowls are said to have been so many in number that the ponds could scarcely hold them, and of such several sorts, and of such strange and various coloured feathers that the most of them the Spaniards knew not, nor had at any time seen the like. There did belong to that house above three hundred persons of service, who had their several charge concerning these fowls; some had care to cleanse the ponds; others were appointed to fish for bait; others served them with meat, and to every kind of fowl they gave such bait as they were wont to feed of in the fields or rivers; others did trim their feathers; others had care to look to their eggs; others to set them abroad; and the principallest office was to pluck the feathers, for of them were made rich mantles, tapestry, targets, tufts of feathers, and many other things wrought with gold and silver.

Besides this house, Montezuma had yet another house within Mexico, appointed only for hawking

SURVEY OF WEST INDIES

fowls, and fowls of rapine. In which house there were many high halls, wherein were kept men, women, and children, such as were dwarfs, crook-backs or any monstrous persons, and with them such as were born white of colour, which did very seldom happen; nay some would deform their children on purpose to have them carried to the King's house, to help to set forth his greatness by their deformity. In the lower halls of this house there were cages for fowls of rapine of all sorts, as hawks, kites, boyters [i.e. vultures] (which are very many in those parts), and of the hawks near a dozen sundry kinds of them. This house had for daily allowance five hundred turkey-cocks, and three hundred men of service, besides the falconers and hunters, which some say were above a thousand men. The hunters were maintained in that house because of the ravenous beasts which were also kept in the lower halls in great cages made of timber, wherein were kept in some lions, in others tigers, in others ounces, in others wolves; in conclusion, there was no four-footed beast that wanted there, only to the effect that the mighty Montezuma might say that he had such things in his house; and all were fed daily with turkey-cocks, deer, dogs, and such like. There were also in another hall great earthen vessels, some with earth, and some with water, wherein were snakes as gross as a man's thigh, vipers, crocodiles which they call caymans, of twenty foot long with scales and head like a dragon; besides many other smaller lizards and other venomous beasts and serpents, as well of the water as of the land. To these snakes and the other venomous beasts they usually gave the blood of men sacrificed to feed them. Others say they gave unto them man's flesh, which the great lizards, or caymans eat very well. But what was wonderful to behold, horrid to see, hideous to hear in this house, was the officers' daily occupations about these beasts, the floor with blood like a jelly, stinking like a slaughter-house, and the roaring of the lions, the fearful hissing of the snakes and adders, the doleful howling and barking of the wolves, the sorrowful yelling of the ounces and tigers, when they would have meat. And yet in this place, which in the night season seemed a dungeon of hell, and a dwelling-place of the Devil, could a heathen prince pray unto his gods and idols, for near to this hall was another of a hundred and fifty foot long and thirty foot broad, where was a chapel with the roof of silver and gold in leaf wainscotted and decked with great store of pearl and stone, as agates, cornelians, emeralds, rubies, and divers other sorts; and this was the oratory where Montezuma prayed in the night season, and in that chapel the devil did appear unto him, and gave him answer according to his prayers, which as they were uttered among so many ugly and deformed beasts, and with the noise of them which represented hell itself, were fitted for a devil's answer.

He had also his armoury, wherein was great store of all kind of such ammunition which they used in their wars as bows, arrows, slings, lances, darts, clubs, swords, and bucklers, and gallant targets more trim than strong, and all made of wood, gilt or covered with leather. The wood whereof they made their armour and targets was very hard and strong; and at their arrows' ends they enclosed a little piece of flint-stone, or a piece of a fish-bone called *libisa*, which was so venomous that if any were hurt with it, and the head remained in the wound, it so festered that it was almost incurable. Their swords were of wood, and the edge thereof was flint-stone, enclosed or joined into a staff; and with these swords they cut spears, yea and a horse's neck at a blow, and could make dents into iron, which seemeth a thing unpossible and incredible. These flints were joined into the staffs with a certain kind of glue, which was made of a root called *zacolt*, and *teuxalli*, which is a kind of strong sand, whereof they made a mixture, and after kneaded it with blood of bats, or rere-mice, and other fowl, which did glue so strong that it scarce ever uncleaved again; and of these Montezuma had in his house of armour great store.

But besides these houses it is wonderful to relate yet many others which that great heathen emperor had for his only recreation and pastime, with excellent fair gardens of medicinal herbs, sweet flowers, and trees of delectable savour. But of one garden more especially it is said that in it there were a thousand personages made and wrought artificially of leaves and flowers. And Montezuma would not permit that in this garden should be any kind of pot-herbs, or things to be sold, saying that it did not appertain to kings to have things of profit among their delights and pleasures, for that such did appertain to merchants. Yet out of Mexico he had orchards with many and sundry fruits; and likewise pleasant houses in woods and forests, of great compass, environed with water, in the which he had fountains, rivers, ponds with fish, rocks and coverts where were harts, bucks, hares, foxes, wolves, and such like, whither he himself seldom went; but the lords of Mexico used to go to sport themselves in them. Such and so many were the houses of Montezuma wherein few kings were equal with him. He had daily attending upon him in his privy guard six hundred noblemen and gentlemen, and each of them three or four servants, and some had twenty servants or more according to their estate; and the most credible report goes that in this manner he had three thousand men attendants in his Court, all which were fed in his house of the meat that came from his table.

There were in those times under the Mexican empire three thousand lords of towns, who had many vassals; but more especially there were thirty of high estate, who were able to make each of them a hundred thousand men of war. And all these noblemen did abide in Mexico certain time of the year in the Court of Montezuma, and could not depart from thence without especial licence of the Emperor, leaving each of them a son or brother behind them for security of rebellion; and for this cause they had generally houses in the city. Such and so great was the Court of Montezuma. Moreover, he spent nothing in the buildings of all these his houses, for he had certain towns that paid no other tribute but only to work and repair continually his houses at their own proper cost, and paid all kind of workmen carrying upon their backs, or drawing in sleds stone, lime, timber, water, and all other necessaries for the work. Likewise they were bound to provide all the wood that should be spent in the Court, which was five hundred men's burdens, and some days in the winter much more. But especially for the Emperor's chimneys they brought the bark of oak trees, which was esteemed for the light. Thus was that great city formerly illustrated with a mighty monarch, his houses, and attendants.

There were then also in Mexico three sorts of streets, very broad and fair; the one sort was only of water, with many bridges, another sort of only earth, and the third of earth and water, the one half being firm ground to walk upon, and the other half for boats to bring provision to the city. The most part of the houses had two doors, the one toward the causeway, and the other toward the water, at the which they took boat to go whither they list. But this water (though so near to the houses) being not good to drink, there is other water fresh and sweet brought by conduit to Mexico from a place called Chapultepec, three miles distant from the city, which springeth out of a little hill, at the foot whereof stood formerly two statues, or images, wrought in stone, with their targets and lances, the one of Montezuma, the other of Axaiaca his father. The water is brought from thence to this day in two pipes built upon arches of brick and stone like a fair bridge; and when the one pipe is foul, then all the water is conveyed into the other, till the first be made clean. From this fountain all the whole city is provided, and the water-men go selling the same water from street to street, some in little boats, others with earthen tankards upon mules' or asses' backs.

The chief and principal division of this city when the Spaniards first conquered it was into two streets, the one was called Tlatelulco, that is to say, a Little Island, and the other Mexico, where Montezuma his dwelling and Court was, signifying in the language a spring. And because of the King's palace there, the whole city was named Mexico. But the old and first name of the city according to some histories was Tenuchtitlan, which signifieth fruit out of a stone, being a compounded name of *tetl*, which in the language is stone, and *nuchtli*, which is a sweet fruit called generally in Cuba, and all other parts of America by the Spaniards, *tunas*; the name of the tree whereon this fruit groweth is called *nopal*. And when this city begun to be founded it was placed near unto a great stone that stood in the midst of the lake, at the foot whereof grew one of these *nopal* trees; which is the reason why Mexico giveth for arms and device the foot of a *nopal* tree springing from a stone according to the first name of the city Tenuchtitlan. But others do affirm that this city hath the name of the first founder of it, called Tenuch, the second son of Iztacmixcoatl, whose sons and descendants did first inhabit all that part of America which is now called New Spain. Mexico is as much as to say a spring or fountain, according to the property of the vowel or speech from whence some judge that city to be so named. But others do affirm that Mexico hath its name from a more ancient time, whose first founders were called Mexiti, for unto this day the Indian dwellers in one street of this city are called of Mexica.

The siege endured from the time the brigantines

came from Tlaxcala three months, and therein were on Cortez his side near 200,000 Indians, who daily increased and came in to help him, 900 Spaniards, fourscore horses only, seventeen or eighteen pieces of ordnance, sixteen or as some say eighteen brigantines, and at least 6,000 canoes. In this siege were slain fifty Spaniards only and six horses, and not above eight thousand of the Indians, Cortez his friends. And on the Mexicans' side were slain at least a hundred and twenty thousand Indians, besides those that died with hunger and pestilence. At the defence of the city were all the nobility, by reason whereof many of them were slain. The multitude of people in the city was so great that they were constrained to eat little, to drink salt water, and to sleep among the dead bodies, where was a horrible stench; and for these causes the disease of pestilence fell among them, and thereof died an infinite number. Whereupon is to be considered their valour, and steadfast determination; for although they were afflicted with such hunger that they were driven to eat boughs, rinds of trees, and to drink salt water, yet would they not yield themselves. And here also is to be noted that although the Mexicans did eat man's flesh, yet they did eat none but such as were their enemies, for had they eaten one another and their own children there would not so many have died with hunger. The Mexican women were highly commended, not only because they abode with their husbands and fathers, but also for the great pains they took with the sick and wounded persons; yea and also they laboured in making slings, cutting stones fit for the same, and throwing stones from the *zoties*; for therein they did as much hurt as their men. The city was yielded to the spoil, and the Spaniards took the gold, plate, and feathers, the Indian friends had all the rest of cloth and other stuff. Thus was that famous city ruinated, and burnt by the Spaniards, and the power of that nation brought under the Spanish subjection.

SURVEY OF WEST INDIES

Cortez having found the air of that city very temperate and pleasant for man's life, and the situation commodious, thought presently of rebuilding it, and of making it the chief seat of justice and court for all that country. But before I come to speak of it as rebuilded and now flourishing, I must add unto what hath been said of Montezuma his former state and houses in it, the greatness of the market-place and temple, which was in it when the Spaniards ruined and destroyed it. The conveniency of the lake about this city gave encouragement to the Mexicans to set apart a most spacious market-place, whither all the country about might resort to buy, exchange, and sell; which was the more easy for them by reason of the abundance of boats which were made only for such traffic. In this great lake there were at that time above two hundred thousand of these little boats, which the Indians call *acalles*, and the Spaniards call them *canoas*, wrought like a kneading trough, some bigger than others according to the greatness of the body of the tree whereof they are made. And where I number two hundred thousand of these boats, I speak of the least, for Mexico alone had above fifty thousand ordinarily to carry and bring unto the city victual, provision, and passengers, so that on the market-days all the streets of water were full of them.

The market is called in the Indian tongue *tianquiztli*; every parish had his market-place to buy and sell in; but Mexico and Tlatelulco only, which are the chiefest cities, had great fairs and places fit for the same; and especially Mexico had one place where most days in the year was buying and selling, but every fourth day was the great market ordinarily. This place was wide and large compassed about with doors, and was so great that a hundred thousand persons came thither to chop and change, as a city most principal in all that region. Every occupation and kind of merchandise had his proper place appointed, which no other might by any means occupy or disturb. Likewise pesterous wares had their place accordingly, such as stone, timber, lime, brick and all such kind of stuff unwrought, being necessary to build withal. Also mats both fine and coarse, of sundry workmanship; also coals, wood, and all sorts of earthen vessels, glazed and painted very curiously. Deer skins, both raw and tanned in hair and without hair, of many colours, for shoemakers, for bucklers, targets, jerkins, and lining of wooden corslets; also skins of other beasts, and fowl in feathers ready dressed of all sorts. The colours and strangeness thereof was a thing to behold. The richest merchandise was salt and mantles of cotton-wool of divers colours, both great and small, some for beds, others for garments and clothing, others for tapestry to hang houses; other cotton cloth was wont to be sold there for linen drawers (which to this day the Indians use), for shirts, table-cloths, towels, and such-like things. There were also mantles made of the leaves of a tree called *metl* and of the palm tree, and coney hair, which were well esteemed, being very warm, but the coverlets made of feathers were the best. They sold thread there made of coney hair, and also skeins of other thread of all colours. But the great store of poultry which was brought to that market was strange to see, and the uses they sold and bought them for; for although they did eat the flesh of the fowl, yet the feathers served for clothing, mixing one sort with another. But the chief bravery of that market was the place where gold and feathers jointly wrought were sold; for anything that was in request was there lively wrought in gold and feathers and gallant colours. The Indians were so expert and perfect in this science that they would work or make a butterfly, any wild beast, trees, roses, flowers, herbs, roots, or any other thing so lively that it was a thing marvellous to behold. It happened many times that one of these workmen in a whole day would eat nothing, only to place one feather in his due perfection, turning and tossing the feather to the light of the sun, into the shade or dark place to see where was his most natural perfection, and till his work were finished he would neither eat nor drink. There are few nations of so much phlegm [fleame] or substance.

The art, or science, of goldsmiths among them was the most curious, and very good workmanship engraven with tools made of flint or in mould. They will cast a platter in mould with eight corners, and every corner of several metal, the one of gold, and the other of silver, without any kind of solder. They will also found or cast a little cauldron with loose handles hanging thereat, as we use to cast a bell; they will also cast in mould a fish of metal, with one scale of silver on his back, and another of gold; they will make a parrot or popinjay of metal that his tongue shall shake and his head move and his wings flutter; they will cast an ape in mould, that both hands and feet shall stir, and hold a spindle in his hand seeming to spin, yea and an apple in his hand as though he would eat it. They have skill also of enamel work and to set any precious stone. But now as touching the market, there was to sell gold, silver, copper, lead, latten, and tin; although there was but very little of the three last metals mentioned.

There were pearls, precious stones, divers and sundry sorts of shells, and bones, sponges, and pedlar's ware. There were also many kind of herbs, roots, and seeds, as well to be eaten as for medicine, for both men, women, and children had great knowledge in herbs, for through poverty and necessity they did seek them for their sustenance and help of their infirmities and diseases. They did spend little among physicians, although there were some of that art, and many apothecaries, who did bring into the market ointments, syrups, waters, and other drugs fit for sick persons. They cure all diseases almost with herbs; yea as much as for to kill lice they have a proper herb for the purpose. The several

THE ENGLISH-AMERICAN

kinds of meats to be sold was without number, as snakes without head and tail, little dogs gelt, moles, rats, long-worms, lice, yea and a kind of earth; for at one season in the year they had nets of mail with the which they raked up a certain dust that is bred upon the water of the lake of Mexico and that is kneaded together like unto ooze [oas] of the sea. They gathered much of this and kept it in heaps, and made thereof cakes like unto brick-bats. And they did not only sell this ware in the market, but also sent it abroad to other fairs and markets afar off; and they did eat this meal with as good a stomach as we eat cheese; yea and they hold opinion that this scum or fatness of the water is the cause that such great number of fowl cometh to the lake, which in the winter season is infinite.

They sold likewise in this market venison by quarters or whole, as does, hares, coneys, and dogs, and many other beasts, which they brought up for the purpose and took in hunting. The great store of sundry kinds of fruits was marvellous, which were there sold, both green and ripe. There is a sort as big as an almond called *cacao* (whereof is the drink called chocolate well known now in Christendom) which is both meat and current money. In these times of the bigger sort six score or seven score, and of the lesser sort two hundred are worth a Spanish real, which is sixpence, and with these the Indians buy what they list, for five, nay for two *cacaos*, which is a very small part of a real, they do buy fruits and the like. There were divers kinds of colours to be sold, which they made of roses, flowers, fruits, barks of trees, and other things very excellent. All the things recited, and many others which I speak not of, were sold in this great market, and in every other market of Mexico; and all the sellers paid a certain sum for their shops or standings to the King, as a custom, and they were to be preserved and defended from thieves and robbers. And for that purpose there went serjeants or officers up and down the market to espy out malefactors. In the midst of this market stood a house, which was to be seen throughout the fair, and there did sit commonly twelve ancient men for judges to dispatch law matters. Their buying and selling was to change one ware for another; one gave a hen for a bundle of maize, others gave mantles for salt or money which was *cacao*. They had measure and strike for all kind of corn, and other earthen measures for honey and oil, and such wines as they made of palm trees, and other roots and trees. And if any measure were falsified, they punished the offenders and brake their measures. This was the civility they had when they were heathens, for buying and selling.

The temple is called in the Mexican language *teucalli*, which is a compound word of *teutl*, which signifieth God, and *calli*, which signifieth a house. There were in Mexico many parish churches with towers, wherein were chapels and altars where the images and idols did stand. All their temples were of one fashion; the like I believe was never seen nor heard of. And therefore it shall be now sufficient to describe the chief and greatest temple, which was as their cathedral church. This temple was square, and did contain every way as much ground as a crossbow can reach level. It was made of stone, with four doors that abutted upon the three causeways, and upon another part of the city that had no causeway, but a fair street. In the midst of this quadern stood a mound of earth and stone square likewise, and fifty fathom long every way, built upward like unto a pyramid of Egypt, saving that the top was not sharp but plain and flat, and ten fathom square. Upon the west side were steps up to the top, in number a hundred and fourteen, which being so many, high, and made of good stone, did seem a beautiful thing. It was a strange sight to behold the priests, some going up, and some down, with ceremonies or with men to be sacrificed. Upon the top of this temple were two great altars, a good space distant the one from the other, and so nigh the edge or brim of the wall that scarcely a man might go behind them at pleasure. The one altar stood on the right hand, and the other on the left; they were but of five foot high; each of them had the back part made of stone, painted with monstrous and foul figures. The chapel was fair and well wrought of mason's work and timber; every chapel had three lofts one above another, sustained upon pillars, and with the height thereof it shewed like unto a fair tower, and beautified the city afar off. From thence a man might see all the city and towns round about the lake, which was undoubtedly a goodly prospect. And because Cortez and his company should see the beauty thereof, Montezuma himself (to make the more ostentation of his greatness and the majesty of his Court) carried the first Spaniards thither, and shewed them all the order of the temple, even from the foot to the top. There was a certain plot or space for the idol priests to celebrate their service without disturbance of any. Their general prayers were made toward the rising of the sun; upon each altar stood a great idol.

Besides this tower which stood upon the pyramid, there were forty towers great and small belonging to other little temples which stood in the same circuit; the which although they were of the same making, yet their prospect was not westward, but other ways, because there should be a difference betwixt the great temple and them. Some of these temples were bigger than others, and every one of a several god; among the which there was one round temple dedicated to the god of the air called Quecalcovatl; for even as the air goeth round about the heavens, even for that consideration they made his temple round. The entrance of that temple had a door made like unto the mouth of a serpent, and was painted with foul and devilish gestures, with great teeth and gums wrought, which was a sight to fear those that should enter in thereat, and especially the Christians unto whom it represented Hell itself with that ugly face and monstrous teeth. There were other *teucallies* in the city, that had the ascending up by steps in three places; and all these temples had houses by themselves with all service belonging to them, and priests, and particular gods.

They had other dark houses full of idols great and small, wrought of sundry metals, which were all bathed and washed with blood, and did shew very black through their daily sprinkling and anointing them with the same, when any man was sacrificed; yea and the walls were an inch thick with blood, and the ground a foot thick of it, so that there was a devilish stench. The priests went daily into those oratories, and suffered none other but great personages to enter in. And when any such went in, they were bound to offer some man to be sacrificed, that those bloody hangmen and ministers of the devil might wash their hands in the blood of those so sacrificed, and might sprinkle their house therewith. For their service in the kitchen they had a pond of water, that was filled once a year, which was brought by the conduit pipes before mentioned from the principal fountain. All the residue of the aforesaid circuit served for places to breed fowls, with gardens of herbs and sweet trees, with roses and flowers for the altars; and this is also the Church of Rome's custom and superstition, to trim and deck their saints and altars with garlands and crowns of roses and other flowers. Such, so great and strange, was this temple of Mexico for the service of the devil, who had deceived those simple Indians. There did reside in this temple and houses joining to it, continually five thousand persons, and all these were lodged and had their living there, for that temple was marvellous rich, and had divers towns only for their maintenance and reparation, and were bound to sustain the same always on foot. These towns did sow corn, and maintain all those five thousand persons with bread, fruit, flesh, fish, and firewood as much as they needed, for they spent more firewood than was spent in the King's Court.

All therefore that hath been mentioned hitherto of Montezuma his houses and gardens, of the spacious market-place and temples of that city was utterly destroyed and brought down to the very ground. But Cortez reedified it again, not only for the situation and majesty, but also for the name and great fame thereof. He divided it among the conquerors, having first taken out places for churches, market-places, town-house, and other necessary plots to build houses profitable for the commonwealth. He separated the dwellings of the Spaniards from the Indians, so that now the water passeth and maketh division betwixt them. He promised to them that were naturals of the city of Mexico plots to build upon, inheritance, freedom, and other liberties, and the like unto all those that would come and inhabit there, which was a means to allure many thither. He set also at liberty Xihuaco, the General Captain, and made him chief over the Indians in the city, unto whom he gave a whole street. He gave likewise another street to Don Pedro Montezuma, who was son to Montezuma the King. All this was done to win the favour of the people. He made other gentlemen seniors of little islands, and streets to build upon, and to inhabit, and in this order the whole situation was reparted, and the work began with great joy and diligence. And when the fame was blown abroad that Mexico should be built again, it was a wonder to see the people that resorted thither hearing of liberty and freedom. The number was so great that in three miles compass was nothing but people, men and women. They laboured sore and did eat little, by reason whereof many sickened, and pestilence ensued, whereof died an infinite number. Their pains was great, for they bare on their backs, and drew after them stones, earth, timber, lime, brick, and all other things necessary in this sort. And by little and little Mexico was built again with a hundred thousand houses, more strong and better than the old building was.

The Spaniards built their houses after the Spanish fashion; and Cortez built his house upon the plot where Montezuma his house stood, which renteth now yearly four thousand ducats, and is called now the palace of the Marqués del Valle, the King of Spain having conferred upon Cortez and his heirs this title from the great valley of Oaxaca. This palace is so stately that (as I have observed before), seven thousand beams of cedar trees were spent in it. They built fair docks covered over with arches for the brigantines; which docks for a perpetual memory do remain until this day. They dammed up the streets of water, where now fair houses stand, so that Mexico is not as it was wont to be, and especially since the year 1634 the water cometh not by far so near the city as it was wont to come. The lake sometimes casteth out a vapour of stench, but otherwise it is a wholesome and temperate dwelling, by reason of the mountains that stand round about it, and well provided through the fertility of the country, and commodity of the lake. So that now is Mexico one of the greatest cities in the world in extension of the situation for Spanish and Indian houses. Not many years after the Conquest it was the noblest city in all India, as well in arms as policy. There were formerly at the least two thousand citizens, that had each of them his horse in his stable with rich furniture for them, and arms in readiness. But now since all the Indians far and near are subdued, and most of them, especially about Mexico, consumed, and there is no fear of their rising up any more against the Spaniards, all arms are forgotten, and the Spaniards live so secure from enemies that there is neither gate, wall, bulwark, platform, tower, armoury, ammunition, or ordnance to secure and defend the city from a domestic or foreign enemy; from the latter they think St John de Ulhua sufficient and strong enough to secure them. But for contractation it is one of the richest cities in the world; to the which by the North Sea cometh every year from Spain a fleet of near twenty ships laden with the best commodities not only of Spain but of the most parts of Christendom. And by the South Sea it enjoyeth traffic from all parts of Peru; and above all it trades with the East Indies, and from thence receiveth the commodities as well from those parts which are inhabited by Portuguese [Portingals], as from the countries of Japan and China, sending every year two great *caracas* with two smaller vessels to the Philippine Islands, and having every year a return of such-like ships.

There is also in Mexico a mint house where money is daily coined, and is brought thither in wedges upon mules from the mines called St Lewis de Zacatecas, standing fourscore leagues from Mexico northward, and yet from Zacatecas forward have the Spaniards entered above a hundred leagues conquering daily Indians, where they discover store of mines; and there they have built a city called Nova Mexico, New Mexico. The Indians there are great warriors, and hold the Spaniards hard to it. It is thought the Spaniard will not be satisfied until he subdue all the country that way, which doubtless reacheth to our plantations of Virginia and the rest being the same continued continent land. There is yet more in Mexico, a fair school, which now is made an university, which the Viceroy Don Antonio de Mendoza caused to be built.

At the rebuilding of this city there was a great difference betwixt an inhabitant of Mexico, and a Conqueror; for a Conqueror was a name of honour, and had lands and rents given him and to his posterity by the King of Spain, and the inhabitant or only dweller paid rent for his house. And this hath filled all those parts of America with proud Dons and gentlemen to this day; for every one will call himself a descendant from a Conqueror, though he be as poor as Job; and ask him what is become of his estate and fortune, he will answer that fortune hath taken it away, which shall never take away a Don from him. Nay, a poor cobbler, or carrier that runs about the country far and near getting his living with half-a-dozen mules, if he be called Mendoza, or Guzman, will swear that he descended from those dukes' houses in Spain, and that his grandfather came from thence to conquer, and subdued whole countries to the Crown of Spain, though now fortune have frowned upon him, and covered his rags with a threadbare cloak. When Mexico was rebuilt, and judges, aldermen, attorneys, town-clerks, notaries, scavengers, and serjeants with all other officers necessary for the commonwealth of a city were appointed, the fame of Cortez and majesty of the city was blown abroad into far provinces, by means whereof it was soon replenished with Indians again, and with Spaniards from Spain, who soon conquered above four hundred leagues of land, being all governed by the princely seat of Mexico. But since that first rebuilding, I may say it is now rebuilt the second time by Spaniards, who have consumed most of the Indians; so that now I will not dare to say there are a hundred thousand houses which soon after the Conquest were built up, for most of them were of Indians. Now the Indians that live there, live in the suburbs of the city, and their situation is called Guadalupe. In the year 1625, when I went to those parts, this suburb was judged to contain five thousand inhabitants; but since most of them have been consumed by the Spaniards' hard usage and the work of the lake. So that now there may not be above two thousand inhabitants of mere Indians, and a thousand of such as they call there mestizoes, who are of a mixed nature of Spaniards and Indians, for many poor Spaniards marry with Indian women, and others that marry them not but hate their husbands, find many tricks to convey away an innocent Uriah to enjoy his Bathsheba. The Spaniards daily cozen them of the small plot of ground where their houses stand, and of three or four houses of Indians build up one good and fair house after the Spanish fashion with gardens and orchards. And so is almost all Mexico new built with very fair and spacious houses with gardens of recreation.

Their buildings are with stone, and brick very strong, but not high, by reason of the many earthquakes, which would endanger their houses if they were above three storeys high. The streets are very broad, in the narrowest of them three coaches may go, and in the broader six may go in the breadth of them, which makes the city seem a great deal bigger than it is. In my time it was thought to be of between thirty and forty thousand inhabitants Spaniards, who are so proud and rich that half the city was judged to keep coaches, for it was a most credible report that in Mexico in my time there were above fifteen thousand coaches. It is a by-word that at Mexico there are four things fair, that is to say, the women, the apparel, the horses, and the streets. But to this I may add the beauty of some of the coaches of the gentry, which do exceed in cost the best of the Court of Madrid and other parts of Christendom; for there they spare no silver, nor gold, nor precious stones, nor cloth of gold, nor the best silks from China to enrich them. And to the gallantry of their horses the pride of some doth add the cost of bridles and shoes of silver.

The streets of Christendom must not compare with those in breadth and cleanness, but especially in the riches of the shops which do adorn them. Above all, the goldsmiths' shops and works are to be admired. The Indians, and the people of China that have been made Christians and every year come thither, have perfected the Spaniards in that trade. The Viceroy

SURVEY OF WEST INDIES

that went thither the year 1625 caused a popinjay to be made of silver, gold, and precious stones with the perfect colours of the popinjay's feathers (a bird bigger than a pheasant), with such exquisite art and perfection, to present unto the King of Spain, that it was prized to be worth in riches and workmanship half a million of ducats. There is in the cloister of the Dominicans a lamp hanging in the church with three hundred branches wrought in silver to hold so many candles, besides a hundred little lamps for oil set in it, every one being made with several workmanship so exquisitely that it is valued to be worth four hundred thousand ducats; and with such-like curious works are many streets made more rich and beautiful from the shops of goldsmiths. To the by-word touching the beauty of the women I must add the liberty they enjoy for gaming, which is such that the day and night is too short for them to end a primera when once it is begun; nay gaming is so common to them that they invite gentlemen to their houses for no other end. To myself it happened that passing along the streets in company with a friar that came with me that year from Spain, a gentlewoman of great birth knowing us to be *chapetons* (so they call the first year those that come from Spain), from her window called unto us, and after two or three slight questions concerning Spain asked us if we would come in and play with her a game at primera.

Both men and women are excessive in their apparel, using more silks than stuffs and cloth. Precious stones and pearls further much this their vain ostentation; a hat-band and rose made of diamonds in a gentleman's hat is common, and a hat-band of pearls is ordinary in a tradesman; nay a blackamoor or tawny young maid and slave will make hard shift but she will be in fashion with her neck-chain and bracelets of pearls, and her ear-bobs of some considerable jewels. The attire of this baser sort of people of blackamoors and mulattoes (which are of a mixed nature, of Spaniards and blackamoors) is so light, and their carriage so enticing, that many Spaniards even of the better sort (who are too too prone to venery) disdain their wives for them. Their clothing is a petticoat of silk or cloth, with many silver or golden laces, with a very broad double ribbon of some light colour with long silver or golden tags hanging down before, the whole length of their petticoat to the ground, and the like behind; their waistcoats made like bodices, with skirts, laced likewise with gold or silver, without sleeves, and a girdle about their body of great price stuck with pearls and knots of gold (if they be any ways well esteemed of), their sleeves are broad and open at the end, of holland or fine China linen, wrought some with coloured silks, some with silk and gold, some with silk and silver, hanging down almost unto the ground; the locks of their heads are covered with some wrought coif, and over it another of network of silk bound with a fair silk, or silver, or golden ribbon which crosseth the upper part of their forehead, and hath commonly worked out in letters some light and foolish love posy; their bare, black, and tawny breasts are covered with bobs hanging from their chains of pearls. And when they go abroad, they use a white mantle of lawn or cambric rounded with a broad lace, which some put over their heads, the breadth reaching only to their middle behind, that their girdle and ribbons may be seen, and the two ends before reaching to the ground almost; others cast their mantles only upon their shoulders, and swaggerers-like, cast the one end over the left shoulder that they may the better jog the right arm, and shew their broad sleeve as they walk along; others instead of this mantle use some rich silk petticoat to hang upon their left shoulder, while with their right arm they support the lower part of it, more like roaring boys than honest civil maids. Their shoes are high and of many soles, the outside whereof of the profaner sort are plated with a list of silver, which is fastened with small nails of broad silver heads. Most of these are or have been slaves, though love have set them loose at liberty to enslave souls to sin and Satan. And there are so many of this kind both men and women grown to a height of pride and vanity, that many times the Spaniards have feared they would rise up and mutiny against them. And for the looseness of their lives, and public scandals committed by them and the better sort of the Spaniards, I have heard them say often who have professed more religion and fear of God, they verily thought God would destroy that city, and give up the country into the power of some other nation.

It seems that religion teacheth that all wickedness is allowable, so the churches and clergy flourish; nay while the purse is open to lasciviousness, if it be likewise opened to enrich the temple walls and roofs, this is better than any their holy water to wash away the filth of the other. Rome is held to be the head of superstition; and what stately churches, chapels, and cloisters are in it? what fastings, what processions, what appearances of devotion? and on the other side, what liberty, what profaneness, what whoredoms, nay what sins of Sodom are committed in it? In so much that it could be the saying of a friar to myself while I was in it, that he verily thought there was no one city in the world wherein were more atheists than in Rome. I might shew this truth in Madrid, Seville, Valladolid, and other famous cities in Spain, and in Italy, in Milan, Genoa, and Naples, relating many instances of scandals committed in those places, and yet the temples mightily enriched by such who have thought those alms a sufficient warrant to free them from Hell and Purgatory. But I must return to Mexico which is *mille testes* of this truth, sin and wickedness abounding in it; and yet no such people in the world toward the Church and clergy, who in their lifetime strive to exceed one another in their gifts to the cloisters of nuns and friars, some erecting altars to their best devoted saints, worth many thousand thousand ducats, others presenting crowns of gold to the pictures of Mary, others lamps, others golden chains, others building cloisters at their own charge, others repairing them, others at their death leaving to them two or three thousand ducats for an annual stipend.

Among these great benefactors to the churches of that city I should wrong my history if I should forget one that lived in my time, called Alonso Cuellar, who was reported to have a closet in his house laid with bars of gold instead of bricks, though indeed it was not so, but only reported for his abundant riches and store of bars of gold which he had in one chest standing in a closet distant from another, where he had a chest full of wedges of silver. This man alone built a nunnery of Franciscan nuns, which stood him in above thirty thousand ducats, and left unto it for the maintenance of the nuns two thousand ducats yearly, with obligation of some Masses to be said in the church every year for his soul after his decease. And yet this man's life was so scandalous that commonly in the night with two servants he would round the city, visiting such scandalous persons whose attire before hath been described, carrying his beads in his hands, and at every house letting fall a bead and tying a false knot, that when he came home in the morning towards break of the day he might number by his beads the uncivil stations he had walked and visited that night. But these his works of darkness came to light, and were published far and near for what happened unto him whilst I was in Mexico; for one night, meeting at one of his stations with a gentleman that was jealous of him, swords on both sides were drawn, the concubine first was stabbed by the gentleman who was better manned and attended; and Cuellar (who was but a merchant) was mortally wounded and left for dead, though afterwards he recovered.

SURVEY OF WEST INDIES

Great alms and liberality towards religious houses in that city commonly are coupled with great and scandalous wickedness. They wallow in the bed of riches and wealth, and make their alms the coverlet to cover their loose and lascivious lives. From hence are the churches so fairly built and adorned. There are not above fifty churches and chapels, cloisters and nunneries, and parish churches in that city; but those that are there are the fairest that ever my eyes beheld, the roofs and beams being in many of them all daubed with gold, and many altars with sundry marble pillars, and others with brazil-wood stays standing one above another with tabernacles for several saints richly wrought with golden colours, so that twenty thousand ducats is a common price of many of them. These cause admiration in the common sort of people, and admiration brings on daily adoration in them to those glorious spectacles and images of saints.

Besides these beautiful buildings, the inward riches belonging to the altars are infinite in price and value, such as copes, canopies, hangings, altar cloths, candlesticks, jewels belonging to the saints, and crowns of gold and silver, and tabernacles of gold and crystal to carry about their sacrament in procession, all which would mount to the worth of a reasonable mine of silver, and would be a rich prey for any nation that could make better use of wealth and riches. I will not speak much of the lives of the friars and nuns of that city, but only that there they enjoy more liberty than in the parts of Europe (where yet they have too much) and that surely the scandals committed by them do cry up to Heaven for vengeance, judgment, and destruction.

In my time in the cloister of the Mercenarian friars which is entitled for the Redemption of Captives, there chanced to be an election of a Provincial to rule over them, to the which all the priors and heads of the cloisters about the country had resorted, and such was their various and factious difference that upon the sudden all the convent was in an uproar, their canonical election was turned to mutiny and strife, knives were drawn, many wounded, the scandal and danger of murder so great, that the Viceroy was fain to interpose his authority and to sit amongst them and guard the cloister until their Provincial was elected.

It is ordinary for the friars to visit their devoted nuns, and to spend whole days with them, hearing their music, feeding on their sweetmeats, and for this purpose they have many chambers which they call *locutorios*, to talk in, with wooden bars between the nuns and them, and in these chambers are tables for the friars to dine at; and while they dine the nuns recreate them with their voices. Gentlemen and citizens give their daughters to be brought up in these nunneries, where they are taught to make all sorts of conserves and preserves, all sorts of needlework, all sorts of music, which is so exquisite in that city that I dare be bold to say that the people are drawn to their churches more for the delight of the music than for any delight in the service of God. More, they teach these young children to act like players, and to entice the people to their churches make these children to act short dialogues in their choirs, richly attiring them with men's and women's apparel, especially upon Midsummer Day, and the eight days before their Christmas, which is so gallantly performed that many factious strifes and single combats have been, and some were in my time, for defending which of these nunneries most excelled in music and in the training up of children. No delights are wanting in that city abroad in the world, nor in their churches, which should be the house of God, and the soul's, not the sense's delight.

The chief place in the city is the market-place, which though it be not as spacious as in Montezuma his time, yet is at this day very fair and wide, built all with arches on the one side where people may walk dry in time of rain, and there are shops of merchants furnished with all sorts of stuffs and silks, and before them sit women selling all manner of fruits and herbs; over against these shops and arches is the Viceroy his palace, which taketh up almost the whole length of the market with the walls of the house and of the gardens belonging to it. At the end of the Viceroy his palace is the chief prison, which is strong of stone work. Next to this is the beautiful street called *La Plateria*, or Goldsmiths Street, where a man's eyes may behold in less than an hour many millions' worth of gold, silver, pearls, and jewels. The street of St Austin is rich and comely, where live all that trade in silks; but one of the longest and broadest streets is the street called Tacuba, where almost all the shops are of ironmongers, and of such as deal in brass and steel, which is joining to those arches whereon the water is conveyed into the city, and is so called for that it is the way out of the city to a town called Tacuba; and this street is mentioned far and near, not so much for the length and breadth of it, as for a small commodity of needles which are made there, and for proof are the best of all those parts. For stately buildings the street called *del Aquila*, the Street of the Eagle, exceeds the rest, where live gentlemen, and courtiers, and judges belonging to the Chancery, and is the palace of the Marqués del Valle from the line of Ferdinando Cortez; this street is so called from an old idol an eagle of stone which from the Conquest lieth in a corner of that street, and is twice as big as London stone.

The gallants of this city shew themselves daily, some on horseback, and most in coaches, about four of the clock in the afternoon in a pleasant shady field called *la Alameda*, full of trees and walks, somewhat like unto our Moorfields, where do meet as constantly as the merchants upon our exchange about two thousand coaches, full of gallants, ladies, and

THE ENGLISH-AMERICAN

citizens, to see and to be seen, to court and to be courted, the gentlemen having their train of blackamoor slaves some a dozen, some half a dozen waiting on them, in brave and gallant liveries, heavy with gold and silver lace, with silk stockings on their black legs, and roses on their feet, and swords by their sides; the ladies also carry their train by their coach's side of such jet-like damsels as before have been mentioned for their light apparel, who with their bravery and white mantles over them seem to be, as the Spaniard saith, *mosca en leche*, a fly in milk. But the train of the Viceroy who often goeth to this place is wonderful stately, which some say is as great as the train of his master the King of Spain. At this meeting are carried about many sorts of sweetmeats and papers of comfits to be sold, for to relish a cup of cool water, which is cried about in curious glasses, to cool the blood of those love-hot gallants. But many times these their meetings sweetened with conserves and comfits have sour sauce at the end, for jealousy will not suffer a lady to be courted, no nor sometimes to be spoken to, but puts fury into the violent hand to draw a sword or dagger and to stab or murder whom he was jealous of, and when one sword is drawn thousands are presently drawn, some to right the party wounded or murdered; others to defend the party murdering, whose friends will not permit him to be apprehended, but will guard him with drawn swords until they have conveyed him to the sanctuary of some church, from whence the Viceroy his power is not able to take him for a legal trial.

Many of these sudden skirmishes happened whilst I lived about Mexico: of which city a whole volume might be compiled, but that by other authors much hath been written, and I desire not to fill my history with trifles, but only with what is most remarkable in it. I may not omit yet from the situation of it upon a lake to tell that certainly the water hath its passage under all the streets of it; for toward the street

SURVEY OF WEST INDIES

of St Austin and the lower parts of the city, I can confidently aver that in my time before the removing of the lake those that died were rather drowned than buried, for a grave could not be digged with an ordinary grave's depth but they met with water, and I was eye-witness of many thus buried, whose coffins was covered with water. And this is so apparent that had not the cloister of the Augustines often been repaired and almost rebuilt, it had quite sunk by this. In my time it was a repairing, and I saw the old pillars had sunk very low, upon the which they were then laying new foundations, and I was credibly informed that that was the third time that new pillars had been erected upon the old which were quite sunk away. This city hath but three ways to come unto it by causeway; the one is from the West, and that causeway is a mile and a half long; another from the North, and containeth three miles in length. Eastward the city hath no entry; but Southward the causeway is five miles long, which was the way that Cortez entered into it, when he conquered it.

The fruit called *nuchtli* (whereof I have spoken before, and some say this city was called Tenuchtitlan from it) though it be in most parts of America, yea and now in Spain, yet in no place there is more abundance of it than in Mexico, and it is absolutely one of the best fruits in it. It is like unto the fig, and so hath many little kernels or grains within, but they are somewhat larger, and crowned like unto a medlar. There are of them of sundry colours, some are green without, and carnation-like within, which have a good taste. Others are yellow, and others white, and some speckled; the best sort are the white. It is a fruit that will last long. Some of them taste of pears, and other some of grapes. It is a cold and a fresh fruit, and best esteemed in the heat of summer. The Spaniards do more esteem them than the Indians. The more the ground is laboured where they grow, the fruit is so much the better. There is yet another kind of this fruit red, and that is nothing so much esteemed, although his taste is not evil, but because it doth colour and dye the eater's mouth, lips, and apparel, yea and maketh the urine look like pure blood. Many Spaniards at their first coming into India, and eating this fruit, were amazed and at their wits' end, thinking that all the blood in their bodies came out in urine; yea and many physicians at their first coming were of the same belief. And it hath happened when they have been sent for unto such as have eaten this fruit, they not knowing the cause and beholding the urine, by and by they have administered medicines to staunch blood; a thing to laugh at, to see physicians so deceived. The skin of the outside is thick and full of little small prickles, and when it is cut downright with one cut to the kernels, with one finger you may uncleave the whole skin round about without breaking it, and take out the fruit to eat. The Spaniards use to jest with it with strangers, taking half a dozen of them, and rubbing them in a napkin, those small prickles which can scarce be seen or perceived stick invisibly unto the napkin, wherewith a man wiping his mouth to drink, those little prickles stick in his lips so that they seem to sow them up together, and make him for a while falter in his speech, till with much rubbing and washing they come off.

There is another fruit twice of the bigness of a great warden, which they call the growing *manjar blanco*, or white meat, which is a dainty dish made by them with the white of a capon, cream, and rice, and sugar and sweet waters, much like unto the which tasteth this fruit. It is as sweet as any honey, and dissolves like melted snow in the mouth into a juice most luscious; within, it is full of hard black kernels or stones, which being cracked are bitter, and these not joined together, but by division one from another, each one having a bag, or little skin, discerning them in their ranks and orders, so that when you cut this fruit in the middle it represents a chequer-board with black and white; the white is sucked or eaten and the kernels thrown away. But I cannot forget that which they call *piña*, or pineapple; not the pineapple of the high pine tree, but a pineapple that groweth upon a lower shrub with prickly leaves, and is bigger than our biggest musk melons [muskmillians] in England, when it is ripe; it is yellow without and within; without it is full of little bunches, and within so juicy and cool that nothing more dangerous than to eat much of it. Before they eat it, they cut it in round slices, and lay it a while in salt and water, and so being scoured half an hour in that salt and water which taketh much of the rawness and coldness from it, and then putting into dishes with more fresh water they eat it thus. But the better way of eating it is preserved, which is absolutely the best preserve in all that country. There is also the grape (though they make not wine of it), the apple, the pear, the quince, the peach, the apricot, the pomegranate, the muskmelon, the plantain, the fig, the walnut, the chestnut, the orange, the lemon both sour and sweet, the citron in great abundance. Most of the fruits of Europe, and as many more which Europe never knew.

About Mexico more than in any other part groweth that excellent tree called *metl*, which they plant and dress as they do their vines in Europe. It hath near forty kinds of leaves, which serve for many uses; for when they be tender they make of them conserves, paper, flax, mantles, mats, shoes, girdles, and cordage. On these leaves grow certain prickles so strong and sharp that they use them instead of saws: from the root of this tree cometh a juice like unto syrup, which being sodden will become sugar. You may also make of it wine and vinegar. The Indians often become drunk with it. The rind roasted healeth hurts and sores, and from the top boughs issueth a gum, which is an excellent antidote against poison. There is nothing in Mexico and about it wanting which may make a city happy; and certainly had those that have so much extolled with their pens the parts of Granada in Spain, Lombardy and Florence in Italy, making them the earthly Paradise, had they been acquainted with the New World and with Mexico, they would have recanted their untruths.

This city is the seat of an Archbishop, and of a Viceroy, who commonly is some great nobleman of Spain, whose power is to make laws and ordinances, to give directions, and determine controversies, unless it be in such great causes which are thought fit to be referred to the Council of Spain. And though there be about the country many governments with several governors, yet they are all subordinate to this Viceroy, and there are at least four hundred leagues of land all governed by the princely seat of Mexico. Most of the governors about the country being the Viceroy his creatures, placed by him, do contribute great gifts and bribes for their preferment; so likewise do all the rest whose right or wrong proceedings depend upon the Viceroy his clemency and mercy in judging the daily appeals of justice which come unto him. The King of Spain allows him out of his Exchequer yearly a hundred thousand ducats whilst he governs; his time being but five years. But commonly with their bribes to the courtiers of Spain, and to the Counsellors for the Estate of the Indies they get a prorogation of five years more, and sometimes of ten. It is incredible to think what this Viceroy may get a year in that place besides his hundred thousand ducats of rent, if he be a man covetous and given to trading (as most of them are), for then they will be masters of what commodities they please, and none else shall deal in them but themselves; as did the Marquess of Serralvo in my time, who was the best monopolist of salt that ever those parts knew. This man was thought to get a million a year, what with gifts and presents, what with his trading to Spain and the Philippines. He governed ten years, and in this time he sent to the King of Spain a popinjay worth half a million, and in one year more he sent the worth of a million to the Count of Olivares, and other courtiers to obtain a prorogation for five years more.

Besides the Viceroy there are commonly six judges and a King's Attorney, who are allowed out of the King's Exchequer yearly twelve thousand ducats apiece rent, besides two *Alcaldes de Corte*, or High Justices, who with the Viceroy judge all Chancery and criminal causes. But these though united together they may oppose the Viceroy in any unlawful and unjustifiable action, as some have done and have smarted for it, yet commonly they dare not. So that he doth what he listeth, and it is enough for him to say, *stat pro ratione voluntas*. This power joined with covetousness in the Viceroy, and threescore thousand ducats yearly joined with pride in the Archbishop, was like to be the ruin of that city in the year 1624. Then was the Count of Gelves Viceroy, and Don Alonso de Zerna Archbishop, whose two powers striving and striking at one another like two flints, had almost brought to combustion that gallant city, and did set on fire the Viceroy his palace, and the prison joining to it.

The story was thus, which may be profitable for other nations, to beware of covetous governors, and proud prelates; and therefore I thought fit to insert it here. The Count of Gelves was in some things one of the best Viceroys and Governors that ever the Court of Spain sent to America, for he was called by the Spaniards *el terrible justiciero, y fuego de ladrones*, that is, terrible for justice, and fire to consume all thieves. For he cleared all the highways of thieves, hanging them as often as they were caught without mercy, and did send out troops and officers to apprehend them, so that it was generally reported that since the Conquest

THE ENGLISH-AMERICAN

unto those days of his there had never been so many thieves and malefactors hanged up as in his time. So in all other points of justice he was severe and upright. But yet covetousness did so blind him to see his own injustice, that before he could see it he had brought the city of Mexico and the whole kingdom to a danger of rebellion. What he would not to be seen in himself, he acted by others his instruments. And one of them was one Don Pedro Mexia, a mighty rich gentleman of Mexico, whom he chose to join with him in monopolizing all the Indian maize and wheat about the country. Don Pedro Mexia of the Indians bought at the price he list their maize, and the wheat of the Spaniards he bought it according to that price at which it is taxed by the law of that land to be sold at in time of famine; which is at fourteen reals a bushel (which is not much there considering the abundance of gold and silver), at which price the farmers and husbandmen, knowing it to be a plentiful year, were glad and willing to sell unto him their wheat, not knowing what the end would be, and others fearing to gainsay him, whom they knew to be the Viceroy's favourite. Thus Don Pedro Mexia filled all his barns which he had hired about the country, and himself and the Viceroy became owners of all the wheat. He had his officers appointed to bring it into the markets upon his warning, and that was when some small remnants that had escaped his fingers were sold, and the price raised. Then hoisted he his price, and doubled it above what it had cost him. The poor began to complain, the rich to murmur, the tax of the law was moved in the Court of Chancery before the Viceroy. But he being privy to the monopoly expounded the law to be understood in time of famine, and that he was informed that it was as plentiful a year as ever had been, and that to his knowledge there was as much brought into the markets as ever had been, and plenty enough for Mexico and all the country.

SURVEY OF WEST INDIES

Thus was the law slighted, the rich mocked, the poor oppressed, and none sold wheat but Don Pedro Mexia his officers for himself and the Viceroy.

When justice would be no father, the people go to their mother the Church; and having understood the business better, and that it was Don Pedro Mexia who did tyrannize and oppress them with the Viceroy his favour, they entreat the Archbishop to make it a case of conscience, and to reduce it to a Church censure. Don Alonso de Zerna, the Archbishop, who had always stomached Don Pedro Mexia and the Viceroy, to please the people granted to them to excommunicate Don Pedro Mexia, and so sent out bills of excommunication to be fixed upon all the church doors against Don Pedro; who not regarding the excommunication, and keeping close at home, and still selling his wheat, raising higher the price than it was before, the Archbishop raised this censure higher against him, adding to it a bill of *cessatio a divinis*, that is, a cessation from all divine service. This censure is so great with them that it is never used but for some great man's sake, who is contumacious and stubborn in his ways, contemning the power of the Church. Then are all the church doors shut up (let the city be never so great), no Masses are said, no prayers used, no preaching permitted, no meetings allowed for any public devotion or calling upon God. Their Church mourns as it were, and makes no shew of spiritual joy and comfort, nor of any communion of prayers one with another, so long as the party continues stubborn and rebellious in his sin and scandal, and unyielding to the Church's censure. And further whereas by this cessation *a divinis*, many churches and especially cloisters suffer in the means of their livelihood, who live upon what is daily given them for the Masses they say, and in a cloister where thirty or forty priests say Mass, so many pieces of eight or crowns in Mexico do daily come in; therefore this censure or *cessatio a divinis* is so inflicted upon the whole Church (all suffering for it as they say in spiritual and some in temporal ways) that the party offending or scandalizing, for whose sake this curse is laid upon all, is bound to satisfy all priests and cloisters which in the way aforesaid suffer, and to allow them so much out of his means, as they might have daily got by selling away their Masses for so many crowns for their daily livelihood. To this would the Archbishop have brought Don Pedro Mexia, to have emptied out of his purse near a thousand crowns daily towards the maintenance of about a thousand priests (so many there may be in Mexico), who from the altar sell away their bread-God to satisfy with bread and food their hungry stomachs. And secondly by the people's suffering in their spiritual comfort, and non-communion of prayers and idolatrous worship, he thought to make Don Pedro Mexia odious to the people. Don Pedro perceiving the spiteful intents of the Archbishop, and hearing the outcries of the people in the streets against him, and their cries for the use and liberty of their churches, secretly retired himself to the palace of the Viceroy, begging his favour and protection, for whose sake he suffered. The Viceroy immediately sent out his orders, commanding the bills of excommunication and cessation *a divinis* to be pulled from the church doors, and to all the superiors of the cloisters to set open their churches, and to celebrate their service and Masses as formerly they had done. But they disobeying the Viceroy through blind obedience to their Archbishop, the Viceroy commanded the Arch-Prelate to revoke his censures. But his answer was that what he had done had been justly done against a public offender and great oppressor of the poor, whose cries had moved him to commiserate their suffering condition, and that the offender's contempt of his first excommunication had deserved the rigour of the second censure; neither of the which he would or could revoke until Don Pedro

SURVEY OF WEST INDIES

Mexia had submitted himself to the Church and to a public absolution, and had satisfied the priests and cloisters who suffered for him, and had disclaimed that unlawful and unconscionable monopoly, wherewith he wronged the whole commonwealth, and especially the poorer sort therein.

Thus did that proud prelate arrogantly in terms exalt himself against the authority of his prince and ruler, contemning his command with a flat denial, thinking himself happy in imitating Ambrose his spirit against the Emperor Theodosius, trusting in the power of his keys, and in the strength of his Church and clergy, which with the rebellion of the meaner sort he resolved to oppose against the power and strength of his magistrate. The Viceroy, not brooking this saucy answer from a priest, commanded him presently to be apprehended and to be guarded to St John de Ulhua, and there to be shipped for Spain. The Archbishop having notice of this the Viceroy his resolution, retired himself out of Mexico to Guadalupe with many of his priests and prebends, leaving a bill of excommunication upon the church doors against the Viceroy himself, and thinking privily to fly to Spain there to give an account of his carriage and behaviour. But he could not flee so fast but the Viceroy his care and vigilancy still eyed him, and with his serjeants and officers pursued him to Guadalupe. Which the Archbishop understanding, he betook himself to the sanctuary of the church, and there caused the candles to be lighted upon the altar, the sacrament of his bread-God to be taken out of the tabernacle, and attiring himself with his pontifical vestments, with his mitre on his head, his crozier in one hand, in the other he took his God of bread, and thus with his train of priests about him at the altar, he waited for the coming of the serjeants and officers, whom he thought with his God in his hand, and with a 'Here I am,' to astonish and amaze, and to make them, as Christ the Jews in the garden, to fall backwards, and to disable them from laying hands upon him. The officers coming into the church went towards the altar where the Bishop stood, and kneeling down first to worship their God made a short prayer; which being ended, they propounded unto the Bishop with courteous and fair words the cause of their coming to that place, requiring him to lay down the Sacrament and to come out of the church, and to hear the notification of what orders they brought unto him in the King's name. To whom the Archbishop replied, that whereas their master the Viceroy was excommunicated he looked upon him as one out of the pale of the Church, and one without any power or authority to command him in the house of God, and so required them as they tendered the good of their souls to depart peaceably, and not to infringe the privileges and immunity of the Church, by exercising in it any legal act of secular power and command; and that he would not go out of the church unless they durst take him and the Sacrament together. With this the head officer, named Tiroll, stood up and notified unto him an order in the King's name to apprehend his person in what place soever he should find him, and to guard him to the port of St John de Ulhua, and there to deliver him to whom by further order he should be directed there, to be shipped for Spain as a traitor to the King's crown, a troubler of the common peace, an author and mover of sedition in the commonwealth. The Archbishop smiling upon Tiroll answered him: 'Thy master useth too high terms, and words which do better agree unto himself; for I know no mutiny or sedition like to trouble the commonwealth, unless it be by his and Don Pedro Mexia his oppressing of the poor. And as for thy guarding me to St John de Ulhua, I conjure thee by Jesus Christ, whom thou knowest I hold in my hands, not to use here any violence in God's house, from whose altar I am resolved not to depart; take heed God punish thee not as he did Jeroboam for stretching forth his hand at the altar against the Prophet; let his withered hand remind thee of thy duty.' But Tiroll suffered him not to squander away the time and ravel it out with further preaching, but called to the altar a priest whom he had brought for that purpose, and commanded him in the King's name to take the Sacrament out of the Archbishop's hand, which the priest doing, the Archbishop unvested himself of his pontificals, and (though with many repetitions of the Church's immunity) yielded himself unto Tiroll, and taking his leave of all his prebends, requiring them to be witnesses of what had been done, he went prisoner to St John de Ulhua, where he was delivered to the custody of the governor of the castle, and not many days after he was sent in a ship prepared for that purpose to Spain to the King and Council, with a full charge of all his carriages and misdemeanours.

Some of the city of Mexico in private began to talk strangely against the Viceroy, and to stomach the banishment of their Archbishop, because he had stood out against so high a power in defence of the poor and oppressed, and these their private grudges they soon vented in public with bold and arrogant speeches against Don Pedro Mexia, and the Viceroy, being set on and encouraged by the priests and prebends, who it seems had sworn blind obedience to their Arch-Prelate, and therewith thought they could dispense with their consciences in their obedience and duty to their magistrate. Thus did those incendiaries for a fortnight together blow the fire of sedition and rebellion, especially amongst the inferior sort of people and the Creoles or native Spaniards, and the Indians and mulattoes, whom they knew brooked not the severe and rigorous justice and judgment of the Viceroy, no nor any government that was appointed over them from Spain; until at a fortnight's end

THE ENGLISH-AMERICAN

Tiroll returned from St John de Ulhua; and then began the spite and malice of all the malcontents to break out, then began a fire of mutiny to be kindled, which was thought would have consumed and buried in ashes that great and famous city. Tiroll was not a little jealous of what mischief the common rabble intended against him, and so kept close, not daring to walk the streets; yet his occasions inviting him to the Viceroy his palace, ventured himself in a coach with drawn curtains, which yet could not blind the eyes of the spiteful and malicious malcontents, who had notice that he was in the coach, and before he could get to the market-place, three or four boys began to cry out, *Judas, Judas, alla va Judas*, 'There goeth Judas that laid his hands upon Christ's Vicar': others joined with them saying, *Ahorquemos a este Judas*, 'Let us hang up this Judas'; the number of boys yet increased, crying aloud and boldly after the coach, *Muera el vellaco descomulgado la muerte de Judas, muera el picaro, muera el perro*, 'Let this excommunicated rogue and dog die the death of Judas'; the coachman lashed the mules, the coach posted, the boys hasted after with stones and dirt, the number increased so that before Tiroll could get through two streets only, there were risen above two hundred boys, of Spaniards, Indians, blackamoors, and mulattoes. With much ado Tiroll got to the Viceroy his palace, posting for his life, and his first care was to wish the porters to shut all the palace gates: for he was fearful of what presently happened, of a more general insurrection and uproar. For no sooner was he got into the Viceroy his house, and the gates shut up, but there were gathered to the market-place (as I was credibly informed by those that saw and observed diligently that day's trouble) above two thousand people, all of inferior rank and quality; and yet the number still increased till they were judged to be about six or seven thousand. They all cried out for Tiroll the Judas, sparing neither stones nor dirt which they did fling at the palace windows.

The Viceroy sent a message to them, desiring them to be quiet, and to betake themselves to their houses, certifying them that Tiroll was not in his palace, but escaped out of a back door. The rude multitude would not be satisfied with this, being now set on by two or three priests who were joined with them, and so they began more violently to batter the palace gates and walls, having brought pikes, and halberds, and long poles; others had got a few pistols, and birding pieces, wherewith they shot, not caring whom they killed or wounded in the palace. It was wonderful to see that none of the better sort, none of the judges, no high justice, no inferior officers durst or would come out to suppress the multitude, or to assist the Viceroy being in so great danger; nay I was told by some shopkeepers who lived in the market-place that they made a laughing business of it, and the people that passed by went smiling and saying, ' Let the boys and youngsters alone, they will right our wrongs, they will find out before they have done both Tiroll and Mexia and him that protects them,' meaning the Viceroy. But amongst them was much noted one priest, named Salazar, who spent much shot and bullets, and more his spirits in running about to spy some place of advantage, which he might soonest batter down. They found it seems the prison doors easier to open, or else with help within they opened them and let out all the malefactors, who joined with them to assault the palace. The Viceroy seeing no help came to him from the city, from his friends, from the judges of the Chancery, from the King's high justices, nor other officers for the peace, went up to the *zoties* of his palace with his guard and servants that attended on him, and set up the Royal Standard, and caused a trumpet to be sounded to call the city to aid and assist their King. But this prevailed not, none stirred, all the chief of the city kept within doors. And when the multitude saw the Royal Standard out, and heard the King's name from the *zoties*, they cried out, and often repeated it, *Viva el Rey, muera el mal gobierno, mueran los descomulgados,* that is to say, ' Our King live long, but let the evil government die, and perish, and let them die that are excommunicated.' These words saved many of them from hanging afterwards, when the business was tried and searched into by Don Martin de Carrillo. And with these words in their mouths, they skirmished with them of the *zoties* at least three hours, they above hurling down stones, and they beneath hurling up to them and some shooting with a few pistols and birding pieces at one another: and mark that in all this bitter skirmish there was not a piece of ordnance shot, for the Viceroy had none for the defence of his palace or person, neither had or hath that great city any for its strength and security, the Spaniards living fearless of the Indians, and (as they think) secure from being annoyed by any foreign nation. There were slain in about six hours in all that this tumult lasted, seven or eight beneath the market-place, and one of the Viceroy his guard and a page in the *zoties* above.

The day drawing to an end, the multitude brought pitch and fire, and first fired the prison, then they set on fire part of the palace, and burnt down the chief gate. This made some of the city, of the gentry, and of the judges to come out, lest the fire should prevail far upon the city, and to persuade the people to desist, and to quench the fire. Whilst the fire was quenching, many got into the palace, some fell upon the Viceroy's stables, and there got part of his mules' and horses' rich furnitures, others began to fall upon some chests, others to tear down the hangings, but they were soon persuaded by the better sort of the city to desist from spoil or robbery, lest by that they should be discovered; others searched about for Don Pedro Mexia, for Tiroll,

PLATE 4

RIOT IN MEXICO CITY
(*From the Dutch Edition of* 1700)

SURVEY OF WEST INDIES

and the Viceroy. None of them could be found, having disguised themselves and so escaped. Whither Don Pedro Mexia and Tiroll went, it could not be known in many days, but certain it was that the Viceroy disguised himself in a Franciscan habit, and so in company of a friar went through the multitude to the cloister of the Franciscans, where he abode all that year (and there I saw him the year after), not daring to come out, until he had informed the King and Council of Spain with what hath happened, and of the danger himself and the city was in, if not timely prevented.

The King and Council of Spain took the business to consideration, and looked upon it as a warning piece to a further mutiny and rebellion, and an example to other parts of America to follow upon any such-like occasion, if some punishment were not inflicted upon the chief offenders. Wherefore the year following, 1625, which was when I went to those parts, the King sent a new Viceroy the Marquess of Serralvo to govern in the place of the Count of Gelves, and especially to aid and assist Don Martin de Carrillo, a priest and inquisitor of the Inquisition of Valladolid, who was sent with large commission and authority to examine the aforesaid tumult and mutiny, and to judge all offenders that should be found in it, yea and to hang up such as should deserve death. I was at Mexico in the best time of the trial, and had intelligence from Don Martin de Carrillo his own ghostly father, a Dominican friar, of the chief passages in the examination of the business; and the result was that if justice should have been executed rightly, most of the prime of Mexico would have suffered, for not coming in to the Royal Standard when called by the sound of the trumpet; the judges some were put out of their places, though they answered that they durst not stir out, for that they were informed that all the city would have risen against them if they had appeared in public.

THE ENGLISH-AMERICAN

The chief actors were found to be the Creoles or natives of the country, who do hate the Spanish government, and all such as come from Spain; and reason they have for it, for by them they are much oppressed, as I have before observed, and are and will be always watching any opportunity to free themselves from the Spanish yoke. But the chief fomenters of the mutiny were found to be the Bishop's party the priests; and so had not Salazar and three more of them fled, they had certainly been sent to the galleys of Spain for galley slaves; this judgment was published against them. There were not above three or four hanged of so many thousands, and their condemnation was for things which they had stolen out of the Viceroy's palace. And because further enquiry into the rebellion would have brought in at least half the city either for actors, or counsellors, or fomenters, the King was well advised to grant a general pardon. The Archbishop's proceedings were more disliked in the Court of Spain than the Viceroy's, and was long without any preferment; though at last, that there might be no exceptions taken by his party, nor cause given for a further stirring the embers to a greater combustion, the Council thought fit to honour him in those parts where he was born, and to make him Bishop of Zamora, a small bishopric in Castile; so that his wings were clipped and from archbishop he came to be but bishop, and from threescore thousand crowns yearly rent he fell to four to five thousand only a year. The Count of Gelves was also sent to Spain, and well entertained in the Court, and therein made Master of the King's Horse, which in Spain is a nobleman's preferment.

And this history shewing the state and condition of Mexico when I travelled to those parts, I have willingly set down, that the reader may by it be furnished with better observations than myself (who am but a neophyte) am able to deduct. Somewhat might be observed from the Viceroy's covetousness; which doubtless in all is a great sin, but much more to be condemned in a prince or governor, whom it may blind in the exercise of justice and judgment, and harden those tender bowels (which ought to be in him) of a father and shepherd to his flock and children.

And thus largely I have described the state and condition of Mexico in the time of Montezuma, and since his death the manner and proportion of it, with the troubled condition I found it in when I went thither, by reason of a mutiny and rebellion caused by an archbishop the year before.

CHAPTER X

Shewing my journey from Mexico to Chiapa southward, and the most remarkable places in the way

My desire is to shew unto my reader what parts of America I travelled through, and did abide in, observing more particularly the state, condition, strength, and commodities of those countries which lie southward from Mexico. It is further my desire, nay the chief ground of this my history, that whilst my country doth here observe an Englishman, become American, travelling many thousand miles there, as may be noted from St John de Ulhua to Mexico, and from thence southward to Panama, and from thence northward again to Cartagena, and to Havana, God's goodness may be admired, and his providence extolled who suffered not the meanest and unworthiest of all his creatures to perish in such unknown countries; to be swallowed by North or South Sea, where shipwrecks were often feared; to be lost in wildernesses where no tongue could give directions; to be devoured by wolves, lions, tigers, or crocodiles, which there so much abound; to fall from steepy rocks and mountains, which seem to dwell in the aerial region, and threaten with fearful spectacles of deep and profound precipices, a horrid and inevitable death to those that climb up to them; to be eaten up by the greedy earth which there doth often quake and tremble, and hath sometimes opened her mouth to draw in towns and cities; to be stricken with those fiery darts of Heaven and thunderbolts which in winter season threaten the rocks and cedars; to be enchanted by Satan's instruments, witches and sorcerers, who there as on their own ground play their pranks more than in the parts of Christendom; to be quite blinded with Romish errors and superstitions, which have double blinded the purblind heathenish idolaters; to be wedded to the pleasures and licentiousness which do there allure; to be glutted with the plenty and dainties of fish, flesh, fowls, and fruits, which do there entice; to be puffed up with the spirit of pride and powerful command and authority over the poor Indians, which doth there provoke; to be tied with the cords of vanity and ambition, which there are strong; and finally to be glued in heart and affection to the dross of gold, silver, pearls, and jewels, whose plenty there doth bind, blind, captivate, and enslave the soul. Oh, I say, let the Lord's great goodness and wonderful providence be observed who suffered not an English stranger in all these dangers to miscarry, but was a guide unto him there in all his travels, discovered unto him as to the spies in Canaan, and as to Joseph in Egypt, the provision, wealth, and riches of that world, and safely guided him back to relate to England the truth of what no other English eye did ever yet behold.

From the month of October until February I did abide with my friends and companions the friars under the command of Friar Calvo in that house of recreation called St Jacintho, and from thence enjoyed the sight of all the towns and of what else was worth the seeing about Mexico. But the time I was there, I was

SURVEY OF WEST INDIES

careful to inform myself of the state of the Philippines, whither my first purposes had drawn me from Spain. It was my fortune to light upon a friar and an acquaintance of some of my friends, who was that year newly come from Manila whither I was going; who wished me and some other of my friends as we tendered our souls' good never to go to those parts, which were but snares and trap-doors to let down to Hell, where occasions and temptations to sin were daily, many in number, mighty in strength, and to get out of them, *labor et opus*, hard and difficult. And that himself, had not he by stealth gotten away (and that to save his soul) certainly he had never come from thence; who had often upon his knees begged leave of his superiors to return to Spain, and could not obtain it. Many particulars we could not get from him, nor the reasons of his coming away. Only he would often say that the friars that live there are devils in private and in those retired places where they live among the Indians to instruct and teach them; and yet in public before their superiors and the rest of friars they must appear saints, they must put on the cloak of hypocrisy to cover their inward devilishness, they must be clothed with sheep's skins, though within they be *lupi rapaces*, ravenous wolves, ravening after their neighbours' wives, and ravening after their neighbours' wealth; and yet with all this unpreparedness, with this outward, seeming, and frothy sanctity, and inward hellishness and deep-rooted worldliness and covetousness, when the superiors command and please to send them, they must go in a disguised manner to Japan or China to convert to Christianity those people though with peril and danger of their lives. Many such-like discourses we got out of this friar; and that if we went to live there we must be subject to the penalties of many excommunications for trivial toys and trifles, which the superiors do lay upon the consciences of their poor subjects, who may as soon strive against the common

THE ENGLISH-AMERICAN

course of nature not to see with their eyes, nor hear with their ears, nor speak with their tongues, as to observe all those things which against sense, reason, and nature with grievous censures and excommunications are charged and fastened upon them. He told us further of some friars that had despaired under those rigorous courses, and hanged themselves, not being able to bear the burden of an afflicted and tormented conscience; and of others that had been hanged, some for murdering of their rigid and cruel superiors; and some that had been found in the morning hanging with their queans at the cloister gates, having been found together in the night, and so murdered and hanged up either by the true husband, or by some other who bare affection to the woman. These things seemed to us very strange, and we perceived that all was not gold that glittered, nor true zeal of souls that carried so many from Spain to those parts; or if in some there were at first a better and truer zeal than in others when they came to the Philippines, and among those strong temptations, we found that their zeal was soon quenched. This reason moved me and three more of my friends to relent in our purposes of leaving of America, and going any further, for we had learned that maxim, *qui amat periculum, peribit in eo*, and *qui tangit picem, inquinabitur ab ea*; he that loveth the danger, shall fall and perish in it; and he that toucheth pitch shall be smeared by it. Wherefore we communed privately with ourselves what course we might take, how we might that year return back to Spain, or where we might abide if we returned not to Spain. For we knew if our Superior Calvo should understand of our purposes to go no further, he would lay upon us an excommunication to follow him, nay and that he would secure us in a cloister prison until the day and time of our departure from Mexico.

Our resolutions we made a secret of our hearts; yet could not I but impart it to one more special and intimate friend of mine, who was an Irish friar, named Thomas de Leon, whom I perceived a little troubled with so long a journey as was at hand, and found often wishing he had never come from Spain; and as soon as I had acquainted him with what I meant to do, he rejoiced and promised to ſtay with me. The time was short which we had to dispose of ourselves; but in that time we addressed ourselves to some Mexican friars and made known unto them that if our Superior Calvo would give us leave, we would willingly ſtay in Mexico, or in any cloiſter thereabouts, until we could better fit ourselves to return to Spain again. But they being natives and born in that country discovered presently unto us that inveterate spite and hatred which they bare to such as came from Spain; they told us plainly that they and true Spaniards born did never agree, and that they knew their superiors would be unwilling to admit of us; yet furthermore they informed us that they thought we might be entertained in the province of Oaxaca, where half the friars were of Spain and half Creoles and natives; but in case we should not speed there, they would warrant us we should be welcome to the province of Guatemala, where almoſt all the friars were of Spain, and did keep under such as were natives born in that country. It did a little trouble us to consider that Guatemala was three hundred leagues off, and that we were ignorant of the Mexican tongue, and unprovided of money and horses for so long a journey. But yet we considered the Philippines to be further, and no hopes there of returning ever again to Chriſtendom; wherefore we resolved to rely upon God's providence only, and to venture upon a three hundred leagues journey with what small means we had, and to sell what books and small trifles we had to make as much money as might buy each of us a horse. But while we were thus preparing ourselves secretly for Guatemala we were affrighted and disheartened with what in the like case to ours happened.

THE ENGLISH-AMERICAN

A friar of our company named Friar Peter Borrallo, without acquainting us or any other of his friends with what he intended, made a secret escape from us, and (as after we were informed) took his way alone to Guatemala. This so incensed our Superior Calvo, that after great search and enquiry after him, he betook himself to the Viceroy begging his assistance and proclamation, in the public market-place, for the better finding out his lost sheep, and alleging that none ought to hide or privily to harbour any friar that had been sent from Spain to the Philippines to preach there the Gospel, for that the aforesaid friars were sent by the King of Spain, whose bread they had eat, and at whose charges they had been brought from Spain to Mexico, and at the same King's charges ought to be carried from Mexico to the Philippines; and therefore if any friar now in the half way should recant of his purpose of going to the Philippines, and should by flight escape from his superior and the rest of his company, the same ought to be punished as guilty of defrauding the King's charges. This reason of Calvo being a politic and State reason prevailed so far with the Viceroy that immediately he commanded a proclamation to be made against whosoever should know of the said Peter Borrallo and should not produce him to his Highness, or should harbour him or any other friar belonging to the Philippines from the time forward until the ships were departed from Acapulco; and that whosoever should trespass against this proclamation should suffer imprisonment at his Highness his will and pleasure, and the penalty of five hundred ducats to be paid in at the King's Exchequer. With this proclamation Calvo began to insult over us, and to tell us we were the King's slaves under his conduct, and that if any of us durst to leave him (for he was jealous of most of us) he doubted not but with the Viceroy his assistance and proclamation he should find both us and Peter Borrallo out to our further shame and confusion. This did very much trouble us, and made my Irish friend Thomas de Leon his heart to faint, and his courage to relent, and utterly to renounce before me his former purposes of staying and hiding himself; yet he protested to me, if I was still of the same mind, he would not discover me, but seeing his weakness I durst not trust him, but made as if I were of his mind. Thus I betook myself to the other three of my friends (of whom one was Antonio Melendez that had been the first cause of my coming from Spain) whom I found much troubled, doubtful, and wavering what course to take.

They considered if we should flee, what a shame it would be to us to be taken and brought back to Mexico as prisoners, and forcedly against our wills to be shipped to the Philippines; they considered further if they went, what a slavish and uncomfortable life they should live in the Philippines, without any hopes of ever returning again to Christendom; yet further they looked upon the Viceroy his proclamation, and thought it hard to break through the opposition and authority of so great a man; and lastly in the proclamation they beheld the estimation that Calvo had of them, as of slaves and fugitives to be cried in a public market-place. But after all these serious thoughts our only comfort was that Peter Borrallo was safely escaped, and (as we were informed) had been met far from Mexico travelling alone towards Guatemala. And we thought, why might not we escape as well as he. Then I told them that my resolution was to stay, though alone I returned either to Spain, or took my journey to Guatemala; the rest were glad to see me resolute, and gave their hands that they would venture as much as I should.

Then we set upon the time when we should take our flight, and agreed that every one should have a horse in readiness in Mexico, and that the night before the rest of our company should depart from Mexico towards Acapulco to take shipping, we should by two and two in the evening leave St Jacintho, and meet in Mexico where our horses stood, and from thence set out and travel all the night, continuing our journey so the first two or three nights and resting in the daytime, until we were some twenty or thirty leagues from Mexico. For we thought the next morning Calvo awaking and missing us would not stop the journey of the rest of his company for our sakes to search and enquire after us; or if he did, it would be but for one day or two at the most till he had enquired for us in Mexico, or a day's journey in some of the common or beaten roads of Mexico, where we would be sure he should not hear of us, for we also agreed to travel out of any common or known road for the first two or three nights. This resolution was by us as well performed and carried on as it had been agreed upon, though some had been fearful that a counsel betwixt four could never be kept secret, nor such a long journey as of nine hundred miles be compassed with such small means of money as was among us, for the maintenance of ourselves and horses; for after our horses were bought, we made a common purse, and appointed one to be the purse-bearer, and found that amongst us all there were but twenty ducats, which in that rich and plentiful country was not much more than here twenty English shillings, which seemed to us but as a morning dew, which would soon be spent in provender only for our horses; yet we resolved to go on, relying more upon the providence of God than upon any earthly means, and indeed this proved to us a far better support than all the dross of gold and silver could have done; and we reckoned that after we had travelled forty leagues from Mexico, and entered without fear into the road, we had for our twenty ducats near forty now in our common purse. The reason was, for that most commonly we went either to friar's cloisters who knew us not, or to rich farms of Spaniards who thought nothing too good for us, and would not only entertain us stately, but at our departure would give us money for one or two days' journey. All our fear was to get safely out of Mexico, for we had been informed that Calvo had obtained from the Viceroy officers to watch in the chiefest roads both day and night until he had departed with his train of friars to Acapulco.

And for all the Viceroy his proclamation we got a true and trusty friend who offered to guide us out of Mexico by such a way as we needed not to fear any would watch for us. So with our friend and a map about us to guide us after he had left us in the morning, we cheerfully set out of Mexico about ten of the clock at night, about the middle of February, and meeting nobody about Guadalupe, which was the way we went out (though the contrary way to Guatemala, which on purpose we followed for fear the true way should be beset), we comfortably travelled all that night, till in the morning we came to a little town of Indians, where we began to spend of our small stock, calling upon the Indians for a turkey and capon to break our fast with our friend and guide before he returned to Mexico. Breakfast being ended, we took our leaves of him, and went to rest, that we might be more able to perform the next night's journey, which was to cross the country towards Atlixco, which is in a valley of twenty miles about at least, and doth give it the name of the valley of Atlixco, and is a valley much mentioned in all those parts, for the exceeding great plenty of wheat that is there reaped every year, and is the chief sustenance and relief of Mexico and all the towns about. In this valley are many rich towns of Spaniards and Indians; but we shunned to enter into them, and went from farm to farm out of the highways, where we found good entertainment of those rich farmers and yeomen, who bare such respect unto the priests that truly they thought themselves happy with our company.

Here we began to shake off all fear, and would no

more like bats and owls fly in the night, but that we might with more pleasure enjoy the prospect of that valley, and of the rest of the country we travelled by day; yet still crossing the country, we went from thence towards another valley called the valley of St Pablo, or Paul's valley, which though it be not as big as the valley of Atlixco, yet is held to be a richer valley, for here they enjoy a double harvest of wheat every year. The first seed they sow is watered, and grows with the common season rain; and the second seed which they sow in summer as soon as their first harvest is in, when the season of rain is past, they water with many springs which fall into that valley from the mountains which round beset it, and let in the water among their wheat at their pleasure, and take it away when they see fit. Here live yeomen upon nothing but their farms, who are judged to be worth some twenty thousand, some thirty thousand, some forty thousand ducats. In this valley we chanced to light upon one farm where the yeoman was countryman to my friend Antonio Melendez, born in Segovia in Spain, who for his sake kept us three days and nights with him. His table was as well furnished as the table of a knight might be, his sideboard full of silver bowls and cups, and plates instead of trenchers; he spared no dainties which might welcome us to his table, no perfumes which might us delight in our chambers, no music (which his daughters were brought up to) which might with more pleasure help to pass away the time. To him Antonio Melendez made known our journey towards Guatemala; and from him we received directions which way to steer our course until we might be throughly free from fear and danger. Here we began to see the great providence of God, who had brought us being strangers to such a friend's house, who not only welcomed us to him, but when we departed gave us a guide for a whole day, and bestowed upon us twenty ducats to help to bear our charges.

SURVEY OF WEST INDIES

From this valley we wheeled about to Tasco, a town of some five hundred inhabitants which enjoyeth great commerce with the country about by reason of the great store of cotton-wool which is there. And here we were very well entertained by a Franciscan friar, who being of Spain made the more of us, knowing we came from thence. Here we got into the road of Oaxaca, and went to Chiautla, which also aboundeth with cotton-wool, but in it we found no entertainment but what our own purses would afford us. Next to this place is a great town called Zumpango, which doth consist of at least eight hundred inhabitants, many of them very rich both Indians and Spaniards. Their commodities are chiefly cotton-wool, and sugar, and cochineal. But beyond this town are the mountains called La Misteca, which abound with many rich and great towns, and do trade with the best silk that is in all that country. Here is also great store of wax and honey; and Indians live there who traffic to Mexico and about the country with twenty or thirty mules of their own, chopping and changing, buying and selling commodities, and some of them are thought to be worth ten, or twelve, or fifteen thousand ducats, which is much for an Indian to get among the Spaniards, who think all the riches of America little enough for themselves. From these mountains of Misteca to Oaxaca we saw little observable, only towns of two or three hundred inhabitants; rich churches, well built, and better furnished within with lamps, candlesticks, crowns of silver for the several statues of saints; and all the way we did observe a very fruitful soil for both Indian and Spanish wheat, much sugar, much cotton-wool, honey, and here and there some cochineal, and of plantains and other sweet and luscious fruit great store; but above all great abundance of cattle, whose hides are one of the greatest commodities that from those parts are sent to Spain. Some reported that about Misteca formerly much gold had been found, and the Indians were wont to use it much, though now they will not be known of any, lest the greediness of the Spaniards bring them to misery and destruction, as it hath their neighbours about them. Also it is reported for certain that there are mines of silver, though as yet the Spaniards have not found them.

There are many mines of iron which the Spaniards will not busy themselves in digging, because they have it cheaper from Spain. From hence we came to the city of Oaxaca, which is a bishop's seat, though not very big, yet a fair and beautiful city to behold. It standeth fourscore leagues from Mexico in a pleasant valley from whence Cortez was named Marqués del Valle, the Marquess of the Valley. This city, as all the rest of America (except the sea towns), lieth open without walls, bulwarks, forts, towers, or any castle, ordnance, or ammunition to defend it. It may consist of at the most two thousand inhabitants, and are governed by a Spanish High Justice called *Alcalde Mayor*, whose power reacheth over all the valley, and beyond it as far as Nixapa, and almost to Tehuantepec, a sea town upon Mar del Sur. The valley is of at least fifteen miles in length, and ten in breadth, where runneth in the midst a goodly river yielding great store of fish. The valley is full of sheep and other cattle, which yield much wool to the clothiers of the City of Angels, store of hides to the merchants of Spain, and great provision of flesh to the city of Oaxaca, and to all the towns about, which are exceeding rich, and do maintain many cloisters of friars, and churches with stately furniture belonging unto them. But what doth make the valley of Oaxaca to be mentioned far and near are the good horses which are bred in it, and esteemed to be the best of all the country. In this valley also are some farms of sugar, and great store of fruits, which two sorts meeting together have cried up the city of Oaxaca for the best conserves and preserves that are made in America.

SURVEY OF WEST INDIES

In the city there are some six cloisters of nuns and friars, all of them exceeding rich; but above all is the cloister of the Dominican friars, whose church treasure is worth two or three millions; and the building of it the fairest and strongest in all those parts, the walls are of stone so broad that a part of them being upon finishing when I was there I saw carts go upon them, with stone and other materials. Here are also two cloisters of nuns, which are talked of far and near not for their religious practices, but for their skill in making two drinks, which are used in those parts, the one called chocolate and the other *atole*, which is like unto our almond milk, but much thicker, and is made of the juice of the young maize or Indian wheat, which they so confection with spices, musk, and sugar, that it is not only admirable in the sweetness of the smell, but much more nourishing and comforting the stomach. This is not a commodity that can be transported from thence, but is to be drunk there where it is made. But the other, chocolate, is made up in boxes, and sent not only to Mexico and the parts thereabouts, but much of it is yearly transported into Spain.

This city of Oaxaca is the richer by reason of the safety they enjoy for the carriage of their commodities to and from the port of St John de Ulhua by the great River Alvarado which runneth not far from it; and although the barques come not to the city of Oaxaca, yet they come up to the Zapotecas, and to St Ildefonso, which is not far from Oaxaca. And the carelessness of the Spaniards here is to be wondered at, that all along this river which runneth up into the heart of their country they have built as yet no castles, towers, or watch-houses, or planted any ordnance, trusting only in this, that great ships cannot come up, as if frigates or smaller barques, such as they themselves use, may not be made to annoy them. But of Oaxaca I shall say no more, but conclude that it is of so temperate an air, so abounding in fruits, and all provision requisite for man's life, so commodiously situated between the North and South Sea, having on the north side St John de Ulhua, and on the south Tehuantepec, a small and unfortified harbour, that no place I so much desired to live in whilst I was in those parts as in Oaxaca, which certainly I had attempted as I travelled by it, had I not understood that the Creole or native friars were many and as deadly enemies unto those that came from Spain as were the Mexicans. And this their spite and malice they shewed whilst we were there, to an ancient and grave old friar, Master in Divinity, who living had been for learning the oracle of those parts.

This old man died when I was there, and because when he lived they could pick no hole in his coat, being dead they searched his chamber, and finding in a coffer some moneys which he had not made known to his Superior when living (which they would reduce to a sin against his professed poverty, called propriety, and subject to the censure of excommunication), they reported that he had died excommunicated, and might not enjoy their Christian burial in the church or cloister, and so ignominiously buried their old divine, and with him his credit and reputation in a grave made in one of their gardens. A thing much talked on as scandalous to all the city and country, which they salved with saying he was excommunicated; but the truth was, he was of Spain, and therefore at his death they would shew their spite unto him. For certainly they could not do it for the sin of propriety which by him had been committed in his life, and to them all may be well said what Our Saviour said to the Jews bringing to him a woman found in adultery to be stoned; 'Whosoever of you is without sin, let him cast the first stone'; for all of them, yea even the best friars that live in America, are some way or other, much or less guilty of the sin of propriety which they profess and vow against. With this which we saw with our eyes,

SURVEY OF WEST INDIES

besides what with our ears we had heard of discords and factions amongst them, we thought Oaxaca was no place for us to live in; so after three days we made haste out of it, and departed towards Chiapa, which lieth three hundred miles from thence. And for our comfort in our further travelling we were informed in Oaxaca that in most towns of the road through that country, the Indians had an order from the High Justice to give unto friars travelling that way either horse to ride on or to carry their carriages, and provision of food freely without money, if they had none, so that at their departure they should write it down in the town book what they had spent, not abiding above four and twenty hours in the town; which expenses of travellers the Indians afterwards at the year's end of their ordinary justice and officers were to give an account of with carrying their town book unto the Spanish justice to whom they belonged, and by so doing these expenses were allowed of to be discharged by the common town purse or treasure, for the which a common plot of ground was allotted to be yearly sown with wheat or maize. With this charitable relief and help of the towns we conceived better of the rest of our long journey, and hoped to compass it with more ease. And so joyfully we went on, and the first place where we made trial of this order was at a great town called Antequera, where we freely called for our fowls and what other provision we saw in the town, fed heartily on them, and the next day when we were to pay and to depart, we called for the town book, subscribed our hands to what we had spent ourselves and horses, and went our way, praising the discretion of the justices of that country, who had settled a course so easy and comfortable for us, especially who had but shallow purses for our long journey. Yet we found in some small towns that the Indians were unwilling, and (as they alleged) unable to extend this charity to us, being four in company, and bringing with us the charge likewise of four horses, which made us sometimes make the longer journey that we might reach unto some great and rich town.

The next to Antequera in that road is Nixapa, which is of at the least eight hundred inhabitants, Spaniards and Indians, standing upon the side of a river, which we were informed was an arm of the great river Alvarado. In this town is a very rich cloister of Dominican friars, where we were well entertained; and in it there is a picture of Our Lady, which superstitiously they fancy to have wrought miracles, and is made a pilgrimage from far and near, and consequently hath great riches and lamps belonging unto it. This is counted absolutely one of the wealthiest places of all the country of Oaxaca; for here is made much indigo, sugar, cochineal; and here grew many trees of *cacao*, and *achiote*, whereof is made the chocolate, and is a commodity of much trading in those parts, though our English and Hollanders make little of it when they take a prize of it at sea, as not knowing the secret virtue and quality of it for the good of the stomach. From hence we went to Aguatulco and Capalita, also great towns standing upon a plain country full of sheep and cattle, abounding with excellent fruits, especially *pinas* and *sandias*, which are as big as pumpkins [pumpions], and so waterish that they even melt like snow in the mouth, and cool the heat which there is great, by reason it is a low and marsh kind of ground, lying near the South Sea.

The next chief town and most considerable after Capalita is Tehuantepec, this is a sea town upon Mar del Sur, and a harbour for small vessels, such as trade from those parts to Acapulco and Mexico, and to Realejo and Guatemala, and sometimes to Panama. Here upon some occasions ships which come from Peru to Acapulco do call in. It is a port no farther safe, than that no English or Holland ships do come thereabouts, which if they did, they would there find

SURVEY OF WEST INDIES

no resistance, but from thence would find an open and easy road over all the country. Upon all this South Sea side from Acapulco to Panama, which is above two thousand miles by land, there is no open harbour but this for Oaxaca, and La Trinidad for Guatemala, and Realejo for Nicaragua, and Golfo de Salinas for small vessels in Costa Rica, and all these unprovided of ordnance and ammunition, all open doors to let in any nation that would take the pains to surround the world to get a treasure. This port of Tehuantepec is the chief for fishing in all that country; we met here in the ways sometimes with fifty, sometimes with a hundred mules together laden with nothing but salt fish for Oaxaca, City of the Angels and Mexico. There are some very rich merchants dwell in it, who trade with Mexico, Peru, and the Philippines, sending their small vessels out from port to port, which come home richly laden with the commodities of all the southern or eastern parts.

From hence to Guatemala there is a plain road along the coast of the South Sea, passing through the provinces of Soconusco and Suchitepequez; but we aiming at Chiapa took our journey over the high rocks and mountains called Quelenes, travelling first from Tehuantepec to Estepec, and from thence through a desert of two days' journey, where we were fain to lodge one night by a spring of water upon the bare ground in open wide fields, where neither town nor house is to be seen, yet thatched lodges are purposely made for travellers. This plain lieth so open to the sea that the winds from thence blow so strongly and violently that travellers are scarce able to sit their horses and mules; which is the reason no people inhabit there, because the winds tear their houses, and the least fire that there breaks out doth a great deal of mischief. This plain yet is full of cattle, and horses and mares, some wild, some tame; and through this windy champaign country with much ado we travelled;

though myself thought I should even there end my days, for the second day being to reach to a town, and my three friends riding before, thinking that I followed them, evening now drawing on they made more haste to find the town. But in the meanwhile my horse refused to go any further, threatening to lie down if I put him to more than he was able. I knew the town could not be far, and so I lighted, thinking to walk and lead my horse, who also refused to be led, and so lay down. With this a troop of thoughts beset me, and to none I could give a flat answer. I thought if I should go on foot to find out the town and my company and leave my horse there saddled, I might both lose myself, and my horse and saddle; and if I should find the town and come in the morning for my horse, the plain was so wide and spacious that I might seek long enough, and neither find him, nor know the place where I left him, for there was nothing near to mark the place, nor where to hide the saddle, neither hedge, tree, shrub, within a mile on any side. Wherefore I considered my best course would be to take up my lodging in the wide and open wilderness with my horse, and to watch him lest he should wander and stray away, until the morning or until my friends might send from the town to see what was become of me; which they did not that night, thinking I had taken my way to another town not far from thence, whither they sent in the morning to enquire for me.

I looked about therefore for a commodious place to rest in, but found no choice of lodgings, everywhere I found a bed ready for me, which was the bare ground; a bolster only or pillow I wanted for my head, and seeing no bank did kindly offer itself to ease a lost stranger and pilgrim, I unsaddled my weary jade, and with my saddle fitted my head instead of a pillow. Thus without a supper I went to bed in my mother's own bosom, not a little comforted to see my tired horse pluck up his spirits, and make much of his supper, which there was ready for him, of short, dry, and withered grass, upon which he fed with a greedy and hungry stomach, promising me by his feeding that the next day he would perform a journey of at least thirty or forty miles. The poor beast fed apace; my careful eye watched him for at least an hour, when upon a sudden I heard such an hideous noise of howling, barking, and crying, as if a whole army of dogs were come into the wilderness, and howled for want of a prey of some dead horse or mule. At first the noise seemed to be a pretty way off from me; but the more I hearkened unto it, the nigher it came unto me, and I perceived it was not of dogs by some intermixed shriekings as of Christains, which I observed in it. An observation too sad for a lone man without any help or comfort in a wilderness, which made my hair to stand upright, my heart to pant, my body to be covered with a fearful sweat as of death. I expected nothing else, not knowing from whence the noise proceeded; sometimes I thought of witches, sometimes of devils, sometimes of Indians turned into the shape of beasts (which amongst some hath been used), sometimes of wild and savage beasts, and from all these thoughts I promised myself nothing but sure death, for the which I prepared myself, recommending my soul to the Lord, whilst I expected my body should be a prey to cruel and merciless beasts; or some instruments of that roaring lion who in the Apostle goeth about seeking whom he may devour. I thought I could not any ways prevail by flying or running away, but rather might that way run myself into the jaws of death; to hide there was no place, to lie still I thought was safest, for if they were wild beasts, they might follow their course another way from me, and so I might escape. Which truly proved my safest course, for while I lay sweating and panting, judging every cry, every howling, and shrieking an alarm to my death, being in this agony and fearful conflict till about midnight, on a sudden the noise ceased, sleep (though but the shadow of death) seized upon my wearied body, and forsook me not, till the morning's glorious lamp shining before my slumbering eyes and driving away death's shadow greeted me with life and safety. When I awaked, my soul did magnify the Lord for my deliverance from that night's danger. I looked about and saw my horse also near the place where I had left him; I saddled him presently with desire to leave that wilderness and to find out my company, and to impart unto them what that night had happened unto me; I had not rid above a mile, when I came to a brook of water, where were two ways, the one straight forward along the desert, where I could discover no town, nor houses, nor trees in a prospect of five or six miles at least; the other way was on the left hand, and that way some two or three miles off I saw a wood of trees, I imagined there might be the town. I followed that way, and within a quarter of a mile my horse began to complain of his poor provender the night before, and to slight me for it; I was fain to light and lead him; and thus again discouraged with my horse, and discomforted for the uncertainty of my way, looking about I spied a thatched house on the one side of the way, and one on horseback, who came riding to me. It was an Indian belonging to that house which was the farm of a rich Indian, and governor of the next town, of whom I asked how far it was to the town of Estepec; he shewed me the trees, and told me that a little beyond them it stood, and that I should not see it until I came unto it. With this I got up again and spurred my sullen jade, until I reached unto the trees, where he was at a stand and would go no further. Then I unsaddled him, and hid my saddle under some low shrubs, and leaving my horse (whom I feared not that any would steal him) I walked unto the town which was not above half a mile from thence, where I found my three friends were waiting for me, and grieved for the loss of me, had sent to another town to enquire for me; it was the least thought they had that I had been a lodger in the desert. When I related unto them and to the Indians the noise and howling that I had heard the Indians answered me that that was common music to them almost every night, and that they were wolves and tigers which they feared not, but did often meet them and with a stick or holloaing did scare them away, and that they were only ravenous for their fowls, colts, calves, or kids. After a little discourse I returned with an Indian to seek my horse and saddle, and in that town I sold my wearied Mexican beast, and hired another to Ecatepec whither we went all four friends again in company.

Where note that in this plain and champaign country of Tehuantepec are five rich and pleasant towns full of fruits and provision of victual, all ending in Tepec, to wit, Tehuantepec, Estepec, Ecatepec, Sanatepec, and Tapanatepec. Now from Ecatepec we could discover the high mountains of Quelenes, which were the subject of most of our discourse to Sanatepec, and from thence to Tapanatepec. For we had been informed by Spaniards and travellers in the way, that they were the most dangerous mountains to travel over that were in all those parts; and that there were on the top of them some passages so narrow, and so high, and so open to the boisterous winds that came from the South Sea, which seemed to lie at the very bottom of them; and on each side of these narrow passages such deep precipices among rocks, that many times it had happened that the wind blowing furiously had cast down mules laden with heavy carriages down the rocks, and likewise horsemen had been blown down, both horse and man. The sight of the rocks and mountains did terrify us, and the report of them did much affright us; so that in all this way we did confer which way to take, whether the road way to Guatemala which lieth under those mountains along the coast by the country of Soconusco, from whence (though out of our way) we might have turned to Chiapa, or whether we should steer our right course to Chiapa over those mountains, which we had been informed we might safely pass over if the winds did not blow too boisterously. We resolved that when we came to Tapanatepec we would choose our way according as the winds did favour or threaten us, but however to Chiapa we would go, because there we had understood was the Superior and Provincial of all the Dominicans of those parts (to whom we ought to address ourselves), and also because we would see that famous and much talked of province of Chiapa. In Sanatepec we met with a friar who gave us stately entertainment, and from thence gave us Indians to guide us to Tapanatepec, and a letter to the chief of the town (which also was at his command) to give us mules to carry us, and Indians to guide us up the mountains. Here the rest of our horses also failed us, but their weariness was no hindrance to us, for the Indians were willing to give us as much or more than they had cost us, because they were true Mexican breed, and all the way we went to Chiapa and through that country to Guatemala the towns were to provide us of mules for nothing. We came to Tapanatepec (which standeth at the bottom and foot of Quelenes) on Saturday night, and with the letter we carried were very much welcomed and entertained well by the Indians.

This town is one of the sweetest and pleasantest of any we had seen from Oaxaca thither, and it seems God hath replenished it with all sorts of comforts which travellers may need to ascend up those dangerous and steepy rocks. Here is great plenty of cattle for flesh, and rich Indians which have farms, called there *estancias*, in some a thousand, in some three or four thousand head of cattle; fowls here are in abundance; fish the best store and choicest of any town from Mexico thither, for the sea is hard by it, and besides there runneth by it a small river which yields divers sorts of fish. From the mountains there fall so many springs of water, that with them the Indians water at their pleasure their gardens which are stored with much herbage and salads. The shade which defends from the heat (which there is great) is the daughter of most sweet and goodly fruit trees, and of orange, lemon, citron, and fig leaves. The Sabbath morning was so calm that we desired to make use of it, lest by longer delays the winds should stay us, or force us to the coast of Soconusco. But the Indians entreated us to be their guest at dinner, not doubting but the weather would hold, and promising us to provide us strong and lusty mules, and provision of fruits, and fried fish, or fowls, or what ourselves desired. We could not refuse this their kind offer, and so stayed dinner with them. After dinner our mules were brought, and two Indians to guide us and carry our provision, which was some fried fish, and a cold roasted capon, with some fruit as much as might suffice us for a day, for the chief ascent and danger is not above seven leagues, or one and twenty English miles, and then beyond the top of the mountains three miles is one of the richest farms for horses, mules, and cattle, in all the country of Chiapa, where we knew we should be welcomed by one Don John de Toledo, who then lived there. Though these mountains shew themselves with several sharp pointed heads, and are many joined together, yet one of them is only mentioned in that country by the travellers, which is called Maquilapa, over the which lieth the way to Chiapa. To this high, steepy, and craggy Maquilapa we took our journey after dinner, and were by the proud mountain that night well entertained, and harboured in a green plot of ground resembling a meadow, which lay as a rib of the one side of that huge and more than Pyrenean monster.

THE ENGLISH-AMERICAN

The Indians comforted us with the shews of fair weather, and told us that they doubted not but the next day at noon we should be at Don John de Toledo his *eſtancia*, or farm. With this we spread our supper upon the green table-cloth, and at that firſt meal eat up our capon and moſt of the provision of our cold fried fish, leaving only a bit for our morning's breakfaſt; the springs of water like conduit-pipes, trickling down the rocks, gave us melodious music to our supper; the Indians fed merrily, and our mules contentedly, and so the fountain nymphs sung us asleep till morning, which seemed to us as calm and quiet as the day before, and encouraged us haſtily to snatch that bit which we had left and so up from breakfaſt, to say merrily, up to Maquilapa. We had not winded the mountain upwards much above a mile, when the higher we mounted, the more we heard the wind from above whiſtling unto us, and forbidding us to go any further. We were now half way up, and doubtful what we should do, whether go forward, or return to Tapanatepec to eat more fish, or to ſtay where we were a while until the weather were more calm, which we thought might be at noon or towards evening. The Indians told us that about a mile further there was a fountain of water, and a lodge made under trees on purpose for travellers that were either benighted or hindered by the winds to compass their journey up the mountain. Thither we went with much ado, hoping the wind would fall; but ſtill the higher we climbed the ſtronger we felt the breath of Æolus, and durſt not like the people called Psilli (of whom Herodotus writeth) march againſt him, leſt as they inſtead of a victory found a grave in the sands where they met to oppose him, so we inſtead of ascending should by a furious blaſt be made to descend into those deep and horrid precipices, which truly threatened death, and offered themselves to be a grave unto our torn and mangled bodies. We liked the fountain very well, and the lodge better for the harbour of trees which compassed it about. The wind kept on breathing, and we stood still fearing, till the day was so far spent that we had no hopes of going back or forward. Of any supper we despaired that night, who would have been glad now to have picked a bone of a capon's leg, or to have sucked a fish's head, and saw there was nothing for us, but only to feed our hungry stomachs with the remembrance of the plenty the night before. Thus gazing one upon another, and sometimes looking down to the fountain, sometimes looking up to the trees, we perceived amongst them a lemon tree, full of small and very sour green lemons. It was not with us as with Tantalus who could neither enjoy the fruit above him, nor the waters beneath him; we could and did most greedily catch and snatch the lemons, which were sauce for no meat, but only to fill an empty stomach; with them we supped and took our rest.

The next morning the wind was rather stronger than calmer, and we as strong the second day as the first in our purpose of staying there, and not turning our backs like cowards. The Indians were also willing to stay yet one day longer; so we fell to our breakfast of lemons which were somewhat cool to a fasting stomach, and relished nothing the better with a draught from the clear fountain. And of what we left on the tree we made our dinner and supper, adding to our water what we saw the Indians did drink, who had their small bags full of powder of their maize, of which first making cakes as dry as biscuit they then grind them to powder, and when they travel carry with them that powder to drink with water. This we thought might be more nourishing to us than lemons and water only, and so for that day we bought of them half a bagful of powder giving for it in our want and necessity four reals, or two English shillings, which out of Maquilapa and that our fear of starving might not be worth above a penny; and yet this was but weak nourishment for our feeble bodies. Thus we waited all Tuesday for the laying of the wind, resolving the next morning either to go up the hill, or down again to Tapanatepec. But on Wednesday morning the wind seeming to be somewhat laid, we purposed to stay till noon hoping then it would be sure travelling; but it ceased not but rather increased a little; whereupon one of our company resolved to go upwards a mile or two on foot, and try the passages, and the danger of the wind, and to bring us word again; for we thought our fear might be greater than the danger, who had heard much talk, but had not as yet seen anything worth our fear. Up therefore went our friend, who stayed from us near two hours, and then returning back he told us he thought we might get up leading our mules by the bridles. But what with further questions and debates time passed away, so that we thought it might be too late; and for that day we put off our journey until the next morning, resolutely purposing to go forwards altogether if the wind were not much increased. So that day we fell again to our green crabby lemons, water, and maize powder, all which we found had much weakened our bodies and feared if we continued there any longer they might hasten our death. Wherefore on Thursday morning (the wind being as the day before) commending ourselves first unto the protection of that Lord whom the winds and sea obey, we mounted up upon our mules (leaving our names written in the bark of a great tree, and the days we stayed there without food) and so went upward.

We perceived no great danger in the wind a great while, but some steps and passages upon stony rocks we feared for the narrowness of them, and there we lighted, thinking ourselves safer upon our own two feet than upon the four feet of a beast. But when we came up to the very top of Maquilapa (which signifies in that tongue, a head without hair) we perceived truly

SURVEY OF WEST INDIES

the danger so much talked of, and wished ourselves again with our green lemons in the way of Tapanatepec, for we found it indeed a head without hair, a top without a tree or branch to shelter a fearful traveller; the passage that lieth open to the sea may be no more than a quarter of a mile, but the height and narrowness of it stupefieth, for if we look on the one side, there is the wide and spacious South Sea lying so deep and low under it that it dazzleth the eyes to behold it; if we look on the other side, there are rocks of at least six or seven miles depth, whose sight doth make the stoutest and hardest heart (though like themselves) to quake and quiver; so that here the sea expects to swallow, there the rocks threaten to tear with a downfall, and in the midst of those dangers in some places the passage is not above an ell broad. We needed better cordials for that quarter of a mile than feeding three days upon green lemons and water, and durst not man ourselves so much as to go through it upon our mules; we lighted, and gave the Indians our mules to lead, and we followed them one by one not daring to walk upright for fear of head giddiness with looking on either side, but bowing our bodies we crept upon our hands and feet as near unto the tracks which beasts and travellers had made as we could without hindering our going. And when we had got to the end of that passage, and where the mountain was broader, and the trees promised relief, we then looked back boldly, and accused of folly both ourselves and all other travellers that sought no other way though ten miles about, to avoid that danger both for man and beast. From thence joyfully we made haste to Don John de Toledo, who made us welcome and gave us some warm broth to comfort our stomachs, which were so weak that no sooner had we eat anything, but presently we cast it up again; till after many sups of broth and wine we recovered strength towards night, and eat our suppers; there we stayed two days; and thus thoroughly refreshed we went to Acapala a very great town of Indians in the province of Chiapa, standing by the same river that passeth by Chiapa, which is called Chiapa de Indios, or Chiapa of the Indians, to distinguish it from another Chiapa, called Chiapa Real, the Royal Chiapa, or Chiapa de Espanoles, Chiapa of the Spaniards.

From Acapala we went first to Chiapa of the Indians, which standeth almost as low as Maquilapa is high, seated upon a river as broad as is the Thames at London, which hath its spring from the mountains called Cuchumatlanes, in the road from Chiapa Real to Guatemala, and runs towards the province of Zoques, where it entereth into the river of Tabasco. But of this Chiapa I will speak a little more in the next chapter, and now only say that here we were joyfully entertained by those friars, who looked upon us as members belonging to the corporation of that their province, and assured us that the Provincial and chief Superior would be very glad of our coming, who wanted Spanish friars to oppose the Creoles and natives who strived to get ahead as they had done in Mexico and Oaxaca. Here we understood that the Provincial was not above one day's journey from thence. Here also we met with our friend Peter Borrallo, who had come before us alone, and made his escape from Mexico: he comforted us much with the good and kind usage which he had found there; yet he told us how Calvo was gone with the rest of his train from Mexico to Acapulco, and from thence was shipped with them to the Philippines; but that at his departure he had writ a letter of bitter complaints unto the Superior of Chiapa and Guatemala against him and us four, desiring the Provincial not to entertain us, but to send us back to Mexico, to be shipped from thence the next year unto the Philippines; which letter was not regarded, but much slighted by the Provincial. After we had been a week feasted in Chiapa, we thought it now fit to present ourselves to the Provincial (whose name was Friar Peter Alvarez) that from him we might receive judgment, and know whether we should stay in that province, or be forced to return to Spain, for in no other part of America we could be entertained.

We found the Provincial in a little town called St Christopher, between Chiapa of the Indians and the Royal Chiapa, recreating himself in the shady walks, which are many sweet and pleasant in that small town; where also there is store of fish, and great abundance of rare and exquisite fruits. He entertained us very lovingly with fair and comfortable words, with a stately dinner and supper, and before we went to bed, to shew his humility he did unto us what Christ to his Disciples, he washed our feet. The first day he said little or nothing unto us concerning our continuing in that country; but the next day he discovered unto us his full resolutions, with many wise and cunning sophisms. For first he read unto us the letter which Calvo had writ unto him against us, glossing upon it how ill we had done in forsaking our first love and calling to the Philippines, and the danger many Indian souls might be in by reason of our not going thither to convert and instruct them, whose gifts and abilities he supposed might have been more profitable and comfortable to those souls than those who in our stead and absence should be sent amongst them. And secondly, he told us how we had frustrated the King of Spain's good hopes of us who had allowed us means and maintenance from Spain to Mexico, hoping that by us many souls of Indians in the Philippines might be saved. Thirdly, he told us that he looked upon us as his prisoners, in whose power it was to imprison us, and to send us prisoners to Mexico to the Viceroy, to be shipped from thence to Manila, according to Calvo his demand. But for the present he would not let us know what he meant to do with us; only he bad us not to be discouraged but to be merry and recreate ourselves, and that after dinner we should know more from him, when he had received an answer to a letter which he had writ unto the city of Chiapa concerning the disposal of our persons. These reasonings of the grave and old Provincial did not a little sad our hearts; for the loss of souls, and King of Spain his intentions and charity charged upon us, and imprisonment spoke of by the by, were words which seemed of a very high strain, and so could hardly be digested by us; this morning's breakfast had quite taken away from us our stomach to our dinner. And thus we departed from the presence of the venerable Friar Peter Alvarez, and betook ourselves to a shady walk under orange trees belonging to the house where this Superior was. In this shade we conferred with ourselves upon the words of Alvarez, and finding them of so high a nature, as involving souls, a King, and imprisonment, we thought verily we should be sent back to Mexico, and from thence like fugitive slaves be forced to the Philippines. Here my hopes of ever more seeing England were lost; Antonio Melendez his heart panted, wished himself again upon the highest top of Maquilapa; another wished himself with old Calvo at sea sailing to Manila, though it were but to help him scrape his rusty gammons of bacon.

The motion was made to make an escape from Alvarez, as we had done from Calvo; but to this answer was made that whithersoever we went, not knowing the country, we should be discovered; and that put case the worst, we should be sent to Mexico, we might better escape in the way than there where we were. At last I told the rest, that I could conceive no hard nor harsh usage from that smiling and loving countenance of the Provincial, nor after that his low and humble act of washing our feet the night before; and that I thought verily he wished us well for having come so far to offer ourselves for fellow-labourers in that harvest of souls belonging to his charge, and

SURVEY OF WEST INDIES

whom we knew wanted such as we were newly come from Spain to oppose the Creoles' or natives' faction in that province; alleging furthermore the example of our friend and companion Peter Borrallo, whom he had already incorporated into that province, and could do no less with us without partiality and acceptation of persons. And lastly, my opinion was, that in case we ought not to be entertained there, yet the Provincial would not send us back to Mexico, there to be disgraced and affronted, but would give way unto us to return to Spain, or whither else we would, with some relief and money in our purses. Whilst we were thus troubled, and in this sad and serious discourse, old Alvarez it seems had been eyeing of us from his window, and as Joseph could not long suppress and keep in the expressions of a loving and tender heart unto his brethren, so this good Superior perceiving that we were troubled with what he had said unto us, sent his companion unto us to comfort us; which we easily perceived by his discourse when he came unto us. For as soon as he came he asked us why we were so sad and melancholy. He told us the Provincial also had observed that we were troubled. 'But,' said he, 'be of good cheer; be confident that the Provincial wisheth you very well, and needeth such as you are, and having come into his dominion to thrust yourselves upon his mercy, by harsh and unkind usage he will not do what martial law forbids a hard-hearted soldier to do unto his enemy upon such terms.' Many such comfortable words did he speak unto us; and told us further that the Provincial had been much censured by the Creole party for entertaining of Peter Borrallo, and that now they would stir worse seeing four more come to weaken their faction, and therefore he desired to be well advised concerning us, and to carry our business with such discretion, as might give little offence to those who were apt to judge and censure the best of all his actions. And finally he did assure us, that we should never be sent back as prisoners to Mexico by the Provincial, who in case he could not entertain us in Chiapa, or Guatemala, would further us with all his favour, and friends, and money in our purses to return again to Spain. These reasons were heart fainting cordials unto us, and stomach preparatives to a good dinner, to which by the sound of a bell we were invited.

When we came in, the loving, smiling, and fatherly countenance of the good Provincial did cheer us more then all the cheer that waited for us upon the table in several dishes, all which were seasoned to our palates with the sauce of the comfort which the Provincial's messenger had brought unto us in the shady orange walk in the garden. The great provision of fish and flesh, with fruits and sweetmeats were yet to us a strong argument that we were very welcome; for what we fed on that day might well become a nobleman's table; besides in many passages of our discourse we perceived that good old Alvarez his heart was overjoyed with our coming to him. Dinner being ended, the Provincial desired to play a game at tables with us round about, saying he would not win our money, because he judged us poor after so long a journey. But thus he settled the game and sport; that if he did win, we should say for him five *Pater Nosters*, and five *Ave Maries*; but if we won, we should win our admittance, and incorporation into that province. This sport pleased us well, for our winnings we judged would be more profitable at that time than to win pounds, and our losings we valued not; besides we were confident all went well with us, when from the favour of the dice we might challenge that favour which with many weary journeys we had come to seek above four hundred miles.

The sport began, and we young blades taking one by one our turns were too hard for the old man, who (as we perceived) would willingly be the loser, that his very losses might speak unto us what through policy and discretion he would not utter with words. Yet we boldly challenged our winnings, which as soon as we had ended our game were now surely confirmed unto us by the return of an Indian messenger, who that morning had been sent to the city of Chiapa for advice and counsel from the Prior and the chief of the cloister concerning our disposal, and now was returned with an answer from the Prior, who in his letter expressed great joy unto the Provincial for our coming, and so from the rest of the seniors of the cloister, and did earnestly beg of the Superior that he would send us to him to be his guests, for that our case had been his own some ten years before, for he had also at Mexico forsaken his company to the Philippines, and fled to Guatemala, where for his learning and good part he had been as a stranger much envied by the Creole faction; but now he hoped he should have some to side with him against such as spited and maligned him. Old Alvarez was much taken with his letter, and told us he must pay what he had lost, and that the next day he would send us to Chiapa, there to abide until he took further care of us, to send us to other parts of the country to learn the Indian languages, that we might preach unto them. This discourse being ended we betook ourselves again to the garden which smelled more of comfort than before dinner, and to our shady walks which now offered us a safer protection than they had done in the forenoon, countenancing that protection which we had gained from the Provincial.

Here we began to praise God, who had looked upon us in our low estate, not forgetting the wise and politic Provincial, who though he had lost his games for our comfort, we would not he should lose our prayers, which there we offered up to God for his health and safety. And so till supper time we continued our discourse in the garden fuller of mirth and

THE ENGLISH-AMERICAN

pleasant jests than we had done before dinner, snatching now and then at the oranges and lemons, which were there both sour and sweet, eating of some, and casting some one at another, but especially at him who had wished himself with Calvo dressing his rusty bacon, whom we strived to beat out of the garden by force of orange and lemon bullets; which sport we continued the more willingly, because we perceived the good Provincial stood behind a lattice in a balcony beholding us, and rejoicing to see our hearts so light and merry. We had no sooner beat Calvo his friend out of the garden, when the bell to supper sounded a retreat to us all, and called us again to meet our best friend Alvarez, who had furnished us a table again like that at noon. After supper he told us that the next morning he would send us to Chiapa, for that the Prior had writ unto him he would meet us in the way with a breakfast at a town called St Philip; wherewith we conceited very highly of ourselves to see that provincials and priors were so forward to feast us. Yet before we went to bed, the Provincial would try again a game at tables with every one of us, to see if now he could beat us that had been too hard for him at noon. The matter of our game was now altered, and what we played for was this; if the Provincial won, we were to be his prisoners (which mystery we understood not till the next day, for the old man was crafty and politic, and knew he could win of us when he listed, for he was an excellent gamester at tables) but if we won of him, he was to give us a box of chocolate, which was a drink we liked very well. The game went on, and we every one of us one by one were losers, yet understood not how we should be his prisoners, but slighted our losses. Yet for all this the merry Provincial told us he was sorry we had lost, and wished we might never be prisoners to a worse enemy than he; and that we should perceive it, but would comfort us each one as a prisoner with a box of chocolate, to drink for his sake, and to

SURVEY OF WEST INDIES

comfort our hearts, when most we should find them discomforted for our losses. We understood not his meaning till the next day at noon, but thought it was a jest and a word of sport and mirth, like many such-like which in his discourse had come from him.

With this we took our leaves, and went to bed with light and merry hearts. In the morning two mules of the Provincial and two of his companion were saddled for us, and at least a dozen Indians on horseback waited for us to conduct us up a steepy hill and through woods to the town of St Philip. After our breakfast the good Provincial embraced us, and bad us farewell, desiring us to pray for him, and not to be discouraged by anything that might befall us, assuring us he wished us very well, and would do what lay in his power for our good; yet so, that he must use policy and discretion to stop the mouths of the Creoles, whom he knew hated both him and us. Thus we departed with waits and trumpets sounding before us, which rebounded an echo all the way up the hill from us to old Alvarez whom we had left in a low bottom compassed about with hills on every side. We had no sooner ascended up to the top of the mountain, when we discovered a little valley, and in it the city of Chiapa of the Spaniards, with two or three small villages, of which one was St Philip at the bottom of the mountain which we were to descend. The trumpets which still went sounding before us were a sufficient and loud alarm to St Philip's inhabitants of our coming, and a warning for the speedier hastening of our second breakfast, for the which the cold morning air (which we found somewhat piercing upon the mountain) had whetted and thorough prepared our stomachs.

We had not got down the mountain half a mile, when we met with a matter of twenty gallant Indians on horseback with their trumpeters sounding before them, and behind them came upon a stately mule the Prior of Chiapa (whose name was Father John Baptist), a merry fat friar, who calling us his brethren fugitives from the Philippines, told us we were welcome to that country, and to him especially, and that in the next St Philip he would shew us better sport than any St Philip in all the Philippine Islands could have shewed us, if we had gone thither. Thus with a pleasant discourse, and many merry conceits from the good Prior we soon came down the hill, where the whole village of St Philip waited for us both men and women, some presenting unto us nosegays, others hurling roses and other flowers in our faces, others dancing before us all along the street, which was strewed with herbs and orange leaves, and adorned with many arches made with flowers and hung with garlands for us to ride under until we came to the church, where for half an hour we were welcomed with the best music from the city of Chiapa, which the Prior had hired to come with him to entertain us. Our music being ended, fat Father John Baptist stood up and made a short speech unto the Indians, giving them thanks for their kind and pompous entertainment of us his special friends, and that their souls might gain by it, he granted unto them a plenary indulgence of all their sins past to be gained by as many of them as should visit that church the next Lord's Day either before or after noon. And thus from the altar we went unto our breakfasting table, which was furnished with many well seasoned dishes of salt and well peppered and spiced meats, all fit to make us relish better a cup of Spanish *Pier Ximeny* which the Prior had provided for us. After our salt meats, came such rare and exquisite sorts of sweetmeats made by John Baptist his best devoted nuns of Chiapa, that the like we had not seen from St John de Ulhua to that place. These were to prepare our stomachs for a cup of chocolate, with the which we ended our breakfast. But whilst all this was gallantly performed by the Prior, it was a hard riddle unto us what he often repeated unto us saying: 'Brethren break your fast well, for your dinner will be the meanest as ever ye did eat in your lives, and now enjoy this sweet liberty which will not last long unto you.' We observed the words, but knew not what to make of them, till we came unto the cloister. After our breakfast the Indians shewed us a little sport in the marketplace, running races on horseback, and playing at *juego de cañas*; which is to meet on horseback, with broad targets to defend their heads and shoulders while passing by they hurl canes, or darts, one at another, which those Indians acted with great dexterity.

Thus the good Prior of Chiapa feasted us, and permitted us to enjoy our liberty as long as it seems it had been agreed upon by letters between him and the Provincial, which was till it might be dinner time in the cloister of Chiapa, where we were to be before noon. The time drew near, and we had from St Philip to the city of Chiapa some two English miles to ride; wherefore the Prior commanded our mules to be brought; the waits and trumpets gave warning to the town of our departure; and so with many horsemen, with dances, music and ringing of bells we were as stately and joyfully conducted out of the town as we had been inducted into it. At the first half-mile's end the Prior gave thanks unto the Indians, and desired them to return, the cloister being near where we expected another kind of entertainment, not using in the city and cloister that pomp and state which in the country might be allowed. The Indians took their leaves of us; and on we went with only two as guides before us. Within half a mile of the city, the Prior and a companion of his stopped, and took out of his pocket an order from the Provincial which he read unto us, to this effect, That whereas we had forsaken our lawful Superior Calvo in the way to the Philippines, and without his licence had come unto the province of Chiapa, he could not in conscience but inflict some punishment upon us before he did enable us to abide there as members under him; therefore he did strictly command the Prior of Chiapa that as soon as we should enter into his cloister, he should shut us up two by two in our chambers, as in prisons, for three days, not suffering us to go out to any place, save only to the public place of refection (called refectory) where all the friars met together to dine and sup, where at noon time we were to present ourselves before all the cloisters sitting upon the bare ground, and there to receive no other dinner but only bread and water; but at supper we might have in our chambers, or prisons, what the Prior would be pleased to allow us. This was the penance enjoined upon us by the wise and cunning Provincial.

This news at the first was but sour sauce, or a dry postpast after a double sumptuous breakfast; it was a doleful ditty to us after our music and dances, to hear of a treble fast after our feast; to hear of imprisonment after so great liberty. We now began to remember the Provincial's winnings at tables the night before, and the mystery thereof, and began to think how comfortable his boxes of chocolate would be unto us after a meal of bread and water. Now we called to mind the short dinner the Prior had told us at St Philip's we were like to have that day, and of the liberty he bad us then make much of. But the good Prior seeing us sad upon a sudden, and our countenances changed, smiled upon us, wishing us not to think the worse of him, nor of the Provincial, who did that out of policy, and to stop the Creoles' mouths, whom he knew would murmur if no punishment were inflicted upon us. He assured us, after our imprisonment, of honours and preferments, and that as long as we were with him, we should want no encouragement; and that after a bread and water dinner he could send us to our chambers a supper that should strongly support our empty stomachs, and fur and line them well for the next four and twenty hours. With these encouragements on we went to the cloister of Chiapa, where we were welcomed by most of the friars, but in some few we noted a frowning and disaffected countenance.

We were no sooner conducted to our chambers, when the bell sounded to dinner for the rest, and cried aloud to us penance with bread and water. Down we went to the common dining place, and thanks being given, the friars sitting round the tables, we four Philippinian Jonahs (so some Creoles were pleased to term us) betook ourselves to the middle of the refectory, where without cushions, stools, seats, or forms, we sat upon the bare ground cross-legged like tailors, acting humility now for our disobedience unto slovenly Calvo. While the first dish was presented round the tables, to each of us was presented a loaf of reasonable bigness, and a pot of pure crystal water, whereof we fed and drank most heartily though with full stomachs from a double breakfast before. Yet even here in this public act of shame and disgrace (which we knew was usual among friars for less faults than ours) we had this comfort, that we had a Prior and Provincial for friends, and that that punishment came from a friendly hand, whose chocolate we had to comfort our fasting bodies; and secondly, we knew that we should have that night in our prison chambers a better supper than any of those before us, who fed upon their three or four dishes.

Thus with my Creole neighbours' company my bread and water went down cheerfully; and dinner being ended, we were again conducted to our chambers, where we drank a cup of old Alvarez his chocolate. The Castilian friars flocked unto our prisons, some to talk with us, some bringing us conserves and sweetmeats, others other dainties, which they had prepared to help our digestion of bread and cold water. Our supper was provided for us according to the promise and generous spirit of the Prior, who also honoured

THE ENGLISH-AMERICAN

our prison that night with his own and two other friars' company supping with us all in one chamber together. And thus we passed our three days of imprisonment merrily and contentedly, wishing we might never suffer harder usage in any prison than we had done in this, which was not to us such a punishment as did bring with it the privation of any liberty of enjoying the company of friends, of feasting with them, but only the privation of the liberty of our legs to walk about those three days; and this rather an ease than a punishment, for that we wanted rather rest than much stirring after so long and tedious a journey as we had compassed from Mexico thither.

We were no sooner set at liberty but we presently found the Provincial and Prior ready to dispose of us so that in lieu of our imprisonment we might receive honour and credit. Two were sent into the country to learn some Indian language, that so they might be beneficed and preach unto the Indians. Myself and another desired to go farther to Guatemala, that there we might practise philosophy and divinity in the famous university of that city. Nothing that we desired was denied unto us, only the time was thought not fit until Michaelmas, because then the schools were renewed, and new orders settled. In the meantime the Provincial, knowing that the Latin tongue is better grounded in England than among the Spaniards (who abuse poor Priscian and daily break his pate with foolish solecisms) and considering the want he had of a master of the Latin tongue to supply a lecture of grammar and syntax to the youths of Chiapa in a school in that cloister, which brought a sufficient yearly stipend unto the convent, desired me to accept of that place until such time as he should take care to send me to Guatemala, promising me all encouragements in the meantime fitting, and that I should when I would go about to see the country (which I much desired) and also that out of the school annuity I should have my allowance for books, and other necessaries. I could not but accept of this good offer; and so with this employment I remained in that city from April to the end of September, where I was much esteemed of by the Bishop and Governor, but especially by the Prior, who would never ride about the country for his recreation, but he would take me with him, whereby I had occasion to note concerning the province, riches, commodities, and government of Chiapa, what in the ensuing chapter I shall faithfully commend unto the press.

CHAPTER XI

Describing the country of Chiapa, with the chiefest towns and commodities belonging unto it

Though Chiapa in the opinion of the Spaniards be held to be one of the poorest countries of America, because in it as yet there have been no mines discovered, nor golden sands found in the rivers, nor any haven upon the South Sea, whereby commodities are brought in and carried out, as to Mexico, Oaxaca, and Guatemala, yet I may say it exceedeth most provinces in the greatness and beauty of fair towns, and yieldeth to none except it be to Guatemala; nay it surpasseth all the rest of America in that one and famous and most populous town of Chiapa of the Indians. And it ought not to be so much slighted by the Spaniards as it is, if they would look upon it as standing between Mexico and Guatemala, whose strength might be all America's strength, and whose weakness may prove dangerous to all that flourishing empire, for the easy entrance into it by the river of Tabasco, or for its near joining and bordering unto Yucatan. Besides, the commodities in it are such as do uphold a constant trading and commerce amongst the inhabitants themselves, and with other neighbouring countries, and from no one part of America doth Spain get more cochineal than from one of the provinces of Chiapa; the towns also being great and populous, by their yearly pole tribute do add much to the King of Spain's revenues.

This country is divided into three provinces, to wit, Chiapa, Zeldales, and Zoques; whereof Chiapa itself is the poorest. This contains the great town of Chiapa of the Indians, and all the towns and farms northward towards Maquilapa, and westward the priory of Comitan, which hath some ten towns, and many farms of cattle, horses, and mules subject unto it; and neighbouring unto it lieth the great valley of Copanabastla, which is another priory reaching towards Soconusco. This valley glorieth in the great river, which hath its spring from the mountains called Cuchumatlanes, and runneth to Chiapa of the Indians, and from thence to Tabasco. It is also famous for the abundance of fish, which the river yieldeth, and the great store of cattle, which from thence minister food and provision both to the city of Chiapa, and to all the adjacent towns. Though Chiapa the city, and Comitan as standing upon the hills, be exceeding cold, yet this valley lying low is extraordinary hot, and from May to Michaelmas is subject to great storms and tempests of thunder and lightning. The head town, where the priory stands, is called Copanabastla, consisting of above eight hundred Indian inhabitants. But greater than this is Izquintenango at the end of the valley and at the foot of the mountains of Cuchumatlanes southward. And yet bigger than this is the town of St Bartholomew northward at the other end of the valley, which in length is about forty miles, and ten or twelve only in breadth. All the rest of the towns lie towards Soconusco, and are yet hotter and more subject to thunder and lightning, as drawing nearer unto the South Sea coast. Besides the abun-

SURVEY OF WEST INDIES

dance of cattle, the chief commodity of this valley consisteth in cotton-wool, whereof are made such store of mantles for the Indians' wearing that the merchants far and near come for them. They exchange them to Soconusco and Suchitepequez for *cacao*, whereby they are well stored of that drink. So that the inhabitants want neither fish (which they have from the river) nor flesh (for that the valley abounds with cattle) nor clothing (for of that they spare to others) nor bread, though not of wheat, for there grows none; but Indian maize they have plenty of; and besides they are exceedingly stored with fowls and turkeys, fruits, honey, tobacco, and sugar-canes. Neither is money here nor in Chiapa so plentiful as in Mexico and Oaxaca; and whereas there they reckon by patacones, or pieces of eight, here they reckon by tostones which are but half patacones. Though the river be many ways profitable to that valley, yet it is cause of many disasters to the inhabitants, who lose many times their children, and their calves and colts drawing near to the water-side, where they are devoured by caymans, which are many and greedy of flesh, by reason of the many prizes they have got.

The city of Chiapa Real is one of the meanest cities in all America, consisting of not above four hundred householders Spaniards, and about an hundred houses of Indians joining to the city, and called *el barrio de los Indios*, who have a chapel by themselves. In this city there is no parish church, but only the cathedral, which is mother to all the inhabitants. Besides, there are two cloisters, one of Dominicans, and the other of Franciscans, and a poor cloister of nuns, which are burdensome enough to that city. But the Jesuits having got no footing there (who commonly live in the richest and wealthiest places and cities) is a sufficient argument of either the poverty of that city, or of want of gallant parts, and prodigality in the gentry, from whose free and generous spirits they like horse-leeches are still sucking extraordinary and great alms for the colleges where they live; but here the merchants are close-handed, and the gentlemen hard and sparing, wanting of wit and courtiers' parts and bravery, and so poor Chiapa is held no fit place for Jesuits. The merchants' chief trading there is in *cacao*, cotton-wool from the adjacent parts of the country, in pedlar's small wares, and in some sugar from about Chiapa of the Indians, in a little cochineal, for commonly the Governor (whose chief gain consisteth in this) will not suffer them to be too free in this commodity, lest they hinder his greedy traffic. These have their shops all together in a little market-place before the cathedral church, built with walks and porches, under which the poor Indian wives meet at five o'clock at evening to sell what slap and drugs they can prepare most cheap for the empty Creole stomachs. The richer sort of these merchants go and send yet further to Tabasco for wares from Spain, such as wines, linen cloth, figs, raisins, olives, and iron, though in these commodities they dare not venture too much, by reason the Spaniards in that country are not very many, and those that are there are such as are loath to open their purses to more than what may suffice nature. So that what are Spanish commodities are chiefly brought for the friars who are the best and jovialles blades of that country.

The gentlemen of Chiapa are a by-word all about that country, signifying great dons (*dones*, gifts or abilities I should say), great birth, fantastic pride, joined with simplicity, ignorance, misery, and penury. These gentlemen will say they descend from some duke's house in Spain, and immediately from the first Conquerors; yet in carriage they are but clowns, in wit, abilities, parts and discourse as shallow-brained as a low brook, whose waters are scarce able to leap over a pebble stone, any small reason soon tries and

SURVEY OF WEST INDIES

tires their weak brain, which is easily at a stand when sense is propounded, and slides on speedily when nonsense carrieth the stream. The chief families in this city are named Cortez, Solis, Velasco, Toledo, Zerna, and Mendoza. One of these, who was thought the chief in my time, called Don Melchor de Velasco, one day fell into discourse with me concerning England, and our English nation, and in the best, most serious, and judicious part of his don-like conference, asked me whether the sun and moon in England were of the same colour as in Chiapa, and whether Englishmen went barefoot like the Indians, and sacrificed one another as formerly did the heathens of that country; and whether all England could afford such a dainty as a dish of *frijoles* (which is the poorest Indians' daily food there, being black and dry Turkey or French beans boiled with a little biting chilli or Indian pepper with garlic, till the broth become as black as any ink); and whether the women in England went as long with child as did the Spanish women; and lastly, whether the Spanish nation were not a far gallanter nation than the English?

When I perceived my don ran farther and farther into his simple and foolish questions, I cut him off suddenly, telling him: 'Sir, it is long since I came out of England, if you give me leave to recollect my memory, I will answer some of these your hard questions the next time we meet' (thinking hereby to try my don's wit further, whether he could perceive I jeered him). To which my simple don replied: 'I pray Sir do, and whensoever you come, you shall be welcome to a dish of *frijoles*.' With this I took my leave of him, and at our farewell, he again desired me to study well his questions, and to return him a speedy answer, whereby I was more confirmed in my conceit of my don, that he was either *tonto* or *bobo*, fool or simple. Yet thought I my best way to answer is to answer a fool according to his folly, and so resolved within two or three days to return unto him some simple answer according to his simple and foolish questions. Therefore speedily I singled out a good occasion of meeting with him at his own house, who welcomed me with much Spanish gravity, and sitting down before Donna Angela, his painted wife and angel, began to answer, or more to jeer his donship. I began with the sun and moon, telling him that they were planets, and had their special influences upon several nations, as all planets have upon man's body. And so they did shew themselves according to the inclination of the people of several kingdoms. And therefore as the Spaniards were much inclined to Venus and to beauty, and not contenting themselves with the natural beauty of their fair ladies, would yet have art add to nature by the skill and use of the best painting colours, so these glorious planets of the sun and moon among the Spaniards, and especially in Chiapa, shewed themselves most comely, bright, glorious and beautiful, working the like inclination to beauty upon, and in all Spaniards. My instance was in the land of the blackamoors, where I told them that their bodies were black, and that among them the sun appeared with a dark and sad visage. Here my don cried out: 'An excellent example.' I gave him yet a second instance from the eclipse of the sun; which being eclipsed, made all the earth, men's faces and bodies seem of a dark, or yellow colour, to shew the proportion or sympathy of sublunary bodies to that high and overmastering planet. To this that good don replied: *Señor no so puede decir mas*, ' Sir, nothing can be answered or said more or better.' *Vengamos ahora a Inglatierra*, ' Let us draw now to England.' To which I answered him, that in England the sun and moon appeared half year of one colour, and half of another; for the women one half year it appeared as in Spain and Chiapa, beautiful and glorious, for that naturally without painting they yielded to none

SURVEY OF WEST INDIES

in beauty. But the other half year it appeared as red as blood, or scarlet; and the reason might easily be guessed at, for that no nation is more warlike and high-spirited than the English, whose very clothes were fiery, wearing more scarlet than any nation in the world; as he might perceive by their coming so much with their ships to the Indian coasts to fight with the Spaniards; and that as they delighted to go in red, and to be like the sun, so naturally they were brought to those seas to single out such ships as from America carried the rich commodity of cochineal, whereof they make more use than Spain itself to dye their clothes and coats withal. Here my don jogged his head, and replied: 'Sir, I thought no nation had been so like the sun as the Spaniards; for I have read that when our ancestors came to conquer these parts, the Indians called them, *hijos del Sol*, that is, sons of the Sun, being comely and gallant, and more like the sun than any other people.' To this I answered him: 'Sir, no doubt but you are like the sun here, and none more glittering and bright, your very hatbands shining with pearls and diamonds like the brightness of the sun; but as I said before the blackamoors are like their sun, so I say, the English is like their sun, which is red, and so do and will affect to wear scarlet, as long as any cochineal is to be found in the Indies.'

Now Don Melchor began to understand me, and told me never man had satisfied him with better reasons than myself. He thanked me heartily, and told me he thought no gentleman in Chiapa could tell so well as himself now why the English ships came so much upon their coasts; and that my discourse had satisfied him to the full. He desired me to go on to his other questions. To his second, demanding whether the English went barefoot like the Indians, I told him I thought that the Count of Gondomar (who had been many years Ambassador from Spain in England) had satisfied all the Spaniards that doubt, who coming from England to Madrid, and being there asked by some courtiers whether London was as big as Madrid, and as well peopled, he made answer that he thought there was scarce a hundred left in London. He proved it from the use and custom of his own countrymen of Spain; who when they are to make a journey, shew themselves two or three days before in colours, walking with boots and spurs, that their friends may take notice that they are departing out of the town or city. So said the Count of Gondomar: 'I think by this there are very few people in London; for when I came from thence I left them all almost in clothes of colours, booted and spurred as ready to depart and take some journey.' 'And truly my don,' quoth I, 'your own Count hath answered for me; yet I say, the English are so far from going barefoot that they go booted, and are all in a readiness to move out of England for any noble and generous design; but above all they are still ready for America, where they know is store and abundance of hides to make them boots to cover the bareness of their legs, that they may not be suspected to be like barefooted Indians.' Here Don Melchor replied: 'I pray Sir, when they come by sea to these parts do they come also booted and spurred? For I should think, when they fight, their spurs should hinder them.' To this his doubt I answered first, as concerning spurs in the ships, with the example of one of his own nation, and of the best divines in Spain, living in my time in Valladolid, called Maestro Nunno (Reader of Divinity in the College of St Gregory, but in his carriage and experience in the world a simple noddy) who being invited by a nobleman to go with him in his coach out of the city a mile or two to a garden of recreation, went hastily about the college to borrow boots and spurs; and when he had put them on, being asked whither he went, and why he put on boots and spurs, answered that he was to go in a coach out of the city, and that he thought the coach and mules would want spurs to go and come the sooner. 'Even so my don,' quoth I, 'the Englishmen come booted and spurred in their ships, to make their ships sail on the swifter. And this is the reason why the English ships sail faster, and when they are in sight turn about quicker than a Spanish galleon, because they are spurred and kicked within.' 'O Sir, I humbly thank you,' said Don Melchor, 'for that by your discourse now I know the truth of what indeed I have often heard say, that the English ships are nimbler and quicker at sea than our heavy galleons.' 'Now as for fighting, the Englishmen's spurs,' said I, 'are no hindrance to them, but rather a great advantage. For they fight with weapons, with their hands, and with their feet, wherein they exceed the Spaniards; for when they have shot with their pieces, or cut down with their swords any enemy, or knocked him with their halberds, then with their feet and spurs they fall upon him and so soon rid him out of the way, that he may no more rise up against them.' 'All you have told me,' said the wise Velasco, 'stands with so much reason, that my judgment is convinced by you.' As for eating and sacrificing one another like the Indians,' I told him, 'that the English filled their bellies so well with fat beef and mutton, fowls, rabbits, partridges, and pheasants, that they had no stomach at all to man's flesh. And that truly for *frijoles* dressed with garlic, that only dainty dish was wanting in England; and that for garlic, three reasons moved the English not to be lavishing of that little they had, first, for fear they should want it for their horses' drenches, secondly, for that they felt not themselves so much troubled with the wind, nor puffed up with windy and vain conceits as other nations did, but thirdly and chiefly they refrained from it among themselves that they might not smell of it, and that by the scent and smell of it afar off at sea they might, when they came to the coast of America, smell out a Spanish ship, and know it from a Hollander. Here my Don Melchor fell into admiration, assuring me he had never heard more solid reasons from any man. Alas poor Creole of Chiapa, thought I, if I had spoken sense, thy shallow brain had not been able to have leaped over it, but after nonsense thou art easily carried away. As for his last question, I told him that was above my reach, for that poor friars ought not to meddle with women, neither had my mother ever told me how long she went with me. But however if Donna Angela would tell me how long she went with her children, I would by the constellations of the Heavens search out against our next meeting how long the English women went with their children. To this my Don Melchor answered that he would not trouble me to study what he thought was not belonging to my profession; but he knew that if I would study that or any other hard and difficult point, I could give him more and better satisfaction than any scholar in that city.

And thus, Reader, by this Don Melchor's wit and ability would I have thee judge of the gentlemen Creoles or natives of Chiapa; and yet as presumptuous they are and arrogant as if the noblest blood in the Court of Madrid ran through their veins. It is a common thing amongst them to make a dinner only with a dish of *frijoles* in black broth, boiled with pepper and garlic, saying it is the most nourishing meat in all the Indies; and after this so stately a dinner they will be sure to come out to the street-door of their houses to see and to be seen, and there for half an hour will they stand shaking off the crumbs of bread from their clothes, bands (but especially from their ruffs when they used them), and from their mustachios. And with their tooth-pickers they will stand picking their teeth, as if some small partridge bone stuck in them; nay if a friend pass by at that time, they will be sure

SURVEY OF WEST INDIES

to find out some crumb or other in the mustachio (as if on purpose the crumbs of the table had been shaken upon their beards, that the loss of them might be a gaining of credit for great house-keeping) and they will be sure to vent out some non-truth, as to say: *A Señor que linda perdiz he comido hoy*, 'O Sir, what a dainty partridge have I eat to-day,' whereas they pick out nothing from their teeth but a black husk of a dry *frijole* or Turkey bean.

Though great in blood and in birth they say they are, yet in their employments they are but rich graziers, for most of their wealth consisteth in farms of cattle and mules. Some indeed have towns of Indians subject unto them, whereof they are called *encomenderos*, and receive yearly from every Indian a certain pole tribute of fowls and money. They have most cowardly spirits for war, and though they will say they would fain see Spain, yet they dare not venture their lives at sea; they judge sleeping in a whole skin the best maxim for their Creole spirits. One hundred fighting soldiers would easily lay low those Chiapa dons, and gain the whole city, which lieth so open to the fields that the mules and asses come in and graze, the streets being very commodious to entertain asses from within, and from without. Yet in this city liveth commonly a Governor, or *Alcalde Mayor*, and a Bishop. The Governor's place is of no small esteem and interest, for that his power reacheth far, and he tradeth much in *cacao* and cochineal, and domineers over both Spaniards and Indians at his will and pleasure. But ill-gotten goods never thrive, as was seen in Don Gabriel de Orellana (Governor of this city and country in my time) who having sent the worth of eight thousand crowns in cochineal, *cacao*, sugar, and hides by the river of Tabasco towards Havana lost it all into the hands of the Hollanders, who doubtless knew how to make better use of it than would have done that tyrannizing Governor. The Bishop's place of that city is worth at least eight thousand ducats a year, which truly he had need of that comes so far from Spain to live in such a city where are such able dons as Don Melchor de Velasco, and where asses are so freely fed and bred. Most of this Bishop's revenues consisteth in great offerings which he yearly receiveth from the great Indian towns, going out to them once a year to confirm their children, whose confirmation is such a means to confirm and strengthen the Bishop's revenues, that none must be confirmed by him who offer not a fair white wax-candle, with a ribbon and at least four reals. I have seen the richer sort offer him a candle of at least six pound weight with two yards of twelvepenny broad ribbon, and the candle stuck from the top to the bottom with single reals round about. Nay the poor Indians make it the chief masterpiece of their vanity to offer proudly in such occasions.

Don Bernardino de Salazar was the Bishop of this city in my time, who desired my company to ride with him his circuit but one month about the towns near to Chiapa, and in this time I was appointed by him to hold the basin wherein the Spaniards and Indians (whilst he confirmed their children) did cast their offerings, which myself and another chaplain did always tell and cast up by good account before we carried the money up into his chamber, and I found that at our return at the month's end he had received one thousand and six hundred ducats of only offerings, besides the fees due to him for visiting the several companies, or sodalities and confraternities, belonging to the saints or souls in their purgatory (which are extraordinary rich there) whereof he and all other bishops in their district take account yearly. This Bishop was (as all the rest are there) somewhat covetous; but otherwise a man of a temperate life and conversation, very zealous to reform whatsoever abuses committed in the church, which cost him his life before I departed from Chiapa to Guatemala. The women of that city it seems pretend much weakness and squeamishness of stomach, which they say is so great that they are not able to continue in the church while a Mass is briefly huddled over, much less while a solemn high Mass (as they call it) is sung and a sermon preached, unless they drink a cup of hot chocolate, and eat a bit of sweetmeats to strengthen their stomachs. For this purpose it was much used by them to make their maids bring to them to church in the middle of Mass or sermon a cup of chocolate, which could not be done to all, or most of them, without a great confusion and interrupting both Mass and sermon. The Bishop perceiving this abuse and having given fair warning for the omitting of it, but all without amendment, thought fit to fix in writing upon the church's doors an excommunication against all such as should presume at the time of service to eat or drink within the church. This excommunication was taken by all, but especially by the gentlewomen, much to heart, who protested if they might not eat or drink in the church they could not continue in it to hear what otherwise they were bound unto.

The chief of them knowing what great friendship there was between the Bishop and the Prior and myself, came to the Prior and me desiring us to use all means we could with the Bishop for the revoking that his excommunication so heavily laid upon them, and threatening their souls with damning judgment for the violation of it. The good Prior and myself laboured all we could, alleging the custom of the country, the weakness of the sex whom it most concerned, and also the weakness of their stomachs, the contempt that might from them ensue unto his person, and many inconveniences which might follow to the breeding of an uproar in the church and in the city, whereof we had some probable conjecture from what already we had heard from some. But none of these reasons would move the Bishop; to which he answered that he preferred the honour of God, and of his house before his own life. The women seeing him so hard to be entreated, began to stomach him the more and to slight him with scornful and reproachful words; others slighted his excommunication, drinking in iniquity in the church, as the fish doth water, which caused one day such an uproar in the Cathedral that many swords were drawn against the priests and prebends, who attempted to take away from the maids the cups of chocolate which they brought unto their mistresses; who at last seeing that neither fair nor foul means would prevail with the Bishop, resolved to forsake the Cathedral, where the Bishop's own and his prebends' eyes must needs be watching over them; and so from that time most of the city betook themselves to the cloister churches, where by the nuns and friars they were not troubled nor resisted, though fairly counselled to obey the command of the Bishop, whose name now they could not brook, and to whose prebends they denied now all such relief and stipend for Masses which formerly they had used to bestow upon them, conferring them all upon the friars who grew rich by the poor impoverished Cathedral. This lasted not long, but the Bishop began to stomach the friars, and to set up another excommunication, binding all the city to resort unto their own cathedral church; which the women would not obey, but kept their houses for a whole month; in which time the Bishop fell dangerously sick, and desired to retire himself to the cloister of the Dominicans, for the great confidence he had in the Prior that he would take care of him in his sickness. Physicians were sent for far and near, who all with a joint opinion agreed that the Bishop was poisoned; and he himself doubted not of it at his death, praying unto God to forgive those that had been the cause of it, and to accept of that sacrifice of his life, which he was willing to offer for the zeal of God's house and honour. He lay not above a week in the cloister, and as soon as he was dead, all his body, his head and face, did so swell that the least touch upon any part of him caused the skin to break and cast out white matter, which had corrupted and overflown all his body. A gentlewoman with whom I was well acquainted in that city, who was noted to be somewhat too familiar with one of the Bishop's pages, was commonly censured to have prescribed such a cup of chocolate to be ministered by the page which poisoned him who so rigorously had forbidden chocolate to be drunk in the church. Myself heard this gentlewoman say of the deceased Bishop, that she thought few grieved for his death, and that the women had no reason to grieve for him, and that she judged, he being such an enemy to chocolate in the church, that which he had drunk at home in his house had not agreed with his body. And it became afterwards a proverb in that country, Beware of the chocolate of Chiapa; which made me so cautious that I would not drink afterwards of it in any house where I had not very great satisfaction of the whole family.

The women of this city are somewhat light in their carriage, and have learned from the Devil many enticing lessons and baits to draw poor souls to sin and damnation; and if they cannot have their wills, they will surely work revenge either by chocolate or conserves, or some fair present, which shall surely carry death along with it. The gentlewoman that was suspected (nay was questioned for the death of the Bishop) had often used to send me boxes of chocolate or conserves, which I willingly received from her, judging it to be a kind of gratuity for the pains I took in teaching her son Latin. She was of a very merry and pleasant disposition, which I thought might consist without sin, until one day she sent unto me a very fair plantain wrapped up in a handkerchief, buried in sweet jasmins and roses; when I untied the handkerchief, I thought among the flowers I should find some rich token, or some pieces of eight, but finding nothing but a plantain, I wondered, and looking further upon it, I found worked upon it with a knife the fashion of a heart with two of blind Cupid's arrows sticking in it, discovering unto my heart the poisoned heart and thoughts of the poisoner that sent it. I thought it a good warning to be wary and cautious of receiving more presents or chocolate from such hands, and so returned unto her again her plantain with this short rhyme cut out with a knife upon the skin *Fruta tan fria, amor no cria*, as much as to say, fruit so cold, takes no hold. This answer and resolution of mine was soon spread over that little city, which made my gentlewoman outrageous, which presently she shewed by taking away her son from school, and in many meetings threatening to play me a Chiapaneca trick. But I remembered the Bishop's chocolate and so was wary, and stayed not long after in that poisoning and wicked city, which truly deserves no better relation than what I have given of the simple dons, and the chocolate-confectioning donnas.

There is yet twelve leagues from this city of Chiapa, another Chiapa which deserveth better commendations. This consisteth most of Indians, and is held to be one of the biggest Indian towns in all America, containing at least four thousand families. This town hath many privileges from the King of Spain, and is governed chiefly by Indians (yet with subordination unto the Spanish government of the city of Chiapa) who do choose an Indian Governor with other inferior officers to rule with him. This Governor may wear a rapier and dagger, and enjoyeth many other liberties which to the rest of the Indians are denied. No town hath so many dons in it of Indian blood as this. Don Philip de Guzman was Governor of it in my time, a very rich Indian, who kept up commonly in his stable a dozen of as good horses for public shews and ostentation as the best Spaniard in the country. His courage was not inferior to any Spaniard, and for defence of some privileges of his town sued in the Chancery of Guatemala the proud and high-minded Governor of the city of Chiapa, spending therein great sums of money till he had overcome him, whereupon he caused a feast to be made in the town, both by water and land, so stately, that truly in the Court of Madrid it might have been acted.

This town lieth upon a great river, whereunto belong many boats and canoes, wherein those Indians have been taught to act sea-fights with great dexterity, and to represent the nymphs of Parnassus, Neptune, Æolus, and the rest of the heathenish gods and goddesses, so that they are a wonder of their whole nation. They will arm with their boats a siege against the town, fighting against it with such courage till they make it yield, as if they had been trained up all their life to sea-fights. So likewise within the town they are as dexterous at baiting of bulls, at *juego de cañas*, at horse-races, at arming a camp, at all manner of Spanish dances, instruments, and music as the best Spaniards. They will erect towers and castles made of wood and painted cloth, and from them fight either with the boats or one against another, with squibs, darts, and many strange fire-works, so manfully that if in earnest they could perform it as well as they do it in sport and pastime the Spaniards and friars might soon repent to have taught them what they have. As for acting of plays, this is a common part of their solemn pastimes; and they are so generous that they nothing think too much to spend in banquets and sweetmeats upon their friars, and neighbouring towns, whensoever they are minded to shew themselves in a public feast.

The town is very rich, and many Indians in it that trade about the country as the Spaniards do. They have learned most trades befitting a commonwealth,

THE ENGLISH-AMERICAN

and practise and teach them within their town. They want not any provision of fish or flesh, having for the one that great river joining unto their town, and for the other many *estancias* (as they call them) or farms abounding with cattle. In this town the Dominican friars bear all the sway, who have a rich and stately cloister with another church or chapel subordinate unto it. The heat here is so great that both friars and Indians commonly wear a linen towel about their necks to wipe off the constant sweat from their faces, which maketh the friars sit longer at their dinner than else they would do, for that at every bit they eat, and draught they drink, they are fain to make a stop to wipe their dropping brows. Yet the evenings are fresh and cool, which are much made of there, and spent in the many walks and gardens which join close unto the river side. Two or three leagues from the town, there are two *ingenios* or farms of sugar, the one belonging to the cloister of the Dominicans of the city of Chiapa; the other unto the cloister of this town, which contain near two hundred blackamoors, besides many Indians, who are employed in that constant work of making sugar for all the country. Hereabouts are bred great store of mules, and excellent horses for any service. The town of Chiapa of the Indians, and all the towns about it, want nothing but a more temperate climate and cooler air, and wheat, which there cannot be sown, yet for Spaniards and such as cannot live without it, it is brought from Chiapa of the Spaniards and from about Comitan; yet this is not generally acknowledged a want by reason of the great plenty of maize which all the towns enjoy, and which is now more used both by Spaniards and dainty-toothed friars than bread of wheat. Yet your poor Spaniards, and some Indians who have got the trick of trading from them, do gain not a little in bringing to these towns biscuits of wheaten bread, which though it be dry and hard, yet because they are novelties to the

SURVEY OF WEST INDIES

Indians, they get by changing them for other commodities especially of cotton-wool, which here is more abounding than in the valley of Copanabaſtla.

Upon this country of Chiapa of the Indians bordereth the province of Zoques, which is absolutely the richeſt part of Chiapa. This reacheth on the one side to Tabasco, and by the river named Grijalva sendeth commonly the commodities which are in it with safety into S John de Ulhua, or Vera Cruz. It trafficketh also with the country of Yucatan by the haven called Puerto Real, which lieth between Grijalva and Yucatan. Yet these two, the River of Tabasco, alias Grijalva, and Puerto Real, though they be commodious to this province of Zoques, yet they are causes of daily fears unto the Spaniards, who well know the weakness of them, and that if a foreign nation should manfully thruſt into that country by any of these two ways, they might so conquer all Chiapa, and from thence pass easily unto Guatemala. But the river of Tabasco lying low, and being somewhat hot, and the towns about it infeſted with many gnats, and the chiefeſt commodity there being but *cacao*, have often discouraged both our English and Hollanders, who have come up some part of the river, and minding more the aforesaid reasons, than what was forward to be had, have turned back, losing a rich country and slighting an eternal name for few and frivolous present difficulties. In this province of Zoques, the towns are not very big, yet they be very rich; the chief commodities are silk and cochineal; whereof the latter is held the beſt of America, and the ſtore of it so great that no one province alone exceeds it. Few Indians there are who have not their orchards planted with the trees whereon the worms breed which yield unto us that rich commodity; not that the Indians themselves eſteem otherwise of it than as they see the Spaniards greedy after it, offering them money for it, and forcing them to the preservation of it in those parts which have proved most successful for this kind. There is great store of silk in this country, in so much that the Indians make it their great commodity to employ their wives in working towels with all colours of silk, which the Spaniards buy, and send into Spain. It is rare to see what works those Indian women will make in silk, such as might serve for patterns and samplers to many school-mistresses in England.

The people of this country are witty, and ingenious, and fair of complexion; the country towards Tabasco is hot, but within in some places very cold. There is also plenty of maize but no wheat; neither is there such plenty of cattle as about Chiapa, but fowls and turkeys as many as in other parts. The province called Zeldales lieth behind this of the Zoques, from the North Sea within the continent, running up towards Chiapa, and reacheth in some parts near to the borders of Comitan north-westward. South-eastward it joins to such Indians which as yet have not been conquered by the Spaniards, who make many invasions upon the Christian Indians, and burn their towns, and carry away their cattle. The chief and head town in this province is called Ococingo, which is a frontier against those heathens. This province is esteemed rich for the Spaniards, who make much of *cacao*, which serveth to make their drink of chocolate, and here is great store of it. There is also another commodity, great among the Spaniards, called *achiote*, wherewith they make their chocolate look of the colour of a brick. Here is also plenty of hogs and bacon, fowls, turkeys, quails, cattle, sheep, maize, honey, and not far from Ococingo, in my time, was setting up an *ingenio*, or farm of sugar, which was thought would prove as well as those about Chiapa of the Indians. The country in most parts is high and hilly; but Ococingo stands in a pleasant valley, enjoying many brooks and streams of fresh water, and therefore hath been thought a fit place for sugar.

SURVEY OF WEST INDIES

Here also in this valley the friars have attempted to sow wheat, which hath proved very good. Thus, Reader, I have shewed you the country of Chiapa, which is compassed about on the one side by Soconusco, and from thence almost to Guatemala, by the province of Suchitepequez, on the other side by Tabasco, and on the other side by Zeldales.

CHAPTER XII

Shewing my journey from the city of Chiapa unto Guatemala, and the chief places in the way

THE time now being come that I was to leave the little city of Chiapa, I took some occasion beforehand to take my leave of my best friends, whose children I had taught, and at my departure I must confess I found them kind and bountiful, except it were Donna Magdalena de Morales, from whom I did not expect, neither did I desire any farewell, or adieu token. But among all, the Governor's wife was most liberal unto me, sending me many boxes of aromatical chocolate, and one extraordinary great box with four several divisions of different conserves gilt over, besides many maple breads, and biscuits made with eggs and sugar, a present it was which might have been sent to a greater man than to a poor worthless mendicant friar, and with this in a handkerchief a dozen pieces of eight. Don Melchor de Velasco yet exceeded her, in words and compliments I mean, but in deeds, he and all the crew of the Creoles must think to come short of them who are born in Spain. The first town I went unto was Theopixca, six leagues from Chiapa, a fair and great town of Indians, who are held to be next unto the Indians of the other Chiapa in sitting and riding a horse. In this town is nothing so considerable as the church, which is great and strong, and the music belonging unto it sweet and harmonious. The vicar or curate of this place was one Friar Peter Martir, a Creole, whom I knew could not endure the Prior nor me, yet he would dissemble a love complimental exceeding well, and in outward shews raise it up to *gradus ut octo*. He knowing my prevalency with the Prior, durst not but give me very good entertainment, which continued two days, until I was weary of his compliments.

The third day I took my leave of him, who would not yet leave me, but would conduct me to Comitan, whither I was invited by the Prior of that cloister, named Friar Thomas Rocolano, a Frenchman, who being a stranger to the Spaniards (for besides him and myself there was no other stranger in that country) desired acquaintance with me, which he began to settle by meeting me at the half way with many Indians on horseback, having provided an arbour where we might more conveniently confer and rest while our chocolate and other refreshments were provided. But the Creole Peter Martir was not a little envious (as I was afterwards informed in the cloister) to see me so much made of and esteemed in the country, yet his fair words and compliments far exceeded the sincerity and down-rightness of my French friend. At Comitan I stayed a whole week, riding about with the Prior unto the Indian towns, and down the hill to the valley of Copanabastla, where I enjoyed much pastime and recreation among the friars and Indians and was feasted after the manner of that country, which knoweth more of an Epicurean diet than doth England, or any part of Europe; nay I am persuaded (and I have heard Spaniards confess it) that Spain hath taken from the Indies since the Conquest many lessons for the dressing of several dishes and completing a feast or banquet. After the week was ended my French friend the Prior conducted me to Izquintenango, to see me well furnished up the mountains of Cuchumatlanes.

This town (as I have formerly observed) standeth

almost at the end of the valley of Copanabastla, and
within two leagues of the Cuchumatlanes. It is one
of the finest Indian towns of all the province of Chiapa,
and very rich, by reason of the much cotton-wool in it,
and especially by reason of its situation, for standing
in the roadway to Guatemala, all the merchants of the
country that trade with their mules that way pass
through this town, and there buy and sell, enriching it
with money and far brought commodities. It is most
plentifully stored with fruits, especially with what
they call *piñas* or pine fruit. It standeth close by the
great river which runneth to Chiapa of the Indians,
and hath its spring not far off from the Cuchumatlanes,
and yet at this town is very broad and deep. No man
nor beast travelling to Guatemala can go into it, or
from Guatemala can go out of it, but by ferrying over.
And the road being much used and beaten by travellers,
and by such as they call *requas* of mules (every *requa*
consisting of fifty or threescore mules) this ferry is
day and night employed and yields much treasure
to the town at the year's end. The Indians of the
town besides the ferry boat, have made many other
little boats, or canoes to go up and down the river.
Hither when the Prior of Comitan had brought me,
we were waited for by the vicar or friar of that town
with the chief and principal Indians, and most of the
canoes. As we ferried over, the little canoes went
before us with the choristers of the church singing
before us, and with others sounding their waits and
trumpets. The friar that lived in this town was called
Friar Geronymo de Guevara, little in stature, but
great in state, pride and vanity, as he shewed himself
in what he had provided for us both of fish and flesh.
A brave professor or vower of mendicancy and poverty
he was, who in twelve years that he had lived in that
town, what by mumming of Masses for the dead and
living, what by shearing and fleecing the poor Indians,
what by trading and trafficking with the merchants

that used that road, had got six thousand ducats, which he had sent to Spain to the Court of Madrid, to trade with them simoniacally for the bishopric of Chiapa, which if he obtained not (yet when I came out of that country the report went that he had obtained it), he would and was well able with a second supply to obtain a better. After two days' feasting with him, he and the Prior of Comitan both joined their power and authority to see me well manned with Indians to the first town of the Cuchumatlanes. A mule was prepared to carry my bedding (which we commonly carried with us in chests of leather called *petacas*), another Indian to carry my *petaquilla* wherein was my chocolate and all implements to make it; and three more Indians to ride before and behind to guide me; but to all these nothing was to be paid (lest a custom of paying should be brought in, for so they doctrined me as a novice in that country) except it were to give them a cup of chocolate if I drank in the way, or when I came to my journey's end. Here I took my leave of my good French friend (who yet continued friendship with me by frequent letters to Guatemala), and of my low but high-minded Guevara, who bad me expect no friendly entertainment until I were well passed over the Cuchumatlanes and arrived at Sacapula, which was four days' journey from thence. Yet he told me I might demand what service I list from the Indians, and call for what I had a mind to eat without paying any money, so that I did write down my expenses in the common town book.

Thus I went away from my friends somewhat heavy having no other company but unknown Indians, leaving a pleasant and delightsome valley behind me, and seeing nothing before me but high and steepy hills and mountains, and considering that in four or five days I should see no more gallant Dominicans and of mine own profession. Now I wished I had the company of my Melendez and other friends, who were a

SURVEY OF WEST INDIES

comfort one to another upon the hills and rocks of Maquilapa. Yet at last I concluded, up English heart and courage, *quondam hæc meminisse juvabit*. Though the mountains seemed high afar off, yet as I travelled on I found the way lie between them very easy and passable, and met now and then *requas* of mules, which were no little comfort unto me to consider, if they being heavily laden could go through those mountains, my mule that had in me but a light burden would easily overcome any danger; it comforted me also to consider that there were towns (though but little ones) where I might rest every night. The further I went, the better and more open I found the road; only the rain and dirt troubled me, which I could not avoid, it being the end of September, or as there they reckon, the end of winter. The first town I came to amongst those mountains was called St Martin, a little place of some twenty houses; I went to the house that belonged to the Franciscan friars (who seldom in the year came to that poverty of house and house room) where I lighted and caused the Indians to be called who were appointed to give attendance to travellers and passengers. I found them very tractable and dutiful, bidding me welcome, bringing me hot water for my chocolate, which I drunk off heartily, and gave unto my Indians of Izquintenango, who refreshed themselves and their mules well for nothing, this being a custom among those towns in the road to welcome one another whensoever they come with travellers. I might have had for my supper anything that place would afford, but I made choice of a pullet, which I thought would be cheapest for the poor Indians. I was glad I had brought with me a good big *frasco*, as they call it, or bottle of wine, for I began already to find the Cuchumatlanes cooler than the valley of Copanabastla. My bed was made in a little thatched *cobe*, and Indian boys appointed to sleep in the next room to me, and to be at hand if in the night I should want anything. Thus having appointed what attendance I had need of in the morning to the next town, discharging the Indians that had brought me from Izquintenango, I went unto my rest, which I took as quietly as if I had been in the company of my best friends.

The next day being accompanied by two Indians, having sent my carriage by another, I took my journey to the next town, which is called Cuchumatlan Grande, because it standeth on the highest part of those mountains, and in the way the Indians shewed me the head-spring or fountain of the great river of Chiapa of the Indians, which is the only remarkable thing in that road. Cuchumatlan Grande is a town a little bigger than St Martin, and of Indians very courteous, who are used and beaten to daily travellers, and so make very much of them. Here I was entertained as the night before; and found the poor Indians willing to give me whatsoever I demanded for my better and safer guiding and conducting the next day, and that night for my supper what I pleased to call for, without any pay, but only writing down my name and expenses with the day and month in their common book of accounts. This are those poor wretches brought to by the friars and commanding justices, though of themselves they have no more than a *milpa* of maize as they term it, or a little Indian wheat plantation, with as much chilli as will suffice them for the year, and what the merchants and travellers give them voluntarily, which is little enough. From this town I would not follow the road to the next, which was a long journey of seven or eight leagues without baiting by the way; and also because I had been informed at Chiapa and at Copanabastla of a strange picture of Our Lady, which was amongst these mountains in a little town of Indians called Chiantla, which in this day's journey being not above a league out of my way, I was resolved to see. The ways were bad, lying out of the road, yet by noon I got to Chiantla, which is a town belonging unto Mercenarian friars, who doubtless would not be able to subsist in so poor a place had they not invented that loadstone of their picture of Mary, and cried it up for miraculous, to draw people far and near, and all travellers from the road to pray unto it, and to leave their gifts and alms unto them for their prayers and Masses. Such an income of treasure and riches hath been from deluded and ignorant souls to this beggarly town, that the friars have had wherewith to build a cloister able to maintain four or five of them. The church is richly furnished, but especially the high altar where the picture standeth in a tabernacle with half a dozen curtains of silk, satin, cloth of gold, with borders of golden lace before it, wearing a rich crown of gold, thickly beset with diamonds and other precious stones. There hang before it at least a dozen rich lamps of silver; and in the vestry of the church are many gowns, candlesticks of silver, censers to burn frankincense before it, besides rich copes, vestments, ornaments for the altar, and hangings for all the church.

To conclude, here is a treasure hid in the mountains; oh that it could be found out to do the Lord service. I was welcomed to this place by those friars, who were strangers unto me; my head was filled that day by them with relations of strange and many miracles or lies, which they told me of that picture; but the heaviness of my head did me good in something, for it made me more drowsy at night and apter to take good rest. The next day I got into the road again, and went to the last town of these Cuchumatlanes called Chautlan, where I stayed all that day and night, and sent before a letter to the Prior of Sacapula of my going thither the next day. In Chautlan I was very kindly used by the Indians, and liked the town the better for the excellent grapes which there I found, not planted like vineyards, but growing up in arbours, which shew that if that land were planted it would certainly yield as good grapes for wine as any are in Spain. They are carried from that place to Guatemala, which stands from it near forty leagues, and are sold about the streets for rarities and great dainties; and well may they, for from Mexico to Guatemala there are none like them. The next morning I made haste to be gone, that I might come sooner to Sacapula, where I was to find those of mine own profession, with whom I knew I might stay and rest a whole week if I pleased. I had not rid above three leagues, when I began to discover at a low and deep bottom, a pleasant and goodly valley laced with a river whose waters receiving the glorious brightness of Phœbus' beams reverberated up to the top of the mountain, a delightsome prospect to the beholders; the more I hasted to that seeming Paradise, the more did the twinkling and wanton stream invite me down the hill; which I had no sooner descended, but I found in an arbour by the water side the Prior of Sacapula himself with a good train of Indians waiting for me with a cup of chocolate. At the first sight I was a little daunted to behold the Prior, who looked most fearfully with a bladder from his throat swelled almost round his neck, which hung over his shoulders and breast, and stayed up his chin, and lifted up his head so that he could scarce look any whither but up to Heaven. In our discourse he told me that disease had been upon him at least ten years, and that the water of that river had caused it in him, and in many others of that town. This made me now as much out of love with the river as above the hill I had liked the good sight of it, and therefore resolved not to stay so long in that place as I had thought, lest the waters should mark me for all my life, as they had done this prior; whose name was Friar John de la Cruz, a Biscayan born, and (like some of that nation) a little troubled with the simples, but a good-hearted man, humble, and well beloved over all the country both by Spaniards and Indians.

PLATE 5

THE HERMITAGE OF THE INDIANS
(*From the Dutch Edition of* 1700)

SURVEY OF WEST INDIES

When I came to the town I discovered many men and women with bladders in their throats like the poor Prior, which made me almost unwilling to drink there any chocolate made with that water, or eat anything dressed with it, until the Prior did much encourage me and told me that it did not hurt all but only some, and those who did drink it cold; wherewith I resolved to stay there four or five days, because of the old Prior's importunity, who would fain have had me continue to live with him, promising to teach me the Indian language in a very short time. But higher matters calling me to Guatemala, I excused myself, and continued there five days with much recreation. The town though it be not in the general very rich, yet there are some Indian merchants who trade about the country and especially to Suchitepequez, where is the chief store of *cacao*, and thereby some of this town of Sacapula have enriched themselves; the rest of the people trade in pots and pans, which they make of an earth there fit for that purpose. But the principal merchandise of this place is salt, which they gather in the morning from the ground that lieth near the river. The air is hot, by reason the town standeth low, and compassed with high hills on every side. Besides many good fruits which are here, there are dates as good as those that come from Barbary, and many trees of them in the garden belonging to the cloister.

After I had here wearied out the weariness which I brought in my bones from the Cuchumatlanes, I departed taking my way to Guatemala, and from Sacapula I went to a town called St Andres, or St Andrews, which standeth six or seven leagues from Sacapula, a great town, but nothing remarkable in it, save only cotton-wool and turkeys, and about it some rich *estancias* or farms of cattle, which are commodiously seated here, it being a plain champaign country. Yet at further end of this plain there is a mountain which discourageth with the sight all such as travel

THE ENGLISH-AMERICAN

to Guatemala; from St Andres I prepared myself for the next day's journey, which was of nine long leagues, to a very great town called by two names, by some Sacualpa, by others Sta Maria Zojabah, to the which I could not go without passing over that mountain. I sent word of going to Zojabah the day before (as is the custom there) that mules and horses might meet me upon the mountain; and the night before I went to a *rancho* (which is a lodge built for travellers to rest when the journey is long) which stood within a league of the mountain by a river, where with the waters' murmur, and refreshing gales, I took good rest.

In the morning having refreshed myself and my Indians with chocolate I set out to encounter with that proud mountain; and when I came unto it I found it not so hard to overcome as I had conceited, the way lying with windings and turnings; but the higher I mounted the more my eyes were troubled with looking to the river below, whose rocks were enough to astonish and make a stout heart tremble. About the middle of the mountain the Indians of Zojabah met with a mule for me and another for my carriage in a narrow passage where the way went wheeling. Here I lighted, whilst the Indians helped one another to unload and load the mule that came of refresh. Out of the narrow way the side of the mountain was steepy, and a fearful precipice of two or three miles to the bottom, almost bare of trees, here and there one only growing. My heart was true unto me, wishing me to walk up a foot until I came unto some broader passage; but the Indians perceiving my fear told me there was no danger, assuring me further that the mule they had brought was sure, and had been well used to that mountain. With their persuasions I got up, but no sooner was I mounted when the mule began to play her pranks and to kick, and to leap out of the way, casting me down and herself, both rolling and tumbling apace to the rocks and death, had not a shrub prevented me, and a tree stopped the mule's blind fury. The Indians cried out, *Milagro, Milagro,* 'Miracle, Miracle,' *Santo, Santo,* 'a Saint, a Saint,' to me so loud as if they would have had their cry reach to Rome to help forward my canonization; for many such miracles have some been noised at Rome, and with further contribution of money have been enrolled in the book and catalogue of saints. Whilst the Indians helped me up and brought the mule again into the way, they did nothing but flatter me with this term saint; which they needed not have done, if as they considered my dangerous fall and stopping at a shrub (which was by chance, and not by miracle) they had further considered my passion and hasty wrath (not befitting a saint) wherewith I threatened to baste their ribs for deceiving me with a young mule not well accustomed to the saddle. But all my hasty words and anger could not discredit me with them, nor lessen their conceit of my holiness and sanctity, who hold the anger and wrath of a priest to be the breath of God's nostrils, and with this their foolish conceit of me, they kneeled before me kissing my hands. The business being further examined, they confessed that they had been mistaken in the mules, having saddled for me that which should have carried my *petacas,* or leathern chests, which was a young mule accustomed only to carriages, and not to the saddle, and upon that which should have been saddled they put my carriage. Whilst they unloaded and loaded again and saddled the right mule, I walked up the hill about a mile, and when they overtook me I got up and rid till I met with my refreshing arbour and chocolate, and many Indians that came to receive me, among whom it was presently noised that I was a saint and had wrought a miracle in the way; with this the rest of the Indians kneeled to me and kissed my hands, and in the way that we went to the town, all their talk was of my sanctity. I was much vexed at their simplicity, but the more they saw me unwilling to accept of that honour, the more they pressed it upon me. When I came to the town I told the friar what had happened, and what the foolish Indians had conceited; at which he laughed, and told me that he would warrant me if I stayed long in the town, all the men and women would come to kiss my hands and to offer their gifts unto me. He knew well their qualities. or else had taught them this superstition with many others; for no sooner had we dined, but many were gathered to the church to see the saint that was come to their town, and that had wrought a miracle in the mountain as he came. With this I began to be more troubled than before at the folly of the simple people, and desired the friar to check and rebuke them, who by no means would, but rather laughed at it, saying, that in policy we ought to accept of any honour from the Indians, for as long as we had credit and an opinion of saints among them, so long we should prevail to do anything with them, yea even to command them and their fortunes at our pleasure. With this I went down with the friar to the church, and sat down with him in a chair in the choir, representing the person of such a saint as they imagined me to be, though in reality and truth but a wretched sinner.

No sooner had we taken our places, when the Indians, men, women, and children, came up by three and four, or whole families to the choir, first kneeling down for my blessing, and then kissing my hands, they began to speak to me in their Indian compliments to this purpose, that their town was happy and doubtless blessed from Heaven by my coming into it, and that they hoped their souls should be much the better if they might partake of my prayers to God for them. And for this purpose some offered unto me money, some honey, some eggs, some little mantles, some plantains, and other fruits, some fowls, and some turkeys. The friar that sat by me I perceived was overjoyed with this, for he knew I was to be gone, and would leave unto him all those offerings. I desired him to make answer unto the Indians in my behalf, excusing me as not well versed in their language (yet the fools if they thought and judged me to be a saint might have expected from me also the gift of tongues), which he did telling them that I had been but a while in that country, and though I understood part of their language, yet could not speak nor pronounce it perfectly, and therefore from me he did give them hearty thanks for the great love they had shewed unto an ambassador of God, witnessing it with so many sorts of offerings, which assuredly should remind him and me of our offerings for them, in our prayers and hearty recommendations of them and their children unto God. Thus was that ceremony ended, the Indians dismissed, and the friar and I went up to a chamber, where he began to tell his eggs and fowls and to dispose of some of them for our supper; he told me he would take them, but at my departure would give me somewhat for them; he bad me keep what money they had given me, and told me I was welcome unto him, and no burdensome guest, but very profitable, who had brought with me store of provision for myself and for him many days after. The money I received came to forty reals, besides twenty which he gave me for the other offerings, which might be worth forty more; all this I got for having a fall from a mule, and for not breaking my neck. I would fain have departed the next morning, but John Vidall (so was the friar named) would not permit me, for that the next journey was of at least ten leagues, and therefore he would have me rest myself the next day.

This town of Zojabah, or Sacualpa is the biggest and fairest of all the towns that belong unto the priory of Sacapula; the Indians are rich, and make of their cotton-wool many mantles, they have plenty of honey, and great flocks of goats and kids; but here, nor in all the towns behind there is no wheat, save only Indian maize. The next day some small offerings fell unto me, but nothing like the day before; and so I told the friar that now the people's devotion was decayed, I would be gone in the morning before day. That night the chief Indians of the town came to offer their service and attendance upon me to a *rancho* or lodge that standeth in the middle way; but I would not accept of the great ones, but desired that I might have three only of the meaner sort to guide me till I met with company from the town whither I was going, and whither I had sent warning of my coming. The time appointed was three of the clock in the morning; at which hour after a little sleep I was called, and having drunk my chocolate, and eat a maple bread with a little conserve, I prepared myself for my journey, and found the Indians ready waiting for me in the yard, with pieces of pine-wood, which burn like torches, and with which they use to travel in the night, and to shew the way to him whom they guide. A little from the town we had some craggy ways, which indeed, had need of lights, but afterwards we came into a plain champaign country, which continued till within a league of the middle way lodge; to the which we were to descend a steep hill. When we came thither (which was about seven in the morning) we found our fresh supply waiting for us, who had set out from their town at midnight to meet us (note the Indians' subjection to their priests' command) and had made us a fire, and warmed water for our chocolate. Which whilst I was drinking, the Indians of Zojabah, who had guided me thither, gave notice to those that came to receive from St Martin (so was the town called whither I was that day minded) of my miracle and sanctity, wishing them to reverence and respect me in the way. But not for this their foolish report did I make the Indians of Zojabah drink every one a cup of chocolate, and so dismissed them; and took forwards my journey to

St Martin. Most of the way was hilly and craggy till we came within two miles of the town; to the which we arrived by noon.

This town is cold, standing high, yet pleasant for the prospect almost to Guatemala; here, and in most of the towns about it, is most excellent wheat. The honey of this town is the best in the country; but above all it furnisheth Guatemala with quails, partridges, and rabbits. It is the first town we enter into belonging to the city and command of Guatemala; which did not a little comfort me, that now I wanted but one good journey to make an end of my long, tedious, and wearisome travelling. The friar of this town named Thomas de la Cruz belonged unto the Dominican cloister of Guatemala; he was a Creole, but yet he entertained me very lovingly. I stayed with him but that night. And in the morning (though I might have gone to dinner to Guatemala) I would needs go by the way to one of the biggest towns in that country, called Chimaltenango, standing in an open valley three leagues from the city, consisting of a thousand housekeepers, and rich Indians who trade much about the country. In this town in my time there was one Indian, who alone had bestowed upon the church five thousand ducats. The church yields to none in the city of Guatemala, and in music it exceeds most about the country. The chief feast of Chimaltenango is upon the 26 day of July (which they call St Anne's day), and then is the richest fair that ever my eyes beheld in those parts of all sorts of merchants and merchandise. It is further set forth with bull-baiting, horse-racing, stage-plays, masks, dances, music, and all this gallantly performed by the Indians of the town.

The friar of this town was a Dominican, belonging to the cloister of the Dominicans of Guatemala, named Alonso Hidalgo, a four-eyed old man, for he always wore spectacles. He was a Spaniard born, but having been brought up in that country from his youth, and having taken his habit and vows in Guatemala amongst the Creoles, he degenerated from his birth and countrymen, hating all such as came from Spain. He was a deadly enemy to the Provincial (aiming indeed himself to be Provincial with the favour of the Creoles) and so I perceived he would have picked a quarrel with me whilst I was with him; he told me I was welcome, though he had little reason to bid any welcome that had come from Spain, who he thought came but to supplant those that had been born and brought up there in their own country, and that for aught he knew, I learning the language of those Indians might one day dispossess him of that town, wherein he had continued above ten years; he inveighed much against the Provincial and Friar John Baptist, the Prior of Guatemala, whom he knew to be my friend. But to all this I answered not a word, respecting his grave and old age, and crystal spectacles. At last he told me that he had heard say that the Indians of Zojabah had cried me up for a saint, which he could not believe of any that came from Spain, much less of me that came from England, a country of heretics; but he feared rather that I might come as a spy, to view the riches of that their country, and betray them hereafter to England, and that in Guatemala there were many rich pieces, especially a picture of Our Lady, and a lamp in the cloister of the Dominicans, which he doubted not but I would be careful to pry into. But all this I put up with a jest, saying, that I would be sure to take notice first of the riches of his chamber in pictures, hangings, and rich cabinets, and that if the English came thither in my time, I would surely conduct them to it; and if he himself would but cause a set of teeth of silver to be set in his gums and jaws instead of those leaden ones (for he was so old that he had lost all his teeth, and had got some of lead in their stead), then surely I would also conduct the English to him as to a rich prize for his teeth, and that I would warrant him he should be well used for his outward and inward riches; and that this my counsel might be profitable and of consequence to him, I told him, for if the English should come, certainly they would try of what metal his teeth were made, thinking that they might be of some rare and exquisite substance found only in that country, and so might cause him to drink such hot and scalding broth (to try whether they were lead) as might melt them in his mouth, and make the melted lead run down his throat, which if they were of silver they would not do. He perceived I jeered him, and so he let me alone; I was glad I had put him out of his former bias of railing; so dinner being ended, I told him I would not stay supper, but go to Guatemala to a light supper in the cloister, for that he had given me such a dinner, as I feared I should not have digested it in few days. I desired him to let me have Indians to guide me to Guatemala, which he willingly performed, peradventure fearing that if I stayed supper with him, I should melt the teeth in his mouth with some scalding cup of my chocolate brought from Chiapa, or that in the night I should rifle or plunder his chamber of his rich idols and ebony cabinets. The Indians being come, I made haste to be gone from that four-eyed beast, being now desirous of a constant rest in Guatemala.

Within a league from this town of Chimaltenango the roadway leaving that open, wide, and spacious valley, contracts and gathereth in itself between hills and mountains standing on each side, and so continueth to the city. From this valley unto Guatemala, neither is there any ascent or descent but a plain, broad, and sandy way. The eye hath much to view, though compassed with mountains, in these two last leagues; for yet it may behold a town of Indians which taketh up most of the way, and is counted as big as Chimaltenango, if not bigger, the houses lying scattered with a distance one from another, mingled with many fair buildings of Spaniards, who resort much thither from the city for their recreation. This town is called Xocotenango, of a fruit named *xocotte*, which is most plentiful there, and all about the country; it is fresh and cooling, of a yellow colour when ripe, and of two sorts, some sweet, and others sour, of the stones whereof the Indians make a fire; they lie so thick in the way, dropping from the trees for want of gathering and spending them all, that the Spaniards have begun to practise the buying of hogs on purpose to let them run about that highway, finding that they fat as speedily and as well with those plums, as our hogs do in England with acorns. All this way are also many fair gardens, which supply the markets of Guatemala with herbs, roots, fruits, and flowers all the year. There are further in this road three water-mills for the corn of the city, whereof the chief and the richest belongs to the Dominican friars of Guatemala, who keep there a friar constantly with three or four blackamoors to do and oversee the work. What will not those friars do to satisfy their covetous minds? Even dusty millers they will become to get wealth. The frontispiece of the church of this town is judged one of the best pieces of work thereabouts; the high altar within is also rich and stately, being all daubed with gold. I made no stay in this place, because I knew I should have many occasions after my settling in the city to come unto it. And thus keeping between the hills I continued on my journey till I came to Guatemala, whose dominions, riches, and greatness the following chapter shall largely shew.

SURVEY OF WEST INDIES

CHAPTER XIII

Describing the dominions, government, riches, and greatness of the city of Guatemala, and country belonging unto it

I HAD not rid on above a mile from the church of Xocotenango, when the hills and mountains seemed to depart one from another, leaving a more spacious object for the eye to behold, and a wider valley to wander in. The fame of that city from Mexico and Chiapa had raised up my thoughts to conceit of some strong walls, towers, forts or bulwarks to keep out an aspiring or attempting enemy. But when I came near and least thought of it, I found myself in it without entering through walls, or gates, or passing over any bridge, or finding any watch or guard to examine who I was; but passing by a new built church, standing near a place of dunghills, where were none but mean houses, some thatched, and some tiled, and asking what town that was, answer was made me that it was the city of Guatemala, and that that, being called St Sebastian, was the only parish church of the city. With this my high conceiting thoughts stooped down to think of some second Chiapa; till having continued on a while by houses on my right hand and dunghills on my left, I came to a broader street having houses on each side, which seemed to promise a city at hand. At my first turning I discovered a proud and stately cloister, which was the place of rest to my wearied body. I surrounded it to find out the back gate, and there lighted, and enquired for the Prior, who bad me very welcome, assuring me that for the Provincial's sake I should want no encouragement, and that he would do for me much more than what the Provincial had signified unto him by letters. He told me he had been brought up in Spain, in the country of Asturias, where many English ships did use to come, and having seen there many of my nation he affected them very much, and to me as one of so good a nation, and as a stranger and pilgrim out of my own country, he would shew all the favour that the utmost of his power would afford. How glad was I to find in him so contrary an opinion to that of four-eyed Hidalgo? And how did he perform his words?

He was the chief Master and Reader of Divinity in the University, his name Master Jacintho de Cabannas, who finding me desirous to follow the schools, and especially to hear from him some lessons of theology, within the first quarter of year, that I had been his constant and attentive auditor, graced me with a public act of conclusions of divinity, which I was to defend under his direction and moderation in the face of the whole University and assembly of doctors and divines, against the tenets of Scotus and Suarez. But the principal and head conclusion was concerning the birth of the Virgin Mary, whom both Jesuits, Suarez, and Franciscans, and Scotists hold to have been born without original sin, or any guilt or stain of it, against whose fond, foolish, and ungrounded fancies, I publicly defended with Thomas Aquinas, and all Thomists, that she (as well as all Adam's posterity) was born in original sin. It was an act, the like whereof had not been so controverted in that University with arguments in *contra*, and their answers and solutions, and with reasons and arguments in *pro* many years before. The Jesuits stamped with their feet, clapped with their hands, railed with their tongues, and condemned it with their mouths for a heresy, saying that in England, where were heretics, such an opinion concerning Christ's mother might be held, and defended by me who had my birth among heretics, but that Master Cabannas, born among Spaniards, and brought up in their Universities, and being the chief Reader in that famous academy should maintain such an opinion, they could not but much marvel and wonder at it. But with patience I told them that strong reasons, and the further authority of many learned

SURVEY OF WEST INDIES

Thomist divines should satisfy their vain and clamorous wondering. The act was ended, and though with Jesuits I could get no credit, yet with the Dominicans, and with Master Cabannas I got so much that I never after lost it for the space of almost twelve years, but was still honoured by the means of this Cabannas and Friar John Baptist, the Prior of Chiapa (who at Christmas ensuing was made Prior of Guatemala) with honours and preferments as great as ever stranger was living among Spaniards. These two above named being at Candlemas or beginning of February that same year at Chiapa, at the election of a new Provincial, would not forget me their poorest friend still abiding in Guatemala, but remembering that the University (which belonged chiefly to the cloister) at Michaelmas would want a new Reader or Master of Arts to begin with logic, continue through the eight books of physics, and to end with the metaphysics, propounded me to the new elected Provincial (whose name was Friar John Ximeno) and to the whole Chapter and Conventicle of the province for Reader of Arts in Guatemala the Michaelmas next ensuing. Their suit for me was so earnest and their authority so great that nothing could be denied them, and so they brought unto me from the Provincial Chapter letters patent from Friar John Ximeno.

This honour conferred upon me a stranger, and newcomer to the province, made the Creolean party and some others (who had aimed at that place and preferment in the University) to stomach me. But to me it was a spur to stir and prick me on to a more eager pursuit of learning, to frequent the academy lessons with more care and diligence; and to spend myself and time, day and night, more in studying, that so I might perform with like honour that which was laid upon me, and answer the expectation of my best and forwardest friends. Three years I continued in this convent and city in obedience to the forecited patents; oftentimes I thought within myself that the honour of my English nation here lay upon me in Guatemala, in not suffering any Spaniard to go beyond me, or to outbrave me with gallant, witty, and well seeming arguments; and so many times I would at nine of the clock at night, when others were gone to bed, take in my chamber a cup of hot chocolate, that with it I might banish sleep from mine eyes, and might the better continue in my study till one or two in the morning, being bound to awake and be up again by six. I was loath in these three years to take upon me any other of such charges which are common in such convents; but especially to preach much, and to hear the confessions of such both men and women as resorted to the church of that cloister, lest hereby my studies might be hindered, and time spent in other ways. Yet the Prior and Master Cabannas would often be very importunate with me, to obtain the Bishop's licence for hearing of confessions, and preaching abroad in the city and country (for in the church of that cloister I might and did sometimes, though seldom, preach with permission of the Provincial) but this I strongly refused, until such time as the Provincial himself came to Guatemala, who hearing me once preach, would by all means have me further licensed and authorised from the Bishop, that so I might not be straitened within the cloister's limits, but abroad in other churches might freely preach, and thereby get some money for the better furnishing myself with books. He therefore commanded me to be examined by five examiners all able divines, for the space of three hours (as is the custom of that Order) and having three hours stood under their hard and rigid questions and examination, having also at the end obtained their approbation, then the Provincial presented me unto the Bishop. Thus with full and ample commission from the Bishop and the Provincial was I settled in Guatemala, to read and preach, where (although I might have continued many years and was offered to read divinity, having in part begun it one quarter of a year) I continued yet but three years and almoſt an half for the reason I shall shew hereafter. So what in that time I could observe of that city, and of the country round about, having had occasions to travel about it both when I lived in Guatemala, and afterwards when I lived for above seven years in the country towns, I shall truly and faithfully recommend unto my Reader.

This city of Guatemala (called by the Spaniards Santiago, or St James of Guatemala) is seated in a valley, which is not above two miles and a half broad, for the high mountains do keep it close in; but in length towards the South Sea it continues a wide and champaign country, opening itself broader a little beyond that town, which to this day is called *la Ciudad Vieja*, or the Old City, ſtanding somewhat above three miles from Guatemala. Though the mountains on each side do ſtrongly environ it, and especially on the eaſt side seem to hang over it, yet none of them are hinderers to travellers, who over them have opened ways easy for man and beaſts though heavily laden with wares of all sorts. The way from Mexico, if taken by the coaſt of Soconusco and Suchitepequez, comes into the city north-weſtward, which is a wide, open, and sandy road; if it be taken by Chiapa, it lieth north-eaſt, and entereth into the city between the mountains, as before hath been noted. Weſtward to the South Sea the way lieth open through the valley and a champaign country. But south or south-eaſt, the entrance is over high and ſteepy hills, which is the common road from Comayagua, Nicaragua, and the Golfo Dulce or sweet gulf, where the ships come yearly and unlade all the commodities which are brought from Spain for Guatemala. This also is the way followed by them who take a journey mere eaſtward from this city.

THE ENGLISH-AMERICAN

But the chiefest mountains which straighten in this city and valley are two, called volcanoes, the one being a volcano of water, and the other a volcano or mountain of fire, termed so by the Spaniards, though very improperly a volcano may be said to contain water, it taking its name from the heathenish God Vulcan, whose profession and employment chiefly was in fire. These two famous mountains stand almost the one over against the other, on each side of the valley; that of water hanging on the south side almost perpendicularly over the city, the other of fire standing lower from it, more opposite to the old city. That of water is higher than the other, and yields a goodly prospect to the sight, being almost all the year green, and full of Indian *milpas*, which are plantations of Indian wheat; and in the small and petty towns which lie some half way up it, some at the foot of it, there are roses, lilies, and other flowers all the year long in the gardens, besides plantains, apricots, and many sorts of sweet and delicate fruits. It is called by the Spaniards, *el volcán del agua*, or the volcano of water, because on the other side of it from Guatemala it springs with many brooks towards a town called Saint Christopher, and especially is thought to preserve and nourish on that side also a great lake of fresh water, by the towns called Amatitlan and Petapa. But on the side of it towards Guatemala and the valley it yields also so many springs of sweet and fresh water as have caused and made a river which runneth along the valley close by the city, and is that which drives the water-mills spoken of before in Xocotenango. This river was not known when first the Spaniards conquered that country; but since (according to their constant tradition) the city of Guatemala standing higher and nearer to the volcano in that place and town which to this day is called *la Ciudad Vieja*, or the Old City, there lived in it then about the year 1534 a gentlewoman called Donna Maria de Castilla, who having lost her husband in the wars, and that same year buried also all her children, grew so impatient under these her crosses and afflictions, that impiously she defied God, saying: 'What can God do more unto me now than he hath done? he hath done his worst without it be to take away my life also, which I now regard not.' Upon these words there gushed out of this volcano such a flood of water as carried away this woman with the stream, ruined many of the houses, and caused the inhabitants to remove to the place where now standeth Guatemala. This is the Spaniards' own tradition, which if true, should be our example to learn to fear and not to defy God, when his judgments shew him to us angry and a God that will overcome, when he judgeth. From that time, and from this their tradition is the town now standing, where first stood Guatemala, called *la Ciudad Vieja*, or the Old City, and hath continued a river which before was not known, having its head and spring from this high volcano, whose pleasant springs, gardens, fruits, flowers and every green and flourishing prospect might be a fair object to a Martial's wit, who here would fancy a new Parnassus, find out new steps of flying Pegasus, and greet the nymphs and Nine Sisters with this their never yet discovered and American habitation.

This volcano or mountain is not so pleasing to the sight (whose height is judged full nine miles unto the top) but the other which standeth on the other side of the valley opposite unto it is unpleasing and more dreadful to behold; for here are ashes for beauty, stones and flints for fruits and flowers, baldness for greenness, barrenness for fruitfulness, for water whisperings and fountain murmurs, noise of thunders and roaring of consuming metals, for running streams, flashings of fire, for tall and mighty trees and cedars, castles of smoke rising in height to out-dare the sky and firmament, for sweet and odoriferous and fragrant smells, a stink of fire and brimstone, which are still in action striving within the bowels of that ever burning and fiery volcano. Thus is Guatemala seated in the midst of a Paradise on the one side and a hell on the other, yet never hath this hell broke so loose as to consume that flourishing city. True it is formerly many years ago it opened a wide mouth on the top, and breathed out such fiery ashes as filled the houses of Guatemala and the country about, and parched all the plants and fruits, and spewed out such stones and rocks which had they fallen upon the city would have crushed it to pieces, but they fell not far from it, but to this day lie about the bottom and sides of it, causing wonder to those that behold them, and taking away admiration from them that admire the force and strength of fire and powder in carrying on a weighty bullet from the mouth of a cannon, whereas here the fire of this mountain hath cast up into the air and tumbled down to the bottom of it such rocks as in bigness exceed a reasonable house, and which not the strength of any twenty mules (as hath been tried) have been able to remove. The fire which flasheth out of the top of this mountain is sometimes more and sometimes less; yet while I lived in the city, on a certain time for the space of three or four days and nights it did so burn that my friend Mr Cabannas confidently avouched to me and others, that standing one night in his window he had with the light of that fire read a letter, the distance being above three English miles. The roaring also of this monstrous beast is not constantly alike, but is greater in the summer time than in the winter, that is, from October to the end of April, than all the rest of the year; for then it seems, the winds entering into those concavities set the fire on work harder than at other times, and cause the mountain to roar and the earth about to quake. There was a time, three years before my coming to that city, when the inhabitants expected nothing but utter ruin and destruction, and durst not abide within their houses for nine days (the earthquakes continuing and increasing more and more) but made bowers and arbours in the market-place, placing there their idol saints and images, especially St Sebastian, whom they hoped would deliver them from that judgment, and for this purpose they daily carried him through the streets in solemn and idolatrous procession and adoration. But all the while I lived there the noise within the mountain, the smoke and flashes of fire without, and the summer earthquakes were such that with the use and custom of them I never feared anything, but thought that city the healthiest and pleasantest place of dwelling that ever I came into in all my travels.

The climate is very temperate, far exceeding either Mexico or Oaxaca. Neither are the two aforenamed cities better stored with fruits, herbs for salad, provision of fish, and flesh, beef, mutton, veal, kid, fowls, turkeys, rabbits, quails, partridges, pheasants, and of Indian and Spanish wheat than is this city: from the South Sea (which lieth in some places not above twelve leagues from it) and from the rivers of the South Sea Coast, and from the fresh lake of Amatitlan and Petapa, and from another lake lying three or four leagues from Chimaltenango, it is well and plentifully provided for of fish. But for beef there is such plenty that it exceeds all parts of America, without exception, as may be known by the hides, which are sent yearly to Spain from the country of Guatemala, where they commonly kill their cattle, more for the gain of their hides in Spain, than for the goodness or fatness of the flesh, which though it be not to be compared to our English beef, yet it is good man's meat, and so cheap, that in my time it was commonly sold at thirteen pound and a half for half a real, the least coin there, and as much as threepence here. Though all about this country there are very great and spacious *estancias*, or farms for breeding only, even near to the Golfo Dulce, where the ships ride that come from Spain,

THE ENGLISH-AMERICAN

yet from Comayagua, St Salvador and Nicaragua is Guatemala stored; but above all are the great *estancias* in the South Sea coast or marsh, where in my time there was a grazier that reckoned up going in his own *estancia* and ground, forty thousand heads of beasts, small and great, besides many which are called there *simarrones*, or wild cattle, which were strayed among the woods and mountains, and could not be gathered in with the rest, but were hunted by the blackamoors like wild boars, and daily shot to death, lest they should too much increase and do hurt. Myself chanced to be present at the fair of the town of Petapa, with a friend named Lope de Chaves (who was as they call there, *obligado*, or charged to provide flesh for six or seven towns thereabouts), who at one bargain, and of one man, bought six thousand head of cattle, great and small, paying one with another eighteen reals, or nine English shillings a head.

The manner and custom of Guatemala for the better providing both beef and mutton for it, and the country towns about, is this. Nine days before Michaelmas, every day proclamation is made about the city for an *obligado*, or one that will be bound to the city and country for competent provision of flesh meat upon forfeiture of such a sum of money to his Majesty, if he fail, as shall be agreed upon between him and the court, and to the inhabitants of the city; if he fail in beef, he is to allow in mutton so many pounds at the same rate as he should have allowed beef. If the *obligado* fail in mutton, he is to allow in fowl flesh, so many pounds and at the same rate as he was to allow the mutton; and this with consideration of the family, what competent allowance of flesh meat shall be judged for a day, or the days that the *obligado* shall fail. Besides this the proclamation is made for whom offers most to his Majesty for one year's obligation. So that sometimes it happeneth that the eight days several men come into the court, offering more and more, till upon the ninth day and last proclamation, the office is settled for one year upon him that hath offered most unto his Majesty. Thus many butchers are not allowed but one only *obligado*, who also is abridged to so many pound for so much money, so that if any other besides him offer to kill or sell, he may follow an action and the court against him. Thus the *obligado* (who commonly is a moneyed man) buyeth by the hundred or by the thousand, as for the present he findeth the expense of the city, without he be himself such a grazier as hath cattle enough of his own. Though mutton be not so plentiful as is beef, yet there never wants from the Valley of Mixco, Pinola, Petapa, and Amatitlan, and the marsh and other places. In the valley afore-named I lived, and was well acquainted with one Alonso Capata, who had constantly going in the valley four thousand sheep. Guatemala therefore is so well stored with good provision, plentiful and cheap, that it is hard to find in it a beggar, for with half a real the poorest may buy beef for a week, and with a few *cacaos* they may have bread of Indian maize, if not of Spanish wheat.

This city may consist of about five thousand families, besides a suburb of Indians called *el Barrio de Sto Domingo*, where may be two hundred families more. The best part of the city is that which joineth to this suburb of Indians, and is called also *el Barrio de Santo Domingo*, by reason of the cloister of Saint Dominic which standeth in it. Here are the richest and best shops of the city, with the best buildings, most of the houses being new, and stately. Here is also a daily *tianguez* (as they call it) or petty market, where some Indians all the day sit selling fruits, herbs, and *cacao*, but at the four in the afternoon, this market is filled for a matter of an hour, where the Indian women meet to sell their country slap (which is dainties to the Creoles) as *atole*, *pinole*, scalded plantains, butter of the *cacao*, puddings made of Indian maize, with a bit of fowl or fresh pork in them seasoned with much red biting chilli, which they call *anacatamales*. The trading of the city is great, for by mules it partakes of the best commodities of Mexico, Oaxaca and Chiapa, and southward of Nicaragua, and Costa Rica. By sea it hath commerce with Peru, by two sea ports and havens, the one called La Villa de la Trinidad, the Village of the Trinity, which lieth southward from it five and twenty leagues; and by another called El Realejo, which lieth five or six and forty leagues from it. It hath traffic with Spain by the North Sea from Golfo Dulce [i.e. Dolce], lying three-score leagues from it.

It is not so rich as other cities, yet for the quantity of it, it yields to none. There were in my time five (besides many other merchants who were judged worth twenty thousand ducats, thirty thousand, fifty thousand, some few a hundred thousand) who were judged of equal wealth, and generally reported to be worth each of them five hundred thousand ducats; the first was Thomas de Siliezer, a Biscayan born, and *Alcalde de Corte*, the King's High Justice, or Chief Officer at Court; the second was Antonio Justiniano, a Genoese born, and one that bore often offices in the city, and had many tenements and houses, especially a great and rich farm for corn and wheat in the Valley of Mexico. The third was Pedro de Lira, born in Castile, the fourth and fifth, Antonio Fernandez, and Bartolome Nunnez, both Portuguese, whereof the first in my time departed from Guatemala for some reasons which here I must conceal. The other four I left there, the three of them living at that end of the city called *Barrio de Santo Domingo*, or the Street of St Dominic, whose houses and presence makes that street excel all the rest of the city, and their wealth and trading were enough to denominate Guatemala a very rich city.

The Government of all the country about, and of all Honduras, Soconusco, Comayagua, Nicaragua, Costa Rica, Vera Paz, Suchitepequez, and Chiapa, is sub-

SURVEY OF WEST INDIES

ordinate unto the Chancery of Guatemala; for although every governor over these several provinces is appointed by the King and Council of Spain, yet when they come to those parts to the enjoyment of their charge and execution office, then their actions, if unjust, are weighed, judged, censured, and condemned by the Court residing in the city. This Court of Chancery consisteth of a president, six judges, one King's attorney, and two chief justices of court. The President, though he have not the name and title of viceroy, as they of Mexico and Peru, yet his power is as great and absolute as theirs. His pension from the King is but twelve thousand ducats a year; but besides this, if he be covetous, he makes by bribes and trading twice as much more, nay what he list, as was seen in the Count de la Gomera, President of that city and Chancery for the space of fourteen years, who departed in old age from Guatemala to the Canaries (where was his house and place of birth) worth millions of ducats. After him succeeded Don Juan de Guzman, formerly President of Santo Domingo, who losing his wife and lady in the way, lost also his former spirit and courage, betaking himself wholly to his devotions, contemning wealth and riches, governing with love and mildness, which made the rest of the judges, who were all for lucre, soon weary him out of his office, continuing in it but five years. His successor (whom I left there when I came away) was Don Gonsalo de Paz y Lorencana, who was promoted from the presidency of Panama to that place, and came into it with such a spirit of covetousness as the like had not been seen in any former president. He forbad all gaming in private houses in the city, which there is much used (though by women not so much as in Mexico) not for that he hated it, but because he envied others what they got and gained by their cards, drawing to himself thereby all that gain, spending sometimes in one night four and twenty pair of cards, appointing a page to assist at the tables, and to see the box well paid for every pair of cards, which for his, and his Court respect, was seldom less than a crown or two for every pair. Thus did he lick up with his cards most of the gamester's gains, and would grudge and pick quarrels with such rich men whom he knew to affect gaming, if they frequented not his Court at night time for that bewitching recreation.

The pension which the King alloweth to every judge of Chancery is four thousand ducats yearly, and three thousand to his attorney, all which is paid out of the King's Exchequer abiding in that city. Yet what besides they get by bribes and trading is so much, that I have heard a judge himself Don Luis de las Infantas say, that though a judge's place at Mexico and Lima be more honourable, yet none more profitable than Guatemala. In my time were such causes at Chancery tried, as had never been, of murders, robberies, and oppressions, and whereas it was expected the offenders some should be hanged, some banished, some imprisoned, some by fines impoverished, bribes took all off, so that I never knew one hanged in that city for the space of above eight years.

The churches though they be not so fair and rich as those of Mexico, yet they are for that place wealthy enough. There is but one parish church and a cathedral which standeth in the chief market-place. All the other churches belong to cloisters, which are of Dominicans, Franciscans, Mercenarians, Augustines, and Jesuits, and two of nuns, called the Conception and St Catharine. The Dominicans, Franciscans, and Mercenarians are stately cloisters, containing near a hundred friars apiece; but above all is the cloister where I lived, of the Dominicans, to which is joined in a great walk before the church the University of the city. The yearly revenues which come into this cloister, what from the Indian towns belonging to it, what from a water-mill, what from a farm for corn, what from an *estancia*, or farm for horses and mules, what from an *ingenio*, or farm of sugar, what from a mine of silver given unto it the year 1633 are judged to be (excepting all charges) at least thirty thousand ducats; wherewith those fat friars feast themselves, and have to spare to build, and enrich their church and altars. Besides much treasure belonging to it, there are two things in it which the Spaniards in merriment would often tell me that the English nation did much enquire after, when they took any ship of theirs at sea, and that they feared I was come to spy them, which were a lamp of silver hanging before the high altar, so big as required the strength of three men to hale it up with a rope; but the other is of more value, which is a picture of the Virgin Mary of pure silver, and of the stature of a reasonable tall woman, which standeth in a tabernacle made on purpose in a Chapel of the Rosary with at least a dozen lamps of silver also burning before it. A hundred thousand ducats might soon be made up of the treasure belonging to that church and cloister. Within the walls of the cloister there is nothing wanting which may further pleasure and recreation. In the lower cloister there is a spacious garden, in the midst whereof is a fountain casting up the water, and spouting it out of at least a dozen pipes, which fill two ponds full of fishes, and with this their constant running give music to the whole cloister, and encouragement to many water-fowls and ducks to bathe and wash themselves therein. Yet further within the cloister, there are other two gardens for fruits and herbage, and in the one a pond of a quarter of a mile long, all paved at the bottom, and a low stone wall about, where is a boat for the friars' recreation, who often go thither to fish, and do sometimes upon a sudden want or occasion take out from thence as much fish as will give to the whole cloister a dinner.

The other cloisters of the city are also rich; but next to the Dominicans is the cloister of nuns called the

Conception, in which at my time there were judged to live a thousand women, not all nuns, but nuns and their serving maids or slaves, and young children which were brought up and taught to work by the nuns. The nuns that are professed bring with them their portions, five hundred ducats the least, some six hundred, some seven, and some a thousand, which portions after a few years (and continuing to the cloister after the nuns' decease) come to make up a great yearly rent. They that will have maids within to wait on them may, bringing the bigger portion, or allowing yearly for their servants' diet. In this cloister lived that Donna Juana de Maldonado, Judge Juan Maldonado de Paz his daughter, whom the Bishop so much conversed withal. She was very fair and beautiful, and not much above twenty years of age, and yet his love blinding him, he strove what he could in my time against all the ancient nuns and sisters, to make her superior and abbess, and caused such a mutiny and strife in that cloister, which was very scandalous to the whole city, and made many rich merchants and gentlemen run to the cloister with their swords drawn, threatening to break in amongst the nuns to defend their daughters against the powerful faction which the Bishop had wrought for Donna Juana de Maldonado: which they had performed if the President Don Juan de Guzman had not sent Juan Maldonado de Paz, the young nun's father, to entreat her to desist in regard of her young age from her ambitious thoughts of being abbess. With this the mutiny both within and without ceased, the Bishop got but shame, and his young sister continued as before under command and obedience, to a more religious, grave, and aged nun than herself.

This Donna Juana de Maldonado y Paz was the wonder of all that cloister, yea of all the city for her excellent voice, and skill in music, and in carriage, and education yielded to none abroad nor within; she was witty, well spoken and above all a Calliope, or

Muse for ingenious and sudden verses; which the Bishop said so much moved him to delight in her company and conversation. Her father thought nothing too good, nor too much for her; and therefore having no other children, he daily conferred upon her riches, as might best beseem a nun, as rich and costly cabinets faced with gold and silver, pictures and idols for her chamber with crowns and jewels to adorn them; which with other presents from the Bishop (who dying in my time left not wherewith to pay his debts, for that as the report went, he had spent himself and given all unto this nun) made this Donna Juana de Maldonado so rich and stately, that at her own charges she built for herself a new quarter within the cloister with rooms and galleries, and a private garden-walk, and kept at work and to wait on her half a dozen blackamoor maids; but above all she placed her delight in a private chapel or closet to pray in, being hung with rich hangings, and round about it costly *laminas* (as they call them) or pictures painted upon brass set in black ebony frames with corners of gold, some of silver, brought to her from Rome; her altar was accordingly decked with jewels, candlesticks, crowns, lamps, and covered with a canopy embroidered with gold; in her closet she had her small organ, and many sorts of musical instruments, whereupon she played sometimes by herself, sometimes with her best friends of the nuns; and here especially she entertained with music her beloved the Bishop. Her chapel or place of devotion was credibly reported about the city to be worth at least six thousand crowns, which was enough for a nun that had vowed chastity, poverty, and obedience. But all this after her decease she was to leave to the cloister; and doubtless with this state and riches she would win more and more the hearts of the common sort of nuns, till she had made a strong party, which by this may have made her abbess. Thus is ambition and desire of command and power crept into the walls of nunneries, like the abominations in the wall of Ezekiel, and hath possessed the hearts of nuns, which should be humble, poor, and mortified virgins.

But besides this one nun, there are many more, and also friars, who are very rich, for if the city be rich (as is this) and great trading in it, they will be sure to have a share. Great plenty and wealth hath made the inhabitants as proud and vicious as are those of Mexico. Here is not only idolatry, but fornication and uncleanness as public as in any place of the Indies. The mulattoes, blackamoors, mestizoes, Indians, and all common sort of people are much made on by the greater and richer sort, and go as gallantly apparelled as do those of Mexico, fearing neither a volcano or mountain of water on the one side, which they confess hath once poured out a flood and river executing God's wrath against sin there committed; neither a volcano of fire, or mouth of hell on the other side, roaring within and threatening to rain upon them Sodom's ruin and destruction; neither the weakness of their habitation, lying wide open on every side, without walls, or works, or bulwarks, to defend them, or without guns, drakes, bullets, or any ammunition to scare away an approaching enemy, who may safely come and without resistance upon them who live as professed enemies of Jesus Christ. This is the city of St James or Santiago de Guatemala, the head of a vast and ample dominion, which extendeth itself nine hundred miles to Nicoya and Costa Rica southward; three hundred miles to Chiapa and Zoques northward; a hundred and fourscore miles to the further parts of Vera Paz, and the Golfo Dulce eastward; and to the South Sea twenty or thirty, in some places forty miles westward.

From Tehuantepec (which is no harbour for any great ships) which standeth from Guatemala at least four hundred miles, there is no landing place for ships nearer to this city than is the village *de la Trinidad*, or of the Trinity. The chief commodities which from

SURVEY OF WEST INDIES

along that coast are brought to Guatemala, are from the provinces of Soconusco and Suchitepequez, which are extreme hot, and subject to thunder and lightning, where groweth scarce any remarkable commodity, save only *cacao, achiote, mechasuchil, vainillas* and other drugs for chocolate, except it be some indigo and cochineal about St Antonio, which is the chief and head town of all the Suchutepeques. But all the coast near joining to Guatemala, especially about a town called Izquinta, or Izquintepeque, twelve leagues from Guatemala, is absolutely the richest part of the dominion of this city; for there is made the greatest part of the indigo which is sent from Honduras to Spain, besides the mighty farms of cattle, which are all along that marsh. Though the living there be profitable and the soil rich, yet it is uncomfortable by reason of the great heat, thunderings and lightnings, especially from May to Michaelmas. If Guatemala be strong (though not in weapons or ammunition) in people, it is strong from hence from a desperate sort of blackamoors, who are slaves in those *estancias* and farms of indigo. Though they have no weapons but a *machete*, which is a short tuck, or lances to run at the wild cattle, yet with these they are so desperate that the city of Guatemala hath often been afraid of them, and the masters of their own slaves and servants. Some of them fear not to encounter a bull though wild and mad, and to grapple in the rivers (which are many there) with crocodiles, or *lagartos*, as there they call them, till they have overmastered them, and brought them out to land from the water.

This hot but rich country runs on by the seaside unto the Village of the Trinity, which (though somewhat dangerous) yet is a haven for ships from Panama, Peru, and Mexico. It serves to enrich Guatemala, but not to strengthen it, for it hath neither fort, nor bulwark, nor castle, nor any ammunition to defend itself. Between this village and the other haven called

Realejo, there is a great creek from the sea; where small vessels do use to come in for fresh water and victuals to St Miguel, a town of Spaniards and Indians, from whence those that travel to Realejo pass over in less than a day to a town of Indians called La Vieja, two miles from Realejo, whither the journey by land from St Miguel is of at least three days. But neither this creek or arm of the sea is fortified (which might be done with one or two pieces of ordnance at most placed at the mouth of the sea's entrance) neither is the Realejo strong with any ammunition, no nor with people, for it consists not of above two hundred families, and most of them are Indians and mestizoes, a people of no courage, and very unfit to defend such an open passage to Guatemala and Nicaragua, which here begins and continues in small and petty Indian towns unto Leon and Granada.

On the north side of Guatemala I shall not need to add to what hath been said of Suchitepequez and Soconusco, and my journey that way from Mexico and Chiapa. The chief side of Guatemala is that on the east, which points out the way to the gulf, or Golfo Dulce, or as others call it St Thomas de Castilla. This way is more beaten by mules and travellers than that on the north side, for that Mexico standeth three hundred leagues from this city, and the gulf but threescore, and no such passages as are in some places in the road to Mexico. Besides the great trading, commerce, and traffic which this city enjoyeth by that gulf from Spain hath made that road exceed all the rest. In July or at furthest in the beginning of August come into that gulf three ships, or two, and frigates, and unlade what they have brought from Spain in *bodegas* or great lodges, built up on purpose to keep dry and from the weather the commodities. They presently make haste to lade again from Guatemala those merchants' commodities of return, which peradventure have lain waiting for them in the *bodegas* two or three months before the ship's arrival. So that these three months of July, August, and September, there is sure to be found a great treasure. And O the simplicity or security of the Spaniards, who appoint no other watch over these their riches, save only one or two Indians and as many mulattoes, who commonly are such as have for their misdemeanours been condemned to live in that old and ruinated castle of S. Thomas de Castilla. True it is, above it there is a little and ragged town of Indians, called S. Pedro, consisting of some thirty families, who by reason of the exceeding heat, and unhealthiness of the air, are always sickly and scarce able to stand upon their legs. But the weakness of this gulf within might well be remedied and supplied at the mouth of the sea, or entrance into it, by one or two at the most good pieces of ordnance placed there. For the entrance into this gulf is but as one should come in at the door of some great palace, where although the door and entrance be narrow, the house within is wide and capacious. Such is this gulf, whose entrance is straitened with two rocks or mountains on each side (which would well become two great pieces, and so scorn a whole fleet, and secure a kingdom of Guatemala nay most of all America) but here being no watch nor defence, the ships come freely and safely in (as have done some both English and Holland ships) and being entered find a road and harbour so wide and capacious as may well secure a thousand ships there riding at anchor, without any thought of fear from St Pedro, or Santo Thomas de Castilla. I have often heard the Spaniards jeer and laugh at the English and Hollanders, for that they having come into this gulf, have gone away without attempting anything further upon the land. Nay while I lived there, the Hollanders set upon Trujillo, the head port of Comayagua and Honduras, and took it (though there were some resistance), the people for the most part flying to the woods, trusting more to their feet than to their hands and weapons (such cowards is all that country full of) and whilst they might have fortified themselves there and gone into the country, or fortifying that have come on to the gulf (all Guatemala fearing it much and not being able to resist them) they left Trujillo contenting themselves with a small pillage, and gave occasion to the Spaniards to rejoice and to make processions of thanksgiving for their safe deliverance out of their enemies' hands.

The way from this gulf to Guatemala is not so bad as some report and conceive, especially after Michaelmas until May, when the winter and rain is past and gone, and the winds begin to dry up the ways. For in the worst of the year mules laden with four hundredweight at least go easily through the steepest, deepest and most dangerous passages of the mountains that lie about this gulf. And though the ways are at that time of the year bad, yet they are so beaten with the mules, and so wide and open, that one bad step and passage may be avoided for a better; and the worst of this way continues but fifteen leagues, there being *ranchos*, or lodges in the way, cattle and mules also among the woods and mountains, for relief and comfort to a weary traveller. What the Spaniards most fear until they come out of these mountains are some two or three hundred blackamoors, *simarrones*, who for too much hard usage have fled away from Guatemala and other parts from their masters unto these woods, and there live and bring up their children and increase daily, so that all the power of Guatemala, nay all the country about (having often attempted it), is not able to bring them under subjection. These often come out to the roadway, and set upon the *requas* of mules, and take of wine, iron, clothing and weapons from them as much as they need, without doing any harm unto the people, or slaves that go with the mules; but rather these rejoice with them, being of one colour, and subject to slavery and misery which the others

PLATE 6

FUNERAL PROCESSION OF THE KING OF MECHAOCAN
(*From the Dutch Edition of* 1700)

[*Face p.* 208

have shaken off; by whose example and encouragement many of these also shake off their misery, and join with them to enjoy liberty, though it be but in the woods and mountains. Their weapons are bows and arrows which they use and carry about them, only to defend themselves if the Spaniards set upon them; else they use them not against the Spaniards, who travel quietly and give them part of what provision they carry. These have often said that the chief cause of their flying to those mountains is to be in a readiness to join with the English or Hollanders, if ever they land in that gulf; for they know, from them they may enjoy that liberty which the Spaniards will never grant unto them.

After the first fifteen leagues the way is better, and there are little towns and villages of Indians, who relieve with provision both man and beast. Fifteen leagues further is a great town of Indians, called Acacabastlan, standing upon a river, which for fish is held the best of all that country. Though here are many sorts, yet above all there is one which they call *bobo*, a thick round fish as long or longer than a man's arm, with only a middle bone, as white as milk, as fat as butter, and good to boil, fry, stew or bake. There is also from hence most of the way to Guatemala in brooks and shallow rivers, one of the best sort of fishes in the world, which the Spaniards judge to be a kind of trout, it is called there *tepemechin*, the fat whereof resembles veal more than fish.

This town of Acacabastlan is governed by a Spaniard who is called *corregidor*; his power extendeth no farther than to the gulf, and to those towns in the way. This governor hath often attempted to bring in those *simarrones* from the mountains, but could never prevail against them. All the strength of this place may be some twenty muskets (for so many Spanish houses there may be in the town) and some few Indians that use bows and arrows, for the defence of the town against the blackamoor *simarrones*.

THE ENGLISH-AMERICAN

About Acacabastlan there are many *estancias* of cattle and mules, much *cacao*, *achiote*, and drugs for chocolate. There is also apothecary drugs, as *zarzaparrilla*, and *cañafistula*, and in the town as much variety of fruits and gardens as in any one Indian town in the country; but above all Acacabastlan is far known, and much esteemed of in the city of Guatemala, for excellent muskmelons, some small, some bigger than a man's head, wherewith the Indians load their mules and carry them to sell all over the country. From hence to Guatemala there are but thirty short leagues, and though some hills there be, ascents and descent, yet nothing troublesome to man or beast. Among these mountains there have been discovered some mines of metal, which the Spaniards have begun to dig, and finding that they have been some of copper, and some of iron, they have let them alone, judging them more chargeable than profitable. But greater profit have the Spaniards lost, than of iron and copper, for using the poor Indians too hardly, and that in this way, from Acacabastlan to Guatemala, especially about a place called El Agua Caliente, The Hot Water, where is a river, out of which in some places formerly the Indians found such store of gold that they were charged by the Spaniards with a yearly tribute of gold. But the Spaniards being like Valdivia in Chile, too greedy after it, murdering the Indians for not discovering unto them where about this treasure lay, have lost both treasure and Indians also. Yet unto this day search is made about the mountains, the river, and the sands for the hidden treasure, which peradventure by God's order and appointment doth and shall lie hid, and kept for a people better knowing and honouring their God. At this place called El Agua Caliente, or The Hot Water, liveth a blackamoor in an *estancia* of his own, who is held to be very rich, and gives good entertainment to the travellers that pass that way; he is rich in cattle, sheep, and goats, and from his farm stores Guatemala and the people thereabout with the best cheese of all that country. But his riches are thought not so much to increase from his farm and cheeses, but from this hidden treasure, which credibly is reported to be known unto him. He hath been questioned about it in the Chancery of Guatemala, but hath denied often any such treasure to be known unto him. The jealousy and suspicion of him is, for that formerly having been a slave, he bought his freedom with great sums of money, and since he hath been free, hath bought that farm and much land lying to it, and hath exceedingly increased his stock; to which he answereth, that when he was young and a slave, he had a good master, who let him get for himself what he could, and that he playing the good husband, gathered as much as would buy his liberty, and at first a little house to live in, to the which God hath since given a blessing with a greater increase of stock.

From this hot water three or four leagues, there is another river called Rio de las Vacas, or the River of Cows, where are a company of poor and country people most of them mestizoes, and mulattoes, who live in thatched houses, with some small stock of cattle, spending their time also in searching for sands of gold, hoping that one day by their diligent search they and their children, and all their country, shall be enriched, and that Rio de las Vacas shall parallel Pactolus, and stir up the wits of poets to speak of it as much as ever they have spoke of that. From this river is presently discovered the pleasantest valley in all that country (where myself did live at least five years) called the Valley of Mixco and Pinola, lying six leagues from Guatemala, being fifteen miles in length, and ten or twelve in breadth. Out of the enclosures this valley is stored with sheep; the ground enclosed is divided into many farms, where groweth better wheat than any in the country of Mexico. From this valley the city is well provided of wheat, and biscuit is made for the ships that come every year unto the gulf. It is called the Valley of Mixco and Pinola from two towns of Indians, so called, standing opposite the one to the other on each side of the valley, Pinola, on the left side from Rio de las Vacas, and Mixco on the right. Here do live many rich farmers, but yet country and clownish people, who know more of breaking clods of earth than of managing arms offensive or defensive.

But among them I must not forget one friend of mine, called Juan Palomeque, whom I should have more esteemed of than I did if I could have prevailed with him to have made him live more like a man than a beast, more like a free man than a bond slave to his gold and silver. This man had in my time three hundred lusty mules trained up in the way of the gulf, which he divided into six *requas*, or companies; and for them he kept above a hundred blackamoor slaves, men, women, and children, who lived near Mixco in several thatched cottages. The house he lived in himself was but a poor thatched house, wherein he took more delight to live than in other houses which he had in Guatemala, for there he lived like a wild *simarron* among his slaves and blackamoors, whereas in the city he should have lived civilly; there he lived with milk, curds, and black, hard and mouldy biscuit, and with a dry *tasajo*, which is dry salted beef cut out in thin slices, and dried in the sun and wind, till there be little substance left in it, such as his slaves were wont to carry to the gulf for their provision by the way, whereas if he had lived in the city he must have eat for his credit what others of worth did eat. But the miser knew well which was the best way to save, and so chose a field for a city, a cottage for a house, company of *simarrones* and blackamoors for citizens, and yet he was thought to be worth six hundred thousand ducats. He was the undoer of all others who dealt with mules for bringing and carrying commodities to the gulf for the merchants; for he having lusty mules, lusty slaves, would set the price or rate for the hundredweight so, as he might get, but others at that rate hiring Indians and servants to go with their mules, might lose. He was so cruel to his blackamoors that if any were untoward, he would torment them almost to death; amongst whom he had one slave called Macaco (for whom I have often interceded, but to little purpose) whom he would often hang up by the arms, and whip him till the blood ran about his back, and then his flesh being torn, mangled, and all in a gore blood, he would for last cure pour boiling grease upon it; he had marked him for a slave with burning irons upon his face, his hands, his arms, his back, his belly, his thighs, his legs, that the poor slave was weary of life, and I think would two or three times have hanged himself, if I had not counselled him to the contrary. He was so sensual and carnal that he would use his own slaves' wives at his pleasure; nay when he met in the city any of that kind handsome and to his liking, if she would not yield to his desire, he would go to her master or mistress, and buy her, offering far more than she was worth, boasting that he would pull down her proud and haughty looks, with one years' slavery under him. He killed in my time two Indians in the way to the gulf, and with his money came off, as if he had killed but a dog. He would never marry, because his slaves supplied the bed of a wife, and none of his neighbours durst say him nay; whereby he hasted to fill that valley with bastards of all sorts and colours, by whom, when that rich miser dieth, all his wealth and treasure is like to be consumed.

Besides the two towns which denominate this valley, there standeth at the east end of it close by the Rio de las Vacas an hermitage, called *Nuestra Señora del Carmel*, or Our Lady of Carmel, which is the parish church to all those several farms of Spaniards living in the valley; though true it is, most constantly they do resort unto the Indian towns to Mass, and in Mixco especially, the Spaniards have a rich sodality of Our Lady of the Rosary, and the blackamoors another. In all the valley there may be between forty and fifty Spanish farms or houses belonging to the hermitage, and in all these houses some three hundred slaves, men and women, blackamoors and mulattoes. Mixco is a town of three hundred families, but in it nothing considerable but the riches belonging unto the two aforenamed sodalities, and some rich Indians, who have learned of the Spaniards to break clods of earth, and to sow wheat, and to traffic with mules unto the gulf. Besides what fowls and great store of turkeys which in this town are bred, there is a constant slaughter house, where meat is sold to the Indians within, and to the farms without, and provision is made for all the *requas* and slaves that go to the gulf with their masters' mules. Besides the six *requas* before named of Juan Palomeque, there are in this valley four brothers, named Don Gaspar, Don Diego, Don Thomas, Don Juan de Colindres, who have each of them a *requa* of threescore mules (though few slaves, and only hired Indians to go with them) to traffic to the gulf, and over all the country as far as Mexico sometimes. Yet besides these there are some six more *requas* belonging to other farms, which with those of the town of Mixco may make up full twenty *requas;* and those twenty *requas* contain above a thousand mules, which only from this valley are employed to all parts of the country by the rich merchants of Guatemala.

But to return again to the town of Mixco, the constant passage through it of these *requas*, of rich merchants, of all passengers that go and come from Spain, hath made it very rich, whereas in the town itself there is no other commodity, except it be a kind of earth, whereof are made rare and excellent pots for water, pans, pipkins, platters, dishes, chafing-dishes, warming-pans, wherein those Indians shew much wit, and paint them with red, white, and several mingled colours, and sell them to Guatemala, and the towns about, which some Creole women will eat by full mouthfuls, endangering their health and lives, so that by this earthly ware they may look white and pale. The town of Pinola in bigness is much like unto Mixco, but a far pleasanter town, more healthy and better seated, standing upon a plain, whereas Mixco stands on the side on a hill, which carrieth the travellers quite out of the sight of the valley. In Pinola there is also a slaughter house, where beef is daily sold, there is plenty of fowls, fruits, maize, wheat (though not altogether so bright as that of Mixco), honey, and the best water thereabouts; it is called in the Indian tongue *Panac* (some say), from a fruit of that name which is very abundant there. On the north and south side of this valley are hills, which are most sown with wheat, which proveth better there than in the low valley. At the west end of it stand two greater towns than Mixco and Pinola, named Petapa and Amatitlan, to the which there are in the midst of the valley some descents and ascents, which they call *barrancas* or bottoms, where are pleasant streams and fountains, and good feeding for sheep, and cattle.

Petapa is a town of at least five hundred inhabitants very rich, who suffer also some Spaniards to dwell amongst them, from whom also those Indians have learned to live and thrive in the world. This town is the passage from Comayagua, St Salvador, Nicaragua, and Costa Rica, and hath got great wealth by the constant goers and comers. It is esteemed one of the pleasantest towns belonging unto Guatemala, for a great lake of fresh water near unto it, which is full of fish, especially crabs, and a fish called *mojarra*, which is much like unto a mullet (though not altogether so big) and eateth like it. In this town there is a certain number of Indians appointed, who are to fish for the city, and on Wednesdays, Fridays, and Saturdays, are bound to carry such a quantity to Guatemala, of crabs and *mojarras*, as the *corregidor* and *regidores*, mayor and aldermen (who are but eight) shall command weekly to be brought.

This town Petapa is so called from two Indian words, *Petap*, which signifieth a mat, and *ha*, which signifieth water, and a mat being the chief part of an Indian's bed, it is as much as to say a bed of water, from the smoothness, plainness, and calmness of the water of the lake. There liveth in it a principal family of Indians, who are said to descend from the ancient kings of those parts, and now by the Spaniards are graced with the noble name of Guzman; out of this family is chosen one to be Governor of the town with subordination unto the city and Chancery of Guatemala. Don Bernabe de Guzman was Governor in my time, and had been many years before, and governed very wisely and discreetly, till with old age he came to lose his sight; and in his place entered his son Don Pedro de Guzman, of whom the rest of the Indians stood in great awe, as formerly they had to his father. Had not these Indians been given to drunkenness (as most Indians are) they might have governed a town of Spaniards. This Governor hath many privileges granted unto him (though none to wear a sword, or rapier, as may the Governor of Chiapa of the Indians) and appoints by turn some of the town to wait and attend on him at dinner and supper, others to look to his horses, others to fish for him, others to bring him wood for his house spending, others to bring him meat for his horses; and yet after all this his attendance, he attends and waits on the friar that lives in the town, and doth nothing concerning the governing of the town and executing of justice but what the friar alloweth and adviseth to be done. There is also great service appointed for this friar, of fishermen, and other attendants in his house, who liveth as stately as any bishop. Most trades belonging to a well settled commonwealth are here exercised by these Indians.

As for herbage, and garden-fruits, and requisites, it hath whatsoever may be found, or desired in the city of Guatemala.

The church treasure is very great, there being many sodalities of Our Lady and other their saints, which are enriched with crowns, and chains, and bracelets, besides the lamps, censers, and silver candlesticks belonging unto the altars. Upon Michaelmas Day is the chief fair and feast of the town, which is dedicated unto St Michael, whither many merchants resort from Guatemala to buy and sell; in the afternoon, and the next day following, bull-baiting is the common sport for that feast with some Spaniards and blackamoors on horseback, and other Indians on foot, who commonly being drunk, some venture, some lose their lives in the sport. Besides this general concourse of people every year at that time, there is every day at five o'clock in the afternoon a *tianguez* or market, upheld by the concourse of the Indians of the town among themselves. Besides the lake, there runneth by this town a river, which in places is easily waded over, and waters the fruits, gardens, and other plantations, and drives a mill which serves most of the valley to grind their wheat.

Within a mile and a half of this town there is a rich *ingenio* or farm of sugar belonging to one Sebastian de Savaletta, a Biscayan born, who came at first very poor into that country, and served one of his countrymen; but with his good industry and pains he began to get a mule or two to traffic with about the country, till at last he increased his stock to a whole *requa* of mules, and from thence grew so rich that he bought much land about Petapa, which he found to be very fit for sugar, and from thence was encouraged to build a princely house, whither the best of Guatemala do resort for their recreation. This man maketh a great deal of sugar for the country, and sends every year much to Spain; he keepeth at least threescore slaves of his own for the work of his farm, is very generous in housekeeping, and is thought to be worth above five hundred thousand ducats. Within half a mile from him there is another farm of sugar, which is called but a *trapiche* belonging unto the Augustine friars of Guatemala, which keeps some twenty slaves, and is called a *trapiche* for that it grinds not the sugar cane with that device of the *ingenio*, but grinds a less quantity, and so makes not so much sugar as doth an *ingenio*. From hence three miles is the town of Amatitlan, near unto which standeth a greater *ingenio* of sugar than is that of Savaletta, and is called the *ingenio* of one Anis, because he first founded it, but now it belongeth unto one Pedro Crespo the postmaster of Guatemala; this *ingenio* seemeth to be a little town by itself for the many cottages and thatched houses of blackamoor slaves which belong unto it, who may be above a hundred, men, women, and children. The chief dwelling house is strong and capacious, and able to entertain a hundred lodgers. These three farms of sugar standing so near unto Guatemala enrich the city much, and occasion great trading from it to Spain.

The town of Amatitlan, though in it there live not so many Spaniards as in Petapa, yet there are in it more Indian families than in Petapa. The streets are more orderly made and framed like a chequer board, they are wide, broad, plain, and all upon dust and sand. This town also enjoyeth the commodity of the lake, and furnisheth with fish the city of Guatemala, upon those days before named of Petapa. And though it standeth out of the road-way, yet it is almost as rich as Petapa. For the Indians of it get much by the concourse of common people, and the gentry of Guatemala, who resort thither to certain baths of hot waters, which are judged and approved very wholesome for the body. This town also getteth much by the salt which here is made, or rather gathered by the lake side, which every morning appeareth like a hoary frost upon the ground, and is taken up and purified by the Indians, and proves very white and good. Besides what they get by the salt, they get also by the *requas* of mules in the valley, and about the country, which are brought to feed upon that salt earth a day, or half a day, until they be ready to burst (the owner paying sixpence a day for every mule) and it hath been found by experience that this makes them thrive and grow lusty and purgeth them better than any drench, or blood-letting. They have further great trading in cotton-wool, more abundance of fruits than Petapa, a fairer market-place with two extraordinary great elm-trees, under which the Indians daily meet at evening to buy and sell. The church of this town is as fair and beautiful as any about Guatemala, the riches and state whereof hath caused the Dominican friars since the year 1635 to make that place the head and priory over the other towns of the valley, and to build there a goodly and sumptuous cloister, in which in my time there was (for I told then most of it, and doubtless since it hath much increased) eight thousand ducats laid up in a chest, with three locks, for the common expenses of the cloister.

Thus, my Reader, I have led thee through the Valley of Mixco and Pinola, Petapa and Amatitlan, which in riches and wealth, what with the great trading in it, what with the sheep and cattle, what with the abundance of mules, what with three farms of sugar, what with the great farms of corn and wheat, what with the churches' treasures yields to no other place belonging unto the dominions of Guatemala I may not forget yet a double wheat harvest (as I may well term it) in this valley. The first being of a little kind of wheat, which they call *trigo tremesino* (a word compounded in Spanish from these two words *tres meses*, or from the Latin *tre menses*) which after three months' sowing is ripe and ready to cut down, and being sowed about the end of August, is commonly harvested in about the end of November, and although in the smallness of it, it seems to have but a little flour, yet it yields as much as their other sorts of wheat, and makes as white bread, though it keep not so well as that which is made of other wheat, but soon groweth stale and hard. The other harvest (which is of two sorts of wheat, one called *rubio*, or red wheat, the other called *blanquilleo*, or white like *Candia* wheat) followeth soon after this first of *tremesino*, for presently after Christmas everyone begins to bring their sickles into the field, where they do not only reap down their wheat, but instead of threshing it in barns, they cause it to be trod by mares enclosed within floors made on purpose in the fields; and when the wheat is trod out of the ears by the mares trampling, who are whipped round about the floors that they may not stand still, but tread it constantly and thoroughly; then the mares being let out of the floors, the wheat is winnowed from the chaff, and put up clean into sacks, and from the field carried to the barns; but the chaff and most of the straw is left to rot in the fields, which they esteem as good as dunging; and further set all the fields on fire, burning the stubble that is left a little before the time of the first showers of rain, which with the ashes left after the burning fatteth the ground, and by them is held the best way to husband or dung their ground. Others that will sow a new and woody piece of land, cause the trees, though timber trees, to be cut down, and sell not a stick of that wood (which is there so plentiful that they judge it would not quit their cost to carry it to Guatemala, though in England it would yield a thousand pounds) but they let it lie and dry, and before the winter rain begins they set on fire all the field, and burn that rich timber, with the ashes whereof that ground becomes so fat and fertile that where upon an acre we sow here three bushels of wheat, or upwards, they sow such ground so thin that they scarce dare

SURVEY OF WEST INDIES

venture a full bushel upon an acre, lest with too much spreading upon the ground it grow too thick, be lodged, and they lose their crop. The like they do unto the pasture of the valley; about the end of March, it is short and withered and dry, and they also set it on fire, which being burnt causeth a dismal sight, and prospect of a black valley; but after the first two or three showers it puts on again its green and pleasant garment, inviting the cattle, sheep, lambs, goats, and kids (which for a while were driven away to other pasturing) to return and sport again, to feed and rest in its new flourishing bosom.

But now it is time I return again back to the other end of this valley, to the Rio de las Vacas (from whence I have viewed the compass of it, and made my long digression from East to West, to the farthest town of Amatitlan) to shew thee, my Reader, the little part of thy way remaining unto Guatemala. True it is, from the hermitage of Our Lady there is a straight way through the middle of the valley leading almost to Amatitlan, and then turning up a hill out of the valley on the right hand, but that hath many ascents and descents, bottoms, falls and risings, and therefore is not the constant road, which from the hermitage pointed on the right hand, observing the town of Mixco, standing but five miles from Guatemala. From Mixco the way lieth up a hill, and leadeth to a town somewhat bigger than Mixco, of Indians called San Lucas, or St Luke, a cold town, but exceeding rich; the temper and coldness of it hath made it the storehouse, or granary, for all the city; for whereas below in the valley the wheat will not keep long without musting, and breeding a worm called *gurgojo*, such is the temper of this town of St Luke, that in it the wheat will keep two or three years ready threshed, with a little turning now and then; and as it lieth will give and yield (as experience taught me there) so that he that hath laid up in that town two hundred bushels of wheat, at the year's end shall find near upon two hundred and twenty bushels. This town therefore receives from the valley most of the harvest, and is full of what we call barns, but there are called *trojas*, without floors, but raised up with stacks and boards a foot or two from the ground, and covered with mats, whereon is laid the wheat, and by some rich monopolists from the city is kept and hoarded two and three years, until they find their best opportunity to bring it out to sale, at the rate of their own will and pleasure. From hence to Guatemala there is but three little leagues, and one only *barranca*, or bottom, and on every side of the way little petty towns, which they call *milpas*, consisting of some twenty cottages. In the middle of the way is the top of a hill, which discovereth all the city, and standeth as overmastering of it, as if with a piece or two of ordnance it would keep all Guatemala in awe. But besides this hill, which is the wide and open road, there stand yet forwarder on the right and left hand other mountains which draw nearer to the city, and what this top peradventure with too much distance, is not able to do or reach, the others certainly would reach with cannon shot, and command that far commanding city. Down this hill the way lies broad and wide, and as open as is the way down Barnet or Highgate Hill; and at the bottom it is more straitened between the mountains, for the space of a bow-shot, which passage also is craggy by reason of stones and some small pieces of rocks which lie in a brook of water that descends from the mountains, and runs towards the city. But at a little hermitage called St John, the way opens again itself, and sheweth Guatemala, welcoming the weary travellers with a pleasant prospect, and easing theirs, or their mules' or horses' feet, what with green walks, what with a sandy and gravelly road unto the city, which never shut gate against any goer or comer, nor forbad their entrance with any fenced walls, or watchmen's jealous questions, but

SURVEY OF WEST INDIES

freely and gladly entertains them either by the back side of the Dominican's cloister, or by the church and nunnery called the Conception. And thus, my Reader, and countryman, I have brought and guided thee from the gulf unto Guatemala, shewing what that way is most remarkable.

I shall not now shew thee any more of this city's dominions toward Nicaragua and the South (having already shewed thee the way as far as Realejo) leaving that until I come to tell thee of my journey homewards, which I made that way. There remains yet the country of the Vera Paz and the way unto it to discover, and so to close up this chapter. The Vera Paz is so called, for that the Indians of that country hearing how the Spaniards had conquered Guatemala, and did conquer the country round about, wheresoever they came, yielded themselves peaceably and without any resistance unto the government of Spain. This country formerly had a bishop to itself distinct from Guatemala, but now is made one bishopric with that. It is governed by an *Alcalde Mayor*, or High Justice sent from Spain, with subordination unto the Court of Guatemala. The head or shire town of it is called Coban, where is a cloister of Dominican friars, and the common place of residence of the *Alcalde Mayor*. All this country as yet is not subdued by the Spaniards, who have now and then some strong encounters with the barbarous and heathen people, which lie between this country and Yucatan; and fain would the Spaniards conquer them, that they might make way through them unto a town called Campin belonging to Yucatan, and settle commerce and traffic by land with that country, which is thought would be a great furtherance to the country and city of Guatemala, and a safer way to convey their goods to Havana than by the gulf, for oftentimes the ships that go from the gulf to Havana are met with by the Hollanders and surprised. But as yet the Spaniards have not been able to bring to pass this their design, by reason they have found strong resistance from the heathenish people, and a hot service to attempt the conquering of them. Yet there was a friar a great acquaintance of mine, called Friar Francisco Moran, who ventured his life among those barbarians, and with two or three Indians went on foot through that country, until he came unto Campin, where he found a few Spaniards, who wondered at his courage and boldness in coming that way. This friar came back again to Coban and Vera Paz, relating how the barbarians hearing him speak their language, and finding him kind, loving, and courteous to them, used him also kindly, fearing (as he said) that if they should kill him, the Spaniards would never let them be at rest and quiet until they had utterly destroyed them. He related when he came back, that the country which the barbarians inhabit is better than any part of the Vera Paz, which is subject to the Spaniards, and spoke much of a valley where is a great lake, and about it a town of Indians, which he judged to be of at least twelve thousand inhabitants, the cottages lying in a distance one from another. This friar hath writ of this country, and hath gone to Spain to the Court to motion the conquering of it, for the profit and commodity that may ensue both to Guatemala and Yucatan, if a way were opened thither. But though as yet on that side the Spaniards and the country of the Vera Paz be straightened by that heathenish people, yet on the other side it hath free passage unto the gulf, and trade there when the ships do come, carrying fowls and what other provision the country will afford for the ships, and bringing from thence wines and other Spanish wares unto Coban. This country is very hilly and craggy, and though there be some big towns in it, they are not above three or four that are considerable.

The chief commodities are *achiote* (which is the best of all the country belonging to Guatemala) and *cacao*, cotton-wool, honey, *cañafistula*, and *zarzaparrilla*, great store of maize, but no wheat, much wax, plenty of fowls and birds of all coloured feathers, wherewith the Indians make some curious works, but not like unto those of Michoacan; here are also abundance of parrots, apes and monkeys which breed in the mountains. The way from Guatemala to this country is that which hitherto hath been spoken of from the gulf, as far as the town of St Luke; and from thence the way keeps on the hills and mountains which lie on the side of the Valley of Mixco. These hills are called Sacatepequez, (compounded of *Sacate* and *Tepec*, the latter signifying a hill, and the former, herb or grass, and thus joined they signify mountains of grass) and among them are these chief towns, first Santiago or St James, a town of five hundred families, secondly, San Pedro or St Peter, consisting of six hundred families, thirdly St Juan, or St John, consisting also of at least six hundred families, and fourthly Sto Domingo Senaco, or St Dominic of Senaco, being of three hundred families. These four towns are very rich, and the two last very cold, the two first are warmer; there are about them many farms of corn and good wheat, besides the Indian maize. These Indians are somewhat of more courage than those of other towns, and in my time were like to rise up against the Spaniards for their unmerciful tyranny over them. The churches are exceeding rich; in the town of Santiago, there was living in my time one Indian, who for only vainglory had bestowed the worth of six thousand ducats upon that church, and yet afterwards this wretch was found to be a wizard and idolater. These Indians get much money by letting out great tufts of feathers, which the Indians use in their dances upon the feasts of the dedication of their towns. For some of the great tufts may have at least threescore long feathers of divers colours; for every feather hiring they have half a real, besides what price they set to every feather if any should chance to be lost.

THE ENGLISH-AMERICAN

From the town of St John, which is the furthest, the way lies plain and pleasant unto a little village of some twenty cottages, called St Raymundo or St Raymond, from whence there is a good day's journey up and down *barrancas*, or bottoms unto a *rancho*, or lodge standing by a river side, which is the same river that passeth by the town of Acacabastlan spoken of before. From this is an ascent or a very craggy and rocky mountain, called the Mountain of Rabinal, where are steps cut out in the very rocks for the mules' feet, and slipping on one or the other side, they fall surely down the rocks, breaking their necks, and mangling all their limbs and joints; but this danger continueth not long nor extendeth above a league and a half, and in the top and worst of this danger there is the comfort of a goodly valley, called El Valle de San Nicholas, St Nicholas his Valley, from an *estancia* called St Nicholas belonging to the Dominicans' cloister of Coban. This valley though it must not compare with that of Mixco and Pinola, yet next after it, it may well take place for only three things considerable in it. The first is an *ingenio* of sugar, called San Geronymo, or St Hierome, belonging unto the Dominicans' cloister of Guatemala, which indeed goeth beyond that spoken of of Amatitlan, both for abundance of sugar made there and sent by mules to Guatemala over that rocky mountain, and for multitude of slaves living in it under the command of two friars, and for the excellent horses bred there, which are incomparably the best of all the country of Guatemala for mettle, and gallantry, and therefore (though mules are commonly used for burdens) are much desired and looked after by the gallants and gentry of the city, who make it a great part of their honour to prance about the streets. The second thing in this valley is the *estancia* or farm of St Nicholas which is as famous for breeding of mules as is St Hierome for horses. The third ornament to it is a town of Indians, called Rabinal, of at least eight hundred families, which hath all that heart can wish for pleasure and life of man. It inclineth rather to heat than cold, but the heat is moderate and much qualified with the many cool and shady walks. There is not any Indian fruit which is not there to be found, besides the fruits of Spain, as oranges, lemons, sweet and sour, citrons, pomegranates, grapes, figs, almonds, and dates; the only want of wheat is not a want to them that mind bread of wheat more than of maize, for in two days it is easily brought from the towns of Sacatepequez. For flesh, it hath beef, mutton, kid, fowls, turkeys, quails, partridges, rabbits, pheasants, and for fish it hath a river running by the houses, which yieldeth plenty both great and small. The Indians of this town are much like unto those of Chiapa of the Indians for bravery, for feasting, for riding of horses, and shewing themselves in sports and pastimes. This town my friend Friar John Baptist, after he had been Prior of many places, and especially of Chiapa and Guatemala, chose to live in to enjoy quietness, pleasure, and content; and in this town was I feasted by him in such a sumptuous, prodigal and lavishing way, as truly might make poor mendicant friars ashamed to come so near unto princes in vanity of life and diet.

From this valley unto the Vera Paz, or Coban, the head town of it, there is nothing considerable, save only one town more called St Christoval or St Christopher, which enjoyeth now a pleasant lake, and bottomless, as is reported. Formerly there being no lake at all, in a great earthquake the earth there opened, and swallowed up many houses, leaving this lake which ever since hath continued. From hence to Coban the ways are bad and mountainous, yet such as through the worst of them those country mules with heavy burdens easily go through. And thus with my pen, Reader, have I gone through most of the bounds and limits of Guatemala, which is more furnished with gallant towns of Indians than is any part of all America;

and doubtless were the Indians warlike, industrious, active for war or weapons, no part in all America might be stronger in people than Guatemala. But they being kept under and oppressed by the Spaniards, and no weapons allowed them, not so much as their natural bows and arrows, much less guns, pistols, muskets, swords, or pikes, their courage is gone, their affections alienated from the Spaniards, and so the Spaniards might very well fear that if their country should be invaded, the multitude of their Indian people would prove to them a multitude of enemies, either running away to another side; or forced to help, would be to them but as the help of so many flies.

CHAPTER XIV

Shewing the condition, quality, fashion, and behaviour of the Indians of the country of Guatemala since the Conquest, and especially of their feasts and yearly solemnities

THE condition of the Indians of this country of Guatemala is as sad, and as much to be pitied as of any Indians in America, for that I may say it is with them, in some sort, as it was with Israel in Egypt. Though it is true there ought not to be any comparison made betwixt the Israelites and the Indians, those being God's people, these not as yet; nevertheless the comparison may well hold in the oppression of the one and the other, and in the manner and cause of the oppression, that being with bitterness, rigour, and hard bondage, and lest they should multiply and increase too much. Certain it is, these Indians suffer great oppression from the Spaniards, live in great bitterness, are under hard bondage, and serve with great rigour; and all this because they are at least a thousand of them for one Spaniard. They daily multiply and increase, in children and wealth, and therefore are feared lest they should be too mighty, and either rise up of them-

SURVEY OF WEST INDIES

selves, or join themselves to any enemy against their oppressors; for both which fears and jealousies they are not allowed the use of any weapons or arms, no not their bows and arrows, which their ancestors formerly used, so that as hereby the Spaniards are secured from any hurt or annoyance from them as an unarmed people, so may any other nation that shall be encouraged to invade that land be secure also from the Indians, consequently the Spaniards' own policy for themselves against the Indians may be their greatest ruin and destruction, being a great people and yet no people; for the abundance of their Indians would be to them as no people, and they themselves (who out of their few towns and cities live but here and there, too thinly scattered upon so great and capacious a land) would be but a handful for any reasonable army; and of that handful very few would be found able or fitting men, and those able men would do little without the help of guns and ordnance; and if their own oppressed people, blackamoors and Indians (which themselves have always feared) should side against them, soon would they be swallowed up both from within and from without. And by this it may easily appear how ungrounded they are, who say it is harder to conquer America now than in Cortez his time, for that there are now both Spaniards and Indians to fight against, and then there were none but bare and naked Indians. This I say is a false ground, for then there were Indians trained up in wars one against another, who knew well to use their bows and arrows, and darts, and other weapons, and were desperate in their fights and single combats, as may appear out of the histories of them; but now they are cowardized, oppressed, unarmed, soon frighted with the noise of a musket, nay with a sour and grim look of a Spaniard, so from them there is no fear. Neither can there be from the Spaniards, who from all the vast dominions of Guatemala are not able to raise five thousand able fighting men, nor to defend so many passages as lie open in several parts of that country, which the wider and greater it is might be advantageous to an enemy, and while the Spaniard in one place might oppose his strength, in many other places might his land be overrun by a foreign nation; nay by their own slaves the blackamoors who doubtless to be set at liberty would side against them in any such occasion; and lastly, the Creoles who also are sore oppressed by them, would rejoice in such a day, and yield rather to live with freedom and liberty under a foreign people than to be longer oppressed by those of their own blood.

The miserable condition of the Indians of that country is such that though the Kings of Spain have never yielded to what some would have, that they should be slaves, yet their lives are as full of bitterness as is the life of a slave. For which I have known myself some of them that have come home from toiling and moiling with Spaniards, after many blows, some wounds, and little or no wages, who have sullenly and stubbornly lain down upon their beds, resolving to die rather than to live any longer a life so slavish, and have refused to take either meat or drink or anything else comfortable and nourishing, which their wives have offered unto them, that so by pining and starving they might consume themselves. Some I have by good persuasions encouraged to life rather than to a voluntary and wilful death; others there have been that would not be persuaded, but in that wilful way have died.

The Spaniards that live about that country (especially the farmers of the Valley of Mixco, Pinola, Petapa, Amatitlan, and those of the Sacatepequez) allege that all their trading and farming is for the good of the commonwealth, and therefore whereas there are not Spaniards enough for so ample and large a country to do all their work, and all are not able to buy slaves and blackamoors, they stand in need of the Indians' help to serve them for their pay and hire; whereupon it hath been considered that a partition of Indian labourers be made every Monday, or Sunday in the afternoon to the Spaniards, according to the farms they occupy, or according to their several employments, calling, and trading with mules, or any other way. So that for such and such a district there is named an officer, who is called *juez repartidor*, who according to a list made of every farm, house, and person, is to give so many Indians by the week. And here is a door opened to the President of Guatemala, and to the judges, to provide well for their menial servants, whom they commonly appoint for this office, which is thus performed by them. They name the town and place of their meeting upon Sunday or Monday, to the which themselves and the Spaniards of that district do resort. The Indians of the several towns are to have in a readiness so many labourers as the Court of Guatemala hath appointed to be weekly taken out of such a town, who are conducted by an Indian officer to the town of general meeting; and when they come thither with their tools, their spades, shovels, bills, or axes, with their provision of victuals for a week (which are commonly some dry cakes of maize, puddings of *frijoles*, or French beans, and a little chilli or biting long pepper, or a bit of cold meat for the first day or two) and with beds on their backs (which is only a coarse woollen mantle to wrap about them when they lie on the bare ground) then are they shut up in the town-house, some with blows, some with spurnings, some with boxes on the ear, if presently they go not in.

Now all being gathered together, and the house filled with them, the *juez repartidor*, or officer, calls by the order of the list such and such a Spaniard, and also calls out of the house so many Indians as by the Court are commanded to be given him (some are allowed three, some four, some ten, some fifteen, some twenty, according to their employments) and delivereth unto the Spaniard his Indians, and so to all the rest, till they be all served; who when they receive their Indians, take from them a tool, or their mantles, to secure them that they run not away; and for every Indian delivered unto them, they give unto the *juez repartidor*, or officer, half a real, which is threepence an Indian for his fees, which mounteth yearly to him to a great deal of money; for some officers make a partition or distribution of four hundred, some of two hundred, some of three hundred Indians every week, and carrieth home with him so many half hundred reals for one, or half a day's work. If complaint be made by any Spaniard that such and such an Indian did run away from him, and served him not the week past, the Indian must be brought, and surely tied to a post by his hands in the market-place, and there be whipped upon his bare back. But if the poor Indian complain that the Spaniards cozened and cheated him of his shovel, axe, bill, mantle, or wages, no justice shall be executed against the cheating Spaniard, neither shall the Indian be righted, though it is true the order runs equally in favour of both Indian and Spaniard. Thus are the poor Indians sold for threepence apiece for a whole week's slavery, not permitted to go home at nights unto their wives, though their work lie not above a mile from the town where they live; nay some are carried ten or twelve miles from their home, who must not return till Saturday night late, and must that week do whatsoever their master pleaseth to command them. The wages appointed them will scarce find them meat and drink, for they are not allowed a real a day, which is but sixpence, and with that they are to find themselves, but for six days' work and diet they are to have five reals, which is half a crown. This same order is observed in the city of Guatemala, and towns of Spaniards, where to every family that wants the service of an Indian or Indians, though it be but to fetch water and wood on their backs, or to go of errands, is allowed the like service from the nearest Indian towns.

It would grieve a Christian's heart to see how by some cruel Spaniards in that week's service those poor wretches are wronged and abused; some visiting their wives at home, whilst their poor husbands are digging and delving; others whipping them for their slow working; others wounding them with their swords, or breaking their heads for some reasonable and well grounded answer in their own behalf; others stealing from them their tools; others cheating them of half, others of all their wages; alleging that their service cost them half a real, and yet their work not well performed. I knew some who made a common practice of this, when their wheat was sown, and they had little to do for the Indians; yet they would have home as many as were due unto their farm, and on Monday and Tuesday would make them cut and bring them on their backs as much wood as they needed all that week, and then on Wednesday at noon (knowing the great desire of the Indians to go home to their wives, for the which they would give anything) would say unto them: ' What will you give me now, if I let you go home to do your own work ?' Whereunto the Indians would joyfully reply and answer, some that they would give a real, others two reals, which they would take and send them home, and so would have much work done, wood to serve their house a week, and money as much as would buy them meat, and *cacao* for chocolate two weeks together; and thus from the poor Indians do those unconscionable Spaniards practice a cheap and lazy way of living. Others will sell them away for that week unto a neighbour that hath present need of work, demanding reals apiece for every Indian, which he that buyeth them will be sure to defray out of their wages. So likewise are they in a slavish bondage and readiness for all passengers and travellers, who in any town may demand unto the next town as many Indians do go with his mules, or to carry on their backs a heavy burden as he shall need, who at the journey's end will pick some quarrel with them, and so send them back with blows and stripes without any pay at all. A *petaca*, or leathern trunk, and chest of above a hundredweight, they will make those wretches to carry on their backs a whole day, nay some two or three days together, which they do by tying the chest on each side with ropes, having a broad leather in the middle, which they cross over the forepart of their head, or over their forehead, hanging thus the weight upon their heads and brows, which at their journey's end hath made the blood stick in the foreheads of some, galling and pulling off the skin, and marking them in the fore-top of their heads, who as they are called *tamemez*, so are easily known in a town by their baldness, that leather girt having worn off all their hair. With these hard usages yet do those poor people make a shift to live amongst the Spaniards, but so that with anguish of heart they are still crying out to God for justice, and for liberty, whose only comfort is in their priests and friars, who many times do quiet them when they would rise up in mutiny, and for their own ends do often prevail over them with fair and cunning persuasions, to bear and suffer for God's sake, and for the good of the commonwealth that hard task and service which is laid upon them. And though in all seasons, wet and dry, cold and hot, and in all ways plain and mountainous, green and dirty, dusty and stony, they must perform this hard service to their commanding masters, their apparel and clothing is but such as may cover the nakedness of their body, nay in some it is such torn rags as will not cover half their nakedness.

Their ordinary clothing is a pair of linen or woollen drawers broad and open at the knees, without shoes (though in their journeys some will put on leathern sandals to keep the soles of their feet) or stockings, without any doublet, a short coarse shirt, which reacheth a little below their waist, and serves more for a doublet than for a shirt, and for a cloak a woollen or linen mantle (called *aiate*) tied with a knot over one shoulder, hanging down on the other side almost to the ground, with a twelvepenny or two shilling hat, which after one good shower of rain like paper falls about their necks and eyes; their bed they carry sometimes about them, which is that woollen mantle wherewith they wrap themselves about at night, taking off their shirt and drawers, which they lay under their head for a pillow; some will carry with them a short, slight, and light mat to lie, but those that carry it not with them, if they cannot borrow one of a neighbour, lie as willingly in their mantle upon the bare ground as a gentleman in England upon a soft down-bed, and thus do they soundly sleep, and loudly snort after a day's work, or after a day's journey with a hundred-weight upon their backs.

Those that are of the better sort, and richer, and who are not employed as *tamemez* to carry burdens, or as labourers to work for Spaniards, but keep at home following their own farms, or following their own mules about the country, or following their trades and callings in their shops, or governing the towns, as *alcaldes*, or *alguaziles*, officers of justice, may go a little better apparelled, but after the same manner. For some will have their drawers with a lace at the bottom, or wrought with some coloured silk or crewel, so likewise the mantle about them shall have either a lace, or some work of birds on it; some will wear a cut linen doublet, others shoes, but very few stockings or bands about their necks; and for their beds, the best Indian Governor or the richest, who may be worth four or five thousand ducats, will have little more than the poor *tamemez*; for they lie upon boards, or canes bound together, and raised from the ground, whereon they lay a broad and handsome mat, and at their heads for man and wife two little stumps of wood for bolsters, whereon they lay their shirts and mantles and other clothes for pillows, covering themselves with a broader blanket than is their mantle, and thus hardly would Don Bernabe de Guzman the Governor of Petapa lie, and so do all the best of them. The women's attire is cheap and soon put on; for most of them also go barefoot, the richer and better sort wear shoes, with broad ribbons for shoe-strings, and for a petticoat, they tie about their waist a woollen mantle, which in the better sort is wrought with divers colours, but not sewed at all, pleated, or gathered in, but as they tie it with a list about them; they wear no shift next their body, but cover their nakedness with a kind of surplice (which they call *guaipil*) which hangs loose from their shoulders down a little below their waist, with open short sleeves, which cover half their arms; this *guaipil* is curiously wrought, especially in the bosom, with cotton, or feathers. The richer sort of them wear bracelets and bobs about their wrists and necks; their hair is gathered up with fillets, without any coif or covering, except it be the better sort. When they go to church or abroad, they put upon their heads a veil of linen, which hangeth almost to the ground, and this is that which costs them most of all their attire, for that commonly it is of Holland or some good linen brought from Spain, or fine linen brought from China, which the better sort wear with a lace about. When they are at home at work they commonly take off their *guaipil*, or surplice, discovering the nakedness of their breasts and body. They lie also in their beds as do their husbands, wrapped up only with a mantle, or with a blanket.

Their houses are but poor thatched cottages, without any upper rooms, but commonly one or two only rooms below, in the one they dress their meat in the middle of it, making a compass for fire, with two or three stones, without any other chimney to convey the smoke away, which spreading itself about the room filleth the thatch and the rafters so with soot that all the room seemeth to be a chimney. The next unto it is not free from smoke and blackness, where sometimes are four or five beds according to the family. The poorer sort have but one room, where they eat, dress their meat, and sleep. Few there are that set any locks upon their doors, for they fear no robbing nor stealing, neither have they in their houses much to lose, earthen pots, and pans, and dishes, and cups to drink their chocolate being the chief commodities in their house. There is scarce any house which hath not also in the yard a stew, wherein they bathe themselves with hot water, which is their chief physic when they feel themselves distempered.

Among themselves they are in every town divided into tribes, which have one chief head, to whom all that belong unto that tribe do resort in any difficult matters, who is bound to aid, protect, defend, counsel, and appear for the rest of his tribe before the officers of justice in any wrong that is like to be done unto them. When any is to be married, the father of the son that is to take a wife out of another tribe goeth unto the head of his tribe to give him warning of his son's marriage with such a maid. Then that head meets with the head of the maid's tribe, and they confer about it. The business commonly is in debate a quarter of a year; all which time the parents of the youth or man are with gifts to buy the maid; they are to be at the charges of all that is spent in eating and drinking when the heads of the two tribes do meet with the rest of the kindred of each side, who sometimes sit in conference a whole day, or most part of a night. After many days and nights thus spent, and a full trial being made of the one and other side's affection, if they chance to disagree about the marriage, then is the tribe and parents of the maid to restore back all that the other side hath spent and given. They give no portions with their daughters, but when they die their goods and lands are equally divided among their sons. If anyone want a house to live in, or will repair and thatch his house anew, notice is given to the heads of the tribes, who warm all the town to come to help in the work, and everyone is to bring a bundle of straw, and other materials, so that in one day with the help of many they finish a house, without any charges more than of chocolate, which they minister in great cups as big as will hold above a pint, not putting in any costly materials, as do the Spaniards, but only a little aniseed, and chilli, or Indian pepper; or else they half fill the cup with *atole*, and pour upon it as much chocolate as will fill the cup and colour it.

In their diet the poorer sort are limited many times to a dish of *frijoles*, or Turkey beans, either black or white (which are there in very great abundance, and are kept dry for all the year) boiled with chilli; and if they can have this, they hold themselves well satisfied; with these beans, they make also dumplings, first boiling the bean a little, and then mingling it with a mass of maize, as we do mingle currants in our cakes, and so boil again the *frijoles* with the dumpling of maize mass, and so eat it hot, or keep it cold; but this and all whatsoever else they eat, they either eat it with green biting chilli, or else they dip it in water and salt, wherein is bruised some of that chilli. But if their means will not reach to *frijoles*, their ordinary fare and diet is their *tortillas* (so they call thin round cakes made of the dough and mass of maize) which they eat hot from an earthen pan, whereon they are soon baked with one turning over the fire; and these they eat alone either with chilli and salt, and dipping them in water and salt with a little bruised chilli. When their maize is green and tender, they boil some of those whole stalks or clusters, whereon the maize groweth with the leaf about, and so casting a little salt about it, they eat it. I have often eat of this, and found it as dainty as our young green peas, and very nourishing, but it much increaseth the blood. Also of this green and tender maize they make a furmety, boiling the maize in some of the milk which they have first taken out of it by bruising it. The poorest Indian never wants this diet, and is well satisfied as long as his belly is thoroughly filled.

But the poorest that live in such towns where flesh meat is sold will make a hard shift but that when they come from work on Saturday night they will buy one half real, or a real worth of fresh meat to eat on the Lord's day. Some will buy a good deal at once, and keep it long by dressing it into *tasajos*, which are bundles of flesh, rolled up and tied fast, which they do when, for example's sake, they have from a leg of beef sliced off from the bone all the flesh with the knife, after the length, form, and thinness of a line, or rope. Then they take the flesh and salt it, (which being sliced and thinly cut, soon takes salt) and hang it up in their yards like a line from post to post, or from tree to tree, to the wind for a whole week, and then they hang it in the smoke another week, and after roll it up in small bundles, which become as hard as a stone, and so as they need it they wash it, boil it and eat it. This is America's powdered beef, which they call *tasajo*, whereof I have often eaten, and the Spaniards eat much of it, especially those that trade about the country with mules; nay this *tasajo* is a great commodity, and hath made many a Spaniard rich, who carry a mule or two loaden with these *tasajos* in small parcels and bundles to those towns where is no flesh at all sold, and there they exchange them for other commodities among the Indians, receiving peradventure for one *tasajo* or bundle, (which cost them but the half part of a farthing) as much *cacao* as in other places they sell for a real or sixpence. The richer sort of people will fare better, for if there be fish or flesh to be had they will have it, and eat most greedily of it, and will not spare their fowls and turkeys from their own bellies. These also will now and then get a wild deer, shooting it with their bows and arrows. And when they have killed it, they let it lie in the wood in some hole or bottom covered with leaves for the space of about a week, until it stink and begin to be full of worms; then they bring it home, cut it out into joints, and parboil it with an herb which groweth there somewhat like unto our tansy, which they say sweeteneth it again, and maketh the flesh eat tender, and as white as a piece of turkey. Thus parboiled, they hang up the joints in the smoke for awhile, and then boil it again, when they eat it, which is commonly dressed with red Indian pepper; and this is the venison of America, whereof I have sometimes eaten, and found it white and short, but never durst be too bold with it, not that I found any evil taste in it, but that the apprehension of the worms and maggots which formerly had been in it troubled much my stomach.

These Indians that have little to do at home, and are not employed in the weekly service under the Spaniards in their hunting, will look seriously for hedgehogs, which are just like unto ours, though certainly ours are not meat for any Christian. They are full of pricks and bristles like ours, and are found in woods and fields, living in holes, and as they say feed upon nothing but ants [emmets] and their eggs, and upon dry rotten sticks, herbs, and roots; of these they eat much, the flesh being as white and sweet as a rabbit, and as fat as is a January hen kept up and fatted in a coop. Of this meat I have also eaten, and confess it is a dainty dish there, though I will not say the same of a hedgehog here; for what here may be poison, there may be good and lawful meat, by some accidental difference in the creature itself, and in that which it feeds upon, or in the temper of the air and climate. This meat not only the Indians but the best of the Spaniards feed on it; and it is so much esteemed

SURVEY OF WEST INDIES

of, that because in Lent they are commonly found, the Spaniards will not be deprived of it, but do eat it also then, alleging that it is no flesh (though in the eating it be in fatness and in taste and in all like unto flesh) for that it feeds not upon anything that is very nourishing, but chiefly upon ants' eggs, and dry sticks. It is a great point of controversy amongst their divines, some hold it lawful, others unlawful for that time; it seems the pricks and bristles of the Indian hedgehog prick their consciences with a foolish scruple.

Another kind of meat they feed much on which is called *iguana*; of these some are found in the waters, others upon the land. They are longer than a rabbit, and like unto a scorpion, with some green, some black scales on their backs. Those upon the land will run very fast, like lizards, and will climb up trees like squirrels, and breed in the roots of trees or in stone walls. The sight of them is enough to affright one; and yet when they are dressed and stewed in broth with a little spice, they make a dainty broth, and eat also as white as a rabbit, nay the middle bone is made just like the backbone of a rabbit. They are dangerous meat, if not thoroughly boiled, and they had almost cost me my life for eating too much of them, not being stewed enough. There are also many water and land tortoises, which the Indians find out for themselves, and also relish exceeding well unto the Spaniard's palate.

As for drinking, the Indians generally are much given unto it; and drink if they have nothing else of their poor and simple chocolate, without sugar or many compounds, or of *atole*, until their bellies be ready to burst. But if they can get any drink that will make them mad drunk, they will not give it over as long as a drop is left, or a penny remains in their purse to purchase it. Among themselves they use to make such drinks as are in operation far stronger than wine; and these they confection in such great jars as come from Spain, wherein they put some little quantity of water, and fill up the jar with some molasses or juice of the sugar-cane, or some honey for to sweeten it; then for the strengthening of it, they put roots and leaves of tobacco, with other kind of roots which grow there, and they know to be strong in operation, nay in some places I have known where they have put in a live toad, and so closed up the jar for a fortnight, or month's space, till all that they have put in him be thoroughly steeped and the toad consumed, and the drink well strengthened, then they open it, and call their friends to the drinking of it (which commonly they do in the night time, lest their priest in the town should have notice of them in the day), which they never leave off until they be mad and raging drunk. This drink they call *chicha*, which stinketh most filthily, and certainly is the cause of many Indians' death, especially where they use the toad's poison with it. Once I was informed living in Mixco, of a great meeting that was appointed in an Indian's house; and I took with me the officers of justice of the town to search that Indian's house, where I found four jars of *chicha* not yet opened; I caused them to be taken out, and broken in the street before his door, and the filthy *chicha* to be poured out, which left such a stinking scent in my nostrils, that with the smell of it, or apprehension of its loathsomeness, I fell to vomiting, and continued sick almost a whole week after.

Now the Spaniards, knowing this inclination of the Indians unto drunkenness, do herein much abuse and wrong them; though true it is, there is a strict order, even to the forfeiting of the wine of anyone who shall presume to sell wine in a town of Indians, with a money mulct besides. Yet for all this the baser and poorer sort of Spaniards for their lucre and gain contemning authority, will go out from Guatemala to the towns of Indians about, and carry such wine to sell and inebriate the natives as may be very advantageous to themselves; for of one jar of wine they will make two at least, confectioning it with honey and water, and other strong drugs which are cheap to them, and strongly operative upon the poor and weak Indians' heads, and this they will sell for current Spanish wine, with such pint and quart measures as never were allowed by justice order, but by themselves invented. With such wine they soon intoxicate the poor Indians, and when they have made them drunk, then they will cheat them more, making them pay double for their quart measure; and when they see they can drink no more, then they will cause them to lie down and sleep, and in the meanwhile will pick their pockets. This is a common sin among those Spaniards of Guatemala, and much practised in the city upon the Indians, when they come thither to buy or sell. Those that keep the *bodegones* (so are called the houses that sell wine, which are no better than a chandler's shop, for besides wine they sell candles, fish, salt, cheese, and bacon) will commonly entice in the Indians, and make them drunk, and then pick their pockets, and turn them out of doors with blows and stripes, if they will not fairly depart. There was in Guatemala in my time one of these bodegoners, or shopkeeper of wine and small ware, named John Ramos, who by thus cheating and tippling poor Indians (as it was generally reported) was worth two hundred thousand ducats, and in my time gave with a daughter that was married, eight thousand ducats. No Indian should pass by his door but he would call him in, and play upon him as aforesaid. In my time a Spanish farmer, neighbour of mine in the Valley of Mixco, chanced to send to Guatemala his Indian servants with half a dozen mules laden with wheat to a merchant, with whom he had agreed before for the price, and ordered the money to be sent unto him by his servant (whom he had kept six years, and ever found him trusty). The wheat being delivered, and the money received (the which mounted to ten pound, sixteen shillings, every mule carrying six bushels, at twelve reals a bushel, as was then the price) the Indian with another mate of his walking along the streets to buy some small commodities, passed by John Ramos his shop, or *bodegon*, who enticing him and his mate in, soon tripped up their heels with a little confectioned wine for that purpose, and took away all his money from the entrusted Indian, and beat them out of his house, who thus drunk being forced to ride home, the Indian that had received the money fell from his mule and broke his neck; the other got home without his mate or money. The farmer prosecuted John Ramos in the court for his money, but Ramos being rich and abler to bribe than the farmer, got off very well, and so had done formerly in almost the like cases. These are but peccadilloes among those Spaniards, to make drunk, rob, and occasion the poor Indian's death; whose death with them is no more regarded nor vindicated than the death of a sheep or bullock that falls into a pit.

And thus having spoken of apparel, houses, eating and drinking, it remains that I say somewhat of their civility, and religion of those who lived under the government of the Spaniards. From the Spaniards they have borrowed their civil government, and in all towns they have one, or two, *alcaldes*, with more or less *regidores* (who are as aldermen or jurats amongst us) and some *alguaziles*, more or less, who are as constables, to execute the orders of the *alcalde* (who is a mayor) with his brethren. In towns of three or four hundred families, or upwards, there are commonly two *alcaldes*, six *regidores*, two *alguaziles mayores*, and six under, or petty, *alguaziles*. And some towns are privileged with an Indian Governor, who is above the *alcaldes* and all the rest of the officers. These are changed every year by new election, and are chosen by the Indians themselves, who take their turns by the tribes or kindreds, whereby they are divided. Their offices begin on New Year's Day, and after that day their election is carried to the city of Guatemala (if in that district it be made) or else to the heads of justice, or Spanish governors of the several provinces, who confirm the new election, and take account of the last year's expenses made by the other officers, who carry with them their town-book of accounts; and therefore for this purpose every town hath a clerk, or scrivener, called *escribano*, who commonly continueth many years in his office, by reason of the paucity and unfitness of Indian scriveners who are able to bear such a charge. This clerk hath many fees for his writings and informations, and accounts, as have the Spaniards, though not so much money or bribes, but a small matter, according to the poverty of the Indians. The Governor is also commonly continued many years, being some chief man among the Indians, except for his misdemeanours he be complained of, or the Indians in general do all stomach him.

Thus they being settled in a civil way of government they may execute justice upon all such Indians of their town as do notoriously and scandalously offend. They may imprison, fine, whip, and banish, but hang and quarter they may not; but must remit such cases to the Spanish governor. So likewise if a Spaniard passing by the town, or living in it, do trouble the peace, and misdemean himself, they may lay hold on him, and send him to the next Spanish justice, with a full information of his offence, but fine him, or keep him about one night in prison they may not. This order they have against Spaniards, but they dare not execute it, for a whole town standeth in awe of one Spaniard, and though he never so heinously offend, and be unruly, with oaths, threatenings, and drawing of his sword, he maketh them quake and tremble, and not presume to touch him; for they know if they do they shall have the worst, either by blows, or by some mis-information which he will give against them. And this hath been very often tried, for where Indians have by virtue of their order endeavoured to curb an unruly Spaniard in their town, some of them have been wounded, others beaten, and when they have carried the Spaniard before a Spanish justice and governor, he hath pleaded for what he hath done, saying it was in his own defence, or for his King and Sovereign, and that the Indians would have killed him, and began to mutiny all together against the Spanish authority and government, denying to serve him with what he needed for his way and journey; that they would not be slaves to give him or any Spaniard any attendance; and that they would make an end of him, and of all the Spaniards. With these and such-like false and lying mis-informations, the unruly Spaniards have often been believed, and too much upheld in their rude and uncivil misdemeanours, and the Indians bitterly curbed, and punished, and answer made them in such cases that if they had been killed for their mutiny and rebellion against the King, and his best subjects, they had been served well enough; and that if they gave not attendance unto the Spaniards that passed by their town, their houses should be fired, and they and their children utterly consumed. With such-like answers from the justices, and credency to what any base Spaniard shall inform against them, the poor Indians are fain to put up all wrongs done unto them, not daring to meddle with any Spaniard, be he never so unruly, by virtue of that order which they have against them.

Amongst themselves, if any complaint be made against any Indian, they dare not meddle with him until they call all his kindred, and especially the head of that tribe to which he belongeth; who if he and the rest together find him to deserve imprisonment, or whipping, or any other punishment, then the officers of justices, the *alcaldes* or mayors, and their brethren the jurats inflict upon him that punishment which all shall agree upon. But yet after judgment and sentence given, they have another, which is their last appeal, if they please, and that is to their priest and friar, who liveth in their town, by whom they will sometimes be judged, and undergo what punishment he shall think fittest. To the Church therefore they often resort in points of justice, thinking the priest knoweth more of law and equity than themselves; who sometimes reverseth what judgment hath been given in the town-house, blaming the officers for their partiality and passion against their poor brother, and setting free the party judged by them; which the priest does oftentimes, if such an Indian do belong to the church, or to the service of their house, or have any other relation to them, peradventure for their wife's sake, whom either they affect, or employ in washing, or making their chocolate. Such, and their husbands, may live lawless as long as the priest is in the town. And if when the priest is absent, they call them to trial for any misdemeanour, and whip, fine, or imprison (which occasion they will sometimes pick out on purpose), when the priest returns, they shall be sure to hear of it, and smart for it, yea, and the officers themselves peradventure be whipped in the church, by the priest's order and appointment; against whom they dare not speak, but willingly accept what stripes and punishment he layeth upon them, judging his wisdom, sentence, and punishing hand the wisdom, sentence, and hand of God; whom as they have been taught to be over all princes, judges, worldly officers, so likewise they believe (and have been so taught) that his priests and ministers are above theirs, and all worldly power and authority. It happened unto me living in the town of Mixco, that an Indian being judged to be whipped for some disorders which he committed, would not yield to the sentence, but appealed to me, saying he would have his stripes in the church, and by my order, for so he said his whipping would do him good as coming from the hand of God.

THE ENGLISH-AMERICAN

When he was brought unto me, I could not reverse the Indian's judgment, for it was just, and so caused him to be whipped, which he took very patiently and merrily, and after kissed my hands and gave me an offering of money for the good he said I had done unto his soul.

Besides this civility of justice amongst them, they live as in other civil and politic and well-governed commonwealths; for in most of their towns there are some that profess such trades as are practised among Spaniards. There are amongst them smiths, tailors, carpenters, masons, shoemakers, and the like. It was my fortune to set upon a hard and difficult building in a church of Mixco, where I desired to make a very broad and capacious vault over the chapel, which was the harder to be finished in a round circumference, because it depended upon a triangle, yet for this work I sought none but Indians, some of the town, some from other places, who made it so complete that the best and skilfullest workmen among the Spaniards had enough to wonder at it. So are most of their churches vaulted on the top, and all by Indians; they only in my time built a new cloister in the town of Amatitlan, which they finished with many arches of stone both in the lower walks and in the upper galleries, with as much perfection as the best cloister of Guatemala had before been built by the Spaniard. Were they more encouraged by the Spaniards, and taught better principles both for soul and body, doubtless they would among themselves make a very good commonwealth. For painting they are much inclined to it, and most of the pictures and altars of the country towns are their workmanship. In most of their towns they have a school, where they are taught to read, to sing, and some to write. To the church there do belong according as the town is in bigness, so many singers, and trumpeters, and waits, over whom the priest hath one officer, who is called *fiscal*; he goeth with a white staff with a little silver cross on the top to represent the church and shew that he is the priest's clerk and officer. When any case is brought to be examined by the priest, this *fiscal* or clerk executeth justice by the priest's order. He must be one that can read and write, and is commonly the master of music. He is bound upon the Lord's Day and other saints' days, to gather to the church before and after service all the young youths, and maids, and to teach them the prayers, sacraments, commandments, and other points of catechism allowed by the Church of Rome. In the morning he and the other musicians, at the sound of the bell, are bound to come to church to sing and officiate at Mass, which in many towns they perform with organs and other musical instruments (as hath been observed before) as well as Spaniards. So likewise at evening at five of the clock they are again to resort to the church, when the bell calleth, to sing prayers, which they call *completas*, or completory, with *Salve Regina*, a prayer to the Virgin Mary. This *fiscal* is a great man in the town, and bears more sway than the mayors, jurats, and other officers of justice, and when the priest is pleased, giveth attendance to him, goeth about his errands, appointeth such as are to wait on him when he rideth out of town. Both he and all that doth belong unto the church are exempted from the common weekly service of the Spaniards, and from giving attendance to travellers, and from other officers of justice. But they are to attend with their waits, trumpets, and music, upon any great man or priest that cometh to their town, and to make arches with boughs and flowers in the streets for their entertainment.

Besides these, those also that do belong unto the service of the priest's house are privileged from the Spaniards' service. Now the priest hath change of servants by the week, who take their turns so that they may have a week or two to spare to do their work. If it be a great town, he hath three cooks allowed him (if a small town, but two), men cooks who change their turns, except he have any occasion of feasting, then they all come. So likewise he hath two or three more (whom they call *chahal*) as butlers, who keep whatsoever provision is in the house under lock and key; and give to the cook what the priest appointeth to be dressed for his dinner or supper; these keep the table-cloths, napkins, dishes, and trenchers, and lay the cloth, and take away, and wait at the table; he hath besides three or four, and in great towns half a dozen, of boys to do his errands, wait at the table, and sleep in the house all the week by their turns, who with the cooks and butlers dine and sup constantly in the priest's house, and at his charges. He hath also at dinner and supper times the attendance of some old women (who also take their turns) to oversee half a dozen young maids who next to the priest's house do meet to make him and his family *tortillas* or cakes of maize, which the boys do bring hot to the table by half a dozen at a time. Besides these servants, if he have a garden he is allowed two or three gardeners; and for his stable, at least half a dozen Indians, who morning and evening are to bring him *sacate* (as there they call it) or herb and grass for his mules or horses, these diet not in the house; but the groom of the stable, who is to come at morning, noon, and evening (and therefore are three or four to change) or at any time that the priest will ride out, these I say and the gardeners (when they are at work) dine and sup at the priest's charges; who sometimes in great towns hath above a dozen to feed and provide for. There are besides belonging to the church privileged from the weekly attendance upon the Spaniards two or three Indians called sacristans, who have care of the vestry and copes, and altar cloths, and every day make ready the altar or altars for Mass; also to every company or sodality of the saints, or Virgin, there are two or three, whom they call *mayor-*

SURVEY OF WEST INDIES

domos, who gather about the town alms for the maintaining of the sodality; these also gather eggs about the town for the priest every week, and give him an account of their gatherings, and allow him every month, or fortnight, two crowns for a Mass to be sung to the saint.

If there be any fishing place near the town, then the priest also is allowed for to seek him fish three or four, and in some places half a dozen Indians, besides the offerings in the church, and many other offerings which they bring whensoever they come to speak unto the priest, or to confess with him, or for a saint's feast to be celebrated, and besides their tithes of everything there is a monthly maintenance in money allowed unto the priest, and brought unto him by the *alcaldes*, or mayors, and jurats, which he setteth his hand unto in a book of the town's expenses. This maintenance (though it be allowed by the Spanish magistrate, and paid in the King's name for the preaching of the Gospel) yet it comes out of the poor Indians' purses and labour, and is either gathered about the town, or taken out of the tribute which they pay unto the King, or from a common plot of ground which with the help of all is sowed and gathered in and sold for that purpose.

All the towns in America, which are civilized and under the Spanish government, belong either to the Crown, or to some other lords, whom they call *encomenderos*, and pay a yearly tribute unto them. Those that are tenants to their lords or *encomenderos* (who commonly are such as descend from the first conquerors) pay yet unto the King some small tribute in money, besides what they pay in other kind of commodities unto their own *encomendero* and in money also. There is no town so poor, where every married Indian doth not pay at the least in money four reals a year for tribute to the King, besides other four reals to his lord, or *encomendero*. And if the town pay only to the King, they pay at least six, and in some places eight reals by statute, besides what other commodities are common to the town or country where they live, as maize (that is paid in all towns), honey, turkeys, fowls, salt, *cacao*, mantles of cotton-wool; and the like commodities they pay who are subject to an *encomendero*, but such pay only money, not commodities to the King. The mantles of tribute are much esteemed of, for they are choice ones, and of a bigger size than others, so likewise is the tribute *cacao, achiote,* cochineal, where it is paid, for the best is set apart for the tribute; and if the Indians bring that which is not prime good, they shall surely be lashed, and sent back for better. The heads of the several tribes have care to gather it, and to deliver it to the *alcaldes* and *regidores*, mayors and jurats, who carry it either to the King's Exchequer in the city, or to the nearest Spanish justice (if it belong to the King), or to the lord, or *encomendero* of the town. In nothing I ever perceived the Spaniards merciful and indulgent unto the Indians, but in this, that if an Indian be very weak, poor, and sickly and not able to work, or threescore and ten years of age, he is freed from paying any tribute. There be also some towns privileged from this tribute; which are those that can prove themselves to have descended from Tlaxcala, or from certain tribes or families of or about Mexico, who helped the first Spaniards in the conquest of that country.

As for their carriage and behaviour, the Indians are very courteous and loving, and of timorous nature, and willing to serve and to obey, and to do good, if they be drawn by love; but where they are too much tyrannized, they are dogged, unwilling to please, or to work, and will choose rather strangling and death than life. They are very trusty, and never were known to commit any robbery of importance; so that the Spaniards dare trust to abide with them in a wilderness all night, though they have bags of gold about them. So for secrecy they are very close, and will not reveal anything against their own natives, or a Spaniard's credit and reputation if they be any way affected to him. But above all unto their priest they are very respective unto him; and when they come to speak unto him, put on their best clothes, study their compliments and words to please him. They are very abundant in their expressions, and full of circumlocutions adorned with parables and similes to express their mind and intention. I have often sat still for the space of an hour, only hearing some old women make their speeches unto me, with so many elegancies in their tongue (which in English would be nonsense, or barbarous expressions) as would make me wonder, and learn by their speeches more of their language than by any other endeavour or study of mine own. And if I could reply unto them in the like phrases and expressions (which I would often endeavour) I should be sure to win their hearts, and get anything from them. As for their religion, they are outwardly such as the Spaniards, but inwardly hard to believe that which is above sense, nature, and the visible sight of the eye; and many of them to this day do incline to worship idols of stocks and stones, and are given to much superstition and to observe cross-ways, and meeting of beasts in them, the flying of birds, their appearing and singing near their houses at such and such times. Many are given to witchcraft, and are deluded by the devil to believe that their life dependeth upon the life of such and such a beast (which they take unto them as their familiar spirit) and think that when that beast dieth they must die, when he is chased their hearts pant, when he is faint they are faint, nay it happeneth that by the devil's delusion they appear in the shape of that beast (which commonly by their choice is a buck, or doe, a lion, or tiger, or dog, or eagle) and in that shape have been shot at and wounded, as I shall shew in the chapter following. And for this reason (as I came to understand by some of them) they yield unto the Popish religion, especially to the worshipping of saints' images, because they look upon them as much like unto their forefathers' idols; and secondly, because they see some of them painted with beasts, as Hierome with a lion, Anthony with an ass, and other wild beasts, Dominic with a dog, Blas with a hog, Mark with a bull, and John with an eagle, they are more confirmed in their delusions, and think verily those saints were of their opinion, and that those beasts were their familiar spirits, in whose shape they also were transformed when they lived, and with whom they died.

All Indians are much affected unto these Popish saints, but especially those which are given to witchcraft, and out of the smallness of their means they will be sure to buy some of these saints and bring them to the church, that there they may stand and be worshipped by them and others. The churches are full of them, and they are placed upon standers gilded or painted, to be carried in procession upon men's shoulders, upon their proper day. And from hence cometh no little profit to the priests; for upon such saints' days, the owner of the saint maketh a great feast in the town, and presenteth unto the priest sometimes two or three, sometimes four or five crowns for his Mass and sermon, besides a turkey and three or four fowls, with as much *cacao* as will serve to make him chocolate for all the whole octave or eight days following. So that in some churches, where there are at least forty of these saints' statues and images, they bring unto the priest at least forty pounds a year. The priest therefore is very watchful over those saints' days, and sendeth warning before hand unto the Indians of the day of their saint, that they may provide themselves for the better celebrating it both at home and in the church. If they contribute not bountifully, then the priest will chide, and threaten that he will not preach. Some Indians through poverty have been unwilling to contribute anything at all, or to solemnize in the church and at his house his saint's day, but then the priest hath threatened to cast his saint's image out of the church, saying that the church ought not to be filled with such saints as are unprofitable to soul and body, and that in such a statue's room one may stand which may do more good by occasioning a solemn celebration of one day more in the year. So likewise if the Indian that owned one of those images die and leave children, they are to take care of that saint as part of their inheritance, and to provide that his day be kept; but if no son, or heirs, be left, then the priest calleth for the heads of the several tribes, and for the chief officers of justice, and maketh a speech unto them, wherein he declareth that part of the church ground is taken up in vain by such an image, and his stander, without any profit either to the priest, the church, or the town, no heir or owner being left alive to provide for that orphan saint, to own it; and that in case they will not seek out who may take charge of him and of his day, the priest will not suffer him to stand idle in his church, like those whom our Saviour in the Gospel rebuked, *quid hic statis tota die otiosi?* for that they stood idle in the market all the day (these very expressions have I heard there from some friars) and therefore that he must banish such a saint's picture out of the church, and must deliver him up before them into the justices' hands to be kept by them in the town-house until such time as he may be bought and owned by some good Christian. The Indians when they hear these expressions begin to fear lest some judgment may befall their town for suffering a saint to be excommunicated and cast out of their church, and therefore present unto the priest some offering for his prayers unto the saint, that he may do them no harm, and desire him to limit them a time to bring him an answer for the disposing of that saint (thinking it will prove a disparagement and affront unto their town if what once hath belonged to the church be now out, and delivered up to the secular power) and that in the meantime they will find out some good Christian, either of the nearest friends and kindred to him or them who first owned the saint, or else some stranger, who may buy that saint of the priest (if he continue in the church) or of the secular power (if he be cast out of the church and delivered up unto them, which they are unwilling to yield to, having been taught of judgments in such a case like to befall them) and may by some speedy feast and solemnity appease the saint's anger towards them, for having been so slighted by the town.

Alas poor Indians, what will they not be brought unto by those friars and priests, who study nothing more than their own ends, and to enrich themselves from the church and altar! Their policies (who are the wise and prudent children of this world spoken of in the Gospel) can easily overtop and master the simplicity of the poor Indians, who rather than they will bring an affront upon their town by suffering any of their saints to be cast out of their church, or to be with money redeemed out of the secular power's hands, will make haste to present unto him an owner of that orphan saint, who for him shall give to the priest not only what he may be prized to be worth in a painter's shop for the workmanship, gold, and colours belonging to him, but besides shall present him what before hath been observed, for the solemnizing of his feast. These feasts bring yet unto the saints more profit than hitherto hath been spoken of; for the Indians have been taught that upon such days they ought to offer up somewhat unto the saints; and therefore they prepare either money (some a real, some two, some more) or else commonly about Guatemala white wax candles, and in other places *cacao*, or fruits, which they lay before the image of the saint, whilst the Mass is celebrating. Some Indians will bring a bundle of candles of a dozen tied together of reals apiece some, some of three or four for a real, and will if they be let alone light them all together and burn them out, so that the priest at the end of the Mass will find nothing but the ends. Therefore (knowing well of the ways of policy and covetousness) he chargeth the church officers, whom I said before were called *mayordomos* to look to the offerings, and not to suffer the Indians who bring candles to light more than one before the saint, and to leave the other before him unlighted (having formerly taught them that the saints are as well pleased with their whole candles as with their burnt candles) that so he may have the more to sell and make money of. After Mass the priest and the *mayordomos* take and sweep away from the saint whatsoever they find hath been offered unto him; so that sometimes in a great town upon such a saint's day the priest may have in money twelve or twenty reals, and fifty or a hundred candles, which may be worth unto him twenty or thirty shillings, besides some ends and pieces. Most of the friars about Guatemala are with those offerings as well stored with candles as is any wax-chandler's shop in the city. And the same candles, which thus they have received by offerings, they need not care to sell them away to Spaniards, who come about to buy them (though some will rather sell them together to such though cheaper, that their money might come in all at once) for the Indians themselves when they want again any candles for the like feast, or for a christening, and for a woman's churching (at which times they also offer candles) will buy their own again of the priest, who sometimes receiveth the same candles and money for them again five or six times. And because they find that the Indians incline very much to this kind of offerings, and that they are so profitable unto them, the friars do much press upon the Indians in their preaching this point of their religion and devotion.

But if you demand of these ignorant but zealous offerers, the Indians, an account of any point of faith, they will give you little or none. The mystery of the Trinity, and of the incarnation of Christ, and our redemption by him is too hard for them; they will only answer what they have been taught in a catechism of questions and answers; but if you ask them if they believe such a point of Christianity, they will never answer affirmatively, but only thus: 'Perhaps it may be so.' They are taught there the doctrine of Rome, that Christ's body is truly and really present in the Sacrament, and no bread in substance, but only the accidents; if the wisest Indian be asked whether he believe this, he will answer: 'Perhaps it may be so.' Once an old woman, who was held to be very religious, in the town of Mixco, came to me about receiving the Sacrament, and whilst I was instructing of her, I asked her if she believed that Christ's body was in the Sacrament, she answered: 'Peradventure it may be so.' A little while after to try her and get her out of this strain and common answer, I asked her what and who was in the Sacrament which she received from the priest's hand at the altar; she answered nothing for a while, and at last I pressed upon her for an affirmative answer, and then she began to look about to the saints in the church (which was dedicated to a saint which they call St Dominic) and, as it seemed, being troubled and doubtful what to say, at last she cast her eyes upon the high altar; but I seeing she delayed the time, asked her again who was in the Sacrament? to which she replied S. Dominic who was the patron of that church and town. At this I smiled, and would yet further try her simplicity with a simple question. I told her she saw S. Dominic was painted with a dog by him holding a torch in his mouth, and the globe of the world at his feet; I asked her whether all this were with St Dominic in the Sacrament? To which she answered: 'Perhaps it might be so'; wherewith I began to chide her, and to instruct her. But mine instruction, nor all the teaching and preaching of those

SURVEY OF WEST INDIES

Spanish priests hath not yet well grounded them in principles of faith; they are dull and heavy to believe or apprehend of God, or of heaven, more than with sense or reason they can conceive. Yet they go and run that way they see the Spaniards run, and as they are taught by their idolatrous priests. Who have taught them much formality, and so they are (as our Formalists formerly in England) very formal, but little substantial in religion.

They have been taught that when they come to confession they must offer somewhat to the priest, and that by their gifts and alms their sins shall be sooner forgiven; this they do formally observe that whensoever they come to confession, but especially in Lent, none of them dareth to come with empty hands; some bring money, some honey, some eggs, some fowls, some fish, some *cacao*, some one thing, some another, so that the priest hath a plentiful harvest in Lent for his pains in hearing their confessions. They have been taught that also when they receive the Communion they must surely every one give at least a real to the priest, (surely England was never taught in America to buy the Sacrament with a two-pence offering, and yet this custom too much practised and pressed upon the people) which they perform so that I have known some poor Indians, who have for a week or two forborne from coming to the Communion until they could get a real offering. It is to be wondered what the priests do get from those poor wretches in great towns by confession and Communion reals in great towns, where they deny the Sacrament to none that will receive it (and in some towns I have known a thousand communicants) and force all above twelve or thirteen years of age to come to confession in the Lent.

They are very formal also in observing Rome's Monday, Thursday, and Good Friday, and then they make their monuments and sepulchres, wherein they set their Sacrament, and watch it all day and night, placing before it a crucifix on the ground, with two basins on each side to hold the single or double reals which everyone muſt offer when he cometh creeping upon his knees and bare-footed to kiss Christ's hands, feet, and side. The candles which for that day and night and next morning are burned at the sepulchre are bought with another contribution-real, which is gathered from house to house from every Indian for that purpose. Their religion is a dear and lick-penny religion for such poor Indians, and yet they are carried along in it formally and perceive it not. They are taught that they muſt remember the souls in Purgatory, and therefore that they muſt caſt their alms into a cheſt, which ſtandeth for that purpose in their churches, whereof the prieſt keepeth the key, and openeth it when he wanteth money, or when he pleaseth. I have often opened some of those cheſts, and have found in them many single reals, some half pieces of eight, and some whole pieces of eight. And because what is loſt and found in the highways muſt belong to somebody, if the true owner be not known, they have been taught that such moneys or goods belong also to the souls departed; wherefore the Indians (surely more for fear or vanity's sake that they may be well thought on by the prieſt) if they find anything loſt will beſtow it upon the souls surer than the Spaniards themselves (who if they find a purse loſt will keep it) and will bring it either to the prieſt or caſt it into the cheſt.

An Indian of Mixco had found a patacon or piece of eight in a highway, and when he came to confession he gave it unto me telling me he durſt not keep it, leſt the souls should appear unto him and demand it. So upon the second day of November which they call All Souls' Day, they are extraordinary foolish and superſtitious in offering moneys, fowls, eggs and maize, and other commodities for the souls' good, but it proves for the profit of the prieſt, who after Mass wipes away to his chamber all that which the poor gulled and deluded Indians had offered unto those souls, which needed neither money, food, nor any other provision, and he fills his purse and pampers his belly with it. A friar that lived in Petapa boasted unto me once that upon their All Souls' Day his offerings had been about a hundred reals, two hundred chickens and fowls, half a dozen turkeys, eight bushels of maize, three hundred eggs, four sontles of *cacao* (every sontle being four hundred grains), twenty clusters of plantains, above a hundred wax candles, besides some loaves of bread, and other trifles of fruits. All which being summed up according to the price of the things there, and with consideration of the coin of money there (half a real, or threepence, being there the least coin) mounts to above eight pounds of our money, a fair and goodly stipend for a Mass, brave wages for half an hour's work; a politic ground for that error of Purgatory, if the dead bring to the living priest such wealth in one day only. Christmas Day with the rest of those holy days is no less superstitiously observed by these Indians, for against that time they frame and set in some corner of their church a little thatched house like a stall, which they call Bethlehem, with a blazing star over, pointing it unto the three sage wise men from the East; within this stall they lay in a crib a child made of wood, painted and gilded (who represents Christ new born unto them), by him stands Mary on the one side, and Joseph on the other, and an ass likewise on the one side and an ox on the other, made by hands, the three wise men of the East kneel before the crib offering gold, frankincense and myrrh, the shepherds stand off aloof offering their country gifts, some a kid, some a lamb, some milk, some cheese, and curds, some fruits, the fields are also there represented with flocks of sheep and goats; the angels they hang about the stall some with viols, some with lutes, some with harps, a goodly mumming and silent stage play, to draw those simple souls to look about, and to delight their senses and fantasies in the church.

There is not an Indian that cometh to see that supposed Bethlehem (and there is not any in the town but doth come to see it) who bringeth not either money or somewhat else for his offering. Nay the policy of the priests hath been such that (to stir up the Indians with their saints' example) they have taught them to bring their saints upon all the holy days until Twelfth Day in procession unto this Bethlehem to offer their gifts, according to the number of the saints that stand in the church, some days there come five, some days eight, some days ten, dividing them into such order that by Twelfth Day all may have come and offered, some money, some one thing, some another. The owner of the saint, he cometh before the saint with his friends and kindred (if there be no sodality or company belonging unto that saint) and being very well apparelled for that purpose, he bows himself and kneels to the crib, and then rising takes from the saint what he bringeth and leaveth it there, and so departs. But if there be a sodality belonging to the saint, then the *mayordomos* or chief officers of that company they come before the saint, and do homage, and offer as before hath been said. But upon Twelfth Day the *alcaldes*, mayors, jurats, and other officers of justice must offer after the example of the saints, and the three wise men of the East (whom the Church of Rome teacheth to have been kings) because they represent the King's power and authority. And all these days they have about the town and in the church a dance of shepherds, who at Christmas Eve at midnight begin before this Bethlehem, and then they must offer a sheep amongst them. Others dance clothed like angels and with wings, and all to draw the people more to see sights in the church than to worship God in spirit and in truth. Candlemas Day is no less superstitiously observed; for then the picture of Mary comes in procession to the altar, and

PLATE 7

THE CHRISTMAS FESTIVAL IN THE CHURCH OF PETAPA
(*From the Dutch Edition of* 1700)

[*Face p.* 262

offereth up her candles and pigeons or turtle-doves unto the priest, and all the town must imitate her example, and bring their candles to be blessed and hallowed; of four or five, or as many as they bring, one only shall be restored back unto them, because they are blessed, all the rest are for the priest, to whom the Indians resort after to buy them, and give more than ordinary, because they are hallowed candles.

At Whitsuntide they have another sight, and that is in the church also. Whilst a hymn is sung of the Holy Ghost, the priest standing before the altar with his face turned to the people, they have a device to let fall a dove from above over his head well dressed with flowers, and for above half an hour, from holes made for that purpose, they drop down flowers about the priest shewing the gifts of the Holy Ghost to him, which example the ignorant and simple Indians are willing to imitate, offering also their gifts unto him. Thus all the year are those priests and friars deluding the poor people for their ends, enriching themselves with their gifts, placing religion in mere policy; and thus doth the Indians' religion consist more in sights, shews, and formalities, than in any true substance. But as sweet meat must have sour sauce, so this sweetness and pleasing delight of shews in the church hath its sour sauce once a year (besides the sourness of poverty which followeth to them by giving so many gifts unto the priest) for, to shew that in their religion there is some bitterness and sourness they make the Indians whip themselves the week before Easter, like the Spaniards, which those simples both men and women perform with such cruelty to their own flesh that they butcher it, mangle and tear their backs, till some swoon, nay some (as I have known) have died under their own whipping, and have self murdered themselves, which the priests regard not, because their death is sure to bring them at least three or four crowns for a Mass for their souls, and other offerings of their friends.

THE ENGLISH-AMERICAN

Thus in religion they are superstitiously led on and blinded in the observance of what they have been taught more for the good and profit of their priests than for any good of their souls, not perceiving that their religion is a policy to enrich their teachers. But not only do the friars and priests live by them and eat the sweat of their brows, but also all the Spaniards, who not only with their work and service (being themselves many given to idleness) grow wealthy and rich, but with needless offices and authority are still fleecing them, and taking from them that little which they gain with much hardness and severity.

The President of Guatemala, the judges of that Chancery, the governors and high justices of other parts of the country, that they may advance and enrich their menial servants, make the poor Indians the subject of their bountifulness towards such. Some have offices to visit as often as they please their towns, and to see what every Indian hath sowed of maize, for the maintenance of his wife and children; others visit them to see what fowls they keep for the good and store of the county; others have order to see whether their houses be decently kept and their beds orderly placed according to their families; others have power to call them out to mend and repair the highways; and others have commission to number the families and inhabitants of the several towns, to see how they increase that their tribute may not decrease, but still be raised. And all this, those officers do never perform but so that for their pains they must have from every Indian an allowance to bear their charges (which indeed are none at all), for as long as they stay in the town they may call for what fowls and provision they please without paying for it. When they come to number the towns, they call by list every Indian and cause his children, sons and daughters, to be brought before them, to see if they be fit to be married, and if they be of growth and age and be not married, the fathers are threatened for keeping them unmarried and as idle livers in the town without paying tribute; and according to the number of the sons and daughters that are marriageable, the father's tribute is raised and increased until they provide husbands and wives for their sons and daughters, who as soon as they are married are charged with tribute; which that it may increase, they will suffer none above fifteen years of age to live unmarried. Nay the set time of age of marriage appointed for the Indians is at fourteen years for the man, and thirteen for the woman, alleging that they are sooner ripe for the fruit of wedlock, and sooner ripe in knowledge and malice, and strength for work and service, than are any other people. Nay sometimes they force them to marry who are scarce twelve and thirteen years of age, if they find them well limbed and strong in body, explicating a point of one of Rome's canons, which alloweth fourteen and fifteen years, *nisi malitia suppleat ætatem.*

When I myself lived in Pinola, that town by order of Don Juan de Guzman (a great gentleman of Guatemala, to whom it belonged) was numbered, and an increase of tributary Indians was added unto it by this means. The numbering it lasted a full week, and in that space I was commanded to join in marriage near twenty couple, which, with those that before had been married since the last numbering of it, made up to the *encomendero* or lord of it an increase of about fifty families. But it was a shame to see how young some were that at that time were forced to marriage, neither could all my striving and reasoning prevail to the contrary, nor the producing of the register book to shew their age, but that some were married of between twelve and thirteen years of age, and one especially who in the register book was found to be not fully of twelve years, whose knowledge and strength of body was judged to supply the want of age. In this manner even in the most free act of the will (which ought to be in marriage) are those poor Indians forced and made slaves by the Spaniards, to supply with tribute the want of their purses, and the meanness of their estates. Yet under this yoke and burden they are cheerful, and much given to feasting, sporting, and dancing, as they particularly shew in the chief feasts of their towns, which are kept upon that saint's day to whom their town is dedicated. And certainly this superstition hath continued also in England from the Popish times, to keep fairs in many of our towns upon saints' days (which is the intent of the Papists to draw in the people and country by way of commerce and trading one with another, to honour, worship, and pray to that saint to whom the town is dedicated) or else why are our fairs commonly kept upon John Baptist, James, Peter, Matthew, Bartholomew, Holy Rood, Lady days, and the like, and not as well a day or two before, or a day or two after, which would be as good and fit days to buy and sell as the other? True it is, our Reformation alloweth not the worshipping of saints, yet that solemn meeting of the people to fairs and mirth and sport upon those days it hath kept and continued, that so the saints and their days may be and continue still in our remembrance.

There is no town in the Indies great or small (though it be but of twenty families) which is not dedicated thus unto Our Lady or unto some saint, and the remembrance of that saint is continued in the minds not only of them that live in the town, but of all that live far and near by commercing, trading, sporting, and dancing, offering unto the saint, and bowing, kneeling, and praying before him. Before this day cometh, the Indians of the town two or three months have their meetings at night, and prepare themselves for such dances as are most commonly used amongst them; and in these their meetings they drink much both of chocolate and *chicha*. For every kind of dance they have several houses appointed, and masters of that dance, who teach the rest that they may be perfected in it against the saint's day. For the most part of these two or three months the silence of the night is unquieted, what with their singing, what with their holloaing, what with their beating upon the shells of fishes, what with their waits, and what with their piping. And when the feast cometh, then they act publicly and for the space of eight days what privately they had practised before. They are that day well apparelled with silks, fine linen, ribbons and feathers according to the dance; which first they begin in the church before the saint, or in the churchyard, and from thence all the octave, or eight days, they go from house to house dancing, where they have chocolate or some heady drink or *chicha* given them. All those eight days the town is sure to be full of drunkards; and if they be reprehended for it they will answer that their heart doth rejoice with their saint in Heaven, and that they must drink unto him that he may remember them.

The chief dance used amongst them is called *toncontin*, which hath been danced before the King of Spain in the Court of Madrid by Spaniards, who have lived in the Indies, to shew unto the King somewhat of the Indians' fashions; and it was reported to have pleased the King very much. This dance is thus performed. The Indians commonly that dance it (if it be a great town) are thirty or forty, or fewer if it be a small town. They are clothed in white, both their doublets, linen drawers, and *aiates*, or towels, which on the one side hang almost to the ground. Their drawers and *aiates* are wrought with some works of silk, or with birds, or bordered with some lace. Others procure doublets and drawers and *aiates* of silk, all which are hired for that purpose. On their backs they hang long tufts of feathers of all colours, which with glue are fastened into a little frame made for the purpose and gilded on the outside; this frame with ribbons they tie about their shoulders fast that it fall not, nor slacken with the motion of their bodies. Upon their heads they wear another less tuft of feathers either in their hats, or in some gilded or painted headpiece, or helmet. In their hands also they carry a fan of feathers, and on their feet most will use feathers also bound together like short wings of birds; some wear shoes, some not. And thus from top to toe they are almost covered with curious and coloured feathers. Their music and tune to this dance is only what is made with a hollow stock of a tree, being rounded and well pared within and without, very smooth and shining, some four times thicker than our viols, with two or three long clefts on the upper side and some holes at the end which they call *tepanabaz*. On this stock (which is placed upon a stool or form in the middle of the Indians) the master of the dance beats with two sticks, covered with wool at the ends, and a pitched leather over the wool that it fall not away. With this instrument and blows upon it (which soundeth but dull and heavy, but somewhat loud) he giveth the dancers their several tunes, and changes, and signs of the motion of their bodies either straight or bowing, and giveth them warning what and when they are to sing. Thus they dance in compass and circle round about that instrument, one following another sometimes straight, sometimes turning about, sometimes turning half way, sometimes bending their bodies and with the feathers in their hands almost touching the ground, and singing the life of that their saint, or of some other. All this dancing is but a kind of walking round, which they will continue two or three whole hours together in one place, and from thence go and perform the same at another house.

This *toncontin* the chief and principal only of the town do dance it; it was the old dance which they used before they knew Christianity, except that then instead of singing the saints' lives they did sing the praises of their

SURVEY OF WEST INDIES

heathenish gods. They have another dance much used, which is a kind of hunting out some wild beast (which formerly in time of heathenism was to be sacrificed to their gods) to be offered up unto the saint. This dance hath much variety of tunes, with a small *tepanabaz*, and many shells of tortoises, or instead of them with pots covered with leather, on which they strike as on *tepanabaz*, and with the sound of pipes; in this dance they use much holloaing and noise and calling one unto another, and speaking by way of stage play, some relating one thing, some another concerning the beast they hunt after. These dancers are all clothed like beasts, with painted skins of lions, tigers, wolves, and on their heads such headpieces as may represent the head of such beasts, and others wear painted heads of eagles or fowls of rapine, and in their hands they have painted staves, bills, swords, and axes, wherewith they threaten to kill that beast they hunt after. Others instead of hunting after a beast, hunt after a man, as beasts in a wilderness should hunt a man to kill him. This man that is thus hunted after must be very nimble and agile, as one flying for his life, and striking here and there at the beasts for his defence, whom at last they catch and make a prey of. As the *toncontin* consists most of walking and turning and leisurely bending their bodies, so this dance doth wholly consist in action, running in a circle round, sometimes out of circle, and leaping and striking with those tools and instruments which they have in their hand. This is a very rude sport, and full of shrieking and hideous noise, wherein I never delighted.

Another Mexican dance they use, some clothed like men, others like women, which in heathenish times they did use with singing praises unto their king or emperor; but now they apply their songs unto the King of Glory, or unto the Sacrament, using these or commonly the like words with very little difference, and some variety of praise.

THE ENGLISH-AMERICAN

Salid Mexicanas, bailad Toncontin.
Cansalas galanas en cuerpo gentil. And again,
Salid Mexicanas, bailad Toncontin.
Al Rey de la gloria tenemos aqui.

Thus they go round dancing, playing in some places very well upon their guitars, repeating now and then all together a verse or two, and calling the Mexican dames to come out to them with their gallant mantles to sing praise unto their King of Glory. Besides these they have, and use our Morris dances, and blackamoor dances with *sonajas* in their hands, which are a round set of small Morris dancing bells, wherewith they make variety of sounds to their nimble feet. But the dance which doth draw to it the people's wondering is a tragedy acted by way of dance, as the death of St Peter, or the beheading of John the Baptist. In these dances there is an Emperor, or a King Herod, with their Queens clothed, another clothed with a long loose coat who represents St Peter, or John the Baptist, who whilst the rest danceth, walketh amongst them with a book in his hands, as if he were saying his prayers, all the rest of the dancers are apparelled like captains and soldiers with swords, daggers, or halberds in their hands. They dance at the sound of a small drum and pipes, sometimes round, sometimes in length forward, and have and use many speeches to the Emperor or King, and among themselves concerning the apprehending and executing the saint. The King and Queen sit sometimes down to hear their pleading against the saint, and his pleading for himself; and sometimes they dance with the rest; and the end of their dance is to crucify St Peter downwards with his head upon a cross, or behead John the Baptist, having in readiness a painted head in a dish which they present unto the King and Queen, for joy whereof they all again dance merrily and so conclude, taking down him that acted Peter from the cross. The

SURVEY OF WEST INDIES

Indians that dance this dance most of them are superstitious for what they do, judging as if it were indeed really acted and performed what only is by way of dance represented. When I lived amongst them it was an ordinary thing for him who in the dance was to act St Peter or John the Baptist to come first to confession, saying they must be holy and pure like that saint, whom they represent, and must prepare themselves to die. So likewise he that acted Herod or Herodias, and some of the soldiers that in the dance were to speak and to accuse the saints, would afterwards come to confess of that sin, and desire absolution as from blood-guiltiness. More particular passages of the Indians according to my experience of them I shall in the chapter following truly relate unto my reader.

CHAPTER XV

Shewing how and why I departed out of Guatemala to learn the Poconchi language, and to live among the Indians, and of some particular passages and accidents whilst I lived there

HAVING read in the University of Guatemala for three years' space a whole course of arts, and having begun to read part of divinity, the more I studied and grew in knowledge, and the more I controverted by way of arguments some truths and points of religion, the more I found the spirit of truth enlightening me, and discovering unto me the lies, errors, falsities, and superstitions of the Church of Rome. My conscience was much perplexed, and wavering, and I desirous of some good and full satisfaction, which I knew might not be had there, and that to profess and continue in any opinion contrary to the doctrine of Rome would bring me to the Inquisition, that rack of tender consciences, and from thence to no less than burning alive, in case I would not recant of what the true spirit had inspired into me. The point of transubstantiation, of Purgatory, of the Pope's power and authority, of the merit of man's works, of his free will to choose all soul-saving ways, the sacrifice of the Mass, the hallowing the Sacrament of the Lord's Supper unto the lay people, the priest's power to absolve from sin, the worshipping of saints though with δουλεία, as they call it, and not with λατρεία, and the Virgin Mary with a higher degree of worship than that of the saints, which they call ὑπερδουλεία, the strange lies and blasphemies which they call miracles recorded in the legend and lives of their saints, the infallibility of the Pope, and council in defining for truth and point of faith what in itself is false and erroneous; these points especially, with many more of Rome's policies, and the lewd lives of the priests, friars, nuns, and those in authority, did much trouble and perplex my conscience, which I knew would be better satisfied if I could return again to my own country of England, where I knew many things were held contrary to the Church of Rome, but what particulars they were I could not tell, not having been brought up in the Protestant Church, and having been sent young over to St Omer's.

Wherefore I earnestly addressed myself to the Provincial, and to the President of Guatemala, for a licence to come home, but neither of them would yield unto it, because there was a strict order of the King and Council that no priest sent by his Majesty to any of the parts of the Indies to preach the Gospel should return again to Spain till ten years were expired. Hereupon I seeing myself a prisoner, and without hopes for the present of seeing England in many years, resolved to stay no more in Guatemala, but to go out to learn some Indian tongue, and to preach in some of their towns, where I knew more money might be got to help me home, when the time should come, than if I did continue to live in the cloister of Guatemala. Yet in the meantime I thought it not unfit to write to Spain to a friend of mine, an English friar in San Lucar, called

PLATE 8

THOMAS GAGE IN THE DOMINICAN HABIT
(Frontispiece of the Dutch Edition of 1700)

SURVEY OF WEST INDIES

Friar Pablo de Londres, to desire him to obtain for me a licence from the Court, and from the General of the Order at Rome, that I might return unto my country. In this season there was in Guatemala, Friar Francisco de Moran, the Prior of Coban in the province of Vera Paz, who was informing the President and whole Chancery how necessary it was that some Spaniards should be aiding and assisting him for the discovery of a way from that country unto Yucatan, and for the suppressing of such barbarous people and heathens as stopped his passage, and did often invade some Indian towns of Christians. This Moran (being my special friend, and having been brought up in Spain in the cloister of San Pablo de Valladolid, where myself was first entered friar) was very desirous of my company along with him, for the better bringing into Christianity those heathens and idolaters, telling me that doubtless in a new country new treasure and great riches was like to be found, whereof no small share and portion should befall him and me for our pains and adventure. I was not hard to be persuaded, being above all desirous to convert to Christianity a people that had never hear of Christ; and so purposed to forsake that honour which I had in the University, for to make Christ known unto that heathenish people. The Provincial was glad to see this my courage, and so, with some gifts and money in my purse, sent me with Moran to the Vera Paz in the company of fifty Spaniards, who were appointed by the President to aid and assist us.

When we came to Coban we were well refreshed and provided for a hard and dangerous enterprise. From Coban we marched to two great towns of Christians called St Peter, and St John, where were added unto us a hundred Indians for our further assistance. From these towns two days' journey we could travel on mules safely among Christians and some small villages; but after the two days we drew near unto the heathens' frontiers, where there was no more open way for mules, but we must trust unto our feet. We went up and down mountains amongst woods for the space of two days, being much discouraged with the thickets and hardness of the way, and having no hope of finding out the heathens. In the night we kept watch and guard for fear of enemies, and resolved yet the third day to go forward. In the mountains we found many sorts of fruits and in the bottoms springs and brooks with many trees of *cacao* and *achiote*. The third day we went on, and came to a low valley, in the midst whereof ran a shallow river, where we found some *milpas* or plantations of maize. These were a testimony unto us of some Indians not far off, and therefore made us keep together and be in readiness if any assault or onset should be made upon us by the heathens. Whilst we thus travelled on, we suddenly fell upon half a dozen poor cottages, covered with boughs and plantain leaves, and in them we found three Indian women, two men, and five young children, all naked, who fain would have escaped, but they could not. We refreshed ourselves in their poor cottages and gave them of our provision, which at the first they refused to eat, howling and crying and puling, till Moran had better encouraged and comforted them, whose language they partly understood. We clothed them and took them along with us, hoping to make them discover unto us some treasure or some bigger plantation. But that day they were so sullen that we could get nothing out of them.

Thus we went on, following some tracks which here and there we found of Indians, till it was almost evening, and then we did light upon above a dozen cottages more, and in them a matter of twenty men, women, and children, from whom we took some bows and arrows, and found there store of plantains, some fish, and wild venison, wherewith we refreshed ourselves These told us of a great town two days' journey off, which made us be very watchful that night. Here I

SURVEY OF WEST INDIES

began with some more of our company to be sick and weary, so that the next day I was not able to go any further; whereupon we resolved to set up our quarters there, and to send out some scouts of Indians and Spaniards to discover the country, who found further more cottages and plantations of maize, of chilli, of Turkey beans, and cotton-wool, but no Indians at all, for they were all fled. Our scouts returned, and gave us some encouragement from the pleasantness of the country; but withal wished us to be watchful and careful, for that certainly the flight of those Indians was a sign that our coming was noised about the country. The next day we purposed to move forward to that plantation which our scouts had discovered, being (as we were informed) safer and more open to foresee any danger ready to befall us. All these plantations lay along by the river, where the sun was exceeding hot, which had caused fevers and a flux in some of us. With much weariness and faintness I got that day to our journey's end, beginning now to repent me of what I was engaged in and on foot, and fearing some sudden danger, by reason our coming was now known by the Indians. The prisoners we had with us began to tell us of some gold that they did sometimes find in that river, and of a great lake yet forward, about which did inhabit many thousand Indians, who were very warlike, and skilful in their bows and arrows. The one encouraged some, the other much discouraged the rest, who wished themselves out of those woods and unknown places, and began to murmur against Moran, who had been the cause of their engagement in that great danger. Our night was set, and I and the rest of the sick Spaniards went to rest, some upon the bare ground, but myself and others in *hamacas*, which are of net-work tied at two posts or trees, and hanging in the air, which with the least stirring of the body rock one asleep as in a cradle. Thus I took my rest till about midnight; at which time our watches gave an alarm against our approaching enemies, who were thought to be about a thousand. They came desperately towards us, and when they saw they were discovered, and our drums beat up, and our fowling pieces and muskets began to shoot, they holloaed and cried out with a hideous noise, which uproar and sudden affrightment added sweat and fear to my fever. But Moran (who came to confess with me, and to prepare himself for death or for some deadly wound) comforted me, wishing me to fear nothing, and to lie still, for that I could do them no good, and that less was my danger than I apprehended because our soldiers had compassed me about, so that on no side the heathens could come in, and flee we could not without the loss of all our lives. The skirmish lasted not above an hour, and then our enemies began to flee back. We took ten of them, and in the morning found thirteen dead upon the ground, and of ours five only were wounded, whereof one died the next day.

In the morning our soldiers began to mutiny and to talk of returning back, fearing a worse and more violent onset that day or the night following, for some of the Indians who were taken told them plainly that if they went not away there would come six or seven thousand against them. They told us further that they knew well that the Spaniards had all the country about, except that little portion of theirs, which they desired to enjoy quietly and peaceably, and not to meddle with us, but rather if we would see their country and go through it as friends, they would let us without doing us any hurt; but if we came in a warlike manner to fight and to bring them into slavery, as we had done their neighbours, they were all resolved to die fighting rather than to yield. With these words our soldiers were divided, some with Moran were of opinion to try the Indians, and to go peaceably through their country till they could come to some town of Yucatan; others were of opinion to fight; others to return back again, considering their weakness against so many thousands of Indians as were in the country. But that day nothing was agreed upon, for that we could not stir by reason of the sick and wounded. So we continued there that night, and as the night before much about the same time the enemies came again upon us, but finding us ready and watching for them, they soon fled. In the morning we resolved to return back, and Moran sent the heathens word that if they would let him go through their country quietly to discover some land of Yucatan, he would after a few months come peaceably unto them with half a dozen Indians, no more, trusting his life upon them; whom he knew if they wronged, all the Spaniards in the country would rise up against them, and not leave one alive. They answered that they would entertain him, and any few Indians well and willingly; all which Moran and they performed according to their agreement the next year following.

Thus we returned that day back the same way that we had come, and I began to find myself better, and my fever to leave me. We carried with us some of those young children which we had taken, to present them unto the President of Guatemala. And in Coban the Prior Moran thought he might first do God good service if he christened those young children, saying that they might become saints, and that afterwards their prayers might prevail with God for the conversion of their parents and of all that country to Christianity. I could not but oppose this his ignorance, which seemed much like unto that of the friars who entered America with Cortez, and increased after the Conquest daily more in number, who boasted to the Emperor that they had some of them made above thirty thousand Indians Christians by baptizing them; which truly they did as sheep are forced to the waters and driven to be washed, so were those first Indians by thousands sprinkled (or if I may use their word, baptized) for they were driven by compulsion and force to the rivers, neither were they first principled in any grounds of belief and Christianity, neither themselves believers, nor children of believing and faithful parents. So would Moran christen these children, though I told him that they ought not to partake of that sacrament and ordinance of Christ, unless they were grounded in articles of Christianity and believed, or were children of believing parents. But as he had been brought up in errors, whereof that Church of Rome is a wide and spacious nest, so he would be obstinate in this point against me and the truth, sprinkling with water those children, and naming them with names of Christians. After this he sent them well apparelled to the President of Guatemala, who commanded them to be kept and brought up in the cloister of the Dominican friars.

I remained after this for a while in Coban, and in the towns about, until such time as the ships came to the gulf; whither I went with Moran to buy wines, oil, iron, cloth and such things as the cloister wanted for the present. At which time there being a frigate ready to depart to Trujillo (some occasions drawing Moran thither) I took ship with him. We stayed not much above a week in that port (which is a weak one, as the English and Hollanders taking of it can witness) but presently we thought of returning back to Guatemala by land through the country of Comayagua, commonly called Honduras. This is a woody and mountainous country, very bad and inconvenient for travellers, and besides very poor; there the commodities are hides, *cañafistula*, and *zarzaparrilla*, and such want of bread that about Trujillo they make use of what they call *cassave*, which is a dry root that being eaten dry doth choke, and therefore is soaked in broth, water, wine or chocolate, that so it may go down. Within the country, and especially about the city of Comayagua (which is a bishop's seat, though a small place of some five hundred inhabitants at the most) there is more store of maize by reason of some Indians, which are gathered to towns, few and small. I found this country one of the poorest in all America. The chief place in it for health and good living is the valley which is called Gracias a Dios, there are some rich farms of cattle and wheat; but because it lieth as near to the country of Guatemala as to Comayagua, and on this side the ways are better than on that, therefore more of that wheat is transported to Guatemala and to the towns about it than to Comayagua or Trujillo. From Trujillo to Guatemala there are between four score and a hundred leagues, which we travelled by land, not wanting in a barren country neither guides nor provision, for the poor Indians thought neither their personal attendance, nor anything that they enjoyed too good for us.

Thus we came again to Guatemala, and were by the friars joyfully entertained, and by the President highly rewarded, and by the city called true Apostles, because we had ventured our lives for the discovery of heathens, and opened a way for their conversion, and found out the chief place of their residence, and sent before us those children to the city who witnessed with being in the cloister our pains and endeavours. Moran was so puffed up with the President's favour and the popular applause that he resolved in Guatemala to venture again his life, and, according to that message which he had sent before to the heathen Indians, to enter amongst them in a peaceable way with half a dozen Indians. He would fain have had me gone with him, but I considered the hardness of the journey, which I thought I should not be able to perform on foot; and also I feared that the barbarians might mutiny against us for those children which we had brought; and lastly I liked not the country, which seemed poor and not for my purpose, to get means sufficient to bring me home to England, which was the chiefest thought and desire of my heart for the satisfaction of my conscience, which I found still unquiet. Wherefore I resolved to forsake the company of my friend Moran, and to desist from new discoveries of heathens, and such difficult undertakings, which might endanger my health and life, and at last bring no profit, but only a little vainglory, fame, and credit in that country. I thought I might better employ my time if I learned some Indian tongue nearer to Guatemala, where I considered the riches of the towns, the readiness of the Indians, and their willingness to further their priest's wants; and lastly, their ignorance in some points of religion, which I thought I might help and clear with some sound doctrine, and with preaching Christ crucified unto them and bringing them unto that rock of eternal bliss and salvation.

I trusted in my friends so much that I knew it would not be hard for me to take my choice of any place about Guatemala, from whence I might facilitate my return to England, and write to Spain, and have every year an answer easier than anywhere else. I opened my mind unto the Provincial (who was then at Guatemala) and he presently and willingly condescended to my request, and counselled me to learn the Poconchi language (whereof I had already got some grounds in the Vera Paz) which is most used about Guatemala, and also is much practised in Vera Paz, and in the country of San Salvador. He promised to send me to the town of Petapa to learn there the language, with a special friend of his named Friar Peter Molina, who was very old, and wanted the help and company of some younger person to ease him in the charge that lay upon him, of so great a town and many travellers that passed that way. The Provincial, as if he had known my mind, pitched upon my very heart's desire; and thus two weeks before Midsummer Day I departed from Guatemala to Petapa, which is six leagues from thence, and there settled myself to learn that Indian tongue.

SURVEY OF WEST INDIES

The friars of those parts that are any way skilful in the Indian languages have composed grammars and dictionaries for the better furthering of others who may supply their places after their decease; but whilst they live are unwilling to teach the languages unto others lest their scholars should after a good and well grounded knowledge of the tongues supplant their own masters, and be means of taking from them that great profit which they have by living as curates in the Indian towns. Yet this old Molina, considering himself in years, and for his good friend's sake the Provincial, was not unwilling to accept of my company, and to impart unto me what knowledge he had got by many years' practice of the Poconchi tongue. He gave me therefore a short abstract of all the rudiments belonging unto it, which did consist chiefly of declining nouns, and conjugating verbs (which I easily learned in the first fortnight that I had been with him) and then a dictionary of Indian words, which was all the rest of my study to get without book until I was able of myself to preach unto the Indians, which with much easiness I obtained by discoursing and conferring with them, what with my private study I had learned.

After the first six weeks Molina writ down for me in the tongue a short exhortation, which he expounded to me, and wished me to learn it without book, which I preached publicly upon the feast of St James. After this he gave me another short exhortation in Spanish, to be preached upon the fifteenth of August, which he made me translate into the Indian tongue, and he corrected in it what he found amiss, wherewith I was a little more emboldened, and feared not to shew myself in public to the Indians. This practice I continued three or four times until Michaelmas, preaching what with his help I had translated out of Spanish, until I was able to talk with the Indians alone, and to make mine own sermons. After Michaelmas, Molina, being not a little vainglorious of what he had done with me in perfecting me in an unknown tongue in so short a space, which was very little above one quarter of the year, writ unto the Provincial acquainting him of what pains he had taken with me, and of the good success of his endeavours, assuring him that I was now fit to take a charge of Indians upon me, and to preach alone, further desiring him that he would bestow upon me some Indian town and benefice, where I might by constant preaching practice and further that which with so much facility I had learned. The Provincial (who had always been my friend) needed not spurs to stir him up to shew more and more his love and kindness unto me; but immediately sent me order to go unto the two towns of Mixco and Pinola, and to take charge of the Indians in them, and to give quarterly an account of what I received thence unto the cloister of Guatemala, unto which all that valley did appertain.

All the Indian towns and the friars that live in them are subordinate unto some cloister; and the friars are called by their Superiors to give up for the cloister's use what moneys they have spared, after their own and their servants' lawful maintenance. Which order yet in Peru is not observed, for there the friars who are once beneficed in Indian towns depend not upon any cloister, but keep all that they get for themselves, and so receive not from their cloisters any clothing, or help for their provision, neither give they any account to their Superiors, but keep, clothe, and maintain themselves with what offerings and other duties fall unto them from the Indians, which is the cause that the friars of Peru are the richest in all the Indies, and live not like friars but rather like lords, and game and dice publicly without control. But the friars of Guatemala, Oaxaca, and Mexico, though they have enough and more than is well suitable to their vow and profession of poverty, yet they enjoy not the liberty of the Peruvian friars in their Indian benefices, for

SURVEY OF WEST INDIES

what is over and above their expenses they give to their Superiors, and from them they receive every month a jar of wine, of an *arrobe* and a half, and every year a new habit with other clothing. Yet with what I have said I must not excuse the friars of Guatemala from liberty, and the enjoyment of wealth and riches; for they also game and sport and spend and fill their bags, and where in their accounts and reckonings to the cloisters they might well give up in a year five hundred crowns besides their own expenses, they give up peradventure three hundred, and usurp the rest for themselves, and their vain and idle uses, and trade and traffic underhand with merchants against their vow of poverty.

With this subordination therefore (which I have shewed) unto the Prior and cloister of Guatemala, was I sent to preach unto the Indians of Mixco and Pinola, from whence for my sake was removed an old friar of almost fourscore years of age, and called to his cloister to rest, who was not able to perform the charge which lay upon him of two towns, three leagues distant one from another. The settled means for maintenance which I enjoyed in these towns, and the common offerings and duties which I received from the Indians was this. In Mixco I was allowed every month twenty crowns, and in Pinola fifteen, which was punctually paid by the *alcaldes* and *regidores*, mayors and jurats, before the end of the month; for which payment the towns sowed a common piece of land with wheat or maize, and kept their book of accounts, wherein they set down what crops they yearly received, what moneys they took in for the sale of their corn, and in the same book I was to write down what every month I received from them; which book at the year's end they were to present to be examined by some officer appointed thereunto by the court of Guatemala. Besides this monthly allowance, I had from the sodalities of the souls in purgatory every week in each town two crowns for a Mass; every month two crowns in Pinola upon the first Sunday of the month from the sodality of the Rosary, and in Mixco likewise every month from three sodalities of the Rosary of the Virgin Mary, which were there belonging unto the Indians, the Spaniards, and the blackamoors, two crowns apiece. Further from two more sodalities belonging to the Vera Cruz, or the Cross of Christ, every month two crowns apiece. And in Mixco from a sodality of the Spaniards belonging to St Nicolas de Tolentino, two crowns every month. And from a sodality of St Blas in Pinola every month two more crowns; and finally in Mixco from a sodality entitled of St Jacintho every month yet two crowns; besides some offerings of either money, fowls or candles upon those days whereon these Masses were sung; all which amounted to threescore and nine crowns a month, which was surely settled and paid before the end of the month. Besides from what I have formerly said of the saints' statues which do belong unto the churches, and do there constantly bring both money, fowls, candles, and other offerings upon their day unto the priest, the yearly revenues which I had in those two towns will appear not to have been small; for in Mixco there were in my time eighteen saints' images, and twenty in Pinola; which brought unto me upon their day four crowns apiece for Mass and sermon and procession, besides fowls, turkeys and *cacao*, and the offerings before the saints, which commonly might be worth at least three crowns upon every saint's day, which yearly amounted to at least two hundred, threescore and six crowns. Besides the sodalities of the Rosary of the Virgin (which as I have before said were four, three in Mixco and one in Pinola), upon five several feasts of the year (which are most observed by the Church of Rome) brought unto me four crowns, two for the day's Mass, and two for a Mass the day following, which they call the anniversary for the dead who had belonged unto those sodalities, which besides those days' offerings (which sometimes were more, sometimes less) and the Indians' presents of fowls and *cacao*, made up yearly four score crowns more. Besides this, the two sodalities of the Vera Cruz upon two feasts of the Cross, the one upon the fourteenth of September, the other upon the third of May, brought four crowns apiece for the Mass of the day, and the anniversary Mass following, and upon every Friday in Lent two crowns, which in the whole year came to four and forty crowns; all which above reckoned was as a sure rent in those two towns. But should I spend time to reckon up what besides did accidentally fall would be tedious.

The Christmas offerings in both those two towns, were worth to me when I lived there at least forty crowns. Thursday and Friday offerings before Easter Day were about a hundred crowns; All Souls' Day offerings commonly worth fourscore crowns; and Candlemas Day offerings commonly forty more. Besides what was offered upon the feast of each town by all the country which came in, which in Mixco one year was worth unto me in candles and money fourscore crowns, and in Pinola (as I reckoned it) fifty more. The communicants (every one giving a real) might make up in both towns at least a thousand reals; and the confessions in Lent at least a thousand more, besides other offerings of eggs, honey, *cacao*, fowls, and fruits. Every christening brought two reals, every marriage two crowns; everyone's death two crowns more at least; and some in my time died who would leave ten or twelve crowns for five or six Masses to be sung for their souls.

Thus are those fools taught that by the priest's singing their souls are delivered from weeping, and from the fire and torments of Purgatory; and thus by singing all the year do those friars charm from the poor Indians and their sodalities and saints an infinite treasure wherewith they enrich themselves and their cloisters; as may be gathered from what I have noted by my own experience in those two towns of Mixco and Pinola (which were far inferior yet to Petapa and Amatitlan in the same valley, and not to be compared in offerings and other church duties to many other towns about that country) which yet yielded unto me with the offerings cast into the chests which stood in the churches for the souls of Purgatory, and with what the Indians offered when they came to speak unto me (for they never visit the priest with empty hands) and with what other Mass stipends did casually come in, the sum of at least two thousand crowns of Spanish money, which might yearly mount to five hundred English pounds. I thought this benefice might be a fitter place for me to live in than in the cloister of Guatemala, wearying out my brains with points of false grounded divinity for to get only the applause of the scholars of the University, and now and then some small profit; which I thought I might look after as well as the rest of my profession, nay with more reason, for that I intended to return to England, and I knew I should have little help for so long a journey in leaving there my friends, if so be that I made not my money my best friend to assist me by sea and land.

My first endeavour was to certify myself from the book of receipts and accounts in the cloister of Guatemala what reckonings my predecessor and others before him had given up to the cloister yearly from Mixco and Pinola, that I might regulate myself and my expenses so as to be able to live with credit, and to get thanks from the cloister by giving more than any before me had given. I found that four hundred crowns had been the most that my old predecessor had given yearly in his accounts; and that before him little more was usually given from those two towns. Whereupon I took occasion once in discourse with the Prior of Guatemala to ask what he would willingly expect from me yearly whilst I lived in those two towns; to which he replied that if I upheld for my part the cloisters usual and yearly revenues, giving what my predecessor had given, he would thank me, and expect no more from me, and that the rest that befell me in those towns I might spend it in books, pictures, chocolate, mules, and servants; to which I made reply that I thought I could live in that benefice creditably enough, and yet give from it more to the cloister than ever any other before me had given, and that I would forfeit my continuing there if I gave not to the cloister every year four hundred and fifty crowns. The Prior thanked me heartily for it, and told me I should not want for wine (wishing me to send for it every month), nor for clothing, which he would every year once bestow upon me. This I thought would save a great part of my charges, and that I was well provided for as long as I lived in the Indies. And here I desire, that England may take notice how a friar that hath professed to be a mendicant, being beneficed in America, may live with four hundred pounds a year clear, and some with much more, with most of his clothing given him besides, and the most charge of his wine supplied, with the abundance of fowls which cost him nothing, and with such plenty of beef as yields him thirteen pound for threepence! Surely well may he game, buy good mules, furnish his chamber with hangings, and rich pictures, and cabinets, yea and fill them with Spanish pistoles, and pieces of eight, and after all trade in the Court of Madrid for a mitre and fat bishopric, which commonly is the end of those proud, worldly, and lazy lubbers.

After I was once settled in these my two towns, my first care was to provide myself of a good mule, which might soon and easily carry me (as often as occasion called) from the one town to the other. I soon found out one, which cost me fourscore crowns, which served my turn very well, to ride speedily the nine miles cross the valley which were between the two towns. Though my chief study here was to perfect myself in the Indian tongue, that I might the better preach unto them, and be well understood, yet I omitted not to search out the Scriptures daily, and to addict myself unto the Word of God, which I knew would profit me more than all those riches and pleasures of Egypt, which for a while I saw I must enjoy till my ten years were fully expired, and licence from Rome or Spain granted for me to return to England, which I began speedily to solicit by means of one Captain Isidro de Zepeda, a Seville merchant and master of one of the ships which came that first year that I was settled in Mixco with merchandise for Guatemala. By this Captain (who passed often through the valley) I writ unto my friends in Spain and had answers, though at first to little purpose, which did not a little increase the troubles of my conscience, which were great, and such whereof the wise man said, 'A wounded conscience who can bear?' My friendship with this Captain Zepeda was such that I broke my mind unto him, desiring him to carry me in his ship to Spain, which he refused to do, telling me the danger he might be in, if complaint should be made to the President of Guatemala, and wishing me to continue where I was, and to store myself with money that I might return with licence and credit. I resolved therefore with David in the 16 Psal. and the 8 V. to set the Lord always before me, and to choose him for my only comfort, and to rely upon his providence who I knew only could order things for my good, and could from America bring me home to the House of Salvation, and to the Household of Faith, from which I considered myself an exile, and far banished. In the meantime I lived five full years in the two towns of Mixco and Pinola. Where I had more occasion to get wealth and money than ever any that lived there before me; for the first year of my abiding there it pleased God to send one of the plagues of Egypt to that country,

PLATE 9

FLYING LOCUSTS
(*From the Dutch Edition of* 1700)

[*Face p.* 288

SURVEY OF WEST INDIES

which was of locusts, which I had never seen till then. They were after the manner of our grasshoppers, but somewhat bigger, which did fly about in number so thick and infinite that they did truly cover the face of the sun and hinder the shining forth of the beams of that bright planet. Where they lighted either upon trees or standing corn, there nothing was expected but ruin, destruction, and barrenness; for the corn they devoured, the leaves and fruits of trees they eat and consumed, and hung so thick upon the branches that with their weight they tore them from the body. The highways were so covered with them that they startled the travelling mules with their fluttering about their head and feet; my eyes were often struck with their wings as I rid along, and much ado I had to see my way, what with a *montero* wherewith I was fain to cover my face, what with the flight of them which were still before my eyes.

The farmers towards the South Sea coast cried out for that their indigo, which was then in grass, was like to be eaten up; from the *ingenios* of sugar the like moan was made, that the young and tender sugar-canes would be destroyed; but above all grievous was the outcry of the husbandmen of the valley where I lived, who feared that their corn would in one night be swallowed up by that devouring legion. The care of the magistrate was that the towns of Indians should all go out into the fields with trumpets, and what other instruments they had to make a noise, and so to affright them from those places which were most considerable and profitable to the commonwealth; and strange it was to see how the loud noise of the Indians and sounding of the trumpets defended some fields from the fear and danger of them. Where they lighted in the mountains and highways, there they left behind them their young ones, which were found creeping upon the ground ready to threaten with a second year's plagues if not prevented, wherefore all the towns were called with spades, mattocks, and shovels to dig long trenches and therein to bury all the young ones.

Thus with much trouble to the poor Indians, and their great pains (yet after much hurt and loss in many places), was that flying pestilence chased away out of the country to the South Sea, where it was thought to be consumed by the ocean, and to have found a grave in the waters, whilst the young ones found it in the land. Yet they were not all so buried, but that shortly some appeared, which not being so many in number as before were with the former diligence soon overcome. But whilst all this fear was, these outcries were made by the country, and this diligence performed by the Indians, the priests got well by it; for everywhere processions were made, and Masses sung for the averting of that plague. In Mixco most of the idols were carried to the field, especially the pictures of Our Lady, and that of St Nicolas Tolentine, in whose name the Church of Rome doth use to bless little breads and wafers with the saint stamped upon them, which they think are able to defend them from agues, plague, pestilence, contagion, or any other great and imminent danger. There was scarce any Spanish husbandman who in this occasion came not from the valley to the town of Mixco with his offering to this saint, and who made not a vow to have a Mass sung unto Saint Nicolas; they all brought breads to be blessed, and carried them back to their farms, some casting them into their corn, some burying them in their hedges and fences, strongly trusting in Saint Nicolas, that his bread would have power to keep the locust out of their fields; and so at the last those simple, ignorant, and blinded souls, when they saw the locusts departed and their corn safe, cried out to Our Lady some, others to Saint Nicolas, *Milagro*, 'a Miracle,' judging the saint worthy of praise more than God, and performing to him their vows of Masses, which in their fear and trouble they had vowed, by which erroneous and idolatrous devotion of theirs I got that year many more crowns than what before I have numbered from the sodalities.

The next year following, all that country was generally infected with a kind of contagious sickness, almost as infectious as the plague, which they call *tabardillo*, and was a fever in the very inward parts and bowels, which scarce continued to the seventh day but commonly took them away from the world to a grave the third or fifth day. The filthy smell and stench which came from them which lay sick of this disease was enough to infect the rest of the house, and all that came to see them. It rotted their very mouths and tongues, and made them as black as a coal before they died. Very few Spaniards were infected with this contagion; but the Indians generally were taken with it. It was reported to have begun about Mexico, and to have spread from town to town, till it came to Guatemala, and went on forwards; and so likewise did the locusts the year before, marching as it were from Mexico over all the country. I visited many that died of this infection, using no other antidote against it save only a handkerchief dipped in vinegar to smell unto, and I thank God I escaped where many died. In Mixco I buried ninety young and old, and in Pinola above an hundred; and for all these that were eight years old, or upwards, I received two crowns for a Mass for their soul's delivery out of Purgatory. But think not that because so many died, therefore the towns growing less my offerings for the future were lessened. The *encomenderos* or lords of the two towns took care for that, who, that they might not lose any part of that tribute which was formerly paid unto them, presently after the sickness was ceased, caused them to be numbered, and (as I have in the chapter before observed) forced to marriage all that were twelve years and upwards of age; which also was a new stream of crowns flowing into my bags, for from every couple that were married I had also two crowns besides other offerings, and in both the towns I married in that occasion above fourscore couple. Truly by all this, I thank the Lord, I was more strengthened in my conceit against the Church of Rome, and not with that greediness of that lucre enticed to continue in it, though I found the preferments there far greater than any might be in the Church of England, where I knew nothing was to be got with singing, or huddling over a Mass. But yet though for the present my profit was great, my eyes were open to see the errors whereby that profit came so plentifully to me, and to all that crew of idolatrous priests.

The judgments ceased not here in that country in my time; but after this contagion there was such an inundation of rain that the husbandmen feared again the loss of all their corn. At noon time the dark clouds for a month together began to thicken and cover the face of the heavens, pouring down such stormy showers as swept away much corn, and many poor cottages of Indians; besides the rain, the fiery thunderbolts breaking through the clouds threatened a doleful judgment to all the country. In the Valley of Mixco two riding together were stricken dead from their mules, the chapel of Our Lady of Carmel in the same valley was burnt to the ground, and likewise two houses at the river of Vacas. In Petapa another flash of lightning, or thunderbolt, fell into the church upon the high altar, cracking the walls in many places, running from altar to altar, defacing all the gold, and leaving a print and stamp where it had gone without any more hurt. In the cloister of the Franciscans in Guatemala, a friar sleeping upon his bed after dinner was stricken dead, his body being left all black as if it had been burnt with fire, and yet no sign of any wound about him. Many accidents happened that year, which was 1632, all about the country. But myself was by the safe protection of the Almighty wonderfully saved;

for being on a Saturday at night in Mixco trembling and fearing, and yet trusting in my God, and praying unto him in my chamber, one flash of lightning or thunderbolt fell close to the church wall to which my chamber joined, and killed two calves, which were tied to a post in a yard, to be slaughtered the next morning. The lightning was so near and terrible that it seemed to have fired all my house, and struck me down unto the ground, where I lay as dead for a great while; when I came again to myself I heard many Indians about my house, who were come to see if either it or the church were set on fire. This stormy season brought me also much profit, for (as formerly) the Spaniards of the valley and the Indians betook themselves to their idol saints carrying them about in procession, which was not done without money, which they call their alms unto their saints, that they may the better be heard and entreated by them.

The summer following there was more than the ordinary earthquakes, which were so great that year in the kingdom of Peru that a whole city called Trujillo was swallowed up by the earth which opened itself, and almost all the people were lost whilst they were at church worshipping and praying unto their saints. The hurt they did about Guatemala was not so much as in other places, only some few mud walls were shaken down, and some churches cracked; which made the people fear and betake themselves again to their saints, and empty their purses before them for Masses and processions, lest the danger should prove as great as was that of the great earthquake which happened before my coming into that country. These earthquakes when they begin are more often than long, for they last but for a while, stirring the earth with three motions, first on the one side, then on the other, and with the third motion they seem to set it right again. If they should continue, they would doubtless hurl down to the ground any steeple or building though never so great and strong. Yet at this time in Mixco some were so violent that they made the steeple bend so much that they made the bells sound. I was so used unto them that many times in my bed I would not stir for them. Yet this year they brought me to such a fear, that had not the Lord been a present refuge to me in time of trouble I had utterly been undone. For being one morning in my chamber studying, so great and sudden was an earthquake, that it made me run from my table to a window, fearing that before I could get down the stairs the whole house might fall upon my head; the window was in a thick wall vaulted upwards like an arch (which the Spaniards hold to be the safest place if a house should fall) where I expected nothing but death. As soon as I got under it, the earthquake ceased, though my heart ceased not to quake with the sudden affrightment. Whilst I was musing and thinking what to do, whether I should run down to the yard, or continue where I was, there came a second shaking worse than the first. I thought with myself if the house should fall the arch would not save my life, and that I should either be stifled or thrown out of the window, which was not very low and near unto the ground, but somewhat high wide open, having no glass casement but wooden shuts (such as there are used), and if I leaped out of the window, I might chance to break a leg, or a limb, yet save my life. The suddenness of the astonishment took from me the best and most mature deliberation in such a case; and in the midst of these my troubled and perplexed thoughts a third motion came as violent as the former, wherewith I had now set one foot in the window to leap down, had not the same Lord by his wonderful providence spoken both to me and to the moving earth, saying, 'Be still and know that am I God'; for certainly had it gone on to a fourth motion, I had by casting down myself broke either my neck, or a leg, or some other joint. Thus was I twice saved by my good God in

Mixco, and in Pinola I was once no less in danger in losing a leg by means of a smaller instrument than is a flea.

This town of Pinola in the Indian language is called *Pancac*; *pan* signifieth in, or amongst, *cac*, signifieth three things, for it signifieth the fire, or a fruit otherwise called *guiava*, or thirdly, a small vermin, commonly called by the Spaniards *nigua*, which is common over all the Indies, but more in some places than in others. Where there are many hogs, there is usually much of this sort of vermin. The Spaniards report that many of the soldiers of Sir Francis Drake died of them, when they landed about Nombre de Dios, and marched up the high mountains of St Pablo towards Panama, who feeling their feet to itch, and not knowing the cause thereof, scratched them so much till they festered, and at last (if this report be true) cost them their lives. Some say they breed in all places, high and low, upon tables, beds, and upon the ground; but experience sheweth the contrary, that they only breed upon the ground, for where the houses are sluttish, and not often swept, there commonly they are most felt; and in that they usually get into the feet and shoes, and seldom into the hands or any other part of the body, argues that they breed upon the ground. They are less than the least flea, and can scarce be perceived, and when they enter into the foot they make it burn and itch; and if then they be looked to, they appear black, and no bigger than the point of a pin, and with a pin may easily be taken out whole; but if part of them be left, the smallest part will do as much harm as the whole and will get into the flesh. When once they are got in, they breed a little bag in the flesh, and in it a great many nits, which increase bigger and bigger to the bigness of a great pea; then they begin again to make the foot itch, which if it be scratched, falleth to festering, and so endangereth the whole foot. Some hold it best to take them out when they cause the first itching and are getting in; but this is hard to do, because they can hardly then be perceived, and they are apt to be broken. Therefore others commonly let them alone until they be got into the flesh, and have bred a bag with nits, which like a blister sheweth itself through the skin, and then with the point of a pin they dig round about the bag, till they can with the pin's point take it out whole, if it be broken it comes to breed again; if it be taken out whole, then they put in a little ear wax, or ashes where the bag lay, and with that the hole is healed up again in a day or two. The way to avoid this vermin's entering into the foot is to lay both shoes and stockings, or whatsoever other clothing, upon some stool or chair high from the ground, and not to go barefoot; which yet is wonderful in the Indians themselves, that though they commonly do go barefoot, yet they are seldom troubled with them, which is attributed to the hardness of their skin; for certainly were they as tender footed and skinned as are those that wear both shoes and stockings, they would be as much troubled with them as these are.

Pancac, or Pinola, is much subject to this vermin, or *nigua*, and I found it by woeful experience, for at my first coming thither not knowing well the quality of it, I let one breed so long in my foot, and continued scratching it, until my foot came to be so festered that I was fain to lie two whole months in a chirurgeon's hand, and at last through God's great mercy and goodness to me I lost not a limb. But that the providence of God may be known to me the worst of all his creatures, living in so far a country from all my friends, and from me may be related unto future generations, before I conclude this chapter I shall further shew both my dangers and deliverances. Though true it is, most of the Indians are but formally Christians, and only outwardly appear such, but secretly are given to witchcraft and idolatry, yet as they were under my charge, I thought by preaching Christ unto them, and

SURVEY OF WEST INDIES

by cherishing them, and defending them from the cruelty of the Spaniards, I might better work upon them to bring them to more knowledge of some truths, at least concerning God and Christ. Therefore as I found them truly loving, kind, and bountiful unto me, so I endeavoured in all occasions to shew them love by commiserating their sufferings, and taking their part against any Spaniard that wronged them, and keeping constantly in my chamber such drugs (as hot waters, aniseed and wine and the like) which I knew might most please them when they came to see me, and most comfort them when they were sick or grieved. This my love and pity towards them had almost in Pinola cost me my life. For an Indian of that town serving a Spaniard named Francisco de Montenegro (who lived a mile and a half from thence) was once so pitifully beaten and wounded by his master, for that he told him he would complain to me that he paid him not his wages, that he was brought home to the town, and had I not out of my charity called for a chirurgeon from Petapa to cure him, he had certainly died. I could not but complain for the poor Indian unto the President of Guatemala, who respecting my complaint, sent for my Spaniard to the city, imprisoned him, and kept him close until the Indian was recovered, and so with a fine sent him back again. In a sermon further I pressed this home unto the neighbouring Spaniards, warning them of the wrongs and abuses which they offered unto the poor Indians, which I told them I would put up no more than any injury done unto myself, for that I looked upon them as neophytes and new plants of Christianity, who were not to be discouraged, but by all means of love encouraged to come to Christ; withal I commanded all the Indians that had any wrong done unto them to come unto me, assuring them that I would make such a complaint for them as should be heard, as they might perceive I had lately done to some purpose. This sermon stuck so in Montenegro his stomach, that (as I was informed) he made an oath that he would procure my death. Though it was told me, yet I could hardly believe it, judging it to be more a bravery and a vain boasting of a Spaniard than anything else; yet by the advice of some friends I was counselled to look to myself, which yet I slighted, until one day the boys and Indians that served in my house came running to my chamber door, wishing me to look to myself, and not to come out, for that Montenegro was come into my yard with a naked sword to kill me. I charged them from within to call the officers of the town to aid and assist me; but in the meanwhile my furious Spaniard, perceiving himself discovered, left the town. With this I thought of securing of myself better, and called for a blackamoor Miguel Dalva, a very stout and lusty fellow who lived from me half a mile, to be about me until I could discover more of Montenegro's designs and malicious intents. The next Sabbath day in the morning being to ride to the town of Mixco, I carried my blackamoor, and half a dozen of Indians in my company, and going through a little wood in the midst of the valley, there I found my enemy waiting for me, who seeing the train I brought, durst do nothing but gave me spiteful languages, telling me he hoped that he should find me alone some time or other. With this I thought fit to delay no longer my second complaint to the President against him, who as before heard me willingly, and after a month's imprisonment banished Montenegro thirty leagues from the valley. And not only from Spaniards was I in danger for the Indians' sake whilst I lived in those towns, but also from some Indians themselves (who were false in religion) I did undergo great perils, and yet was still delivered.

In Pinola there were some who were much given to witchcraft, and by the power of the Devil did act strange things. Amongst the rest there was one old woman named Martha de Carrillo, who had been by some of the town formerly accused for bewitching many; but the Spanish justices acquitted her, finding no sure evidence against her; with this she grew worse and worse, and did much harm. When I was there, two or three died, withering away, declaring at their death that this Carrillo had killed them, and that they saw her often about their beds, threatening them with a frowning and angry look. The Indians for fear of her durst not complain against her, nor meddle with her; whereupon I sent word unto Don Juan de Guzman, the lord of that town, that if he took not order with her, she would destroy his town. He hearing of it, got for me a commission from the Bishop and another officer of the Inquisition, to make diligent and private enquiry after her life and actions; which I did, and found among the Indians many and grievous complaints against her, most of the town affirming that certainly she was a notorious witch, and that before her former accusation she was wont whithersoever she went about the town to go with a duck following her, which when she came to the church would stay at the door till she came out again, and then would return home with her, which duck they imagined was her beloved devil and familiar spirit, for that they had often set dogs at her and they would not meddle with her, but rather run away from her. This duck never appeared more with her since she was formerly accused before the justice, which was thought to be her policy that she might be no more suspected thereby. This old woman was a widow, and of the poorest of the town in outward shew, and yet she always had store of money, which none could tell which way she might come by it.

Whilst I was thus taking privy information against her (it being the time of Lent, when all the town came to confession) she among the rest came to the church to confess her sins, and brought me the best present and offering of all the town, for whereas a real is common she brought me four, and besides a turkey, eggs, fish, and a little bottle of honey. She thought thereby to get with me a better opinion than I had of her from the whole town; I accepted of her great offering, and heard her confession, which was on nothing but trifles, which could scarce be judged sinful actions. I examined her very close of what was the common judgment of all the Indians, and especially of those who dying had declared to myself at their death that she had bewitched them, and before their sickness had threatened them, and in their sickness appeared threatening them with death about their beds, none but they themselves seeing her. To which she replied weeping, that she was wronged; I asked her how she being a poor widow without any sons to help her, without any means of livelihood had so much money, as to give me more than the richest of the town, how she came by that fish, turkey, and honey, having none of this of her own about her house; to which she replied, that God loved her and gave her all these things, and that with her money she had bought the rest. I asked her of whom; she answered that out of the town she had them. I persuaded her much to repentance, and to forsake the Devil and all fellowship with him; but her words and answers were of a saintly and holy woman, and she earnestly desired me to give her the Communion with the rest that were to receive the next day. Which I told her I durst not do, using Christ's words, 'Give not the children's bread unto dogs, nor cast your pearls unto swine'; and that it would be a great scandal to give the Communion unto her, who was suspected generally, and had been accused for a witch. This she took very ill telling me that she had many years received the Communion, and now in her old age it grieved her to be deprived of it; her tears were many, yet I could not be moved with them, but resolutely denied her the Communion, and so dismissed her.

At noon when I had done my work in the church,

I bad my servants go to gather up the offerings, and gave order to have the fish dressed for my dinner which she had brought; but no sooner was it carried into the kitchen when the cook looking on it found it full of maggots and stinking, so that I was forced to hurl it away. With that I began to suspect my old witch, and went to look on her honey, and pouring it out into a dish, I found it full of worms; her eggs I could not know from others, there being near a hundred offered that day; but after as I used them we found some rotten, some with dead chickens within; the next morning the turkey was found dead; as for her four reals, I could not perceive whether she had bewitched them out of my pocket, for that I had put them with many others which that day had been given me, yet as far as I could, I called to memory who and what had been given me, and in my judgment and reckoning I verily thought that I missed four reals. At night when my servants the Indians were gone to bed, I sat up late in my chamber betaking myself to my books and study, for I was the next morning to make an exhortation to those that received the Communion. After I had studied a while, it being between ten and eleven of the clock, on a sudden the chief door in the hall (where in a lower room was my chamber, and the servants', and three other doors) flew open, and I heard one come in, and for a while walk about; then was another door opened which went into a little room, where my saddles were laid; with this I thought it might be the blackamoor Miguel Dalva, who would often come late to my house to lodge there, especially since my fear of Montenegro, and I conjectured that he was laying up his saddle. I called unto him by his name two or three times from within my chamber, but no answer was made; but suddenly another door that went out to a garden flew also open, wherewith I began within to fear, my joints trembled, my hair stood up, I would have called out to the servants, and my voice was as it were stopped with the sudden affrightment. I began to think of the witch, and put my trust in God against her, and encouraged myself and voice calling out to the servants, and knocking with a cane at my door within that they might hear me, for I durst not open it and go out. With the noise which I made the servants awaked and came out to my chamber door; then I opened it, and asked them if they had not heard somebody in the hall, and all the doors opened. They said they were asleep, and heard nothing, only one boy said he heard all, and related unto me the same that I had heard. I took my candle then in my hand and went out into the hall with them to view the doors, and I found them all shut, as the servants said they had left them. Then I perceived that the witch would have affrighted me, but had no power to do me any harm; I made two of the servants lie in my chamber, and went to bed. In the morning early I sent for my *fiscal*, the clerk of the church, and told him what had happened that night; he smiled upon me, and told me it was the widow Carrillo, who had often played such tricks in the town with those that had offended her, and therefore he had the night before come unto me from her desiring me to give her the Communion lest she should do me some hurt, which I denied unto him as I had done to herself. The clerk bad me be of good cheer, for he knew she had no power over me to do me any hurt. After the Communion that day some of the chief Indians came unto me, and told me that old Carrillo had boasted that she would play me some trick or other, because I would not give her the Communion. But I to rid the town of such a limb of Satan sent her to Guatemala, with all the evidences and witnesses which I had found against her unto the President and Bishop, who commanded her to be put in prison, where she died within two months.

Many more Indians there were in that town who

were said in my time to do very strange things. One called John Gonzalez was reported to change himself into the shape of a lion, and in that shape was one day shot in the nose by a poor harmless Spaniard who chiefly got his living by going about the woods and mountains and shooting at wild deer and other beasts to make money of them. He espied one day a lion, and having no other aim at him but his snout behind a tree, he shot at him; the lion ran away. The same day this Gonzalez was taken sick; I was sent for to hear his confession; I saw his face and nose all bruised, and asked him how it came. He told me then that he had fallen from a tree and almost killed himself; yet afterwards he accused the poor Spaniard for shooting at him; the business was examined by a Spanish justice; my evidence was taken for what Gonzalez told me of his fall from a tree; the Spaniard was put to his oath, who sware that he shot at a lion in a thick wood, where an Indian could scarce be thought to have any business; the tree was found out in the wood whereat the shot had been made and was still marked with the shot and bullet, which Gonzalez confessed was to be the place, and was examined how he neither fell nor was seen by the Spaniard when he came to seek for the lion thinking he had killed him; to which he answered that he ran away lest the Spaniard should kill him indeed. But his answers seeming frivolous, the Spaniard's integrity being known, and the great suspicion that was in the town of Gonzalez his dealing with the Devil, cleared the Spaniard from what was laid against him.

But this was nothing to what after happened to one John Gomez, the chiefest Indian of that town of near fourscore years of age, the head and ruler of the principallest tribe among the Indians, whose advice and counsel was taken and preferred before all the rest, who seemed to be a very godly Indian, and very seldom missed morning and evening prayers in the church, and had bestowed great riches there. This Indian very suddenly was taken sick (I being then in my other town of Mixco) the *mayordomos*, or stewards of the sodality of the Virgin, fearing that he might die without confession and they be chid for their negligence, at midnight called me up at Mixco, desiring me to go presently and help John Gomez to die, whom also they said desired much to see me and to receive some comfort from me. I judging it a work of charity, although the time of the night were unseasonable, and the great rain at the present might have stopped my charity, yet I would not be hindered by either of them, and so set forth to ride nine miles both in the dark and wet. When I came to Pinola being thorough wet to the skin, I went immediately to the house of old sick Gomez, who lay with his face all muffled up, thanked me for my pains and care I had for his soul; he desired to confess, and by his confession and weeping evidenced nothing but a godly life and a willing desire to die and to be with Christ. I comforted him and prepared him for death, and before I departed, asked him how he felt himself; he answered that his sickness was nothing but old age and weakness. With this I went to my house, changed myself and lay down a while to rest, when suddenly I was called up again to give Gomez the extreme unction, which the Indians (as they have been ignorantly taught) will not omit to receive before they die. As I anointed him in his nose, his lips, his eyes, his hands and his feet, I perceived that he was swelled, and black and blue, but made nothing of it judging it to proceed from the sickness of his body; I went again home being now break of the day, when after I had taken a small nap, some Indians come to my door for to buy candles to offer up for John Gomez his soul, whom they told me was departed, and was that day to be buried very solemnly at Mass. I arose with drowsy eyes after so unquiet a night's rest, and walked to the church, where I saw the grave was preparing.

SURVEY OF WEST INDIES

I met with two or three Spaniards who lived near the town and were come to Mass that morning, who went in with me to my chamber, and with them I fell into discourse about John Gomez, telling them what comfort I had received at his death, whom I judged to have lived very holily, and doubted not of his salvation, and that the town would much want him, for that he was their chief guide and leader, ruling them with good advice and counsel. At this the Spaniards smiled one at another, and told me I was much deceived by all the Indians, but especially by the deceased Gomez, if I judged him to have been a saint and holy man. I told them that they as enemies to the poor Indians judged still uncharitably of them; but that I who knew very well their consciences, could judge better of them than they. One then replied, that it seemed I little knew the truth of John Gomez his death by the confession which he had made unto me, and that I seemed to be ignorant of the stir which was in the town concerning his death. This seemed so strange unto me that I desired them to inform me of the truth. Then they told me that the report went that John Gomez was the chief wizard of all the wizards and witches in the town, and that commonly he was wont to be changed into the shape of a lion, and so to walk about the mountains. That he was ever a deadly enemy to one Sebastian Lopez an ancient Indian, and head of another tribe, and that both of them two days before had met in the mountain, Gomez in the shape of a lion, and Lopez in the shape of a tiger, and that they fought most cruelly till Gomez (who was the older, and weaker) was tired, much bit and bruised, and died of it. And further that I might be assured of this truth, they told me that Lopez was in prison for it, and the two tribes striving about it; and that the tribe and kindred of Gomez demanded from Lopez and his tribe and kindred satisfaction, and a great sum of money, or else did threaten to make the case known unto the Spanish power and authority, which yet they were unwilling to do if they could agree and smother it up among themselves, that they might not bring an aspersion upon their whole town. This seemed very strange unto me, and I could not resolve what to believe, and thought I would never more believe an Indian if I found John Gomez to have so much dissembled and deceived me. I took my leave of the Spaniards and went myself to the prison, where I found Lopez with fetters. I called one of the officers of the town, who was *alguazil mayor*, and my great friend, unto my house, and privately examined him why Lopez was kept so close prisoner; he was loath to tell me fearing the rest of the Indians, and hoping the business would be taken up and agreed by the two tribes, and not noised about the country which at that very instant the two *alcaldes* and *regidores*, mayors and jurats, with the chief of both tribes were sitting about in the town-house all that morning. But I seeing the officer so timorous, was more desirous to know something, and pressed more upon him for the truth, giving him an inkling of what I had heard from the Spaniards before. To which he answered that if they could agree amongst themselves, they feared no ill report from the Spaniards against their town; I told him I must know what they were agreeing upon amongst themselves so closely in the town-house. He told me, if I would promise him to say nothing of him (for he feared the whole town if they should know he had revealed anything unto me) he would tell me the truth. With this I comforted him, and gave him a cup of wine, and encouraged him, warranting him that no harm should come unto him for what he told me.

Then he related the business unto me as the Spaniards had done, and told me that he thought the tribes amongst themselves would not agree, for that some of Gomez his friends hated Lopez and all such as were so familiar with the Devil, and cared not if Gomez his dissembling life were laid open to the world; but others, he said, who were as bad as Lopez and Gomez, would have it kept close, lest they and all the witches and wizards of the town should be discovered. This struck me to the very heart, to think that I should live among such people, whom I saw were spending all they could get by their work and labour upon the church, saints, and in offerings, and yet were so privy to the counsels of Satan; it grieved me that the Word I preached unto them did no more good, and I resolved from that time forward to spend most of my endeavours against Satan's subtlety, and to shew them more than I had done the great danger of their souls who had made any compact with the Devil, that I might make them abandon and abjure his works, and close with Christ by faith. I dismissed the Indian, and went to the church, to see if the people were come to Mass; I found there nobody but only two who were making Gomez his grave. I went back to my chamber troubled much within myself, whether I should allow him a Christian burial who had lived and died so wickedly, as I had been informed. Yet I thought I was not bound to believe one Indian against him, nor the Spaniards, whom I supposed spoke but by hearsay.

Whilst I was thus musing, there came unto me at least twenty of the chiefest of the town with the two mayors, jurats, and all the officers of justice, who desired me to forbear that day the burying of John Gomez, for that they had resolved to call a crown officer to view his corpse and examine his death, lest they all should be troubled for him, and he again unburied. I made as if I knew nothing, but enquired of them the reason; then they related all unto me, and told me how there were witnesses in the town who saw a lion and a tiger fighting, and presently lost the sight of the beasts, and saw John Gomez and Sebastian Lopez much about the same place parting one from another; and that immediately John Gomez came home bruised to his bed, from whence he never rose more, and that he declared upon his deathbed unto some of his friends that Sebastian Lopez had killed him: whereupon they had him in safe custody. Further they told me that though they had never known so much wickedness of these two chief heads of their town whom they had much respected and followed, yet now upon this occasion, from the one tribe and the other, they were certainly informed that both of them did constantly deal with the Devil, which would be a great aspersion upon their town, but they for their parts abjured all such wicked ways, and prayed me not to conceive the worse of all for a few, whom they were resolved to persecute, and suffer not to live amongst them. I told them I much liked their good zeal, and encouraged them as good Christians to endeavour the rooting out of Satan from their town, and they did very well in giving notice to Guatemala, to the Spanish power, of this accident, and that if they had concealed it they might all have been punished as guilty of Gomcz his death, and agents with Satan and his instruments. I assured them I had no ill conceit of them, but rather judged well of them for what they were agreed to do. The crown officer was sent for who came that night and searched Gomez his body; I was present with him, and found it all bruised, scratched, and in many places bitten and sore wounded. Many evidences and suspicions were brought in against Lopez by the Indians of the town, especial by Gomez his friends, whereupon he was carried away to Guatemala, and there again was tried by the same witnesses, and not much denying the fact himself, was there hanged. And Gomez, though his grave was opened in the church, he was not buried in it but in another made ready for him in a ditch.

In Mixco I found also some Indians no less dissemblers than was this Gomez, and those of the chiefest and richest of the town, who were four brothers called

Fuentes, and half a score more. These were outwardly very fair tongued, liberal, and free handed to the church, much devoted to the saints, great feasters upon their day, and yet in secret great idolaters. But it pleased God to make me his instrument to discover and bring to light the secrecy of their hidden works of darkness, which it seemed the privacy of a thick wood and mountain had many years hid from the eyes of the world. Some of these being one day in the company of other better Christians drinking hard of their *chicha*, boasted of their god, saying that he had preached unto them better than I could preach, nay that he had plainly told them that they should not believe anything that I preached of Christ, but follow the old ways of their forefathers, who worshipped their gods aright, but now by the example of the Spaniards they were deluded, and brought to worship a false god. The other Christians hearing of this began to wonder, and to enquire of them where that god was, and with much ado, promising to follow their ways and their god, got out of them the place and mountain where they might find him. Though this in drunkenness were agreed upon, yet in soberness the good Christians thought better of what they had agreed upon, slighted what before in drinking they heard, and yet it was not kept by them so close but that it came to the ears of a Spaniard in the valley, who finding himself touched in conscience, came to Mixco to me, and told me what he had heard, that some Indians of that town followed an idol, and boasted that he had preached unto them against my doctrine and for the ways of the former heathens. I thanked God for that he was pleased to undermine the secret works of Satan daily; and desired the Spaniard to tell me by whom he came to know of this. He told me the Indian's name from whom he had it, and that he was afraid to discover the Indians, and to tell me of it. I sent for the Indian before the Spaniard, who confessed unto me that he had heard of such a thing; but knew that if he did discover the Indians they with the power of the Devil would do him much harm; I told him, if he were a true Christian he ought to fight against the Devil and not to fear him who could do him no harm if God were with him and he closed by faith with Christ, and that the discovery of that idol might be a means for the converting of the idolaters, when they should see the small power of their false god against the true God of the Christians. Further I told him plainly, that if he did not tell me who the Indians were, and where their idol was, that I would have him to Guatemala, and there make him discover what he knew. Here the Indian began to tremble, and told me the Fuentes had boasted of such an idol, whom they called their god, and gave some signs of a fountain and of a pine tree at the mouth of a cave in such a mountain. I asked him if he knew the place, or what kind of idol it was; he told me that he had often been in that mountain, where he had seen two or three springs of water, but never was in any cave. I asked him if he would go with me and help me to find it out; he refused still fearing the idolaters, and wished me not to go, for fear if they should be there, they might kill me rather than be discovered. I answered him that I would carry with me such a guard as should be able to defend me against them, and my faith in the true living God would secure me against that false god.

I resolved therefore with the Spaniard to go to search out the cave the next day, and to carry with me three or four Spaniards and my blackamoor Miguel Dalva, and that Indian. I told him I would not suffer him to go home to his house that day, for fear he should discover in the town my design and purpose, and so we might be prevented by the idolaters, who certainly that night would take away their idol. The Indian still refused, till I threatened him to send for the officers of justice, and to secure his person; with this he yielded, and that he might have no discourse with anybody in the town, nor with the servants of my house, I desired the Spaniard to take him home to his house, and to keep him there close that day and night, promising to be with him the next morning. I charged the Spaniard also with secrecy, and so dismissed him with the Indian. That day I rid to Pinola for the blackamoor Miguel Dalva, and brought him to Mixco with me, not telling him what my intent was; I went also to four neighbouring Spaniards, desiring them to be in a readiness the next morning to go a little way with me for the service of God, and to meet me at such a neighbour's house, and that if they would bring their fowling pieces we might chance to find some sport where we went, and as for provision of wine and meat, I would provide sufficiently. They promised to go with me, thinking that although I told them it was for the service of God, my purpose only was to hunt after some wild deer in the mountains. I was glad they construed my action that way, and so went home, and provided that night a good gammon of bacon, and some fowls roasted, cold, and others boiled, well peppered and salted, for the next day's work. Where I had appointed my Indian to be kept, I met with the rest of my company, and from thence we went together to the place of the idolaters' worshipping, which was some six miles from Mixco towards the town of St John Sacatepequez. When we came into the wood we presently met with a deep *barranca*, or bottom, where was a running water, which encouraged us to make there diligent search, but nothing could be found; from thence we ascended up out of the *barranca*, and found after much time spent a spring of water, and looked carefully about it, but could find no cave. Thus in vain we searched till the evening, and fearing lest we might lose our way and ourselves, if the night overtook us, my friends began to speak of returning homewards. But I considering that as yet we had not gone over one half part of the wood, and to go home and come again might make us to be noted and spoken of, we thought it our best way to take up our lodging that night in the wood, and in that bottom which we first searched, where was good water for to drink chocolate, and warm lying under the trees, and so in the morning to make our second search. The company was very willing to yield unto it, and the calm night favoured our good intentions. We made a fire for our chocolate, and supped exceeding well of our cold meat, and spent most part of the night in merry discourse, having a watchful eye over our Indian, lest he should give us the slip, and committing him to the charge of Miguel Dalva.

In the morning we prayed unto God, beseeching him to guide us that day in the work we went about, and to discover unto us the cave of darkness and iniquity where lay hid that instrument of Satan, that so by his discovery glory might be given unto our true God, and shame and punishment brought upon his enemies. We entered again into the thick wood up a steepy hill, and having throughly searched all the south side of it, we went on to the north side, where we found another deep descent, which we began to walk down looking on every side, and not in vain; for almost half a mile from the top we found some marks of a way that had been used and trodden, which we followed until we came to another spring of water; we searched narrowly about it, and found some pieces of broken earthen dishes and pots, and one piece of a chafing dish, such as the Indians use to burn frankincense in in the churches before their saints. We verily imagined that these were pieces of some such instruments wherewith the idolaters performed their duty unto their idol, and we were the more comforted for that we knew that earthen ware had been made in Mixco; the pine tree which immediately we discovered confirmed our hopes. When we came unto it we made very little more search, for near at hand was the cave, which was dark within, but light at the mouth, where we found more earthen ware, with ashes in them, which assured us of some frankincense that had been burned. We knew not how far the cave might reach within, nor what might be in it, and therefore with a flint we struck fire and lighted a couple of candles and went in; at the entering it was broad, and went a little forward, but when we were in, we found it turn on the left hand towards the mountain, and not far; for within two rods we found the idol standing upon a low stool covered with a linen cloth. The substance of it was wood, black shining like jet, as if it had been painted or smoked, the form was of a man's head unto the shoulders, without either beard or mustachios; his look was grim with a wrinkled forehead and broad startling eyes. We feared not his frowning look, but presently seized upon him; and as we lifted him up we found under him some single reals, which his favourites had offered unto him; which made us search more diligently the cave; and it was not amiss, for we found upon the ground more single reals, some plantains and other fruits, wax candles half burned, pots of maize, one little one of honey, little dishes wherein frankincense had been burned, whereby I perceived the idolaters and Christians both agreed in their offerings; and had I not been informed that they called this idol their god, I could have blamed them no more than the rest of the towns who worship, kneel before, and offer such offerings unto their saints made of wood, and some no handsomer than was this idol, which I thought might have been some beast's shape; but being the shape and form of a man, they might have named him by the name of some saint, and so some way have excused themselves, which they could not do, nor would they do it, in that they persisted in this error that he was their god, and had spoken and preached unto them, and being afterwards asked by me whether it were the picture of any saint, such as were in Mixco, and other churches, they answered, No, but that he was above all the saints in the country.

We were very joyful to see that we had not spent our time in vain; we cut down boughs of trees, and filled the cave with them and stopped the mouth of it up, and came away, making the Indian that went with us carry the idol on his back wrapped up in a cloth, that it might not be seen or perceived as we went. I thought it fit to delay the time till night, and then to enter into Mixco, that the Indians might see nothing. So I stayed at one of the Spaniard's houses till it were late, and desired him to warn from me all the Spaniards thereabouts to be at Mixco church the next Sabbath (fearing lest the idolaters might be many, and rise up against me) that I had somewhat to say unto them and their blackamoors concerning their sodalities, for I would not have them know of the idol till they heard of it and saw it in the church, lest it should come to the Indians' hearing, and so the idolaters might absent themselves. At night I took my Indian, and Miguel Dalva with me, and went home, and shutting up the idol in a chest till the next Sabbath, I dismissed the Indian, charging him to say nothing, for he knew if he did what harm might come unto him from the idolaters, and I knew few words now would suffice, for that he feared himself if it should be known that he had been with me. I kept Miguel Dalva with me, who was desirous to see the end of the business, and prepared myself against the next Sabbath to preach upon the 3 v. of the 20 of *Exodus*: 'Thou shalt have none other gods before me,' though it were a text nothing belonging to the Gospel of the day, from whence commonly in the Church of Rome the texts and subjects of sermons are deducted; but I judged that text most seasonable for the present occasion. On the Sabbath day in the morning, when the pulpit was made ready by him who had care of the church and altars, I caused Miguel Dalva to carry under his cloak the idol, and to leave it in the pulpit upon the ground that it might not be seen, till such time as I should think fit in my sermon to produce it, and to watch about the church till the congregation came in, that none might see it or take it away. Never was there a greater resort from abroad to that church than that day of Spaniards and blackamoors, who by the warning I sent unto them expected some great matter from me, and of the town very few were absent, the Fuentes and all the rest that were suspected to be that idol's favourites (little thinking that their god was brought from his cave, and now lay hid in the pulpit to shame them) came also that day to church. I commanded Miguel Dalva to be himself near the pulpit at sermon time, and to warn those Spaniards that knew the business, and some more blackamoors his friends, to be also near the pulpit stairs.

Thus Mass being ended, I went up to preach; when I rehearsed the words of my text, I perceived both Spaniards and Indians began to look one upon another, as not being used to sermons out of the Old Testament. I went on laying open this command of God, for having no other gods before him, so that the doctrine might seem to convince all that were there present, as well saint-worshippers as indeed that idol's worshippers, if the cause of my preaching upon that subject had not diverted their eyes from themselves to behold their own guiltiness of idolatry, and to look only upon those who worshipped a piece of wood for God, and not, as they did, for a saint (which yet in my judgment was much alike). After I had spoken what I thought fit concerning that horrible sin, and shewed that no creature could have the power of God (who was the Creator of all things) neither could do good or harm without the true living God's commission, especially inanimate creatures as stocks and stones, who by the hands and workmanship of man might have eyes, and yet were dead idols, and see not, might have ears and not hear, might have mouths and not speak, might have hands and not work, nor help or defend with them such as worshipped them, and bowed down unto them.

Thus having half finished my sermon, I bowed myself down in the pulpit, and lifted up the black, grim, and staring devil, and placed that Dagon on one side of the pulpit, with my eyes fixed upon some of the Fuentes and others, who I perceived changed their colour, blushed, and were sore troubled looking one upon another. I desired the congregation to behold what a god was worshipped by some of them, and all to take notice of him, if any knew what part of the earth was the dominion of this god, or from whence he came. I told them that some had boasted that this piece of wood had spoken and preached against what I had taught of Christ, and that therefore he was worshipped by them for God, and they had offered money, honey, and of the fruits of the earth unto him, and burnt frankincense before him in a secret and hidden cave under the earth, shewing thereby that they were ashamed to own him publicly, and that he lurking in the darkness of the earth shewed certainly that he belonged to the Prince of Darkness. I challenged him there in public to speak for himself, or else by silence to shame and confound all his worshippers. I shewed them how being but wood he had been made and fashioned by the hands of man, and therefore was but a dead idol. I spent a great deal of time arguing with him, and defying Satan who had used him as his instrument, daring the Devil himself to take him from that place which I had confined him to if he could, to shew what little power he or Satan had against the power of my faith in Christ. After much arguing and reasoning according to the shallow capacity of the Indians present, I told them if that their god had power to deliver him from that execution which I had intended againſt him (which was there publicly to have him cut in pieces and burnt) they should not believe the Gospel of Jesus Chriſt; but if they saw no power at all in him againſt me the weakeſt inſtrument of the true living God, then I beseeched them to be converted unto that true God who created all things, and to embrace salvation by his Son the only Mediator and Saviour Jesus Chriſt, and to renounce and abjure from that time all heathenish idolatry of their forefathers, assuring them for what was paſt I would intercede for them, and secure them from what punishment might be inflicted upon them by the President and Bishop, and if they would come to me I would spend my beſt endeavours for the helping and furthering of them in the way of Chriſtianity.

And thus concluding without naming any person, I went down out of the pulpit, and caused the idol to be brought after me, and sending for an axe and for two or three great pans of coals, I commanded him to be hewn in very small pieces, and to be caſt in the fire and burned before all the people in the midſt of the Church. The Spaniards cried out joyfully *Victor, Victor*, and others repeated, *Gloria á nueſtro Dios*, ' Glory to our God,' the idolaters held their peace and spake not then a word. But afterwards they acted moſt spitefully againſt me, and conspired day and night to get me at some advantage, and to kill me. I writ to the President of Guatemala informing him of what I had done; and to the Bishop (as an inquisitor to whom such cases of idolatry did belong) to be informed from him of what course I should take with the Indians who were but in part yet discovered unto me, and those only by the relation of one Indian. From both I received great thanks for my pains in searching the mountain and finding out the idol, and for my zeal in burning of it. And as touching the Indian idolaters their counsel unto me was that I should further enquire after the rest and discover as many as I could, and endeavour to convert them to the knowledge of the true God by fair and sweet means, shewing pity unto them for their great blindness, and promising them upon their repentance pardon from the Inquisition, which considering them to be but new plants useth not such rigour with them which it useth with Spaniards if they fall into such horrible sins. This advice I followed, and sent privately for the Fuentes to my chamber, and told them how merciful the Inquisition was unto them, expecting their conversion and amendment. They seemed somewhat stubborn and angry for that I had burned that god, whom not only they, but many others in the town, and also in the town of Saint John Sacatepequez did worship. I used reasons to persuade them no honour was due unto it, as to a god. But one of them boldly replied, that they knew that it was a piece of wood and of itself could not speak, but seeing it had spoken (as they were all witnesses) this was a miracle whereby they ought to be guided, and they did verily believe that God was in that piece of wood, which since the speech made by it was more than ordinary wood, having God himself in it, and therefore deserved more offerings and adoration than those saints in the church, who did never speak unto the people. I told them that the Devil rather had framed that speech (if any they had heard) for to deceive their souls and lead them to Hell; which they might easily perceive from the doctrine which I was informed he had preached against Christ the only begotten son of God, whom the Father loveth and in whom he is well pleased, and against whom he certainly would not speak in that idol. Another answered boldly, our forefathers never knew what Christ was until the Spaniards came unto that country, but they knew there were gods, and did worship them, and did sacrifice unto them; and for aught they knew this god of theirs belonged in old times unto their forefathers. 'Why then,' said I unto them, 'he was a weak god who by my hands hath been burned.' I perceived that at that time there was no reasoning with them, for they were stubborn and captious, and so I dismissed them. Had not God most graciously protected me against these my enemies I had certainly been murdered by them; for a month after the burning of the idol, when I thought all had been forgotten, and that the idolaters were quiet, then they began to act their spite and malice, which first I discovered by a noise which once at midnight I heard of people about my house, and at my chamber door, to whom I called out from my bed, not daring to open, but could have no answer from them. I perceived they would have come in by force, for they pushed hard at the door. Whereupon I took suddenly the sheets from off my bed, tying them with a strong knot together, and with another to a bar of the window, making myself ready to fall down by them to the ground, and so to flee in the dark night, if they had used violence to come in. The sheets being thus prepared, and they still at the door thrusting without any word from them, I thought by calling and crying out aloud I might affright them away. Wherefore with a shrill voice I called first to my servants, who were but boys, and lay at the further end of a long gallery, then I cried out to the neighbouring houses to come and assist me against thieves. The servants had heard the noise and were awake, who presently at my call came out; and with their coming my enemies ran down the stairs, and were heard no more that night. But I perceiving which way their spite and malice was bent, thought fit to be no more alone in the night with boys only in so great a house as was that of Mixco; whereupon the next day I sent for my trusty friend Miguel Dalva who was able to fight alone with any half dozen of Indians, wishing him to bring with him what weapons he could get for my defence. I kept him with me a fortnight; and the next Sabbath I gave warning in the church that whosoever came in the night to my house to affright me, or to do me any other mischief, should look to himself, for that I had weapons both offensive and defensive.

Though for a while I heard no more of them, yet they desisted not altogether from their evil and malicious intents; for, knowing that Miguel Dalva did not lie in the same chamber with me, a fortnight after (I being till about midnight with my candle studying) they came up the stairs so softly that I heard them not; but the blackamoor being awake it seems perceived that they were coming up, and softly arose up from a long table were he lay upon a mat, and took in his hand a couple of brick-bats of many which lay under the table for a work which I had in hand, and as he opened the door made a little noise, which was to them an item to flee down the stairs, and to run (as they thought) for their lives. The blackamoor did also run after them, and finding they had got too much advantage of him, and not knowing which way they might take, sent after them with a fury his two brick-bats, wherewith he supposed he did hit one of them, for the next day walking about the town he met with one of the Fuentes having a cap on his head, and he enquired of some Indians what he ailed, and he understood by them that his head was broke, but how they knew not. They perceiving that I was thus guarded by Miguel Dalva, desisted from that time from coming any more in the night unto my house, but yet desisted not from their spite and malice and from acting mischief against me. For a month after when I thought that all had been forgotten, and they seemed outwardly to be kind and courteous, there came a messenger to me from the oldest of them, named Pablo de Fuentes, to tell me that he was very sick, and like to die, and desired me to go to comfort and instruct him in the truth, for that he truly desired to be converted. I conceived very great joy at this news, and doubted not of the truth and certainty of it, and prayed to God to direct me in the conversion of that soul; and so with haste and good zeal I went unto his house, where soon my joy and comfort was turned into bitterness; for when I came to the door of his house, and was with one step entered, I found all the brothers of Pablo Fuentes, and some others who were suspected to be idolaters, sitting round the room; and missing Pablo, I withdrew my foot a little, and asked them where he was, mistrusting somewhat to see them there all gathered together; but when I perceived that they stood not up, nor answered me a word, nor so much as took off their hats to me, then I began to fear indeed, and to suspect some treachery; and so I turned back resolving to go home again. But no sooner was I turned, but behold Pablo Fuentes (who by his message had feigned both sickness and conversion) came from behind his house with a cudgel in his hand, lifting it up to strike at me. Had I not catched hold of his stick with both my hands, and prevented the intended blow, certainly he had struck me down. But whilst he and I were striving for the stick who should be master of it, the rest of the Indians who were sitting in the house came out into the yard (which being a public place was more comfort to me than if they had compassed me about within the house) and beset me round, some pulling me one way, some another, tearing my clothes in two or three places, another to make me let go my hand from the stick with a knife run me into the hand (which to this day a small scar doth witness) and certainly had we not been in a public yard that party would also have run his knife into my sides; another seeing I would not let go the stick, took hold if it with Pablo and both together thrust it against my mouth, and with such strength that they broke some of my teeth, and filled my mouth with gore blood, with which blow I fell, but soon recovered myself and arose, they laughing at me, but not daring to do me any more harm for fear they should be seen, as God would have seen what already they had done; for a mulatto slave to a Spaniard in the valley, at that very time when I was down and rising, passed by, and hearing me cry out for help to the neighbours (who lived somewhat far off that might help and succour me, for all the houses thereabouts were of the brothers the Fuentes) came into the yard, and seeing me all in blood thought I had been mortally wounded, and calling them murderers ran along the street crying: 'Murder, murder in Pablo Fuentes his yard,' till she came to the market-place and town-house, where she found the mayors and jurats sitting, and a couple of Spaniards, who when they heard of my danger, with drawn swords came presently running with all the officers of justice to the yard of Pablo Fuentes to aid and assist me; but in the meanwhile the idolaters perceiving the outcry of the mulatto, began to fall away and to hide themselves; Pablo Fuentes going to shut up his house also to absent himself, I held him hard to it, striving with him that he might not escape away till some help came unto me. The Spaniards when they came and saw me all in a blood, made furiously to Pablo Fuentes with their naked swords, whom I stopped desiring them not to hurt him, lest what harm they did unto him should be imputed unto me. I wished the justice not to fear him though he were a rich Indian, and as they would answer before the President of Guatemala to lay hold of him, and to carry him to prison, which they presently performed. I made the Spaniards and the mulatto to witness under writing by way of information what they had seen, what blood about my clothes, what wound in my hand, what blow in my mouth they had found, and sent with speed to the President of Guatemala this their information.

The business was soon noised about the valley, whereupon most of the Spaniards came to offer their help and aid unto me; Miguel Dalva also chancing to be near at a Spaniard's house in the same valley came with the rest, who would have done that night some mischief among the Indians if I had not prevented them. I desired them to depart and go home to their houses, telling them I feared nothing, and that Miguel Dalva his company would be guard enough unto me. But they would by no means yield unto this, saying that night might prove more dangerous unto me than I imagined, and that I needed a stronger guard than of one man alone, for they conceived that the idolaters knowing what already they had done, and fearing what grievous punishment might be inflicted upon them from the President of Guatemala, seeing themselves lost and undone men, might desperately that night rescue their brother out of prison, and attempt some mischief against me, and so flee away. Which I could not be brought to fear, or to believe any such thing of their cowardly spirits, nor that they would flee away for that they had houses and land there in and about the town, yet I was willing for one night to yield to have a stronger guard of Spaniards than at other times I had had with the blackamoor Miguel Dalva alone. After supper they kept watch about my house till such time as they perceived all was still, and the Indians abed, and then they set a watch about the prison that Pablo Fuentes might not be taken out, and after this (pretending that they were in danger as well as I being but about a dozen, if the town should all rise and mutiny by the suggestion of the idolaters, who most of them were rich and powerful with the rest, which yet I feared not) they would needs go and raise up the two *alcaldes* or mayors alone, with two more petty officers to make search about the town for the rest of the Fuentes and other known idolaters, that being found they might secure them in the prison to appear at Guatemala, and prevented from doing any mischief either that night, or at any other time. With this stir which they made, and their care of me, they suffered me not to take any rest that night; but went and called up the *alcaldes* and two officers and brought them to my house, desiring me to signify unto them how fit and necessary it was to search for the rest of the Indians. The poor *alcaldes* trembled to see so many Spaniards at that time in my house with naked swords, and durst not but do what they thought best to be done, and so from my house about midnight they walked about the town, searching such houses as they most suspected might conceal any of the Fuentes, or of the rest that had been that day in the rebellion and mutiny against me. They could find none at home, till at last coming to the house of one Lorenzo Fuentes, one of the brothers, they found all that had been in the conspiracy against me gathered together drinking and quaffing. The house being beset there was no flying nor escaping, and seeing the Spaniards' naked swords, they durst not rebel, who doubtless (as we were afterwards informed) would have made a great stir in the town that night, and were met together to rescue Pablo their brother, and to do me some mischief and fly, not knowing that I was so strongly manned and guarded by the Spaniards. There were ten of them, and were presently without any noise in the town carried to the prison, and there shut up, and guarded by the Spaniards.

In the morning the President of Guatemala (who then was Don Juan de Guzman, a religious governor) taking into his consideration what the day before I had writ unto him, and judging my danger to be great, sent a Spanish *alguazil*, or officer of justice, with a very large commission to bring prisoners to the city all those Indians who the day before had been in rebellion against me, and in case they could not be found, then to seize upon what goods soever of theirs could be found in Mixco. But with the diligence of the Spaniards the night before they were all in a readiness for him, and paying the *alguazil* first his charges (which he demanded as he listed) and bearing the charges of Miguel Dalva, and two or three more Spaniards, who were commanded in the King's name to be aiding and assisting the officer for the safer carrying them to Guatemala, they were horsed and had away that day to the President, who committed them close prisoners, and afterwards commanded them to be whipped about the streets, banished two of them from Mixco to the Gulf of St Thomas de Castilla, and would have banished them all had they not humbled themselves, and desired me to intercede for them, promising to amend their lives, and to make me great satisfaction if they might return again to their town, and that if ever more they did stir against me they would yield to be hanged and to lose all their goods. With this the President (fining them yet to pay twenty crowns apiece to the church to be employed in what I should think fittest) sent them back; who, as they had promised, came unto me, and humbled themselves before me with much weeping, with many expressions, shewing their sorrow from their hearts for what they had done, casting all upon the Devil, whom they confessed had been great with them in tempting them, whom also now they did abjure and renounce, promising to live as good Christians, and never more to worship any god but one. I was very much taken with their deep sorrow expressed with many tears, and endeavoured to instruct them in the true knowledge of Christ, whom now I found they were very willing to embrace.

I lived not very long after in that town; but for the time I did continue in it I found a great change and alteration in their lives, which truly made me apt to judge that their repentance was unfeigned. And these former particulars of a few Indians of those two towns, I have not here inserted to bring an aspersion upon all that nation (which I do very much affect, and would willingly spend the best drops of blood in my veins to do them good, and to save their souls), but to cause rather pity and commiseration towards them, who after so many years' preaching have been made as yet but formal and outward Christians, and by the many saints of wood which they have been taught to worship by the priests have rather been inclined to the superstition and idolatry of their forefathers, and to trust to living creatures, and bow to inanimate stocks and stones, which they daily see performed publicly in their churches. Certainly they are of a good and flexible nature, and (were those idols of saints' statues removed from their eyes) might be brought easily to worship one only God; and whereas they so willingly lavish out their small means and what they labour for in offerings to the priests and to their saints, and in maintaining lazy singing lubbers, they without doubt would be free enough to true ministers of God's Word, who should venture their lives to beat down those false gods, and set up Jesus Christ, and him that sent him into the world to save such as truly believe in him.

The year that this stir happened in Mixco, I received from Rome, from the General of the Dominicans Order, licence to come home to England; at which I rejoiced much, for now I was even weary with living among the Indians, and grieved to see the little fruit I reaped amongst them, and that for fear of the Inquisition I durst not preach a new gospel unto them, which might make them true, real, and inward Christians; and lastly, for that I perceived that Antonio Mendez de Satomayor (who was lord of the town of Mixco) did stomach me for having caused two of his town to be banished, and publicly affronted the Fuentes for their idolatry, which he thought was a great aspersion laid upon his Indians.

All which well considered I writ unto the Provincial (who was then in Chiapa) of my desire to return home to mine own country, for the which I had a licence sent unto me from Rome. But he having heard of what good I had done in the town of Mixco, in reducing some idolaters, burning their idol, and venturing my life in so good a cause, and also for the perfect knowledge which now I had of the Poconchi tongue, would by no means yield that I should go; but with fair and flattering words encouraged me to stay, where he doubted not but I did, and I might yet do, God much more good service; and that he might the better work upon me, he sent me a patent of vicar of the town and cloister of Amatitlan, where at the present there was a new cloister abuilding to separate all that valley from the cloister of Guatemala. He desired me to accept of that small preferment, not doubting but that I speaking so well the Indian language might prevail much in that place, and better than another to further the building of that new cloister; which work would be a good step for him to advance me afterwards to some better preferment. Although I regarded neither that present superiority, nor any better honour which might afterwards ensue unto me, I thought the time which God had appointed for my returning to England was not yet come; for that if the Provincial and with him the President of Guatemala (for so much I conjectured out of the Provincial's letter) should both oppose and hinder my departure from that country, it would be very hard for me to take my journey any way, and not be discovered and brought back. Whereupon I resolved to stay the Provincial's coming to Guatemala, and there to confer with him face to face, and to shew him some reasons that moved me to leave that country, and to seek again mine own wherein I was born. So for the present I accepted of the town of Amatitlan, where I had more occasions of getting money than in the other two, where I had lived five full years; for albeit that town alone was bigger than both Mixco and Pinola together, and the church fuller of saints' pictures and statues, and very many confraternities and sodalities belonged unto it; besides this from without the town I had great comings in from the *ingenio* of sugar, which, I related before, stood close unto that town, from whence I had daily offerings from the blackamoors and Spaniards that lived in it; and besides this I had under my charge another lesser town called St Christoval de Amatitlan, standing two leagues from great Amatitlan.

This town of St Christoval, or St Christopher, is called properly in that language, *Palinha*, *ha* signifying water, and *pali* to stand upright, and is compounded of two words which express water standing upright; for the town standeth on the back side of the volcano of water which looketh over Guatemala, and on this side sendeth forth many fountains, but especially spouteth forth from a high rock a stream of water, which as it falleth from high with a great noise and downfall, the rock standing upright over the bottom where it falleth, and causeth a most pleasant stream by the town's side, it hath moved the Indians to call their town *Palinha*, from the high and upright standing rock from whence the water falleth. In this town there are many rich Indians, who trade in the coast of the South Sea; the town is as an arbour shadowed with many fruitful trees; but the chief fruit here is the *piña*, which groweth in every Indian's yard, and with the nearness of the *ingenio* of sugar are by the Spaniards thereabouts much made up in preserves, some whole, some in slices, which is the daintiest and most luscious preserve that I ever did eat in that country. The Indians of this town get much by boards of cedar, which they cut out of many cedar trees, which grow on that side of the volcano, which they sell to Guatemala and all about the country for new buildings.

Between great Amatitlan and this town the way is plain, and lieth under a volcano of fire which formerly was wont to smoke as much as that of Guatemala, but having formerly burst out at the top, and there opened a great mouth, and cast down to the bottom mighty stones (which to this day are to be seen) it hath not since been any ways troublesome unto the country. In this way there was in my time a new *trapiche* of sugar erecting up by one John Baptista of Guatemala, which was thought would prove very useful and profitable unto the aforesaid city. I had yet for the time that I lived in Amatitlan another very little village at my charge, called Pampichi, at the bottom of a high mountain on the other side of the lake over against it, which was but a chapel of ease unto great Amatitlan, unto which I went not above once in a quarter of a year, and that for pastime and recreation; for this village is well in that language a compound also of *pam*, in, and *pichi*, flowers, for that it standeth compassed about with flowers, which make it very pleasant, and the boats or *canoas*, which do constantly stand near the doors of the houses, invites to much pleasure of fishing and rowing about the lake.

And thus whilst I lived in Amatitlan I had the choice of three places wherein to recreate myself, and because the charge of many souls lay in my hands I had one constantly to help me. The town of Amatitlan was as the Court in respect of the rest, where nothing was wanting that might recreate the mind and satisfy the body with variety and change of sustenance, both for fish and flesh. Yet the great care that did lie upon me in the work and building of the cloister made me very soon weary of living in that great and pleasant town; for sometimes I had thirty, sometimes twenty, sometimes fewer, and sometimes forty, workmen to look unto, and to pay wages to on Saturday nights, which I found wearied much my brain, and hindered my studies, and was besides a work which I delighted not in, nor had any hopes ever to enjoy it. And therefore after the first year that I had been there I betook myself unto the Provincial who was in Guatemala, and again earnestly besought him to peruse the licence which I had from Rome to go to England mine own country for to preach there (for that was the chief ground of letting me go home, as the General largely expressed) where I doubted not but I might do God great service, and in conscience I told him I thought I was bound to employ what parts God had bestowed upon me rather upon my own countrymen than upon Indians and strangers. The Provincial replied unto me that my countrymen were heretics, and when I came amongst them they would hang me up. I told him, I hoped better things of them, and that I would not behave myself among them so as to deserve hanging, not daring to tell him what was in my heart concerning points of religion. After a long discourse I found the Provincial inexorable, and half angry, telling me that he and that whole province had cast their eyes upon me, and honoured me, and were ready and willing to promote me further, and that I would shew myself very ungrateful unto them if I should forsake them for my own nation and people, whom I had not known from my young and tender age. I perceived there was no more to be said, and all would be in vain, and so resolved to take my best opportunity, and with my licence from Rome, to come away unknown unto him. But for the present I humbly beseeched him to remove me from Amatitlan, for that I found myself unable to undergo that great charge, and too weak for that strong work that was then building. With much ado he would be brought to this, alleging what an honour it was to be a founder and builder of a new cloister, in whose walls my very name would be engraven to posterity; all which I told him I regarded not, but esteemed more of my health and a quiet mind than of such preferments and vanities. Upon which at last he condescended to my request, and gave me order to go to Petapa, and that the vicar of Petapa should go to finish the work of Amatitlan.

In Petapa I lived above a twelvemonth, with great ease, pleasure, and content for all things worldly and outward, but within I had still a worm of conscience, gnawing this gourd that shadowed and delighted me with worldly contentment. Here I grew more and more troubled concerning some points of religion, daily wishing with David that I had the wings of a dove that I might flee from that place of daily idolatry into England, and be at rest. I resolved therefore to put on a good courage, and rely wholly upon my God, knowing that the journey was hard and dangerous, and might bring shame and trouble unto me if I should be taken in the way flying and brought back to Guatemala; here I weighed the affliction and reproach which might ensue unto me, after so much honour, pleasure, and wealth which I had enjoyed for about twelve years in that country. So for faith and a safe conscience I now purposed likewise with Moses to forsake Egypt, not fearing the wrath of the President, the King's own deputy, nor of the Provincial, and my best friends, but to endure all this (if I should be taken) as seeing him who is invisible. I thought this was a business not to be conferred with flesh and blood, lest the best friend knowing of it should betray me; yet on the other side, I thought it hard to flee alone without some friend for the first two or three days' journey; and besides having many things to sell away to make money of, I thought I were better to employ some trusty friend than to do all alone. I thought of none fitter than Miguel Dalva, whom by long experience I knew to be true and trusty, and that a small money matter would content him; whom I sent for to Pinola, and charging him with secrecy, I told him I had a journey for my conscience' sake to make to Rome (I would not tell him that I intended England, lest the good old blackamoor should grieve thinking never more to see me, and for the love he bare me, and interest he had many times from me, he should by discovering my intent seek to stop me), which I would have none to know of but himself, not doubting but to return again, as he knew many had taken the like journey, and returned within two years.

The blackamoor offered himself to go with me, which I refused, telling him that the seas would be too hard for his old age to endure, and that as a blackamoor in foreign countries he might be stopped and apprehended for a fugitive; which reason he liked well, and offered himself to go with me as far as the sea side, for which I thanked him and employed to sell me away some mules, wheat, and maize which I had, and what else might well pass through his hands. As for many rich pictures which hung in my chamber, I thought the town of Petapa would buy them for their church, and propounded it unto the Governor, who willingly accepted of them. Most of my books, chests, cabinets, quilts, and many good pieces of household-stuff, by the pains and industry of Miguel (whom I kept with me for the space of two months before I came away) I sold to Guatemala, reserving only two *petacas* or leathern chests, with some books and a quilt for my journey. When I had sold all that I intended, I found I had in Spanish money near nine thousand pieces of eight, which I had got in twelve years that I lived in that country. So much money I thought would be too cumbersome for a long journey; whereupon I turned above four thousand of them into pearls and some precious stones, which might make my carriage the lighter; the rest I laid up some in bags, some I sewed into my quilt, intending in the way to turn them into Spanish pistoles. Thus the chief provision being made of money, I took care for chocolate and some conserves for the way, which were soon provided. Now because I considered that my flight the first week must be with speed, and that my chests could not post day and night as myself intended to do, I thought of sending my carriage four days at least before me; and not daring to trust any Indian of Petapa, I sent to Mixco for one special Indian friend whom I had there, who knew the way that I was to travel very well; to whom I opened my mind, and offered what money I knew would well content him, and at midnight sent him away with two mules, one for himself and another for my chests, wishing him to keep on travelling towards St Miguel, or Nicaragua till I overtook him. I gave him the advantage of four days and nights, and then resolutely with my good blackamoor in my company, leaving the key of my chamber in my door, and nothing but old papers within, when all the Indians were fast asleep I bad adieu unto Petapa, and to the whole valley, and to all my friends throughout America.

CHAPTER XVI

Shewing my journey from the town of Petapa into England; and some chief passages in the way

THE chief thing which troubled me in my resolved purpose to come home was the choice of the safest way; which made me utterly forsake the gulf (though the easiest way of all, and that sea nearest to the place where I lived) for that I knew I should meet there with many of my acquaintance, and the setting out of the ships was so uncertain that before they departed, order might come from Guatemala to stop me; if I should go by land through Comayagua to Trujillo, and there wait for the ships, likewise I feared lest the Governor of that place by some item from the President of Guatemala might examine me, and send me back, and that the masters of the ships might have charge given them not to receive me into their ships. If I should go back to Mexico and Vera Cruz, then I called to mind how I was troubled in that long journey when I came first to Chiapa in company of friends, and that now alone I should certainly be much put to it, for I would not carry Miguel Dalva so far by land with me. Wherefore rejecting these three ways, I chose the fourth, which was by Nicaragua and the Lake of Granada; and therefore I deferred my journey till the week after Christmas, knowing that the time of the frigates' setting out from that lake to Havana was commonly after the middle of January, or at Candlemas at the furthest, whither I hoped to reach in very good time. Now, that I might by no means be suspected to have taken this way, before I went I left by the hand of Miguel Dalva a letter to a friend of his to be delivered to the Provincial in Guatemala four days after my departure, wherein I kindly took my leave of him, desiring him not to blame me nor to seek after me; and whereas I had a sufficient licence from Rome, and could not get his, that I thought I might with a safe conscience go where I was born, leaving linguists enough to supply my place amongst the Indians. And because he should not make enquiry after me by Nicaragua, I dated and subscribed my letter to him from the town of St Antonio Suchitepequez, which was the way to Mexico and quite contrary to Nicaragua.

The next day after Twelfth Day, being the seventh of January, 1637, at midnight I set out of Petapa upon a lusty mule (which afterwards in the way I sold for fourscore pieces of eight) with Miguel Dalva alone; and the first part of the way being very hilly we could not go so fast as our hearts would have posted; for it was break of day before we could get to the top of the mountain, which is called Cerro Redondo, or the round hill; which is much mentioned in that country for the good pasture there which serveth for the cattle and sheep, when the valleys below are burnt and no grazing left for beasts. This hill is also a great refuge to travellers, for there they find good entertainment in a *venta*, where wine and provision is sold, and is a great lodge for to lay up dry what carriages they bring; there is besides one of the best *estancias* or farms of

SURVEY OF WEST INDIES

cattle in the country, where of goat's and ewe's milk is made the best cheese thereabouts. This round hill or mountain is five leagues from Petapa, where I feared I might meet with some people of Petapa, and therefore the day now dawning I made haste by it, leaving in the lodge asleep many Indians, who attended on two Spanish *requas* of mules, which that day were to go to Petapa; four leagues further from this Cerro Redondo is a town of Indians called Los Esclavos, or the Slaves, not that now they are more slaves than the rest of the Indians, but because in the old time of Montezuma the Emperor, and the Indian kings that were under him, the people of this town were more slaves than any other, for from Amatitlan (which is so called from *amat*, which in the Mexican tongue signifieth letter, and *itlan* which signifieth town, for that it was the Town of Letters as some say, for a rind of a tree, whereon they were wont formerly to write and express their minds, or because it was the place whither from all parts letters were sent to be carried about the country, and to Peru) these Indians of the town of Esclavos, or slaves, were commanded as slaves to go all about the country with letters, or whatsoever else they should be charged with; and they were bound constantly to send every week so many of their town (as were appointed) unto Amatitlan, there to wait and attend the pleasure of that town for the conveying of letters, or any carriages, to other parts.

This town of Los Esclavos standeth in a bottom by a river, over the which the Spaniards have built a very strong stone bridge to go in and out of the town, for otherwise with mules there is no passing by reason of the violent and rapid stream of the water, and many rocks in the river, from which the water falleth down with great force. From this town (where we only stayed to drink a cup of chocolate and to bait our mules) we went on that day to Aguachapa, being ten leagues further, and not far from the South Sea, and the port called De la Trinidad; whither we came towards evening, having that day and part of the night travelled about threescore English miles up hills, and upon stony ways from the Esclavos unto this town; which is much mentioned in that country for two things. The one is for the earthen ware which is made there (as some think) exceeding that of Mixco. The other is for a place within a mile and a half from the town, which the Spaniards do credibly report and believe to be a mouth of Hell. For out of it there is constantly ascending a thick black smoke smelling of brimstone, with some flashes now and then of fire; the earth from whence this smoke ariseth is not high, but low. None ever durst draw nigh to find out the truth and ground of it; for those that have attempted to do it have been stricken down to the ground and like to lose their lives. A friend of mine a friar (whom I thought verily I might believe) upon his oath affirmed unto me that travelling that way with a Provincial he resolved to go unto the place, and satisfy himself of the ground and cause of the strange talk which was everywhere about the country concerning that smoke. He went within a quarter of a mile of it, and presently, he said, he heard a hideous noise, which together with the stench of the fiery smoke and brimstone, struck him into such a fear that he was like to fall to the ground, and retiring himself back with all speed was taken with a burning fever, which was like to cost him his life. Others report that drawing near unto it, they have heard great cries as it were of men and women in torment, noise of iron, of chains, and the like, which (how simply I leave it to my judicious Reader) maketh them believe that it is a mouth of Hell. Of my knowledge I will say no more, but that I saw the smoke, and asked the Indians what was the cause of it, and if ever they had been near unto it. And they answered me, that they could not imagine what might be the cause of it, neither durst they draw nigh unto it; and that they had seen travellers attempting to go near it, and that they were all stricken either to the ground, or with some sudden amazement, or fever. I told them that I would walk thither myself, and they desired me that I would not, if I loved my life. It was not yet for all this report the fear of being so near the Spaniard's Hell (as they call it) that made me haste with speed out of that town, but fear of some messenger that might come after me to stop my journey. For at midnight I departed from thence, and went to break my fast to a great town called Chalchuapan, where the Indians made very much of me, being Pocomanes who spake the Poconchi or Pocoman tongue which I had learned. They would willingly have had me to stay with them and preach unto them the next Sabbath, which I would have done had not a better design called upon me to make haste.

Here I was troubled how I should get through St Salvador, which was a city of Spaniards, and wherein there was a cloister of Dominicans, whom I feared most of all, because I was known by some of them. My resolution was therefore when I came near unto the city to turn out of my way to a Spaniard's farm as if I had lost my way, and there to delay the time till evening in drinking chocolate, discoursing, and baiting my mules well, that so I might travel all that night, and be out of the reach of that city and friars (who lived in Indian towns about it) the next morning early. This city of St Salvador is poor, not much bigger than Chiapa, and is governed by a Spanish Governor. It standeth forty leagues at least from Guatemala, and towards the North Sea side is compassed with very high mountains, which are called Chuntales, where the Indians are very poor. In the bottom where the city standeth there are some *trapiches* of sugar, some indigo made, but the chief farms are *estancias* of cattle. Towards evening I departed from that farm where I had well refreshed myself and my mule, and about eight of the clock I rid through the city not being known by anybody. My purpose was to be the next morning at a great river called Rio de Lempa, some ten leagues from St Salvador, for within two leagues of it there lived in an Indian town a friar belonging to the cloister of St Salvador who knew me very well. But such haste I made that before break of the day I passed through that town, and before seven of the clock I was at the river, where I found my Indian of Mixco ready to pass over with my carriage, who that morning by three of the clock had set out of that town two leagues off. I was not a little glad to have overtaken my chests, wherein was most of my treasure. There I sat down a while by the river whilst my mules grazed, and my Indian struck fire and made me chocolate.

This River of Lempa is held the broadest and biggest in all the jurisdiction belonging unto Guatemala; there are constantly two ferry boats to pass over the travellers, and their *requas* of mules. This river is privileged in this manner, that if a man commit any heinous crime or murder on this side of Guatemala, and San Salvador, or on the other side of St Miguel, or Nicaragua, if he can flee to get over this river, he is free as long as he liveth on the other side, and no justice on that side whither he is escaped can question or trouble him for the murder committed. So likewise for debts he cannot be arrested. Though I thanked God I neither fled for the one, or for the other, yet it was my comfort that I was now going over to a privileged country, where I hoped I should be free and sure, and that if anyone did come after me, he would go no further than to the River of Lempa. My blackamoor did much laugh at this my conceit, and warranted me that all would do well. We ferried safely over the river; and from thence went in company with my Indian to a little small town of Indians two leagues off, where we made the best dinner that we had done from the town of Petapa, and willingly gave rest to all our mules till four of the clock in the afternoon; at which time we set forth to another small town little above two leagues off, through a plain, sandy, and champaign country. The next day we had but ten leagues to travel to a town called St Miguel, which belongeth unto Spaniards, and though it be not a city, yet is as big almost as San Salvador, and hath a Spanish Governor; in it there is one cloister of nuns, and another of Mercenarian friars, who welcomed me unto their cloister; for here I began to shew my face, and to think of selling away the mule I rid on, being resolved from hence to go by water or an arm of the sea, to a town in Nicaragua called La Vieja. I would here have dismissed my Indian, but he was loath to leave me until I got to Granada, where he desired to see me shipped. I refused not his kind offer, because I knew he was trusty and had brought my chests well thither, and knew well the way to Granada. So I sent him by land to Realejo, or to La Vieja, which stand very near together and thirty leagues by land from St Miguel, and myself stayed that day and till the next day at noon in that town, where I sold the mule I rid on, because I knew that from Realejo to Granada I could have of the Indians a mule for nothing for a day's journey. My blackamoor's mule I sent also by land with the Indian, and the next day went to the gulf, being three or four miles from St Miguel, where that afternoon I took boat with many other passengers, and the next morning by eight in the morning was at La Vieja, which journey by land would have taken me near three days. The next day my Indian came at night, and we went to Realejo (as I have observed before), a haven very weak and unfortified on the South Sea; where if I would have stayed one fortnight I might have taken shipping for Panama, to go from thence to Portobello, and there stay for the galleons from Spain. But I considered that the galleons would not be there

THE ENGLISH-AMERICAN

till June or July, and that so I should be at great charges in staying so long. But afterwards I wished I had accepted of that occasion, for I was at last forced to go to Panama, and Portobello. From hence to Granada I observed nothing but the plainness and pleasantness of the way, which with the fruits and fertility of all things may well make Nicaragua the Paradise of America. Between Realejo and Granada standeth the city of Leon, near unto a volcano of fire, which formerly burst out at the top, and did much hurt unto all the country about; but since that it hath ceased, and now letteth the inhabitants live without fear. Sometimes it smokes a little, which sheweth that as yet there is within some sulphurous substance.

Here it was that a Mercenarian friar thought to have discovered some great treasure, which might enrich himself and all that country, being fully persuaded that the metal that burned within that volcano was gold; whereupon he caused a great kettle to be made, and hung at an iron chain to let it down from the top, thinking therewith to take up gold enough to make him bishop and to enrich his poor kindred. But such was the power and strength of the fire within, that no sooner had he let down the kettle, when it fell from the chain and from his hands being melted away.

This city of Leon is very curiously built, for the chief delight of the inhabitants consisteth in their houses, and in the pleasure of the country adjoining, and in the abundance of all things for the life of man more than in any extraordinary riches, which there are not so much enjoyed as in other parts of America. They are contented with fine gardens, with variety of singing birds, and parrots, with plenty of fish and flesh, which is cheap, and with gay houses, and so lead a delicious, lazy, and idle life, not aspiring much to trade and traffic, though they have near unto them the lake, which commonly every year sendeth forth some frigates to Havana by the North Sea, and Realejo on the South Sea, which to them might be very commodious for any dealing and rich trading in Peru, or to Mixco, if their spirits would carry them so far. The gentlemen of this city are almost as vain and phantastical as are those of Chiapa. And especially from the pleasure of this city is all that province of Nicaragua called by the Spaniards, Mahomet's Paradise.

From hence the way is plain and level to Granada, whither I got safely and joyfully, hoping that now I had no more journey to make by land, till I should land at Dover in England, and from thence post up to London. Two days after I had arrived at this place and rested myself, and enjoyed the pleasant prospect of the lake, I began to think of dismissing my Indian and blackamoor. But true and faithful Miguel Dalva would by no means leave me till he saw me shipped and that I had no more need of him by land. Likewise the Indian would willingly have stayed, but by no means I would permit him, for that I considered he had a wife and children to look to at home. He was as willing to return afoot as to ride, because he would have me sell my mules, and make what money I could of them; but I seeing the good nature of the Indian, would recompense his love with as much money as might be more beneficial to him than a tired mule; which might have died in the way under him, and left him on foot; so I gave him money enough to bear his charges home, and to hire mules at his own pleasure, and some to spare, when he came home. The Indian with many tears falling from his eyes, saying he feared he should never more see me, took his leave of me the third day after we arrived at Granada. My blackamoor and I being left alone, first began to think of selling away the two mules, which had brought thither the Indian and my chests, for which I got fourscore and ten pieces of eight after so long a journey, and thought they were well sold. I would have had Miguel have sold away that whereon he rid (which was his own), and offered to buy him another that might better carry him back, but the loving and careful blackamoor would not suffer me to be at such charges, considering the long journey which I was to make.

After this, we hearing that the frigates were not like to depart in a fortnight, thought of viewing well that stately and pleasant town a day or two, and then to betake ourselves to some near Indian town, where we might be hid (lest by the great resort of *requas* of mules, which at that time brought indigo and cochineal from Guatemala to the frigates, we should be discovered), and might now and then come to the town to treat concerning my passing in one of the frigates to Havana or to Cartagena. What in that town we observed was two cloisters of Mercenarian and Franciscan friars, and one of nuns, very rich; and one parish church, which was as a cathedral, for the Bishop of Leon did more constantly reside there than in the city. The houses are fairer than those of Leon, and the town of more inhabitants, among whom there are some few merchants of very great wealth, and many of inferior degree very well to pass, who trade with Cartagena, Guatemala, San Salvador, and Comayagua, and some by the South Sea to Peru and Panama. But at this time of the sending away the frigates that town is one of the wealthiest in all the north tract of America; for the merchants of Guatemala fearing to send all their goods by the Gulf of Honduras, for that they have been often taken by the Hollanders between that and Havana, think it safer to send them by the frigates to Cartagena, which passage hath not been so much stopped by the Hollanders as the other. So likewise many times the King's treasure, and revenues (when there is any report of ships at sea, or about the Cape of St Anthony) are this way by the Lake of Granada passed to Cartagena.

That year that I was there, before I betook myself to an Indian town, in one day there entered six *requas* (which were at least three hundred mules) from St Salvador and Comayagua only, laden with nothing else but indigo, cochineal and hides; and two days after from Guatemala came in three more, the one laden with silver (which was the King's tribute from that country), the other with sugar, and the other with indigo. The former *requas* I feared not; but the latter made me keep close within my lodging, lest going abroad I should be known by some of those that came from Guatemala; who after they had delivered what they brought, presently departed, and with their departure set me at liberty, who for their sakes was a voluntary prisoner within mine own lodging. But fearing lest more of these *requas* might come and affright me, I went to a town out of the road, a league from Granada, and took my pleasure up and down the country where I was much feasted by the Mercenarian friars, who enjoy most of those towns. Amongst these I heard much of the passage in the frigates to Cartagena, which did not a little dishearten and discourage me. For although, whilst they sail upon the lake they go securely and without trouble, yet when they fall from the lake to the river (which there they call El Desaguadero) to go out to the sea, *hic labor, hoc opus est*, here is nothing but trouble, which sometimes makes that short voyage to last two months; for such is the fall of the waters in many places amongst the rocks that many times they are forced to unlade the frigates, and lade them again with help of mules which are there kept for that purpose by a few Indians that live about the river, and have care of the lodges made for to lay in the wares, whilst the frigates pass through those dangerous places to another lodge, whither the wares are brought by mules, and put again into the frigates. Beside this trouble (which must needs be tedious to a passenger, to be thus stopped, who would willingly come soon to his journey's end) the abundance of gnats is such which maketh him to take no joy in his voyage, and the heat in some places so intolerable that many do die before they get out to the sea. Though all this was terrible to me to hear, yet I comforted myself that my life was in the hands of the Lord, and that the frigates did commonly every year pass that way, and seldom any were loſt.

I went now and then to Granada to bargain for my passage, and to know when the frigates would for certain set out, and to provide myself of some dainties and chocolate for my journey, having agreed with a maſter of a frigate for my diet at his table. The time was appointed within four or five days; but suddenly all was crossed with a ſtrict command from Guatemala that the frigates should not go out that year, because the President and whole Court was informed for certain that some English or Holland ships was abroad at sea, and lay about the mouth of the river of Desaguadero waiting for the frigates of Granada, and that the said were sometimes lurking about the Islands of St John, and St Catharine (which then was our Providence), which made all the merchants of the country to fear and sweat with a cold sweat, and the President to be careful for the King's revenues, leſt the loss of them should be imputed to his wilful negligence, in ſtopping the frigates whilſt he might, and had warning given. This was but sad news unto me, who knew not for the present which way to dispose of myself. I began to think of the ship that was at Realejo ready to set out to Panama, thinking that would now be my beſt course, but enquiring after it I was for certain informed by some merchants that it was newly gone. Then my eyes looked upon Comayagua and Truxillo, and upon the ships of Honduras, but these were but vain and troubled thoughts, arising from a perplexed heart, for the ships were also gone from thence, without some small vessel or frigate might be there with news from Havana or Cartagena (for those places send often word and notice of what ships are abroad at sea)

THE SPANISH MAIN, NEW GRANADA AND POPAYAN

SURVEY OF WEST INDIES

but this also was a mere chance, and not to be trusted unto, as my friends did advise and counsel me. Whereupon my perplexity more and more increased; only my comfort was that there were more passengers besides myself who I knew must take some course, and whom I also resolved to follow by sea or land. Amongst us all we were once resolving to hire a frigate to carry us only to Cartagena, but this would not be granted, for nobody would hazard his vessel and life for our sakes.

Whilst we were thus distressed and perplexed enquiring about Granada of the merchants what course we might take to get to Spain that year, or to meet with Havana or Cartagena, one that wished us well counselled us to go to Costa Rica, where at Cartago we should be sure to hear of some vessels bound for Portobello, either from the river called de los Anzuelos, or from the river called Suere, from whence every year went out some small frigates to carry meal, bacon, fowls, and other provision for the galleons to Portobello. This we thought was hard and difficult, and of near a hundred and fifty leagues, over mountains and through deserts, where we should miss the pleasure, variety, and dainties of Guatemala and Nicaragua, and after all this peradventure might miss of an opportunity of any frigate bound to Portobello. Yet so unwilling were we all to return to Guatemala from whence we came, that we would rather go forward, and undergo any difficulties, so that at last we might find any shipping to convey us where we might meet with the galleons, which we knew were not to come to Portobello till the month of June or July. We therefore agreed four of us, three Spaniards and myself, to go to Costa Rica, and there to try our fortune. They had each of them (as myself had) carriage for one mule, and none to ride on; but thought it their best way to buy each of them a mule to carry them, which they hoped after their journey to sell again at

Costa Rica, and to get money by them, and for their carriages to hire mules and Indians from town to town, who also might serve to guide us through many dangerous places and passages, which we understood were in the way. Now I wished I had my mule which I sold at San Miguel, or any one of the two which I sold before in Granada. But for my money I doubted not, with the help of my blackamoor, but I should find one for my purpose. I furnished myself very speedily, for fifty pieces of eight, of one which I feared not would perform my journey. My good and trusty blackamoor would willingly have gone on with me, and further round the world if I would have permitted him, but I would not; but thanked him heartily for what he had done, and gave him money enough in his purse, and dismissed him, hoping that the company of the three Spaniards would be sufficient comfort unto me.

Thus with one Indian to guide us we set four of us out of Granada, enjoying for the two first days more of the pleasure of that Mahomet's Paradise, Nicaragua, finding the way for the most part plain, the towns pleasant, the country shady, and everywhere fruits abounding. The second day after we set out we were much affrighted with a huge and monstrous cayman or crocodile, which having come out of the lake (which we passed by) and lying cross a puddle of water bathing himself, and waiting for some prey, as we perceived after, whom we not knowing well at the first, but thinking that it had been some tree that was felled or fallen, passed close by it; when on a sudden we knew the scales of the cayman, and saw the monster stir and move, and set himself against us; wherewith we made haste from him, but he thinking to have made some of us his greedy prey, ran after us, which when we perceived, and that he was like to overtake us, we were much troubled, until one of the Spaniards (who knew better the nature and quality of that beast than the rest) called upon us to turn on one side out of the way, and to ride on straight for a while, and then to turn on another side, and so to circumflex our way, which advice of his without doubt saved mine, or some of the others' lives, for thus we wearied that mighty monster and escaped from him, who (had we rid out straightway) had certainly overtaken us, and killed some mule or man, for his straight forward flight was as swift as our mules could run; but whilst he turned and wheeled about his heavy body, we got ground and advantage till we left him far behind us; and by this experience we came to know the nature and quality of that beast, whose greatness of body is no hindrance to run forward as swift as a mule; but otherwise, as the elephant once laid down is troubled to get up, so this monster is heavy and stiff, and therefore much troubled to turn and wind about his body. We praised God who had that day delivered us, and riding for a while by the side of the lake we were watchful that we might not fall again into the like danger. But the greatness of this Lake of Granada may from hence be known, in that the second and third day of our journey, being at least threescore miles from whence we set out, we now and then found our way lying by it. After that we had wholly lost the sight of it, we began to enter into rough and craggy ways, declining more to the South than to the North Sea. And in all the rest of our journey to Cartago we observed nothing worth committing to posterity, but only mighty woods and trees on the South Sea side, very fit for to make strong ships, and many mountains and desert places, where we lay sometimes two nights together, either in woods or open fields, far from any town or habitation of Indians, yet for our comfort in these so desert places we had still a guide with us, and found lodges, which by the command of the nearest justices had been set up for such as travelled that way.

We came at last through thousand dangers to the city of Cartago, which we found not to be so poor as in richer places, as Guatemala and Nicaragua, it was reported to be. For there we had occasion to enquire after some merchants for exchange of gold and silver, and we found that some were very rich, who traded by land and sea with Panama, and by sea with Portobello, Cartagena, and Havana, and from thence with Spain. This city may consist of four hundred families, and is governed by a Spanish governor; it is a bishop's see, and hath in it three cloisters, two of friars, and one of nuns. Here we began to enquire after that which had brought us through so many mountains, woods, and deserts, to wit, after some speedy occasion of shipping ourselves for Portobello or Cartagena; and according to our desires we understood of one frigate almost ready to set out from the river called De los Anzuelos, and another from the River Suere; and being well informed that Suere would be the best place for us to travel unto by reason of more provision in the way, more towns of Indians, and *estancias* of Spaniards, we resolved within four days after we had rested in Cartago to undertake a new journey towards the North Sea. We found that country mountainous in many places, yet here and there some valleys where was very good corn, Spaniards living in good farms, who as well as the Indians bred many hogs; but the towns of Indians we found much unlike to those which we had left behind in Nicaragua and Guatemala; and the people in courtesy and civility much differing from them, and of a rude and bold carriage and behaviour towards us; yet they are kept under by the Spaniards, as much as those whom I have formerly spoken of about Guatemala. We came in so good a time to the River Suere that we stayed there but three days in a Spanish farm near unto it, and departed.

The master of the frigate was exceeding glad of our company, and offered to carry me for nothing, but for my prayers to God for him, and for a safe passage; which he hoped would not be above three or four days'

SURVEY OF WEST INDIES

sailing. What he carried was nothing but some honey, hides, bacon, meal, and fowls. The greatest danger he told us of, was the setting out from the river (which runs in some places with a very strong stream, is shallow and full of rocks in other places) till we come forth to the main sea. Whither we got out safely and had not sailed on above twenty leagues when we discovered two ships making towards us; our hearts began to quake, and the master himself of the frigate we perceived was not without fear, who suspected that they were English, or Holland ships; we had no guns nor weapons to fight with, save only four or five muskets and half a dozen swords; we thought the wings of our nimble frigate might be our best comfort, and flying away our chiefest safety. But this comfort soon began to fail us, and our best safety was turned into near approaching danger; for before we could fly on five leagues towards Portobello, we could from our top mast easily perceive the two ships to be Hollanders, and too nimble for our little vessel, which presently one of them (which being a man-of-war was too much and too strong for our weakness) fetched up, and with a thundering message made us strike sail. Without any fighting we durst not but yield, hoping for better mercy. But O, what sad thoughts did here run to and fro my dejected heart, which was struck down lower than our sail! How did I sometimes look upon death's frighting visage! But if again I would comfort and encourage myself against this fear of death; how then did I begin to see an end of all my hopes of ever more returning to my wished and desired country! How did I see that my treasure of pearls, precious stones, and pieces of eight, and golden pistoles, which by singing I had got in twelve years' space, now within one half hour ready to be lost with weeping, and become a sure prey to those who with as much ease as I got them, and with laughing, were ready to spoil me of all that with the sound of flutes, waits, and organs I had so long been hoarding up! Now I saw I must forcedly and feignedly offer up to a Hollander what superstitious, yea also forced and feigned, offerings of Indians to their saints of Mixco, Pinola, Amatitlan, and Petapa had for a while enriched me. My further thoughts were soon interrupted by the Hollanders who came aboard our frigate with more speed than we desired. Though their swords, muskets and pistols did not a little terrify, yet we were somewhat comforted when we understood who was their chief captain and commander, and hoped for more mercy from him, who had been born and brought up amongst Spaniards, than from the Hollanders, who as they were little bound unto the Spanish nation for mercy, so did we expect little from them. The captain of this Holland ship which took us was a mulatto born and bred in Havana, whose mother I saw and spoke with afterwards that same year, when the galleons struck into that port to expect there the rest that were to come from Vera Cruz. This mulatto, for some wrongs which had been offered unto him from some commanding Spaniards in Havana, ventured himself desperately in a boat out to the sea, where were some Holland ships waiting for a prize, and with God's help getting unto them, yielded himself to their mercy, which he esteemed far better than that of his own countrymen, promising to serve them faithfully against his own nation, which had most injuriously and wrongfully abused, yea and (as I was afterwards informed) whipped him in Havana.

This mulatto proved so true and faithful in his good services unto the Hollanders, that they esteemed much of him, married him to one of their nation, and made him captain of a ship under that brave and gallant Hollander whom the Spaniards then so much feared, and named *Pie de Palo*, or Wooden Leg. This famous mulatto it was that with his sea soldiers boarded our frigate, in the which he had found little worth his labour had it not been for the Indians' offerings which I carried with me, of which I lost that day the worth of four thousand patacones or pieces of eight in pearls and precious stones, and near three thousand more in money. The other Spaniards lost some hundreds apiece, which was so rich a prize that it made the Hollanders' stomach loath the rest of our gross provision of bacon, meal and fowls, and our money tasted sweeter unto them than the honey which our frigate also afforded them. Other things I had (as a quilt to lie on, some books, and *laminas*, which are pictures in brass, and clothes) which I begged of that noble captain the mulatto, who considering my orders and calling, gave me them freely, and wished me to be patient, saying that he could do no otherwise than he did with my money and pearls, and using that common proverb at sea,—*oy por mi, mañana por ti*, today fortune hath been for me, tomorrow it may be for thee.

I had some comfort left in a few pistoles, some single, some double, which I had sewed up in my quilt (which the captain restored unto me, saying it was the bed I lay in) and in the doublet which I had at that present, which mounted to almost a thousand crowns, and in their searching was not found out. After the captain and soldiers had well viewed their prize, they thought of refreshing their stomachs with some of our provision; the good captain made a stately dinner in our frigate, and invited me unto it, and knowing that I was going towards Havana, besides many other *brindis* or healths, he drank one unto his mother, desiring me to see her, and to remember him unto her, and how that for her sake he had used me well and courteously in what he could; and further at table he said that for my sake he would give us our frigate that we might return again to land, and that I might find out from thence some safer way and means to get to Portobello, and to continue on my journey unto Spain. After dinner I conferred with the captain alone, and told him that I was no Spaniard, but an Englishman born, shewing him the licence which I had from Rome to go to England, and that therefore I hoped, not being of an enemy nation to the Hollanders, he would restore unto me what goods were mine. But all this was of little consequence with him, who had already taken possession of mine, and all other goods in the ship: he told me I must suffer with those amongst whom I was found, and that I might as well claim all the goods in the ship for mine. I desired him then to carry me along with him to Holland, that from thence I might get to England, which also he refused to do, telling me that he went about from one place to another, and knew not when he should go to Holland, and that he was daily ready to fight with any Spanish ship, and if he should fight with the Spaniards whilst I was in his ship, his soldiers in their hot blood might be ready to do me a mischief, thinking I would do them harm if in fight they should be taken by the Spaniards. With these his answers I saw there was no hope of getting again what now was lost, therefore (as before) I commended myself again to God's providence and protection.

The soldiers and mariners of the Holland ship made haste that afternoon to unlade the goods of our frigate into their man-of-war, which took them up that, and part of the next day, whilst we as prisoners were wafting up and down the sea with them. And whereas we thought our money had satisfied them enough, and to the full, we found the next day that they had also a stomach to our fowls and bacon, and wanted our meal to make them bread, and our honey to sweeten their mouths, and our hides for shoes and boots, all which they took away, leaving me my quilt, books, and brass pictures, and to the master of the frigate some small provision, as much as might carry us to land, which was not far off, and thus they took their leaves of us, thanking us for their good entertainment.

And we weary of such guests, some praying to God that they might never entertain the like again, some cursing them all, and especially the mulatto to hell, calling him *renegado*; some thanking God for their lives which were given them for a prey, we all returned again to Suere from whence we had set out, and going up the river were almost like to be cast away, and lose our lives after we had lost our goods. When we came to land, the Spaniards about the country pitied our case and helped us with alms, gathering a collection for us. The three Spaniards of my company lost all their money and most of their best clothes, yet they had reserved some bills of exchange for money to be taken up at Portobello; which I wished I had also for what I had lost. For the present we knew not what course to take; we thought of going to Rio de los Anzuelos, but we were informed that certainly the frigates there were either gone, or would be gone before we could get thither; and if they stayed not with the news of the Hollanders' ships at sea, they either already were or would be their prize, as we had been. We resolved therefore with the charitable assistance of the Spaniards about the country to return again to Cartago, and from thence to take some better directions. In the way we conferred what we had saved, the Spaniards bragged yet of their bills of exchange, which would yield them money at Cartago, I would not let them know what I had saved, but somewhat I told them I had kept; and we agreed all the way we went to signify nothing but poverty and misery, that the Indians and Spaniards in the way might pity and commiserate us, and our great losses. When we came to Cartago we were indeed much pitied, and collections were made for us; and as it was expected from me that I should sing again at the altars and that I should preach wheresoever I came, so by these two ways, of singing and of huddling over *Dominus vobiscum* and the rest of the Mass, and by accepting of what sermons were recommended unto me, I began again to store myself with moneys. Yet I knew that in such a poor country as that was, where I was little known, I could not possibly get enough to bring me home with credit into England; and therefore the cunning enemy finding me to stand upon my credit, began strongly to tempt me to return again to Guatemala (where I doubted not but I should be welcomed and entertained by my friends) and to settle myself there until I had again by sacrilegious, base, superstitious, and idolatrous means and works, made up a new purse to return with credit home.

But I perceiving that God already had shewed himself angry, and justly taken from me what by unlawful means I had in twelve years obtained, bad Satan avaunt, purposing never more to return to the flesh pots of Egypt, and to go still homewards, though in the way I did beg my bread. Yet (lest I might be suspected amongst the Spaniards, and troubled for not exercising my orders and function) I resolved to take what as to a stranger and traveller for preaching or any other exercise might be offered unto me.

Thus with courage resolving to go on still towards England, I enquired at Cartago which way I might get to Portobello. But this door of hope was afst shut up; though my trust in God's providence was not weakened. In this season there came to Cartago some two or three hundred mules unsaddled or unloaden with some Spaniards, Indians, and blackamoors, from the parts of Comayagua and Guatemala to convey them to Panama by land, over the mountains of Veragua, there to be sold. This is the yearly and only trading by land which Guatemala, Comayagua, and Nicaragua, hath with Panama over that narrow isthmus lying between the North and South Sea, which is very dangerous by reason of the craggy ways, rocks, and mountains, but more especially by reason of many heathens, barbarians and savage people, which as yet are not conquered by the Spaniards, and sometimes do great hurt and mischief, and kill those that with mules pass through their country, especially if they misdemean themselves, or please them not well. Yet for all these difficulties I was entertaining a thought to go along with those mules and Spaniards, which were now on their way by land to Panama. The three Spaniards were half of the same mind; but the providence of God who better ordereth and disposeth man's affairs than he himself disappointed these our thoughts for our good and safety, as after we were informed; for we heard for certain at Nicoya that some of those mules and Spaniards were killed by the barbarians and savage Indians, amongst whom my life might have been lost if I had attempted that hard and dangerous journey; from which many well-wishers at Cartago did dissuade me, both for the danger of the Indians, and for the difficulties of the ways and mountains, which they told me the weakeness of my body would never endure. After we had wholly desisted from this land journey, the best counsel that we had from some merchants our friends, was to try whether Mar del Sur, or the South Sea, would favour our design and journey better than the Mar del Norte, or the North Sea had done; who wished us to go to Nicoya, and from thence to Chira, and to the Golfo de Salinas, where they doubted not but we should find shipping to Panama. We were willing to follow any good advice and counsel, yet we knew that this was the last shift which we could make, and the *non plus ultra* of our hopes, and that if here we should be disappointed, we could expect no other way ever to get to Panama, except we should venture our lives most desperately over the mountains of Veragua, and by land without any guide or company through the country of the barbarians (who before had slain some Spaniards passing that way), or else should return again all the way that we had come to Realejo, where our hopes might be frustrated, and peradventure no shipping found for Panama, without a year's waiting for it.

We resolved therefore to follow this our friend's counsel, and to go yet to Nicoya, and from thence to Golfo de Salinas, where laughing, I told the three Spaniards of my company that if we were disappointed, we would like Hercules set up a pillar to eternize our fame, with our names, and this inscription upon it, *Non plus Ultra*, for that beyond it there was no other port, haven, or place, to take shipping to Panama; neither could any man have done more (nor ever did any Englishman in that country do more than myself) than we had done, but especially myself, who from Mexico had thus travelled by land to Nicoya at least six hundred leagues, or eighteen hundred English miles straight from North to South, besides what I had travelled from Vera Cruz to Mexico, and from Guatemala to Vera Paz, and to Puerto de Cavallos, or Golfo Dulce, and from thence to Trujillo, and from thence back again to Guatemala, which was at least thirteen or fourteen hundred English miles more, which I thought to eternize upon a pillar at Nicoya. But what there was not erected, I hope here shall be eternized, and that this my true and faithful history shall be a monument of three thousand and three hundred miles travelled by an Englishman, within the mainland of America, besides other sea navigations to Panama, from Portobello to Cartagena, and from thence unto Havana.

The way which we travelled from Cartago to Nicoya was very mountainous, hard, and unpleasant, for we met with few *estancias* of Spaniards, and few Indian towns, and those very poor, small, and all of dejected and wretched people. Yet Nicoya is a pretty town, and head of a Spanish government, where we found one Justo de Salazar, *Alcalde Mayor*, who entertained us very well, and provided lodgings for us for the time that we should abide there, and comforted us with hopeful words, that though for the present there was no ship or frigate in the Gulf of Salinas, yet he doubted not but very shortly one would come from Panama thither, for salt and other commodities, as yearly they were wont. The time of the year when we came thither was a fit time for me to get again some moneys after my great loss; for it was in Lent, which is the friars' chiefest harvest, who (as I have before observed) then by confessions and by giving the Communion get many money offerings.

The time, and the Franciscan friar who had the pastorship and charge of that town, were both very commodious unto me, who could not refuse as long as I stayed there to exercise my function, lest I should bring a just cause of suspicion and aspersion upon myself. The friar of the town was a Portuguese, who about three weeks before my coming thither had had a very great bickering and strife with Justo de Salazar, the *Alcalde Mayor*, for defending the Indians, whom Salazar did grievously oppress, employing them in his, and his wife's service as slaves, and not paying them what for the sweat of their brows was due unto them, and commanding them to be from their home and from their wives, and from their church upon the Sabbath, working for him as well that day as any other. Which the friar not enduring, charged them in the pulpit not to obey any such unlawful commands from their *Alcalde Mayor*. But Justo de Salazar (who had been trained up in wars and fighting, and had served formerly in the castle of Milan) thought it a great disparagement unto him now to be curbed by a friar, and by such a one to be interrupted in his government of the Indians, and in the ways of his own lucre and gain. Therefore after many bitter words and defiances, which had passed between him and the friar, he came one day resolutely to the friar's house with his sword drawn; and certainly had not the friar been assisted by some of the Indians, he had killed him.

The friar being as hot as he, and standing upon his calling, orders, and priesthood, presuming that he durst not touch him violently, lest his privilege should bring an excommunication upon the striker and offender, would not flee from him, but dared him boldly; which was a strong provocation to Salazar's heat and passion, and caused him to lift up his sword and aim his blow and stroke at the friar, which fell so unhappily that with it he struck off two of the friar's fingers, and had undoubtedly seconded another blow more hurtful and dangerous to the friar had not the Indians interposed themselves, and shut up their priest into his chamber. Justo was for this action excommunicated, yet for that he was a man of high authority he soon got off his excommunication from the Bishop of Costa Rica, and sent his complaint to the Chancery of Guatemala against the friar, where with friends and money he doubted not but to overcome the mendicant priest, as it happened after; for (as I was informed) he caused the friar to be sent for up to the Court, and there prevailed so much against him that he got him to be removed from Nicoya. In this season the friar kept his house and chamber, and would by no means go out to the church, either to say Mass, or to preach, or hear confessions (all which that time of the year did require of him) but had got one to help him; who alone not being able to perform so great a charge of many hundred Indians, Spaniards, blackamoors, and mulattoes, who from the country without, and from the town within, expected to have their confessions heard, their sins absolved, the word preached, and the Communion to be given them, hearing of my coming desired me to assist and help him, and that for my pains I should have my meat and drink at his table, and a crown daily for every Mass, and whatsoever else the people should voluntarily offer, besides the sermons, which should be well rewarded unto me. I stayed in this town from the second week of Lent until Easter week, where what with three sermons at ten crowns apiece, what with my daily stipend and many other offerings, I got about an hundred and fifty crowns.

The week before Easter news came of a frigate from Panama to Golfo de Salinas, which much comforted us, who already began to mistrust the delay. The master of the frigate came to Nicoya, which is as Court thereabouts; and with him the three Spaniards and myself agreed for our passage to Panama. About Chira, Golfo de Salinas, and Nicoya, there are some farms of Spaniards, few and very small Indian towns, who are all like slaves employed by the *Alcalde Mayor*, to make him a kind of thread called *pita*, which is a very rich commodity in Spain, especially of that colour wherewith it is dyed in these parts of Nicoya, which is a purple colour; for the which the Indians are here much charged to work about the seashore, and there to find out certain shells wherewith they make this purple dye.

There are also shells for other colours, which are not known to be so plentifully in any other place as here. About Chira and Golfo de Salinas the chief commodities are salt, honey, maize, some wheat, and fowls, which every year they send by some few frigates to Panama, which from thence come on purpose to fetch them with this purple coloured thread, or *pita*, which I have spoken of. The frigate which came when I was there was soon laden with these commodities, and with it we set out hoping to have been at Panama within five or six days. But as often before we had been crossed, so likewise in this short passage we were striving with the wind, sea, and *corrientes*, as they are called (which are swift streams as of a river) four full weeks. After the first day that we set out, we were driven with a wind and storm towards Peru, till we came under the very equinoctial line, where what with excessive heat, what with mighty storms, we utterly despaired of life. But after one week that we had thus run towards death, it pleased God to comfort us again with hopes of life, sending us a prosperous gale, which drove us out of that equinoctial heat and stormy sea towards the islands of Perlas, and Puerta de Chame, lying on the south side of the mountains of Veragua, from whence we hoped within two days at the most to be at rest and anchor at Panama. But yet these our hopes were frustrated, for there our wind was calmed, and we fell upon those strong *corrientes* or streams, which drave us back in the night for the space of almost a fortnight as much as we had sailed in the day. Had not God again been merciful here unto us, we had certainly perished in this our striving with the stream; for although we wanted not provision of food, yet our drink failed us so that for four days we tasted neither drop of wine or water, or anything that might quench our thirst, save only a little honey which we found did cause more thirst in us, which made me and some others to drink our own urine, and to refresh our mouths with pieces of lead bullets, which did for a while refresh, but would not long have sufficed Nature, had not God's good providence sent us such a wind which in the day drave us quite off from those *corrientes*.

Our first thoughts were then to strike either to the continent, or some island of many which were about us to seek for water, finding our bodies weak and languishing; which the captain of the ship would by no means yield unto, assuring us that that day he would land us at Panama; but we not being able to sail on without drink, unless we should yield to have our dead and not live bodies landed where he promised, thought it no good purchase though we might buy all Panama with our lives, which we judged could not hold out another day; and seeing that the wind began to slacken, we all required him to strike into some island for water, which he stubbornly refused and denied to do; whereupon the three Spaniards and some of the mariners mutinied against him with drawn swords, threatening

SURVEY OF WEST INDIES

to kill him if he betook not himself presently to some island. The good master thought it bad sport to see swords at his breast, and so commanded his ship to be turned to two or three islands, which were not above two or three hours sail from us. When we drew nigh unto them, we cast our anchor and our cock-boat, and happy was he that could first cast himself into it to be rowed to land to fill his belly with water. The first island we landed upon was on that side unhabitable, where we spent much time running to and fro, over-heating ourselves and increasing our thirst; thus whilst one ran one way, and another tried another to find out some fountain, our hopes being frustrated, and I lost in the wood, and my shoes torn from my feet, with stony rocks, and many thorns and bushes in other places, my company betook themselves to the cock-boat to try another island, leaving me alone and lost in the wood; out of which at last when I came, and found the cock-boat gone from the shore, I began to consider myself a dead man, thinking that they had found water and were gone to ship, and not finding me would hoist up their sails for Panama. Thus being dejected I cried out to the ship, which I perceived could not possibly hear my weak voice, and running up and down the rocks to see if I could discover the cock-boat, I perceived it was not with the ship, and espied it at the next island. With this I began to hope better things of them that they would call for me when they had gotten water; so I came down from the rocks to the plain shore, where I found a shade of trees and amongst them some berries (which might have been poison, for I knew them not) wherewith I refreshed my mouth for a while; but my body so burned that I thought there with heat, weakness, and faintness I should have expired and given up the ghost. I thought by stripping myself naked and going into the sea unto my neck, I might thus refresh my body, which I did, and coming out again into the shade,

THE ENGLISH-AMERICAN

I fell into a deep sleep, in so much that the cock-boat coming for me, and the company holloaing unto me, I awaked not, which made them fear that I was dead or lost; till landing, one searched for me one way, and another another, and so they found me, who might have been a prey to some wild beast, or slept till the frigate had gone away, and so have perished in a barren and unhabitable island. When they awaked me, I was glad to see my good company, and the first thing I enquired for was if they had got any water; they bad me be of good cheer and arise, for they had water enough, and oranges and lemons from another island, where they met with Spaniards that did inhabit it. I made haste with them to the boat, and no sooner was I entered into it but they gave me to drink as much as I would. The water was warm and unsettled, for they could not take it up so but that they took of the gravel and bottom of the fountain, which made it look very muddy; yet for all this (as though my life had depended upon it) I drank up a whole pot of it; which no sooner had I drank but such was the weakness of my stomach that it presently cast it up again not being able to bear it. With this they wished me to eat an orange or a lemon; but them also did my stomach reject; so to our frigate we went, and in the way I fainted so that the company verily thought I would die before we got aboard. When we came thither I called again for water, which was no sooner down my stomach but presently up again; they had me to bed with a burning fever upon me; where I lay that night expecting nothing but death, and that the sea should be my grave.

The master of the ship seeing the wind was turned, began to be much troubled, and feared that with that wind he should never get to Panama. He resolved to venture upon a way which never before he had tried; which was to get between the two islands which we had searched for water, knowing that the wind, which on this side was contrary, on the other side of the islands would be favourable unto him. Thus towards the evening he took up anchor and hoisted up his sails, and resolved to pass his frigate between the two islands; which how dangerous and desperate an attempt it was, the event witnessed. I lay in this season (as I may truly say) upon my death-bed, not regarding which way the master of the ship, or fortune, carried me, so that the mercy of the Lord carried my soul to Heaven. No sooner had the frigate steered her course between the narrow passage of the two islands, when being carried with the stream too much to the one side of the land it ran upon a rock, so that the very stern was lifted up, and almost cast out of the pilot's hands, who cried out not to God, but unto the Virgin Mary saying; *Ayudad nos Virgen Santissima, que si no aqui nos perecemos*, 'Help us, O most holy Virgin, for if not, here we perish.' This, and the outcry of all that were in the frigate gave unto me an alarm of death; from the which yet it pleased God by the means and diligence of the painful mariners to deliver me and all the company, for with much ado most part of that night they haled from the cock-boat the frigate off from the rock, after the stream had made it three several times to strike upon it. After a very troublesome night in the morning we got our little ship out of all danger and from between the two islands on the other side of them, where we sailed prosperously towards Panama. That morning my stomach recovered some of its lost strength, and I began to eat and to drink, and to walk about, rejoicing much to see those pleasant islands which we sailed by. In the evening we got to Puerto de Perico; where we cast anchor, expecting to be searched in the morning; but that night (the master of our ship having gone to shore) the wind turned and blew so strong that we lost our anchor, and were driven back almost to La Pacheque and feared we should be carried out into the Ocean again so far that we should with great difficulty get to Panama. But that God whom the sea and winds do obey turned again that contrary wind into a prosperous gale, wherewith we came once more unto Perico; and being searched we went on with full sail to Panama. Being near the port and without an anchor in our ship the wind once more blew us back and had not the ship master sent us an anchor, we had gone again to Pacheque or further. But with that anchor we stayed all that night at Perico, wondering among ourselves that so many crosses should befall us, which made some say that we were bewitched; others, that certainly there was amongst us some excommunicated person, whom they said if they knew of they would hurl him overboard.

Whilst they were in this discourse, the wind turned yet again, and we levying our anchor went on to Panama, whither it pleased God that time safely to conduct us in. I being now well strengthened made no stay in that frigate, which I thought would have been my last abiding place in this world, but went to land, and betook myself to the cloister of the Dominicans, where I stayed almost fifteen days viewing and reviewing that city; which is governed like Guatemala by a President and six judges, and a Court of Chancery, and is a bishop's see. It hath more strength towards the South Sea than any other port which on that side I had seen, and some ordnances planted for the defence of it; but the houses are of the least strength of any place that I had entered in; for lime and stone is hard to come by, and therefore for that reason, and for the great heat there, most of the houses are built of timber and boards; the President's house, nay the best church walls, are but boards, which serve for stone and brick, and for tiles to cover the top. The heat is so extraordinary that a linen cut doublet, with some slight stuff or taffeta breeches is the common clothing of the inhabitants. Fish, fruits, and herbage for salads is more plentiful there than flesh; the cool water of the

SURVEY OF WEST INDIES

coco is the women's best drink, though chocolate also, and much wine from Peru be very abounding. The Spaniards are in this city much given to sin, looseness and venery especially, who make the blackamoors (who are many, rich, and gallant) the chief objects of their lust. It is held to be one of the richest places in all America, having by land and by the river Chagres commerce with the North Sea, and by the South, trading with all Peru, East Indies, Mexico, and Honduras. Thither is brought the chief treasure of Peru in two or three great ships, which lie at anchor at Puerto de Perico some three leagues from the city; for the great ebbing of the sea at that place especially suffereth not any great vessel to come nearer, where daily the sea ebbs and falls away from the city two or three miles, leaving a mud which is thought to cause much unhealthiness in that place, being seconded with many other muddy and moorish places about the town. It consisteth of some five thousand inhabitants, and maintaineth at least eight cloisters of nuns and friars. I feared much the heats, and therefore made as much haste out of it as I could. I had my choice of company by land and water to Portobello. But considering the hardness of the mountains by land, I resolved to go by the river Chagres; and so at midnight I set out from Panama to Venta de Cruces, which is ten or twelve leagues from it. The way is thither very plain for the most part, and pleasant in the morning and evening.

Before ten of the clock we got to Venta de Cruces, where live none but mulattoes and blackamoors, who belong unto the flat boats that carry the merchandise to Portobello. There I had very good entertainment by that people, who desired me to preach unto them the next Sabbath day, and gave me twenty crowns for a sermon and procession. After five days of my abode there, the boats set out, which were much stopped in their passage down the river; for in some places we found the water very low, so that the boats ran upon the gravel, from whence with poles and the strength of the blackamoors they were to be lifted off again; sometimes again we met with such streams that carried us with the swiftness of an arrow down under trees and boughs by the river side, which sometimes also stopped us till we had cut down great branches of trees. Had not it pleased God to send us after the first week plentiful rain, which made the water run down from the mountains and fill the river (which otherwise of itself is very shallow) we might have had a tedious and longer passage; but after twelve days we got to the sea, and at the point landed at the castle to refresh ourselves for half a day. Certainly the Spaniards trust to the streams and shallowness of that river, which they think will keep off any foreign nation from attempting to come up to Venta de Cruces and from thence to Panama, or else they would strengthen more and fortify that castle, which in my time wanted great reparations, and was ready to fall down to the ground. The Governor of the castle was a notable wine-bibber, who plied us with that liquor the time that we stayed there, and wanting a chaplain for himself and soldiers, would fain have had me stayed with him; but greater matters called me further, and so I took my leave of him, who gave us some dainties of fresh meat, fish, and conserves, and so dismissed us. We got out to the open sea, discovering first the Escudo de Veragua, and keeping somewhat close unto the land we went on rowing towards Portobello, till the evening which was Saturday night; then we cast anchor behind a little island, resolving in the morning to enter in Portobello. The blackamoors all that night kept watch for fear of Hollanders, whom they said did often lie in wait thereabouts for the boats of Chagres; but we passed the night safely, and next morning got to Portobello, whose haven we observed to be very strong with two castles at the mouth and constant watch within them, and another called St Miguel further in the port.

When I came into the haven I was sorry to see that as yet the galleons were not come from Spain, knowing that the longer I stayed in that place, greater would be my charges. Yet I comforted myself that the time of the year was come, and that they could not long delay their coming. My first thoughts were of taking up a lodging, which at that time were plentiful and cheap, nay some were offered me for nothing with this caveat, that when the galleons did come I must either leave them or pay a dear rate for them. A kind gentleman, who was the King's Treasurer, falling in discourse with me promised to help me, that I might be cheaply lodged even when the ships came, and lodgings were at the highest rate. He, interposing his authority, went with me to seek one, which at the time of the fleets being there, might continue to be mine. It was no bigger than would contain a bed, a table, and a stool or two, with room enough besides to open and shut the door, and they demanded of me for it during the aforesaid time of the fleet, sixscore crowns, which commonly is a fortnight. For the town being little, and the soldiers that come with the galleons for their defence at least four or five thousand, besides merchants from Peru, from Spain, and many other places to buy and sell, is the cause that every room, though never so small, be dear; and sometimes all the lodgings in the town are few enough for so many people, which at that time do meet at Portobello. I knew a merchant who gave a thousand crowns for a shop of reasonable bigness to sell his wares and commodities that year that I was there, for fifteen days only, which the fleet continued to be in that haven. I thought it much for me to give the sixscore crowns which were demanded of me for a room, which was but as a mouse hole, and began to be troubled, and told the King's Treasurer that I had been lately robbed at sea, and was not able to give so much and be besides at charges for my diet, which I feared would prove as much more. But not a farthing would be abated of what was asked; whereupon the good Treasurer pitying me, offered to the man of the house to pay him threescore crowns of it, if so be that I was able to pay the rest, which I must do, or else lie without in the street. Yet till the fleet did come I would not enter into this dear hole, but accepted of another fair lodging which was offered me for nothing. Whilst I thus expected the fleet's coming, some money and offerings I got for Masses and for two sermons which I preached at fifteen crowns apiece. I visited the castles, which indeed seemed unto me to be very strong; but what most I wondered at was to see the *requas* of mules which came thither from Panama, laden with wedges of silver; in one day I told two hundred mules laden with nothing else, which were unladen in the public market-place, so that there the heaps of silver wedges lay like heaps of stones in the street, without any fear or suspicion of being lost. Within ten days the fleet came, consisting of eight galleons and ten merchant ships, which forced me to run to my hole. It was a wonder then to see the multitude of people in those streets which the week before had been empty.

Then began the price of all things to rise, a fowl to be worth twelve reals, which in the main land within I had often bought for one; a pound of beef then was worth two reals, whereas I had had in other places thirteen pound for half a real, and so of all other food and provision, which was so excessive dear that I knew not how to live but by fish and tortoises, which there are very many, and though somewhat dear, yet were the cheapest meat that I could eat. It was worth seeing how merchants sold their commodities, not by the ell or yard, but by the piece and weight, not paying in coined pieces of money, but in wedges which were weighed and taken for commodities.

This lasted but fifteen days, whilst the galleons were lading with wedges of silver and nothing else; so that for those fifteen days, I dare boldly say and avouch, that in the world there is no greater fair than that of Portobello, between the Spanish merchants and those of Peru, Panama, and other parts thereabouts.

Don Carlos de Ybarra, who was the Admiral of that fleet, made great haste to be gone; which made the merchants buy and sell apace, and lade the ships with silver wedges; whereof I was glad, for the more they laded, the less I unladed my purse with buying dear provision, and sooner I hoped to be out of that unhealthy place, which of itself is very hot, and subject to breed fevers, nay death, if the feet be not preserved from wetting when it raineth; but especially when the fleet is there, it is an open grave ready to swallow in part of that numerous people which at that time resort unto it, as was seen the year that I was there when about five hundred of the soldiers, merchants, and mariners, what with fevers, what with the flux caused by too much eating of fruit and drinking of water, what with other disorders lost their lives, finding it to be to them not *Porto bello*, but *Porto malo*. And this is usual every year; and therefore for the relief and comfort of those that come sick from sea, or sicken there, a great and rich hospital is in the town, with many friars called *De la Capacha*, or by others *De Juan de Dios*, whose calling and profession is only to cure and attend upon the sick, and to bear the dead unto their graves. The Admiral, fearing the great sickness that year, made haste to be gone, not fearing the report that was of some three or four Holland or English ships abroad at sea, waiting (as it was supposed) for some good prize out of that great and rich fleet. This news made me begin to fear, and to think of securing myself in one of the best and strongest galleons; but when I came to treat of my passage in one of them, I found that I could not be carried in any under three hundred crowns, which was more than my purse was able to afford. With this I thought to address myself to some master of a merchant's ship, though I knew I could not be so safe and secure in any of them as in a galleon well manned and fortified with soldiers and guns of brass; yet I hoped in God, who is a strong refuge to them that fear him, and in this occasion provided for me a cheap and sure passage. For meeting one day with my friend the Treasurer, he again pitying me as a stranger and lately robbed, commended me to the master of a merchant ship, called 'St Sebastian,' whom he knew was desirous to carry a chaplain with him at his own table. I no sooner addressed myself unto him, using the name and favour of his and my friend the Treasurer, but presently I found him willing to accept of my company, promising to carry me for nothing, and to board me at his own table, only for my prayers to God for him and his; offering further to give me some satisfaction for whatsoever sermons I should preach in his ship. I blessed God, acknowledging in this also his providence, who in all occasions furthered my return to England. The ships being laden, we set forth towards Cartagena; and the second day of our sailing we discovered four ships which made the merchant ships afraid, and to keep close to the galleons, trusting to their strength more than their own. The ship I was in was swift and nimble under sail, and kept still under the wings either of the Admiral or of some other of the best galleons; but all the other merchants ships were not so, but some slowly came on behind, whereof two were carried away by the Hollanders in the night, before ever we could get to Cartagena.

The greatest fear that I perceived possessed the Spaniards in this voyage was about the Island of Providence, called by them Sta Catalina, or St Catharine, from whence they feared lest some English ships should come out against them with great strength. They cursed the English in it, and called the island the den of thieves and pirates, wishing that their King of Spain would take some course with it, or else that it would prove very prejudicial to the Spaniards, lying near the mouth of the Desaguadero, and so endangering the frigates of Granada, and standing between Portobello and Cartagena, and so threatening the galleons, and their King's yearly and mighty treasure.

Thus with bitter invectives against the English and the Island of Providence, we sailed on to Cartagena, where again we met with the four ships which before had followed us and had taken away two of our ships, and now at our entering into that port threatened to carry away more of our company; which they might have done, if they would have ventured to have come upon the ship wherein I went, which at the turning about the land point to get into the haven, ran upon the shore, which if it had been rocky, as it was sandy and gravelly, had certainly there been cast away by keeping too near unto the land, from which danger by the care of the mariners, and their active pains we were safely delivered, as also from the ships which followed us as far as they durst for fear of the cannon shot of the castle; and thus we entered into the haven of Cartagena, and stayed there for the space of eight or ten days; where I met with some of my countrymen their prisoners, who had been taken at sea by the Spaniards, and belonged unto the Island of Providence; among whom was the renowned Captain Rouse, and about a dozen more, with whom I was glad to meet, but durst not shew them too much countenance, for fear of being suspected; yet I soon got the good will of some of them, who, being destined to Spain, were very desirous to go in the ship wherein I went, which desire of theirs I furthered, and was suitor unto my captain to carry four of them in his ship, which for my sake he willingly yielded unto; amongst these was one Edward Layfield (who afterwards setting out of St Lucar for England, was taken captive by the Turks, and since from Turkey writ into England unto me to help to release him) with whom both at Cartagena, and in the way in the ship, I had great discourse concerning points of religion, and by him came to know some things professed in England, which my conscience (whilst I lived in America) much inclined unto. I was much taken with his company, and found him very officious unto me, whose kindness I requited by speaking for him in the ship to the masters and mariners, who otherwise were ready and forward to abuse him and the rest of the English company as prisoners and slaves.

At Cartagena we heard a report of threescore sail of ships of Hollanders waiting for the galleons, which struck no little fear into the Spaniards; who called a council whether our fleet should winter there, or go on to Spain. It proved to be but a false report of the inhabitants of Cartagena, who for their own ends and lucre would willingly have had the ships and galleons to have stayed there; but Don Carlos de Ybarra replied that he feared not a hundred sail of Hollanders, and therefore would go on to Spain, hoping to carry thither safely the King's treasure. Which he performed and in eight days arrived at Havana, where we stayed eight days longer, expecting the fleet from Vera Cruz. In which time I viewed well that strong castle manned with the twelve guns, called the Twelve Apostles, which would do little hurt to an army by land, or marching from the river of Matanzas.

I visited here the mother of that mulatto, who had taken away all my means at sea; and spent much time in comforting my poor countrymen the prisoners; but especially that gallant Captain Rouse, who came unto me to complain of some affronts which had been offered unto him by Spaniards in the ship wherein he came; which he not being able to put up, though a prisoner unto them desired to question in the field, challenging his proud contemners to meet him if they durst in any

SURVEY OF WEST INDIES

place of Havana, (a brave courage in a dejected and imprisoned Englishman to challenge a Spaniard in his country, a cock upon his own dunghill), which as soon as I understood by Edward Layfield, I desired to take up, fearing that many would fall upon him cowardly and mince him small in pieces. I sent for him to the cloister where I lay, and there had conference with him, prevailing so far as that I made him desist from his thoughts of going into the field, and shewing his manhood in such a time and place, where his low condition of a prisoner might well excuse him. The rest of my poor countrymen were here much discouraged and in some want; whom I relieved (especially Layfield) and encouraged as much as I was able.

I chanced here to have occasion to take a little physic before I went again to sea, and thereby I learned what before I never knew, to wit, the diet which on such a day the best physicians of Havana prescribe unto their patients. Whereas after the working of my physic I expected some piece of mutton, or a fowl, or some other nourishing meat, my physician left order that I should have a piece of roasted pork, which seeming unto me a diet contrary to that day's extremity, I began to refuse it, alleging to my doctor the contrary course of all nations, the natural quality of that meat to open the body. To which he replied, that what pork might work upon man's body in other nations, it worked not there, but the contrary; and so he wished me to feed upon what he had prescribed, assuring me that it would do me no hurt. Now as hog's flesh there is held to be so nourishing, so likewise no other meat is more than it and tortoises, wherewith all the ships make their provision for Spain. The tortoises they cut out in long thin slices, as I have noted before of the *tasajos*, and dry it in the wind after they have well salted it, and so it serveth the mariners in all their voyage to Spain, which they eat boiled with a little

THE ENGLISH-AMERICAN

garlic, and I have heard them say that to them it tasted as well as any veal. They also take into their ships some fowls for the masters' and captains' tables, and live hogs, which would seem to be enough to breed some infection in the ship, had they not care to wash often the place where such unclean beasts lie. In the ship where I was passenger, was killed every week one for the masters', pilots', and passengers' table.

Thus all things being made ready for the ships' provision to Spain, and the merchants' goods and the King's revenue being shipped in nine days that we abode there, we now wanted nothing but only the company of the fleet from Vera Cruz, which should have met us there upon the eight day of September. But Don Carlos de Ybarra, seeing it stayed longer than the time appointed, and fearing the weather, and the new moon of that month which commonly proveth dangerous in the Gulf of Bahama, resolved to stay no longer, but to set out to Spain. On a Sabbath day therefore in the morning we hoisted sails (being in all seven and twenty ships with those which had met with us there from Honduras and the islands), and one by one we sailed out of Havana to the main sea, where we that day wafted about for a good wind, and also waiting for our guide, which was not yet come out of Havana to guide us through the Gulf of Bahama. But that night we wished ourselves again in Havana, thinking that we were compassed about with a strong fleet of Hollanders; many ships came amongst us, which made us provide for a fight in the morning. A council of war was called, and all that night watch was kept, the guns prepared, red cloths hung round the ships, orders sent about both to the galleons and to the merchants' ships what posture and place to be in. That which I was in was to attend the Admiral, which I hoped would be a strong defence unto us. Our men were courageous and ready to fight, though I liked not such martial business and discourse; but for me a place was prepared where I might lie hid, and be safe among some barrels of biscuit; I had all the night enough to do to hear the confessions of those in the ship, who thought they could not die happily with the shot of a Holland bullet until they had confessed all their sins unto me, who towards morning had more need of rest than of fighting, after the wearying of my ears with hearing so many wicked, grievous, and abominable sins. But the dawning of the day discovered our causeless fear, which was from friends, and not from any enemies or Hollanders; for the ships which were joined unto us in the night were as fearful of us, as we of them, and prepared themselves likewise to fight in the morning, which shewed unto us their colours, whereby we knew that they were the fleet which we expected from Vera Cruz to go along with us to Spain. They were two and twenty sail, which little thought to find us out of Havana, but within the haven lying at anchor, waiting for their coming, and therefore in the night feared us much more than we them. But when the day cleared our doubts, fears, and jealousies, then began the martial colours to be taken down; the joyful sound of trumpets with the help of Neptune's kingdoms echoed from ship to ship, the boats carried welcoming messages from one to another, the Spanish *brindis* with *Buen viaje, Buen pasaje*, was generally cried out, the whole morning was spent in friendly acclamations and salutations from ship to ship. But in the midst of this our joy, and sea greetings, we being now in all two and fifty sail (yet we not knowing well how many they were from Vera Cruz, nor they how many we were from Havana), two ships were found amongst us, whether English or Hollanders we could not well discover, but the English prisoners with me told me they thought one was a ship of England called the 'Neptune' which having got the wind of us, singled out a ship of ours, which belonged to Dunkirk and from St Lucar or Cadiz had been forced to the King's service in that voyage to the Indies, laden with sugars, and other rich commodities to the worth of at least fourscore thousand crowns; and suddenly giving her a whole broad side (receiving a reply only of two guns) made her yield, without any hope of help from so proud and mighty a fleet, for that she was somewhat far straggled from the rest of the ships. The whole business lasted not above half an hour: but presently she was carried away from under our noses; the Spaniards changed their merry tunes into *Voto á Dios* and *Voto á Cristo*, in raging, cursing, and swearing, some reviling at the captain of the ship which was taken, and saying that he was false and yielded on purpose without fighting, because he was forced to come that voyage; others cursing those that took her, and calling them *hijos de puta, borrachos, infames ladrones,* bastards, drunkards, infamous thieves, and pirates; some taking their swords in their hands, as if they would there cut them in pieces, some laying hold of their muskets as if they would there shoot at them, others stamping like madmen, and running about the ship as if they would leap overboard, and make haste after them; others grinding their teeth at the poor English prisoners that were in the ship, as if they would stab them for what (they said) their countrymen had done. I must needs say I had enough to do to hold some of those furious and raging brains from doing Layfield some mischief, who more than the rest would be smiling, arguing, and answering their outrageous nonsense. Order was presently given to the Vice-Admiral and two more galleons to follow and pursue them; but all in vain, for the wind was against them, and so the two ships laughing and rejoicing as much as the Spaniards cursed and raged, sailed away *con viento en popa*, with full sail, gallantly boasting with so rich a prize taken away from two and fifty ships, or (as I may say) from the chiefest, and greatest strength of Spain.

SURVEY OF WEST INDIES

That afternoon the fleet of Vera Cruz took their leave of us (not being furnished with provision to go on to Spain with us), and went into Havana; and we set forwards towards Europe, fearing nothing for the present but the Gulf of Bahama; through which we got safely with the help and guidance of such pilots which our Admiral Don Carlos had chosen, and hired for that purpose.

I shall not need to tell thee my Reader of the sight which we had of St Augustine, Florida, nor of many storms which we suffered in this voyage, nor of the many degrees we came under, which made us shake with cold more than the frost of England do in the worst of winter; only I say that the best of our pilots not knowing where they were, had like to have betrayed us all to the rocks of Bermuda one night, had not the breaking of the day given us a fair warning that we were running upon them. For which the Spaniards instead of giving God thanks for their delivery out of that danger, began again to curse and rage against the English which inhabited that island, saying that they had enchanted that and the rest of those islands about, and did still with the Devil raise storms in those seas when the Spanish fleet passed that way. From thence when we had safely escaped, we sailed well to the islands called Terceras [i.e. Azores], where fain we would have taken in fresh water (for that which we had taken in at Havana now began to stink, and look yellow, making us stop our noses whilst we opened our mouths), but rigid Don Carlos would not pity the rest of his company, who led us by the islands; and that night following we all wished ourselves in some harbour of them; for (though in their conceit those islands were not enchanted by Englishmen, but inhabited by holy and idolatrous Papists) we were no sooner got from them when there arose the greatest storm that we had in all our voyage from Havana to Spain, which lasted full eight days, where we lost one ship and endangered two galleons, which shot off their warning pieces for help, and made us all stay and wait on them, till they had repaired their tacklings and main mast.

We went on sometimes one way, sometimes another, not well knowing where we were, drinking our stinking water by allowance of pints, till three or four days after the storm was ceased we discovered land, which made all cry out, *Hispania, Hispania,* 'Spain, Spain'; whilst a council was summoned by the Admiral to know what land that was, some sold away barrels of biscuit, others of water, to those that wanted (everyone thinking that it was some part of Spain), but the result of the wise council was, after they had sailed nearer to the land, and had laid and lost many wagers about it, that it was the Island of Madeira, which made some curse the ignorance of the pilots, and made us all prepare ourselves with patience for a longer voyage. It pleased God from the discovery of this island to grant us a favourable wind to Spain, where within twelve days we discovered Cadiz; and some of the ships there left us, but most of them went forward to San Lucar, as did the ship wherein I went; when we came near to the dangerous place which the Spaniards call La Barra, we durst not venture our ships upon our pilots' own knowledge, but called for pilots to guide us in, who greedy of their lucre came out in boats almost for every ship one. Upon the eight and twentieth of November, 1637, we cast anchor within St Lucar de Barrameda about one of the clock in the afternoon, and before evening other passengers and myself went ashore (having first been searched) and although I might presently have gone to the cloister of St Dominic, where my old friend Friar Pablo de Londres was yet living, whom I knew would be glad of my coming from the Indies, yet I thought fit the first night to enjoy my friends' company both Spaniards and English (who had come so long a voyage with me), in some ordinary, and to take my rest better abroad than I should do in a cloister, where I expected but a poor friar's supper, a hard and mean lodging, many foolish questions from old Friar Pablo de Londres concerning the Indies, and my abode there so many years, and finally the noise of bells and rattlers to rouse up the drowsy friars from their sleep to matins at midnight. That night therefore I betook myself to an English ordinary, where I refreshed myself and my poor prisoners (who by the master of the ship were committed to my charge that night and forwards upon my word, so as to be forthcoming when they should be called), and the next morning I sent my honest friend Layfield with a letter to the cloister to old Pablo de Londres, who upon my summons came joyfully to welcome me from the Indies, and after very little discourse told me of ships in the haven ready to set out for England. The old friar being of a decrepit and doting age, thought every day a year that I stayed there and suspended my voyage for England, and (not knowing the secrets of my heart) judged already that the conversion or turning of many Protestant souls to Popery waited for my coming, which made him hasten me, who was more desirous than he to be gone the next day, if I might have found wind, weather, and shipping ready. But God, who had been with me in almost ninety days' sailing from Havana to San Lucar, and had delivered me from many a storm, prepared and furthered all things in a very short time for the last accomplishment of my hope and desire, to return to England my native soil, from whence I had been absent almost for the space of four and twenty years.

My first thought here in St Lucar was to cast off now my friar's weed, which was a white coat or gown hanging to the ground girded about with a leathern belt, and over it from the shoulders downward a white scapulary (so called there), hanging shorter than the gown both before and behind, and over that a white hood to cover the head, and lastly, over that a black cloak with another black hood; both which together, the black and white, make the friars of that profession look just like magpies, and is acknowledged by the Church of Rome itself in a verse which they feign of Mr Martin Luther (with what just ground I know not), saying of his former life and profession before his conversion, *Bis Corvus, bis Pica fui, ter fune ligatus*, 'I was twice a crow, twice a magpie, and thrice was bound or tied with a cord'; by a crow meaning an Augustine friar, who is all in black; by a magpie, meaning a Dominican, and by bound with a rope or cord, meaning a Franciscan, who indeed is girded about with a cord made of hemp. I applying the allegory of this black and white habit otherwise unto myself, and in the outward black part of it seeing the foulness and filthiness of my life and idolatrous priesthood in the exercise of that profession and orders which from Rome I had received; and in the white inward habit considering yet the purity and integrity of those intentions and thoughts of my inward heart, in pursuance whereof I had left what formerly I have noted, yea all America, which, had I continued in it, might have been to me a mine of wealth, riches, and treasure; I resolved here therefore to cast off that hypocritical cloak and habit, and to put on such apparel whereby I might no more appear a wolf in sheepskin, but might go boldly to my country of England, there to shew and make known the candour of my heart, the purity and sincerity of my thoughts, which had brought me so far, by a public profession of the pure truths of the Gospel without any invention or addition of man unto it. With the small means therefore which was left me after so long and almost a whole year's journey from Petapa to St Lucar (having yet about a hundred crowns) I gave order for a suit of clothes to be made by an English tailor, which I willingly put on, and so prepared myself for England.

SURVEY OF WEST INDIES

Three or four ships were in readiness, who had only waited for the fleet to take in some commodities, especially some wedges of silver, of which I was with old Pablo de Londres in doubt which to choose. The first that went out was thought should have been my lot, in the which my friend Layfield embarked himself (for all the English prisoners were there freed to go home to their country) and from which the great providence of God diverted me, or else I had been this day with Layfield a slave in Turkey; for the next day after this ship set out it was taken by the Turks, and carried away for a rich prize, and all the English in it for prisoners to Algiers. But God (who I hope had reserved me for better things) appointed for me a safer convoy home in a ship (as I was informed) belonging to Sir William Courteen, under the command of an honest Fleming named Adrian Adrianzen living at Dover then, with whom I agreed for my passage and diet at his table. This ship set out of the bar of St Lucar the ninth day after my arrival thither, where it waited for the company of four ships more, but especially for some Indian wedges of silver, which upon forfeiture of them it durst not take in within the bar and haven.

And thus being now clothed after a new fashion and ready to lead a new life; being now changed from an American into the fashion of an Englishman, the tenth day after my abode in San Lucar I bad adieu to Spain and all Spanish fashions, factions, and carriages, I bad farewell to my old Friar Pablo de Londres, with the rest of my acquaintance, and so in a boat went over the bar to the ship, which that night in company of four more set forward for England. I might observe here many things of the goodness of Adrian Adrianzen, and his good carriage towards me in his ship, which I will omit, having much more to observe of the goodness of God, who favoured this our voyage with such a prosperous wind, and without any storm at all, that in thirteen days we came to Dover, where I landed, the ship going on to the Downs. Others that landed at Margaret were brought to Dover, and there questioned and searched; but I, not speaking English but Spanish, was not at all suspected, neither judged to be an Englishman; and so after two days I took post, in company of some Spaniards and an Irish colonel, for Canterbury, and so forward to Gravesend. When I came to London, I was much troubled within myself for want of my mother tongue (for I could only speak some few broken words), which made me fearful I should not be acknowledged to be an Englishman born. Yet I thought my kindred (who knew I had been many years lost) would some way or other acknowledge me, and take notice of me, if at the first I addressed myself unto some of them, until I could better express myself in English. The first therefore of my name whom I had notice of was my Lady Penelope Gage, widow of Sir John Gage, then living in St Johns; to whom the next morning after my arrival to London I addressed myself for the better discovery of some of my kindred; whom though I knew to be Papists, and therefore ought not to be acquainted with my inward purpose and resolution, yet for fear of some want in the meantime, and that I might by their means practice myself in the use of my forgotten native tongue, and that I might enquire what child's part had been left me by my father, that I might learn some fashions, and lastly, that in the meantime I might search into the religion of England, and find how far my conscience could agree with it, and be satisfied in those scruples which had troubled me in America, for all these reasons I thought it not amiss to look and enquire after them. When therefore I came unto my Lady Gage she believed me to be her kinsman, but laughed at me, telling me that I spake like an Indian or Welshman, and not like an Englishman; yet she welcomed me home, and sent me with a servant to a brother's lodging in Long

Acre, who being in the county of Surrey and hearing of me, sent horse and man for me to come to keep Christmas with an uncle of mine living at Gatton; by whom as a lost and forgotten nephew, and now after four and twenty years returned home again, I was very kindly entertained, and from thence sent for to Cheam, to one Mr Fromand, another kinsman with whom I continued till after Twelfth Day, and so returned again to London to my brother.

Thus, my good Reader, thou seest an American, through many dangers by sea and land now safely arrived in England; and thou mayest well with me observe the great and infinite goodness and mercy of God towards me a wicked and wretched sinner.

CHAPTER XVII

Shewing how, and for what causes, after I had arrived in England, I took yet another journey, to Rome and other parts of Italy, and returned again to settle myself in this my country.

Now Reader, as the stone that is falling, the nearer it cometh to its centre more haste it maketh, so I the nearer I am coming to the conclusion of this my history more haste I desire to make in this last chapter, for the completing and finishing of it. With brevity therefore I will relate some of my travels in Europe, in which I will yield to many of my nation, but for America, and my travels and experience there, I dare boldly challenge all travellers of my country. After my return to London from Surrey, I began to expostulate with my younger brother (knowing he had been present at my father's death, and had a chief hand in the ordering and executing his last will and testament), concerning what child's part was left unto me. To which he made me answer, that my father had indeed left him, and my brother the colonel, and two others sons by a second wife, and my own sister, every one somewhat, but to me nothing, nay that at his death he did not so much as remember me; which I could not but take to heart, and called to mind the angry and threatening letter which I had received from him in Spain, because I would not be a Jesuit. Though for the present I said nothing, yet afterwards in many occasions I told my brother I would have the will produced, and would by course of law demand a child's part; but he put me off, assuring me I should never want amongst others my friends and kindred, with whom he knew I should be well accommodated as long as I continued in England. After few days that I had been in London, my kinsman at Cheam desired me to come to live with him; where I continued not long; for my uncle at Gatton invited me to his house, offering me there meat, drink, lodging, horse and man, with twenty pound a year, which he promised in other ways to make as good as thirty. Here I continued a twelvemonth, refining myself in my native tongue, and (though altogether unknown to my uncle and kindred) searching into the doctrine and truth of the Gospel professed in England; for which cause I made many journeys to London, and then privately I resorted to some churches, and especially to Paul's Church, to see the service performed, and to hear the Word of God preached, but so that I might not be seen, known, or discovered by any Papist. When in Paul's Church I heard the organs, and the music, and the prayers and collects, and saw the ceremonies at the altar, I remembered Rome again, and perceived little difference between the two churches. I searched further into the Common-Prayer, and carried with me a Bible into the country on purpose to compare the prayers, epistles, and Gospels, with a Mass Book, which there I had at command, and I found no difference but only English and Latin, which made me wonder, and to acknowledge that much remained still of Rome in the Church of England, and that I feared my calling was not right. In these my scruples coming often to London, and conversing with one Dade, Popham and Crafts, Connel and Brown, English and Irish Dominican friars, I found their ways and conversations base, lewd, light and wanton, like the Spanish and Indian friars, which made me again reflect upon the Popish Church, upheld by such pillars. I came yet to the acquaintance of one Price, Superior to the Benedictine monks, whom I found to be a mere statesman, and a great politician, and very familiar, private, and secret with the Archbishop of Canterbury, William Laud; in conversation with my brother (who belonged then unto one Signor Con, the Pope's Agent, and was in such favour at the Court that he was sent over by the Queen with a rich present to a Popish idol named our Lady of Sichem in the Low Countries), I heard him sometimes say that he doubted not but to be shortly curate and parish priest of Covent Garden, sometimes that he hoped to be made bishop in England, and that then I should want for nothing, and should live with him till he got me another bishopric; by which discourse of his, and by his and other priests' favour at Court and with the Archbishop, I perceived things went not well, Spanish Popery was much rooted, Protestant religion much corrupted, and the time not seasonable for me to discover my secret intents and purpose of heart. At this time coming once from Surrey to London, I chanced to be discovered and known to one of the State officers, a pursuivant, who had a large commission for the apprehending of seminary priests and Jesuits, named John Gray, who meeting me one day in Long Acre, followed and dogged me as far as Lincoln's Inn wall, where he clapped me on the shoulders, and told me that he had a commission against me, to apprehend me, and carry me to the Council Table or to one of His Majesty's Secretaries. To whom I spoke in Spanish (thinking thereby to free myself out of his hands for a Spaniard): but this would not do, for he replied he knew me to be an Englishman born, and by the name of Gage, and brother to Colonel Gage and Mr George Gage, and that before he left me I must speak in English to him. He carried me to a tavern, and there searched my pockets for letters and money, which in discourse he told me was too little for him (not being above twelve shilling) and that I must go with him to answer before one of His Majesty's Secretaries. I told him that I would willingly go before the Archbishop of Canterbury, or before Sir Francis Windebanke; at which he smiled, saying, I knew well whom to make choice of to favour and protect me, but he would carry me to none of them, but to Secretary Cooke. I fearing the business might go hard with me, and knowing him to be greedy of money, told him that I would give him anything that might content him, and so offered him twelve shillings then about me, and my word to meet him in any place the next day, with a better and fuller purse. He accepted of my money for the present, and further offer for the day following, and appointed the Angel Tavern in Long Acre (knowing that I lodged thereabout), to be the place of our meeting, and so dismissed me. I being free from him, went immediately to my brother and told him what had happened unto me, what money I had already given unto him, and what I had promised the next day following. My brother hearing me began to chafe and vex, and to fall into furious words against John Gray, calling him knave and rogue, and that he could not answer what he had done, and that he would have his commission taken from him, chiding me for that I had given him any money, and calling me young novice and unexperienced in the affairs of England. This seemed strange to me, that my brother should not only not fear a pursuivant, but should threaten to take away the commission from him, who was appointed to search for and find out priests and Jesuits. Yet I told him I would according to my word and promise meet him the next day, and satisfy him for his fair carriage towards me; to which my brother would by no means yield, but said he would meet him; which he accordingly performed, and although for my sake and promise he gave him some money, yet he brought him before Signor Con, and there himself and the Pope's Agent with him spake most bitter words unto him, and threatened him very much if ever again he durst meddle with me.

After this my brother carried me to one Sir William Howard, a Papist knight, living at Arundel gate over Clement's Church, who was very familiar with Sir Francis Windebanke, telling him what had happened unto me, and desiring him to carry me with him in his coach to Sir Francis, and to get his protection for me. Secretary Windebanke, understanding who I was, told me I should fear no pursuivant of them all, and that if I lived quietly in England nobody should trouble me, and that John Gray was a knave, and wished me if ever he meddled with me again to come unto him. Though for the present this was good and commodious for me to have such favour and protection, yet I perceived this my brother's power, and this conniving at priests and Jesuits could not be useful for me if I should publish my mind and purpose to alter my religion. I was therefore much troubled in mind and conscience, which I found was curbed with the great power of the Papists. I resolved therefore to go again out of England, and to travel in some other countries amongst both Papists and Protestants, and to try what better satisfaction I could find for my conscience at Rome in that religion, or in France and Germany amongst the Protestants. I writ therefore to the General of the Dominicans at Rome (without whose licence I could not go thither) that he would be pleased to send me his letters patent to go to confer some points with him; which he willingly granted unto me. I wanted not money from my uncle (who commended unto me some business to be dispatched for him at Rome) for so long a journey, other friends also helped me; but my chief trust was upon my brother Colonel Gage, then in the Low Countries, whom I knew not, nor had seen him from a child. I had no other pass to take shipping at Dover, but only the letter of a Papist in London (by means of one Popham, a Dominican friar) to Sir John Manwood his lady, who was then Governor of Dover Castle, and with the aforesaid letter suffered me not to be troubled, examined, or searched, but gave order that I should freely and quietly pass over in the packet boat to Dunkirk, wherewith in four hours with a good wind I arrived, and from thence by Nieuport and Bruges went to Ghent; not far from whence my brother with his regiment lay in field against the Hollander. He was glad to see me, and knowing what journey I was minded to take, furnished me with more money, and for my uncle's business recommended me to the Marquess de Serralvo (then at Brussels) and to other great men, desiring them to give me their letters to their friends at Rome; from them I got a letter to Don Francisco Barbarini, the Pope's nephew, and one of the chief Cardinals then in Rome, likewise to Cardinal Cucua, and Cardinal Albornos, both Spaniards. With these letters I thought I should have occasion of some conversation with these pillars of the Church of Rome, and in discourse might pry into the hearts and ways of them, and see whether in them were more policy than religion. By reason of the wars between France and the Low Countries, I durst not make my journey the nearest and shortest way through France; but though there were wars also in Germany, I thought that would be my safest way, and I desired much to look into the Protestant and Lutheran Church in that country. Whereupon I resolved from Brussels to go to Namur, and from thence by water to Liége, and from thence to Cologne in Germany. From Liége to Cologne though we were twelve in company, we were much troubled with soldiers; yet God still delivered me and brought me safe to Cologne, from whence by the river Rhine I went in boat to Frankfort in September at the time of that great fair, where I knew I should meet company of merchants to any part of Italy. In all my travels I never made a more pleasant journey than that which I made by the river Rhine, where I had occasion to see many fair and goodly cities. In Frankfort there I began to take notice of the Lutheran Church, and for the space of a fortnight that I stayed there had many thoughts of discovering myself there, and disclaiming Popery, thinking that there I might be sure and safe, and lie hid and unknown to my brothers and kindred, who in England would not suffer me to live a Protestant. Yet again I considered how hard it would be for me a stranger to subsist there, and to get any livelihood, for the which I must first get the native tongue, and though many points that were opposite to the Church of Rome pleased me, yet in some points of that religion my conscience was not satisfied. At the end of the fair I sought out for company, and found near a dozen wagons which were upon setting out towards Augsburg with goods of merchants, who had also hired a convoy of thirty soldiers to go along with them; which I thought would be safe company for me. With them, and many other passengers and travellers that went in the wagons, and on foot by them, I went as far as the famous and gallant city of Augsburg; from whence forward there was no great danger, neither in what part belonged to the Duke of Bavaria, nor in the county of Tirol; from whence we passed some four together to Trent; where I was taken with the first ague that ever in my life I remembered I had, which continued seven months upon me. I thought from thence to have continued my journey by land to Venice, but my ague

THE ENGLISH-AMERICAN

suffered me to go but to Verona; from whence I turned to Milan, and so to Genoa, leaving my good company, that from Genoa I might go by sea to Leghorn, and so likewise to Rome. After a fortnight's stay in Genoa, I went with the galleys of the great Duke of Florence to Leghorn, where I found no boats ready [to set out] to Rome, and so in the meantime, whilst they were preparing, I went to Pisa and Florence to see those brave cities, and returned again to Leghorn, where I found many boats ready to set out to Rome.

The first night and day we had a fair wind to Piombino; but there it turned, and continued contrary for almost three weeks. At last it pleased God to send us a fair wind wherewith we went out many boats and feluccas in company together, thinking all had been friends; but when we came near to the Castle of Montalto, most of the boats having got before us, two that went in company with the boat wherein I was suddenly set upon us, and shewed themselves to be French pirates, who robbed us all, and took from me all the money I had, which was not then above five pound, leaving me some bills of exchange which I had to take up money at Rome: after we were robbed we called in at Civita Vecchia for relief, where I met with a good English merchant, who freely bestowed upon me provision both of wine and meat, as much as would well suffice me and a friend to Rome, whither we got in a day and night. When I came to Rome I delivered my letters to the cardinals; of whom the two Spaniards I found proud and stately; but Don Francisco Barbarini (who was entitled the Protector of England), I found more tractable, kind, and loving. I perceived by his discourse that he knew much of England, and desired to know more; and propounded unto me many questions concerning the state of this kingdom, and especially concerning the Archbishop of Canterbury, whom he seemed to affect; and yet sometime again would say he feared he would cause some great disturbance in our kingdom, and that certainly for his sake and by his means the King had dissolved lately the Parliament (which was that which before this now sitting was so suddenly dissolved by his Majesty) which he feared Scotland and most of the people of England would take very ill. He asked me further what conceit the people had of the said Archbishop; and whether they did not mistrust that he complied much with the Court of Rome. And lastly, he told me that he thought the creating of an English cardinal at Rome might be of great consequence for the conversion of the whole kingdom. I laid up in my heart all this discourse, and well perceived some great matters were in agitation at Rome, and some secret compliance from England with that Court, which I purposed to discover more at large among some friends there.

After this discourse with the cardinal I was invited to the English College to dinner by one Father Fitzherbert, who was then Rector, a great statesman and politician, with whom I had also great discourse concerning my brother Colonel Gage, concerning my travels in America, and lastly concerning England; whereof I perceived little discourse could be had in Rome except the Archbishop William Laud had his part and share in it. The Jesuit began highly to praise the Arch-Prelate for his moderate carriage towards Papists and priests, boasting of the free access which one Simons, alias Flood, a Jesuit, had unto him at all hours, and in all occasions; and to extol him the more, he brought in the Archbishop Abbot, whom he cried down as much for a cruel enemy and persecutor of the Church of Rome, and of all Papists and priests. 'But the now Archbishop,' said he, ' is not only favourable unto us there, but here desireth to make daily demonstrations of his great affection to this our Court and Church; which he shewed not long since in sending a Common-Prayer book (which he had composed for the Church of Scotland), to be first viewed and approved of by our Pope and cardinals. Who perusing it, liked it very well for Protestants to be trained in a form of prayer and service; yet considering the state of Scotland, and the temper and tenets of that people, the cardinals (first giving him thanks for his respect and dutiful compliance with them) sent him word that they thought that form of prayer was not fitting for Scotland, but would breed some stir and unquietness there, for that they understood the Scots were aversed from all set forms, and would not be tied and limited to the invention of man's spirit, having (as they thought) the true and unerring Spirit of God in them, which could better teach and direct them to pray. All this,' said Father Fitzherbert, 'I was witness of, who was then sent for by the cardinals (as in all like occasions, and affairs concerning England) to give them my opinion concerning the said Common-Prayer book, and the temper of the Scots. But the good Archbishop,' quoth he, 'hearing the censure of the cardinals concerning his intention and form of prayer, to ingratiate himself the more into their favour, corrected some things in it, and made it more harsh and unreasonable for that nation; which we already hear they have stomached at, and will not suffer it in many parts to be read; and we justly fear that this his Common-Prayer book, and his great compliance with this Court will at last bring strife and division between the two kingdoms of Scotland and England.'

And this most true relation of William Laud, late Archbishop of Canterbury (though I have often spoken of it in private discourse and publicly preached it at the lecture of Wingham in Kent), I could not in my conscience omit it here; both to vindicate the just censure of death, which the now sitting Parliament have formerly given against him for such-like practices and compliance with Rome; and secondly to reprove the ungrounded opinion and error of some ignorant and malignant spirits, who to my knowledge have since his death highly exalted him, and cried him up for a martyr. At the same time, whilst I was at Rome, I understood of another great business concerning England, then in agitation amongst the cardinals, and much prosecuted by this Fitzherbert and one Father Courtney a Jesuit, son to one Sir Thomas Leeds; which was, to create one of the English nation cardinal, that so the conversion of England, what by the assistance of William Laud, what by the power of a higher person, and what by the authority of the said cardinal, might be more fully and earnestly plotted and endeavoured. This business was much agitated in England by Signor Con, at whose house in Long Acre were many meetings of the chief gentry of the Papists. In Rome, Sir William Hamilton, then agent for the Queen, vied much for the said cardinal's cap, and got a great number of friends to further this his ambitious design. But he was too young, and some scandal of a gentlewoman, who stuck too close to him, made the red cap unfit for his head; and secondly, because a greater than he, to wit Sir Kenelm Digby, was appointed by the Queen to be her agent there; who sent before him his chaplain, a great politician and active priest, named Fitton, to take up his lodgings and make way and friends for his ambitious preferment; who in his daily discourse cried up his master Digby for cardinal, and told me absolutely that he doubted not but he would carry it. But though he had great favour from the Queen, and was her agent, yet he had strong antagonists in Fitzherbert, Courtney, and the rest of the crew of the Jesuits, who looked upon that honour and red cap as better becoming one of their profession, and fitter for a head which had formerly worn a four cornered black cap, to wit, Sir Toby Mathy. But in case the said cap should fall from Sir Toby his head, then they would help and further a third, whose birth and nobility should advance him before Sir Kenelm Digby, to wit, Walter Mountague, the old Earl of Manchester his son at that time.

And thus it was a general and credible report in Rome that either a Digby, a Mathy, or a Mountague, should that year be made cardinal. Whereby I perceived that England was coming near to Rome, and that my design of professing and following the truth in England was blasted, and that in vain I had come from America for satisfaction of my conscience in England. I was more troubled now than ever; and desired to try all ways, if I could be better satisfied concerning the Popish religion in Rome, Naples, or Venice (whither I went) than I had been in America and among the Spaniards. But I found such exorbitances and scandals in the lives of some cardinals of Rome whilst I was there, especially in Don Antonio Barbarini, and Cardinal Burgesi, who at midnight was taken by the *corchetes*, or officers of justice, in uncivil ways, and came off from them with money, that I perceived the religion was but as I had found it in America, a wide and open door to looseness and policy, and the like in Naples and Venice, which made me even hate what before I had professed for religion, and resolve that if I could not live in England and there enjoy my conscience, that I would live in France for a while, until I had well learned that tongue, and then associate myself unto the best reformed Protestant Church. Whereupon I obtained from the General of the Dominicans this ensuing order to live in the cloister of Orleans, intending from thence at my best opportunity to go to Paris, Lyons, or some other place, and shake off my magpie habit, and to live and die in France in the true Protestant and reformed religion as professed there.

SURVEY OF WEST INDIES

In Dei Filio sibi dilecto Reverendo Patri fratri Thomæ Gageo *Provinciæ Anglicanæ Ordinis Prædicatorum,* Frater Nicolaus Rodulfius *totius ejusdem Ordinis Magister Generalis ac servus in Domino salutem.*

Conventui nostro Aurelianensi Provinciæ nostræ Franciæ de probo & optimo Patre Sacerdote providere cupientes, Tenore præsentium, & nostri authoritate officii te supra nominatum Reverendum Patrem Fratrem Thomam Gageum *revocamus a quovis alio Conventu, & assignamus in dicto Conventu nostro Aurelianensi assignatumque declaramus, in Nomine Patris, & Filii, & Spiritus Sancti,* Amen. *Mandantes Rdo. admodum Patri Magistro Priori illius, ut te benigne recipiat, & cum omni charitate tractet. In quorum fidem his officii nostri sigillo munitis propria manu subscripsimus. Datum Suriani die nono Aprilis,* 1640.

Frater Nicolaus   Frater Ignatius Ciantes
Magister Ordinis.   Magister Provincialis
                            Angliæ, & Socius.

The form whereof (as also the manner of sending friars from one cloister to live in another, commonly called by them an assignation) is in English as followeth.

To our Beloved in the Son of God, the Reverend Father Friar Thomas Gage, of the English Province, of the Order of Preachers, Friar Nicholas Rodulfius of the same whole Order Master General, and Servant in the Lord, health and greeting.

We being willing and desirous to provide for our Convent of Orleans, of our Province of France, of an honest and very good father and priest; by tenour of these present, and by the authority of our Office do recall you the above-named Reverend Friar Thomas Gage from any other convent, and do assign you in our said Convent of Orleans, and declare you to be assigned, in the Name of the Father, and of the Son, and of the Holy Ghost. Amen. Commanding the very Reverend Father Master Prior thereof that he receive you courteously, and entertain you with all love and charity. In witness whereof with our own hand we have subscribed these being sealed with the seal of our Office. Dated at Soriano the ninth day of April, 1640.

    Friar Nicholas Master
      of the Order.

                    Friar Ignatius Ciantes Master
                        Provincial of England and
                        Companion.

Yet after I had got this order, I bethought myself further that I would try one way, which was to see if I could find out a miracle, which might give me better satisfaction of the Romish religion than had the former experience of my life, and the lives of the priests, cardinals, and all such with whom I had lived in Spain and America. I had heard much of a picture of Our Lady of Loretto, and read in a Book of Miracles or lies concerning the same that whosoever prayed before that picture in the state of mortal sin, the picture would discover the sin in the soul by blushing, and by sweating. Now I framed this argument to myself, that it was a great sin, the sin of unbelief, or to waver and stagger in points of faith; but in me (according to the tenets of Rome) was this sin, for I could not believe the point of transubstantiation, and many others; therefore (if the miracles which were printed of the aforesaid Lady of Loretto were true, and not lies) certainly she would blush and sweat when such an unbeliever as I prayed before her. To make this trial I went purposely to Loretto, and kneeling down before God, not with any faith I had in the picture, I prayed earnestly to the true searcher of all hearts, that in his Son Jesus Christ he would mercifully look upon me a wretched sinner, and inspire and enlighten me with his spirit of truth, for the good and salvation of my soul. In my prayer I had a fixed and settled eye upon the lady's picture, but could not perceive that she did either sweat or blush, wherewith I arose up from my knees much comforted and encouraged in my resolution to renounce and abandon Popery, and saying within myself as I went out of the church, surely if my Lady neither sweat nor blush, all is well with me, and I am in a good way for salvation, and the miracles written of her are but lies. With this I resolved to follow the truth in some Protestant church in France, and to relinquish error and superstition. Upon which good purpose of mine, I presently perceived the God of truth did smile, with what I heard he was ordering in England by an army of Scotland raised for reformation, and by a new Parliament called to Westminster, at which I saw the Papists and Jesuits there began to tremble, and to say that it would blast all their designs, and all their hopes of settling Popery; William Laud his policy was now condemned and cursed, Con was dead at Rome, the cardinal's cap for one of the three aforenamed was no more spoken of, Fitton was daunted, Fitzherbert and Courtney quite disheartened, Sir Kenelham Digby his agency and coming to Rome put off and suspended, and with all this good news I was much heartened and encouraged to leave off my journey to France, and to return to England, where I feared not my brother nor any kindred, nor the power of the Papists, but began to trust in the protection of the Parliament, which I was informed would reform religion, and make such laws as should tend to the undermining of all the Jesuits' plots, and to the confusion and subversion of the Romish errors and religion. I was too weak of body to make my journey by land (by reason of my long ague which had but newly left me) and so resolved

THE ENGLISH-AMERICAN

to go to Leghorn to find out shipping there; where I found four or five ships of English and Hollanders ready to set out, but were bound to touch at Lisbon in their way. I bargained with one Captain Scot for my passage, first to Lisbon, intending there to make a second bargain. We had no sooner sailed on as far as to the coast of France joining to the duchy of Savoy but presently from Cannes came out part of a fleet, lying there under the command of the Bishop of Bordeaux to discover us, and take us for a lawful prize. I might say much here of the valour of the good old Captain Scot, who, seeing all the other ships had yielded to the French men-of-war, would upon no terms yield to be their prize (which they challenged because we were bound for Lisbon, then their enemy's country) but would fight with them all, and at last rather blow up his ship than to deliver the goods which had been entrusted to him by the merchants of Leghorn. We were in a posture to fight, our guns ready, and mariners willing to die that day, which was heavy news to me. After much treaty between the French and our valorous captain, who still held out and would not yield, there came up to us two ships to give us the last warning that if we yielded not, they would immediately set our ship on fire. With this all the passengers and many more in the ship desired the captain to yield upon some fair articles for the securing of what goods he had for England, and should appear were not any way for the strengthening of any enemies to the state and kingdom of France. With much ado our captain was persuaded, and we were carried with the rest into Cannes for a lawful prize. I seeing that the ships were like to be stayed there long, obtained the Bishop of Bordeaux his pass to go to Marseilles, and from thence by land through France. Which being granted, I went by water to Toulon, and from thence to Marseilles, and so in company of carriers to Lyons, and from thence to Paris, Rouen, and Dieppe, where in the first packet boat to Rye I passed over to England, where I landed upon Michaelmas Day the same year that this present Parliament began to sit the November following. My brother's spirit I found was not much daunted with the new Parliament, nor some of the proudest Papists, who hoped for a sudden dissolving of it. But when I saw their hopes frustrated by His Majesty's consent to the continuing of it, I thought the acceptable time was come for me, wherein I ought not to dissemble any further with God, the world, and my friends, and so resolved to bid adieu to flesh and blood; and to prize Christ above all my kindred, to own and profess him publicly maugre all opposition of hell and kindred to the contrary. I made myself first known to Doctor Brunnick, Bishop of Exeter, and to Mr Shute of Lombard Street, from whom I had very comfortable and strong encouragements. The Bishop of Exeter carried me to the Bishop of London then at Fulham, from whom I received order to preach my recantation sermon at Paul's: which done, I thought I must yet do more to satisfy the world of my sincerity, knowing that converts are hardly believed by the common sort of people unless they see in them such actions which may further disclaim Rome for ever for the future. Whereupon I resolved to enter into the state of marriage (to which God hath already given his blessing) which the Church of Rome disavows to all her priests. What I have been able to discover for the good of this state I have done, and not spared (when called upon) to give in true evidence upon my oath against Jesuits, priests, and friars; for the which (after a fair invitation from my brother Colonel Gage to come over again to Flanders, offering me a thousand pound ready money) I have been once assaulted in Aldersgate Street; and another time like to be killed in Shoe Lane by a captain of my brother's regiment, named Vincent Burton, who (as I was after informed) came from Flanders on purpose to make me away or convey me over, and with such a malicious design followed me to my lodging, lifting up the latch and opening the door (as he had seen me done) and attempting to go up the stairs to my chamber without any enquiry for me, or knocking at the door; from whom God graciously delivered me by the weak means of a woman my landlady, who stopped him from going any further; and being demanded his name, and answering by the name of Steward, and my landlady telling him from me that I knew him not, he went away chafing and saying that I should know him before he had done with me. But he that knoweth God well shall know no enemy to his hurt; neither have I ever since seen or known this man. I might here also write down the contents of a threatening letter from mine own brother, when he was colonel for the King of England and Governor of Oxford, which I forbear with some tender consideration of flesh and blood. At the beginning of the wars I confess I was at a stand as a neophyte and new plant of the Church of England concerning the lawfulness of the war; and so continued above a year in London spending my own means till at last I was fully satisfied, and much troubled to see that the Papists and most of my kindred were entertained at Oxford, and in other places of the King's dominions; whereupon I resolved upon a choice for the Parliament cause, which now in their lowest estate and condition I am not ashamed to acknowledge. From their hands and by their order I received a benefice, in the which I have continued almost four years preaching constantly for a thorough and godly reformation intended by them, which I am ready to witness with the best drops of blood in my veins, though true it is I have been envied, jealousied, and suspected by many; to whom I desire this my history may be a better witness of my sincerity, and that by it I may perform what our Saviour Christ spoke to Peter, saying; 'And thou being converted strengthen thy brethren.' I shall think my time and pen happily employed if by what here I have written I may strengthen the perusers of this small volume against Popish superstition whether in England, other parts of Europe, Asia, or America; for the which I shall offer up my daily prayers unto him, who (as I may well say) miraculously brought me from America to England, and hath made use of me as a Joseph to discover the treasures of Egypt, or as the spies to search into the land of Canaan, even the God of all nations, to whom be ascribed by me and all true and faithful believers, Glory, Power, Majesty and Mercy for evermore. *Amen.*

INDEX

Abbot, Archbishop, 391
Acacabastlan, 209, 210, 226
Acapala, 136
Achiote, 124
Adrianzen, Adrian, 381
Agriculture in Guatemala, 219
Agua Caliente, 210
Aguachapa, 335
Aguatulco, 124
Albornos, Cardinal, 388
Alixco, 117
Alvarez, Friar Peter (Provincial of Chiapa), 137
Amatitlan, 218, 329, 335
Angels, the City of, 50-52
Antequera, 123
Anzuelos, River, 348
Atole, 121
Augsburg, 389
Axaiaca, 70

Baptist, Father John, 143, 144, 189
Barbarini, Don Francisco, 388, 390
Borrallo, Peter, 114, 136, 139
Brown, 385
Brunnick, Dr, 399
Burgesi, Cardinal, 394
Burton, Vincent, 399

Cabannas, Jacintho de, 188
Cacao as money, 76
Cadiz, 12, 378
Calvo, Friar Antonio, 10, 12, 114, 136, 137
Canterbury, Archbishop of. *See* Laud
Capalita, 124

Carding and dicing among the friars, 41
Carrillo, Don Martin, 14, 106, 107
Carrillo, Martha de, 298-302
Cartagena, 371
Cartago, 347, 353
Cayman, danger from, 346
Cedar used by the Spaniards, 58
Cerro Redondo, 334
Chagres, River, 365
Chalchuapan, 337
Chapultepec, 59, 70
Chautlan, 175
Cheam, 383
Chiantla, 174
Chiapa of the Indians, 136, 150, 164
Chiapa Province, Provincial of, 137-142; description of, 151, 159
Chiapa Real, Prior of, 143, 144; imprisonment in, 147; gentlemen of, 152; Bishop of, 160
Chiautla, 119
Chicha, 242
Chimaltenango, 183
Chira, 359
Chocolate taken by ladies in church, 161
Chuntales, mountains, 337
Churches and the Indians, 254
Coacuacoyocin, 54, 55
Coban, 223, 224, 273
Colindres, Dons Gaspar, Diego, Thomas, and John de, 214
Comitan, 150, 170
Con, Signor, 385, 387, 393
Connel, 385
Conquerors, descendants of, 82

403

INDEX

Copanabastla, 150, 170
Cortez, Hernando, at St John de Ulhua, 31; at Segura de la Frontera, 44; at Tlaxcala, 48; at Texcoco, 54; siege of Mexico, 57, 72; rebuilding of Mexico, 80; property of, 81, 91, 120
Courtney, Father, 393
Crafts, 385
Creoles, dislike of Spaniards, 122, 139; ignorance of, 152-158; cowardice of, 159
Cruz, Friar John de la, 176
Cruz, Thomas de la, 183
Cuchumatlan Grande, 174
Cuchumatlanes, 136, 150, 171, 172
Cucua, Cardinal, 388
Cuellar, Alonso, 88
Cueva, Friar John, 24, 26
Curtin (Courteen), Sir William, 381

Dalva, Miguel, 298, 311, 319, 331, 341
Dances of the Indians, 266
Defences, lack of, in the towns, 81, 120, 125
Desaguadero, River, 343
Deseada, 16, 18
Digby, Sir Kenelm, 393
Dominica, 18
Dorados, 16, 27
Drake, Sir Francis, 295
Dress, 85, 234
Drunkenness of the Indians, 243
Dutch pirates, 349

Earthquakes, 293
Ecatepec, 129
Elizabeth, Queen, 62
Encomenderos, the, 251
England, return to, 382, 399; stay in, 384
Englishmen, meeting with, 371

Feather-work, 225
Fernandez, Antonio, 198

Festivals on board, 16
Fitton, 393
Fitzherbert, Father, 391
Flight from Mexico, 115
Flight from Petapa, 334
Flood, 391
Food, lack of nourishment of, 61
Frankfort, 389
French, taken prisoner by, 398
Friars, luxury and wantonness of, 33, 40, 90; carding and dicing, 41; exploitation of the Indians, 256
Fromand, Mr, 383
Fruit, descriptions of, 25, 44, 60, 93, 95, 124
Fuentes, the brothers, 309, 320

Gage, Colonel Henry, 388, 399
Gage, Lady Penelope, 382
Gallantry in Mexico, 91
Gatton, 383, 384
Gelves, Conde de, 14, 97, 107, 108
Ghent, 388
Goldsmiths in Mexico, 75, 85
Golfo Dulce. *See* St Thomas de Castilla
Gomera, Count de la, 199
Gomez, John, 303
Gonzalez, John, 303
Granada, 341
Gray, John, 385
Grijalva, River, 167
Guacocingo, 52
Guadalupe, 83, 101
Guadeloupe, landing at, 18
Guatemala, University of, 188; description of city, 190; provisioning of, 194-198; government of, 198; wealth of, 198; cloisters of, 200; description of province, 205
Guetlavac, 58
Gurvara, Friar Geronymo de, 171
Guzman, Don Bernabe, 216
Guzman, Don Juan, 199, 265

INDEX

Hamilton, Sir William, 393
Havana, 372
Hedgehogs as food, 240
Hell, Spaniard's, 336
Hidalgo, Alonso, 183
Hollander. *See* Dutch pirates
Howard, Sir William, 387

Idolaters at Mixco, 308
Iguana, the, 241
Indian language, Gage learns, 281
Indians, the priests and, 38, 49, 248; languages of, 48, 281; treatment by Spaniards, 84, 228-234; entertainment of travellers, 123; in Chiapa, 164-165; dress, 234; domestic arrangements, 235-237; food, 238; drunkenness, 242; government, 244; tribute, 251, 265; and religion, 253, 258-263; devotion to churches, 254; dances of, 266
Izquinta, 205
Izquintenango, 150, 170

Jalapa, 40
Juego de cañas, 145, 165
Justiniano, Antonio, 198

La Rinconada, 43
La Vieja, 206, 339
Laud, William, 385, 391, 392, 393
Layfield, Edward, 371, 381
Leeds, Sir Thomas, 393
Lempa, River, 338
Leon, 340
Leon, Thomas de, 10, 113, 115
Lewis the mulatto, 20, 21, 22, 24
Lira, Pedro de, 198
Locusts, 289
Londres, Friar Pablo, 13, 273, 379
Lopez, Sebastian, 305
Loretto, Our Lady of, 396

Los Esclavos, 335
Luther, Martin, 380

Madeira, 378
Maldonado y Paz, Juana de 202
Manchester, Earl of, 394
Manwood, Lady, 388
Maquilapa mountain, 131
Marie Galante, 18
Market-place of Mexico, 73, 90
Martir, Friar Peter, 170
Mathy (Matthew), Sir Toby, 393
Maxixca, 46, 48
Melendez, Antonio, 5, 115, 118, 138
Metl, the, 95
Mexia, Don Pedro de, 98-107
Mexico City, siege of, 56, 71; Montezuma's palaces and Court, 65-70; origin of name, 71; market-place, 73, 90; temple, 77; rebuilding by Cortez, 80; description of streets, churches, etc., 81, 84, 89, 91; Guadalupe, 83, 101; ostentation in dress, 85; religion in, 87; gallantry in, 91; government of, 96; Viceroy, 96; strife between Archbishop and Viceroy, 97
Mexico, Lake of, 62-65
Miraculous picture of Our Lady, 174
Misteca mountains, 119
Mixco, 211-215, 283-326
Molina, Friar Peter, 280
Montenegro, Francisco de, 297
Montezuma, his palaces, 65, 66; armoury, 68; Court, 69
Moran, Friar Francisco, 224, 273
Mountague, Walter, 394

Nahualh language, 48
Nicoya, 356
Nigua, the, 295
Nixapa, 124

405

INDEX

Nuchtli, 93
Nunnez, Bartolome, 198

Oaxaca, description of, 120-121; valley of, 120
Obligado, office of, 196
Ococingo, 168
Orellana, Don Gabriel de, 159
Orleans, assignation to, 395
Otomir language, 48

Palomeque, Juan, 212
Panama, 364
Papists, power of, 387
Paz y Lorencana, Don Gonsalo de, 199
Perico, Puerto de, 363
Petapa, 215, 330
Philippines, description of, 111; decision not to go to, 112
Piña, the, 95
Pinola, 210-215, 283-326
Pinomer language, 48
Pirates, 349, 376, 390
Pita, 359
Plantain, the, 25
Poconchi language, 281
Popham, 385, 388
Pork prescribed, 373
Portobello, 366
Porto Rico, 27
Prayer Book, 392
Price, 385
Protestantism, examination of, 389
Providence Island, 370
Psilli, the, 132
Puerto Real, 167

Quelenes mountains, 125, 129

Rabinal, 226
Ramos, John, 243
Realejo, 206, 339
Religion in Mexico, 87; Indians and, 253, 258-263
Rhine, the, 389
Rocolano, Friar Thomas, 170

Rome, journey to, 389, 390 sojourn in, 390-394
Rouse, Captain, 371, 372

Sacapula, 177
Sacualpa. See Zojabah
St Andrews, 177
St Bartholomew, 150
St Christopher, 137, 227, 328
St Domingo Senaco, 225
Saint, Gage considered a, 179
Saint Jacintho, 59, 110
St James, 225
St John de Ulhua, arrival at, 31 Prior of St Dominic, 33; description, 34
St John Sacatepequez, 225
St Luke, 221
St Martin, 173, 182
St Miguel, 206, 339
St Pedro, 207, 225
St Philip, 143, 144
St Salvador, 337
St Thomas de Castilla, 206, 207
Salazar, 105, 108
Salazar, Don Bernadino de (Bishop of Chiapa), 160
Salazar, Justo de, 356-358
Salinas, Golfo de, 357, 359
San Lucar, 378
San Nicholas, El Valle de, 226
Sanatepec, 130
Sandias, 124
Sta Catalina, 370
Sapote, the, 44
Satomayor, Antonio Mendez de, 326
Savaletta, Sebastian de, 217
Scot, Captain, 398
Scottish rebellion, 397
Segura de la Frontera, 44
Serralvo, Marqués de, 14, 96, 107, 388
Shute, Mr, 399
Sichem, Lady of, 385
Siege of Mexico, 56, 71
Siliezer, Thomas de, 198

INDEX

Simarrones, the, 208
Slaves, Indians as, 231
Sport, 165
Suere, River, 348

Tabardillo, 291
Tabasco, River, 167
Tamemez, the, 234
Tapanatepec, 130
Tasajo, 239
Tasco, 119
Taxation of the Indians, 251, 265
Tehuantepec, 124
Tenuchtitlan. *See* Mexico
Tepanabaz, the, 268, 269
Terceras Islands, the, 377
Texcoco, 54-58
Theopixca, 169
Tiburon, the, 28
Tiroll, 102-107
Tlatelulco, 71, 73
Tlaxcala, 46-50
Toledo, Don John de, 135
Toncontin, the, 267
Trinity, Village of the, 205
Truxillo, 207

Vacas, Rio de las, 211
Valdivia, 210

Valle, Marqués del. *See* Cortez
Velasco, Don Melchor de, 153, 169
Venta de Cruces, 365
Vera Cruz. *See* St John de Ulhua
Vera Paz, 223
Viceroy of Mexico, the, 96
Vidall, John, 181
Villa, Friar Matthew de la, 5, 11, 12
Volcanoes, 192, 340

Water, failure of, 360
Windebanke, Sir Francis, 387
Witchcraft, 298-308

Ximeno, Friar John, 189
Xocotenango, 186

Ybarra, Don Carlos de, 12, 369
Yucatan, expedition to, 273-277

Zacatecas, 82
Zeldales, 168
Zepeda, Captain Isidro de, 288
Zerna, Don Alonso (Archbishop of Mexico), 97-103, 108
Zojabah, 178, 181
Zoques, 167

THE BROADWAY TRAVELLERS

Edited by Sir E. DENISON ROSS
and EILEEN POWER

"Lucky is the lover and collector of books on travel who has the whole handsome red bound volumes of this series on his shelves."—*Daily Telegraph.*

The Discovery and Conquest of Mexico. By *Bernal Diaz del Castillo*, 1517-21. Translated by *Professor A. P. Maudslay*. 15 plates and maps, 15*s*. net.

"Something more than an historical document of the first importance. His narrative is also captivatingly readable, so that one's interest and admiration are equally divided between the stupendous events he records and the charming revelations he makes of his own character."
—*Saturday Review.*

Letters of Hernando Cortes, 1519-26. Translated by *J. Bayard Morris*. 14 plates and maps, 15*s*. net.

"The reader has to wonder how the deeds related could possibly have been accomplished, and marvel at the courage of such a small band of men."—*Times Literary Supplement.*

The English American : a New Survey of the West Indies, 1648. By *Thomas Gage*. Edited by *Professor A. P. Newton, D.Litt.* 12 plates, 15*s*. net.

"His narrative is immensely interesting. Of all the excellent *Broadway Travellers* we have not read anything better."—*Saturday Review.*

The True History of Hans Staden, 1557. Translated by *Malcolm Letts*. Illustrated, 10*s*. 6*d*. net.

"The present translation of his adventures among the Brazilian cannibals now make Staden's story available to a larger public, and the story warrants it, not only because of its sensational qualities."
—*New Statesman.*

Travels in Persia, 1627-9. By *Thomas Herbert*. Edited by *Sir William Foster*, C.I.E. 13 plates, 15s. net.

"One of the best of seventeenth century travel narratives."—*Times*.
"This delightful classic."—*Saturday Review*.

Travels of Ibn Battuta, 1324-54. Translated by *H. A. R. Gibb*. 8 plates, 15s. net.

"One of the most fascinating travel-books of all time."—*Times Literary Supplement*. "The entire book, beautifully translated, has intense interest. The account of the court of the Sultan at Delhi is as exciting as anything of the kind I ever read."—ARNOLD BENNETT, in *Evening Standard*.

Memorable Description of the East-Indian Voyage, 1618-25. By *Willem Ysbrantsz Bontekoe*. Translated by *Mrs. C. B. Bodde-Hodgkinson* and *Professor Pieter Geyl, Lit.D.* 10 plates, 7s. 6d. net.

"Fire and shipwreck, fights ashore and afloat, the pitting of ceaseless patience and resource against fate, these things make one understand why this book, famous in its original tongue, has but to be savoured in translation to gain an equal popularity."—*Manchester Guardian*.

Travels into Spain. By *Madame d'Aulnoy*, 1691. Edited by *R. Foulché-Delbosc*. 4 plates, 21s net.

"Of all literary fakes this is surely the most impudent, ingenious and successful. Despite its factual falseness, it is intellectually and emotionally the real thing."—*Saturday Review*.

Travels and Adventures of Pero Tafur. (1435-1439). Translated by *Malcolm Letts*. 8 plates, 12s. 6d. net.

"A document of unique interest, it is a picture of Europe at the most critical moment of its history."—SIR EDMUND GOSSE, in *Sunday Times*.

Akbar and the Jesuits. Translated from the "Histoire" of *Father Pierre du Jarric, S.J.*, by *C. H. Payne*. 8 plates, 12s. 6d. net.

"A serious and intensely interesting piece of work."—*Guardian*.

Don Juan of Persia, a Shi'ah Catholic, (1560-1604). Translated by *Guy le Strange*. 3 Maps, 12s. 6d. net.

"The record of an intrepid Persian nobleman who undertook a special diplomatic mission to various Courts of Europe in the interests of his King. A fine story of gallant adventure."—*New Statesman*.

The Diary of Henry Teonge, Chaplain on board H.M.'s Ships *Assistance, Bristol,* and *Royal Oak* (1675-1679). Edited by *G. E. Manwaring.* 8 plates, 12*s.* 6*d.* net.

"This diary is history; and more can be learnt from it of actual life under Charles II than from many able academic books."—*Observer.*

Memoirs of an Eighteenth-Century Footman: the Life and Travels of John Macdonald (1745-1779). Edited by *John Beresford.* 8 plates, 10*s.* 6*d.* net.

"Exceedingly entertaining travels, instinct with life."—*Times Literary Supplement.* "Simply packed with interest."—*Sunday Times.*

Nova Francia: a Description of Acadia, 1606. By *Marc Lescarbot.* Edited by *H. P. Biggar.* 2 maps, 12*s.* 6*d.* net.

"The early beginnings of the French settlement of Acadia are delightfully narrated. The book is full of gaiety and sound information."—*Spectator.*

Travels in Tartary, Thibet, and China, (1844-6). By *E. R. Huc* and *M. Gabet.* Introduction by *Professor Paul Pelliot.* With a map. 2 vols, 25*s.* net.

"One of the most alluring travel books ever written. To read it is like seeing the scenes described. The edition is admirable."—ARNOLD BENNETT in *Evening Standard.*

Clavijo's Embassy to Tamerlane, (1403-6). Translated by *Guy le Strange.* 7 maps and plans, 15*s.* net.

"So keen and intelligent an observer and so lively a retailer of travel gossip that a popular edition of his work has long been overdue. . . . this remarkable book."—*New Statesman.*

Commentaries of Captain Ruy Freyre de Andrada, 1647. Edited by *C. R. Boxer.* 8 plates and maps, 15*s.* net.

"The main interest of this most vivacious chronicle lies in the account it gives of the siege and capture of the island-fortress of Ormuz, which was the Portuguese Gibraltar."—*Spectator.*

Jahangir and the Jesuits. By *Fernao Guerreiro, S. J.* Translated by *C. H. Payne, M.A.* 4 plates, 12*s.* 6*d.* net.

"Full of splendour and strange scenes."—*New Statesman.*

Jewish Travellers, from the Ninth to the Eighteenth Century. Translated by *Elkan Adler.* 8 plates and map, 15*s.* net.

"Narratives full of interesting and curious information presented in a readable and scholarly version."—*Manchester Guardian.*

The Travels of Marco Polo. Translated from the text of *L. F. Benedetto* by *Professor Aldo Ricci*. 11 plates and maps, 21*s*. net.

"For most readers the *Broadway Travellers* edition of this most famous of travel books will supersede all others in English."—*Discovery*.

Travels in India. By *Captain Basil Hall, R.N., F.R.S.* Edited by *Professor H. G. Rawlinson*. 4 plates, 10*s*. 6*d*. net.

"Contains very interesting pictures of life in India during the latter days of 'The Company' and some remarkable scenes of extraordinary interest. His vivid narrative offers his reader only too much to think about."—*Spectator*.

The Travels of an Alchemist. Translated by *Arthur Waley*. With a map, 10*s*. 6*d*. net.

"An account of the journey of Ch'ang-Ch'un from China to the Hindukush in the early thirteenth century. A highly fascinating book, written as brightly as the best modern journalism."—*Everyman*.

The First Englishmen in India. Edited by *J. Courtenay Locke*. 4 plates, 10*s*. 6*d*. net.

"Here are the narratives of the sturdy Elizabethan merchants who travelled to India and whose reports of their experiences led to the founding of the East India Company."—*Spectator*.

An Account of Tibet: the Travels of *Ippolito Desideri*, of Pistoia, S. J., 1712-27. Edited by *Filippo De Filippi*. 16 plates, 25*s*. net.

"The present publication, in English, is the first edition of the whole work. It will be a classic of travel and a monument of heroic devotion. Desideri was intelligent, observant, humorous, sympathetic, and Franciscan in his charity and faith. He was interested in everything he saw. Many of his descriptions of the country might have come out of a modern book. The *Broadway Travellers* is a fine series, but no volume yet published in it exceeds this in interest or is fuller of surprises."—*Sunday Times*.

Sir Anthony Sherley and his Persian Adventure. By *Sir E. Denison Ross*. 10 plates and maps, 8vo, 12*s*. 6*d*. net.

"Rich in material that is interesting to the historian and to the student of the customs, religion, and culture of the times."—*Scotsman*.

Published by
GEORGE ROUTLEDGE & SONS, LTD.
Broadway House, Carter Lane, London, E.C.4

For Product Safety Concerns and Information please contact our EU
representative GPSR@taylorandfrancis.com
Taylor & Francis Verlag GmbH, Kaufingerstraße 24, 80331 München, Germany